The Distressed Investing Playbook

The Distressed Investing Playbook

HOW THE SMART MONEY PROFITS WHEN COMPANIES FAIL AND MARKETS GO HAYWIRE

Joseph E. Sarachek

Copyright © 2025 by Joseph E. Sarachek. All rights reserved. No part of this book may be used or reproduced in any manner whatsoever without written permission except in the case of brief quotations embodied in critical articles and reviews.

979-8-9985851-0-4 (paperback)
979-8-9985851-1-1 (e-book)
Sarachek Publishing Inc.
670 White Plains Rd
Scarsdale, NY 10583
Library of Congress Control Number: 2025907358
Printed in the United States of America

To my wife, Heather, and kids, Jake, Sydney, Josh, Jason & Spencer:
I love you guys more than I love distressed investing.

To my loving dog, Cruz, my most fearsome, patient, loyal friend and protector: between your bark and your bite, there's no one else I'd rather have at my side in battle.

To G-d: please bless my friends, family, and colleagues with good health and outsized distressed investing returns so we can solve the world's problems.

To my students in the Executive MBA program at NYU Stern: you inspired me to write this book and to give 110% every time I step into the classroom.
Now, inspire us all with your future successes.

Disclaimer

This book is intended for informational and educational purposes only and should not be construed as investment, financial, legal, or tax advice. The strategies and concepts discussed herein are based on the author's personal experiences, research, and opinions. While every effort has been made to ensure the accuracy and completeness of the information presented, neither the author nor the publisher assumes any responsibility for errors, omissions, or consequences resulting from the use of this material.

Investing in distressed assets involves significant risks, including, but not limited to, loss of principal, illiquidity, valuation inaccuracies, legal uncertainties, and exposure to unpredictable market conditions. Readers are strongly advised to conduct their due diligence and seek professional advice from qualified financial, legal, or tax professionals before making investment decisions.

The examples and case studies provided are for illustrative purposes only and may not indicate future results or apply to individual circumstances. Past performance is not indicative of future results, and the distressed investing landscape is inherently volatile and subject to rapid changes.

The author expressly disclaims liability for any financial losses or legal actions incurred due to following the information or strategies outlined in this book. The reader assumes full responsibility for their investment decisions and associated outcomes.

By reading this book, you acknowledge and agree that investing in distressed assets carries inherent risks that may not be entirely predictable or preventable, and no specific outcome is guaranteed.

Contents

Preface: "Good Morning, Chickens" xvii
    The Art of the Deal: Bankruptcy 301 xviii
    A High-Stakes Playbook xx

Chapter 1: Why Distressed Investing? 1
    The Market Beckons 2
    Getting Started 3
    The Six Rules for Distressed Investing (as Followed by Industry All-Stars) 4
        Rule 1: Buy at the Right Price or Be Damned 5
        Rule 2: Do Your Homework 5
        Rule 3: Debt Comes First 6
        Rule 4: Protect Yourself 6
        Rule 5: Bankruptcy Sales Offer Advantages 6
        Rule 6: Take Advantage of Uncertainty 7
    Bankruptcy in 2025: Things Are Heating Up 8
    Key Insights 9

Chapter 2: Bankruptcy 101 11
    The Bankruptcy Landscape: Fundamentals 12
    Bankruptcy Parties 13
    Bankruptcy Levers 16
    Professionals in Bankruptcy Cases 19
    Restructuring Support Agreements (RSAs) 20
    Case Study in Reorganization: J.Crew 22
    Key Insights 26

Chapter 3: Types of Distressed Assets 29
    Trade Claims 29
    Three Different Bankruptcy Stories: JCPenney, Nortel Networks, and Lehman Brothers 31
        How to Buy Trade Claims 33
    Special Situation Investments 34

CONTENTS

Distressed Real Estate Notes...36
    How to Access Distressed Real Estate Notes...38
Operating Businesses...39
    Turnaround Strategies...40
Case Study A: Manufacturing Business with High Debt and Low Margins...41
Case Study B: Cabinet Manufacturer with High Margins and Strong Management...42
Risky Business...43
Key Insights...44

Chapter 4: Getting on First Base: Sourcing Distressed Opportunities...45
    The "Getting on First Base" Approach...46
    Who You Know: Leveraging Your Network...47
    Industry You Know: Using Sector Expertise to Spot Opportunities...49
    What You Know: Using Public Information to Gain an Edge...50
        Trade Publications and Industry News Sources...51
        Google and AI Keywords...51
        A Digital Gold Mine: Public Information Sources...51
    Networking and Cold Outreach...53
    Brokers and Firms...54
    Navigating Ethical Considerations...54
    The "Getting on First Base" Approach in Action...56
    Fall in Love with Making Money, Not Your Hobbies...57
    Conclusion: The Harder You Work, The Luckier You Get...58
    Key Insights...58

Chapter 5: Analyzing and Valuing Distressed Assets...61
    Understanding the Distressed Company Structure...63
        Healthy vs. Distressed Balance Sheets...63
    The Distressed Investing Waterfall...65
    Building a Financial Model...66
        Liquidation Analysis: The Fundamental Valuation Method...66
            Rule #1: Determine the Liquidation Value of an Asset...66
            Rule #2: Anticipate Changes to the Balance Sheet...67
            Rule #3: Do Your Due Diligence...68
        American Airlines Liquidation Analysis...68
        Titan Solar Liquidation Analysis...70
        Important Features of Liquidation Analyses...72
    Discounted Cash Flow (DCF) Analysis...72
    Comparable Company Analysis...74
    Evaluating Collateral, Liens, and Risks to Recovery...75
    Advanced Strategies in Distressed Investing: Beyond Traditional Valuation...77

CONTENTS

Case Studies from Industry: Highlighting the Value of Bottom-Up Research 79
    Revlon's Bankruptcy Case 79
    Five Forces Analysis 79
    PG&E's 2019 Bankruptcy Filing 82
Key Insights 83

Chapter 6: Acquisition Mechanisms and Strategy 85
  Asset vs. Stock Acquisitions: The First Fork in the Road 86
    Asset Deals 87
    Stock Deals 87
  Pacific Ethanol: Stock Acquisition, Asset Deal, or Funding a Stand-Alone Reorganization? 88
    The Pros and Cons of Each 89
    The Outcome 89
  UCC Article 9 Sales 89
  Section 363 Sales 91
    A Balloon Maker Goes Pop 92
  Receiverships 93
  Summary of Mechanisms 95
  Choosing the Right Mechanism 95
  Final Thoughts 96
  Key Insights 96

Chapter 7: Advanced Bankruptcy Strategies and Industry Case Studies 99
  Getting J-Screwed 99
  Liability Management Exercises (LMEs): The New Battleground 100
  Uptier Transactions: The Art of Leapfrogging Creditors 100
  Drop-Down Transactions: The Shell Game 101
  The Serta Mattress Decision: Courts Draw a Line 102
  Investment Implications: Navigating the New Landscape 102
  Tax Considerations: The Hidden Value Drivers 103
    Net Operating Losses (NOLs): The Valuable Tax Asset 103
    Cancellation of Debt Income (COD): The Bankruptcy Exception 104
  Strategic Implications for Investors 104
  The "Texas Two-Step" and Mass Tort Liabilities 105
  The Scrub Island Case: Navigating Complex Restructurings 107
  Special Considerations 108
  Small Business Bankruptcies: Subchapter V 110
  Industry-Specific Factors in Bankruptcy: Challenges and Opportunities for Investors 111
    Retail: Adapting to a Changing Consumer Landscape 111
    Energy: The Volatility of Commodities and Asset Valuation 111
    Healthcare: Navigating Regulation and Patient-Centered Restructuring 112

CONTENTS

    Hospitality: Balancing Real Estate Value and Brand Strength 112
    The Bigger Picture: Industry-Specific Knowledge Is a Competitive Advantage 113
  Conclusion: The Investor's Mindset 113
  Key Insights 114

Chapter 8: Managing Bankruptcy Cases 117
  Brooks Brothers: The Ripple Effects of Retail Collapse 118
  The Anatomy of a Bankruptcy 119
    First-Day Motions: Setting the Stage 120
    Debtor-in-Possession (DIP) Financing: A Lifeline for Debtors 121
    Brooks Brothers's Zero-Interest DIP Financing 122
  GWG Holdings Case: DIP Financing and Strategic Maneuvers in Bankruptcy 124
    DIP Financing and the Battle for Control 125
    Executory Contracts and Their Role in the Restructuring 126
    Outcome: Who Won and Who Lost? 126
  The QualTek Case: Using Cash Collateral to Access Working Capital 127
  Treatment of Executory Contracts: Assuming or Rejecting Ongoing Agreements 130
  Plans of Reorganization: Charting a Path Forward 131
  Wrapping Up 134
  Key Insights 134

Chapter 9: The Trade Claims Playbook: Rules, Risks, and Rewards 137
  Understanding Trade Claims 138
  Types of Trade Claims 140
  The Rationale Behind Investing in Trade Claims 141
  The Trade Claim Market Landscape 142
  Final Thoughts 143
  Key Insights 143

Chapter 10: Trade Claims Investing Strategies 145
  The Trade Claim Investor's Mindset 146
  Uncovering Trade Claims 146
  Online Marketplaces and Platforms 147
  Conducting Due Diligence 149
    Assessing the Debtor's Financial Condition and Prospects 149
    Analyzing the Bankruptcy Case and Potential Outcomes 150
  Investing Strategies for Trade Claims 151
  Timing Considerations 151
  Executing and Managing Trade Claim Investments 152
  Monitoring the Bankruptcy Case and Claim Status 153

CONTENTS

    Exit Strategies 153
    Case Study: Sears Bankruptcy 154
    Final Thoughts 158
    Key Insights 158

Chapter 11: Investing in Fraudulent Bankruptcies 161
    Investing in Fraud Cases: The Madoff Payoff 163
    Courting Controversy: Clawback and Trustee Fees 165
    The Stanford International Bank Scandal 168
    The Enron Scandal: Complexities in Bankruptcy Claims Trading 170
    The Collapse of MF Global: A Tale of Reckless Bets and Missing Funds 172
    Lessons from Fraud, Collapse, and Recovery 174
    Key Insights 175

Chapter 12: Crypto: A Unique Opportunity in Distressed Investing 177
    The Genesis of Crypto Distress: Mt. Gox 178
        How Mt. Gox Established Themes and Implications for Future Crypto Cases 179
    Cred: A Tale of Alleged Fraud and Misrepresentation 180
    Widespread Crypto Crises: A Chain Reaction 181
    Celsius Network: Rapid Rise, Sudden Fall 182
    Voyager Digital: Overextension and Poor Risk Management 183
    From Voyager to FTX: A Fall That Shook the Crypto World 184
        Sam Bankman-Fried and the Rise of FTX 184
        Revelations and the Beginning of the End 185
        Bankruptcy and Unraveling of the Scheme 186
        A Watershed Moment for Crypto 186
        The Surprising FTX Asset Recovery 187
        An Unprecedented Recovery Effort 187
        A Caveat for Creditors 188
        A Legacy for the Industry 189
    Lessons from Crypto Distressed Investing 189
    Key Insights 191

Chapter 13: Turning Chaos into Opportunity 193
    Active vs. Passive Investing Approaches 193
        The Salad Oil Scandal: Young Warren Buffett Proves His Chops 194
        Passive Investing: Walter Schloss and the Rise of Index Funds 196
    Debt vs. Equity: A Distressed Investor's Dilemma 198
    Case Study: Bed Bath & Beyond 199
    Taking Control Through Distressed Investments 202

CONTENTS

 Asset Stripping Considerations 204
 Restructuring Approaches. 205
  Out-of-Court Restructurings 206
  The Holdout Problem. 207
 Legal Considerations in Distressed Investing 209
 Third-Party Non-Debtor Releases. 209
 Case Study: Supreme Court Decision in Purdue Pharma 209
 Litigation Funding: Opportunities and Risks in Distressed Investing. 211
 Conclusion 212
 Key Insights. 212

Chapter 14: The Distressed Investing Playbook in Action 215
 Lessons from the Masters of Distressed Investing 218
 Case Studies: The Playbook in Action 219
  Start Small; Learn from Experience. 219
  Lessons Learned from Failure: When the Playbook Breaks Down 221
  Mid-Market Example: The Turnaround Specialist 222
 Navigating Risks. 222
  Valuation and Collateral Risks 223
  Disclosure Risk and the Fine Print. 224
  Timing and Execution Risks 225
 The Psychology of Successful Distressed Investing 225
 Key Insights. 226

Chapter 15: Bringing It All Together: Your Complete Playbook. 229
 The Distressed Investing Decision Framework. 229
  Your Distressed Investing Toolkit 231
 Your Next Steps 232
 The Next 2008 Financial Crisis 233
 Conclusion: Prepare for Opportunity 233
 Key Insights. 235

Appendix 237
Glossary 239
Endnotes. 247
Works Cited 249
Index 251
Acknowledgments. 265

Preface: "Good Morning, Chickens"

Things I love:

G-d, and my family. I have a large family—my wife and our five kids.

I love my country, but I also love other countries. I love my mini dachshund, Cruz. He's twelve years old and comes to work with me every day, always barking at Rob, the postman.

I love sports. I love the Islanders, the Giants, the Knicks, and the Yankees, even though. they're not the dynasty they used to be.

I like golf, but I don't love it. Yes, I play a round now and then for fun, but it's also a bit of a headache or heartache.

I'm a former Cornell University college rower, and I love rowing. I love the beach, but I love the mountains, too.

When it comes to making money, I love the bankruptcy business. And the part of bankruptcy I love most is distressed investing, which involves buying and selling assets that are part of a bankruptcy case. It's been my passion for the entirety of my thirty-six-year career, and I love it.

I believe that after you finish reading the pages of this book, you will also come to love it. When you gain some fundamental knowledge of how the law and claims systems work in the United States, you can make enormous, life-changing gains.

Contrary to what you might think, buying distressed assets is easy to understand. It's true that bankruptcy falls within the domain of our code-based legal system. But if you have first-hand knowledge of any industry, whatever it is—healthcare, real estate, boxing, wine bars, or canned food products—you can make sense of distressed assets. If you've observed an industry cycling up and down, through good times and bad, you have the capacity to buy distressed assets for less than you could at, let's call it, retail.

I'm a student of history. Throughout history, great fortunes have been made in buying distressed assets. As you will learn soon, "it's all in the buy." What you pay for distressed assets determines your fate. Conrad Hilton is known worldwide as a hotel magnate, but did you know he made his fortune by buying distressed debt from banks during the Great Depression and using it to acquire hotel properties?

Cornelius Vanderbilt never built a single railroad company. The fortune he amassed, a sum that in 2024 purchasing power would make him richer than Elon Musk or Bill Gates, came through his buying of undercapitalized railroad companies.

Warren Buffett is known as one of the world's greatest investors, but he's really a value investor; that is, he is a distressed investor at his core.

Presumably, neither you nor I are in the same league as Warren Buffett. However, there are daily opportunities to buy assets at 30 cents on the dollar and then turn around and sell them for 85 cents on the dollar (to give one example of distressed investing), which is a 183% gain. In this book, I will teach you where to find these assets, when to buy them, how to trade them, and what it takes to play and win this game.

Over the past four decades, I've been in the room with some of the very best and worst players. I've learned what works and what doesn't. I've seen shrewd millionaires walk away penniless and savvy young gamers come away with bargain-basement deals.

First, you have to understand that distressed investing is a discipline. Second, you have to be willing to engage in the process, which sometimes means allowing yourself to get the stuffing knocked out of you in a room full of bankers and lawyers.

The Art of the Deal: Bankruptcy 301

For an illustrative example, we can look at none other than President Donald Trump and his negotiation of the Plaza Hotel's debt in 1992. (This was long before Trump had contemplated a political career, and, as such, this story is not meant as a political statement, just a colorful anecdote.)

Trump is not technically a distressed investor, but over the course of his career he's frequently found himself in situations where distressed investors lurk, often uncomfortably close. He has experienced the agony and ecstasy of being forced to grapple with shrewd, sophisticated, experienced professionals over heavily leveraged assets more than a few times.

The series of events leading up to Trump's forced appearance in a crowded law firm conference room was many years in the making. It began with his purchase of the Plaza Hotel in 1988 for $400 million using significant debt. Later that year, he decided to finance the completion of the five-star Taj Mahal casino in Atlantic City, mostly with high-interest, 14% per annum junk bonds, amassing another $675 million in debt. With the United States entering a recession in 1990, this proved to be bad timing. Trump soon found himself needing another $675 million from a consortium of seventy-two lenders to save a combination of his assets, including the Trump Shuttle airline, the Plaza, and his Atlantic City casinos.

Unfortunately for him, the funds still weren't enough to see him through the economic downturn. The Taj Mahal was put into bankruptcy in 1991, and Manhattan real estate values continued plunging. Interest payments accrued, and by 1992, he owed $550 million on the Plaza alone.

At the time, I was a young associate in the bankruptcy department at a Park Avenue law firm, just five years out of New York Law School. For me and my colleagues in the strange world that is bankruptcy law, Trump's travails were kind of like watching the Olympics. We couldn't get enough of all the twists and turns.

PREFACE: "GOOD MORNING, CHICKENS"

As it turned out, Trump's high-stakes negotiations with a small army of lenders and lawyers were taking place just a couple of blocks away from my firm. They had gathered to restructure the mountain of debt he'd taken on to acquire the Plaza Hotel, his highly leveraged trophy asset. It should have been a humbling moment, but you wouldn't have known it from his demeanor.

Legend would have it that when Trump strolled into the packed conference room that day, his first words were something like, "Good morning, chickens." I wasn't there, but several reliable, independent sources gave me details about the meeting. Considering all that has happened in the ensuing years, this line certainly rings true.

With so much at stake, why start an important bankruptcy meeting by calling creditor representatives "chickens"? I can think of at least four reasons.

First, it instantly threw everyone off guard. Bankers and lawyers prepare for these kinds of encounters with studied sobriety, arming themselves with documents and evidence. With one word, Trump had them off balance.

Second, it was a funny, quirky remark that caused people to pause. No one walked into the meeting that morning expecting to be labeled a chicken. I can only imagine the bemused expressions on the bankers' faces.

Third, the term "chicken" is colorful. It doesn't immediately evoke hostility. Think about what Trump *didn't* say. He could have said, "Good morning, idiots," or replaced the word "idiots" with any number of different profanities. Lawyers love a good fight, and opening with a taunt would have only energized them.

What does one retort to being called a chicken? "Well, you're a chicken, too!"? No, it doesn't work. By calling the bankers and lawyers in that room chickens, Trump subtly implied that he somehow had the upper hand. Why? Because chickens are harmless, innocent birds that often wind up being plucked, roasted, and eaten.

Fourth, Trump's words suggested he was fearless, compared to the cowardly or risk-averse "chicken" bankers and lawyers. In American culture, being a "chicken" goes against national mythology; after all, we are from the "Land of the Free and the Home of the Brave."

Even back then, Trump had acting ability. Also, most people don't realize that he was honing his habit of calling people unflattering nicknames many decades before the 2016 presidential campaign, when U.S. Senators Sanders and Warren became "Crazy Bernie" and "Pocahontas," respectively. Labeling opponents and critics is a serious negotiating strategy that serves a purpose—especially when it comes to the high-stakes world of debt negotiation.

The "chickens" line landed like a punch. It disrupted the flow of the meeting at the outset, resetting the tone for how the proceedings would go. It was an audacious way to take some negotiating leverage back, and it worked.

After filling the stunned and silent conference room with his words, he launched into a rant about New York City real estate and the value of having the "Trump name" on it. Eventually, it all became too much for his audience. As folklore has it, one high-powered lawyer for the banks known for his curt demeanor finally interrupted and told Trump to "Sit the f--k down and shut the f--k up"—all while picking his nose.

PREFACE: "GOOD MORNING, CHICKENS"

(When a meeting of this type veers off course, *that's* how an astute legal tactician neutralizes an opponent. What incredible theater!)

Trump being Trump, perhaps he figured his swagger and salesmanship could convince the "chickens" to slash the interest rates on his debt and give him more time. Suffice it to say that didn't happen. Nevertheless, considering his poor bargaining position, Trump made out about as well as anyone could. He was denied most of the accommodations and relief he requested and gave up a 49% stake in the hotel to the creditors, but he got a repurchase option, which meant they gave him an opportunity to buy the stake back if he could come up with the money. And he ultimately got to keep his plane and yacht, a remarkable concession.

Here's a guy whose debt exceeds a billion dollars, yet he had the audacity to negotiate for and keep these symbols of wealth. Why did they let him? Because in the grand scheme of things, a plane worth $3 or $10 million and a yacht worth $20 million do little to offset a half-billion-dollar hotel property bleeding red ink. On a pragmatic level, the time and effort required to separate him from those assets wasn't worth it. Give credit where credit is due. Trump's bravado probably got him terms no ordinary bankrupt businessperson could dream of.

This story is a powerful lesson for any distressed investor: Having a deep understanding of leverage and the psychology of your counterparts can yield unexpected advantages, even when your position seems hopeless. Most debtors don't walk out of a room like that still owning their yachts, planes, or even automobiles, unless they know how to navigate the fine line between corporate and personal liability.

The kind of person who can hold their own in a creditor's meeting is the exact sort who is drawn to distressed investing. They possess a high tolerance for risk and the temperament to dance along a razor's edge. They relish the fact that when egos clash and billions are on the line, the drama rivals any Broadway show.

All that said, distressed investing requires more than just raw bravado. Success in this field isn't about throwing bankers and lawyers off balance with bold words. It also requires preparation and the ability to strategize. Trump's unconventional tactics may have worked for him, but they are not a reliable blueprint for many if not most. An effective distressed investor needs a solid grasp of the market and the legal frameworks they're operating in, not to mention a precise sense of timing.

A High-Stakes Playbook

That's where this book comes in. It is a playbook for the high-stakes world of distressed investing, much like the ones coaches have for football teams. My goal is to give you the plays you need for successful distressed investing. Some people may be more or less emotionally suited to handle intense pressure when it spontaneously arises. But more often than not, it is preparation, not just temperament, that separates the winners from the losers in this game.

In the pages that follow, I will walk you through the investing process step-by-step, just as I do with the students in the MBA classes I teach at New York University. Not that academic credentials are required to be a successful investor in distressed debt. Anyone can do this type of investing. The deals are out there if you know where to look and how to acquire them.

We'll explore how fortunes are lost when once-mighty companies spiral into bankruptcy and how wise investors pick up the pieces by buying assets thought to be worthless and selling them at a profit.

You'll learn essential insider tricks, such as how to:

- acquire everything from real estate to business loans at killer discounts in times of distress.
- value distressed assets using proven frameworks like liquidation and cash flow analysis.
- navigate critical bankruptcy processes, from claims to cramdowns and more.
- source the very best turnaround opportunities even before others spot them.
- assess red flags and mitigate risks inherent to this edgy area of finance.

I'll be your fly on the wall as famous investors and corporate flameouts take center stage. You'll discover how some financiers have made out like bandits via distressed investing; hear delicious, lesser-known details from famous bankruptcy cases; and learn from the chess-like legal battles over Enron's and FTX's financial carcasses in the wake of their massive frauds.

Do you have what it takes to profit from the Chapter 11 pressure cooker?

Let's find out.

CHAPTER 1

Why Distressed Investing?

What if I told you there was a way to buy commercial real estate for pennies on the dollar? Or lend money out at 40% interest while borrowing at 5%? Or purchase a manufacturing business with $100 million in assets, $50 million in revenue, and $2 million in cash flow for just $2 million? Opportunities like these may sound too good to be true, but they exist in the world of distressed investing.

Opportunities to buy distressed assets emerge when the overall economy and markets struggle, making them a powerful diversification tool for smoothing out portfolio returns across cycles. As equities and commodities crash, and companies fall on hard times and plummet in value, distressed investors get busy doing deals. They see opportunity amidst the chaos.

Their operating principle is simple (and familiar to anyone with even a basic understanding of investing): buy low and sell high. But finding value where others see only trouble requires a keen eye, plenty of creativity, and nerves of steel.

At its core, distressed investing is bargain hunting, scooping up assets "on the cheap" from those desperate or eager to sell. The upside potential can be enormous once markets recover and values rebound to normal levels. Of course, with great potential reward also comes significant risk. Separating the genuine diamonds in the rough from the lumps of coal takes skill and the ability to do rigorous analysis.

That said, distressed assets may offer more transparency to potential buyers than public stock and bond markets. Public securities, meant to be bought and sold with a click, provide only the information required by securities laws, and most investors have no say in how they are structured. Contrast that with buyers of distressed assets, however, who often get direct access to company management, allowing them to ask tough questions and kick the tires before making a deal or agreeing to a purchase. This feature provides a margin of safety and the chance to investigate whether value truly is hidden or nonexistent.

The profiles of history's greatest distressed investors provide valuable insights and inspiration for those just starting out, which is why I will showcase so many throughout this book. Take Conrad Hilton, the hotel magnate (see Fig. 1). During the Great Depression, he scooped up distressed debt from struggling banks, using it to acquire hotel properties for a fraction of their value. In one famous deal, he bought the Waldorf Astoria's bonds for a measly 4.5 cents on the dollar and flipped them for 85 cents, a 1,789% gain. That's turning $22,500 into $425,000.

Or consider Cornelius Vanderbilt, the railroad tycoon. As I mentioned in the preface, contrary to popular belief, he never laid a single track himself. Instead, he rolled up smaller, undercapitalized railroad companies on the cheap and combined them into a powerful network.

More recently, hedge funds and distressed debt funds have been flocking to the bankrupt remains of cryptocurrency giant FTX. At first, customer claims (or "trade claims") were being sold for 10 cents on the dollar. However, as more information emerged about the value of the assets, claims rocketed up to 90 cents and past 100, all in the span of a year. As soon as crypto prices started rising and it became apparent that FTX's assets were bargains, institutional investors rushed to get as large a share as they could.

Figure 1: Conrad Hilton, Founder of Hilton Hotels

Pioneering titans and today's powerhouses of commerce provide a masterclass in the three core pillars of distressed investing: 1) Buy Low/Sell High; 2) Be Creative; and 3) Move Fast. By and large, the individuals who thrived learned through trial and error, but you already have a leg up, namely, this playbook.

Every investment involves a degree of risk, but most people avoid distressed investments because they fear the unknown. Knowledge and information can help overcome that fear.

My goal is to shift your mindset from passively reading about distressed opportunities to actively developing the insight and confidence needed to join the 0.1% of investors who seize them.

The Market Beckons

Of course, the sorts of investors mentioned above benefited from immense scale, backing, and connections. But even if you are not on Warren Buffett's speed dial, distressed opportunities are everywhere, often close to home.

Consider that distressed investing covers many asset types across industries (see Fig. 2). These include trade claims, real estate loans, operating businesses, and special situations. Trade claims are debts one company owes to another, often purchased at a discount. Real estate loans may involve distressed properties and mortgages, particularly in overleveraged markets.

WHY DISTRESSED INVESTING?

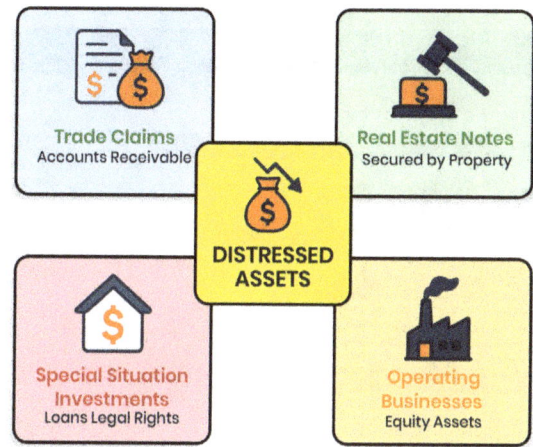

Figure 2: Types of Distressed Assets

Operating businesses can be companies attempting to restructure through bankruptcy or asset sales. Special situations refer to event-driven opportunities such as litigation financing or the modification of contracts that affect asset values.

I will examine each of these categories in detail in later chapters. For now, it is worth knowing that the United States dominates the distressed landscape, both in deal volume and in accessibility. The U.S. bankruptcy system, with its transparent and established legal framework, supports a steady flow of transactions.

Although the United States holds about 30% of the world's total debt, opportunities also exist in other markets. In 2019, Japan and China ranked next in global debt levels (see Fig. 3). But debt volume alone does not determine opportunity. Non-performing loans and distressed assets vary in quality depending on local economies and legal systems. Investors must weigh potential returns against the additional risks of unfamiliar markets.

As a general principle, focusing first on the U.S. market makes sense. The combination of available deals, legal certainty, and lower operational risk makes it a sound place to begin.

Getting Started

So, where do you start as a novice distressed investor? I advise focusing first on industries and situations you know something about. If you've worked in healthcare, chances are you'll have a major leg up analyzing distressed hospital systems or overleveraged biotech firms. Likewise, real estate professionals should scour their local property markets for potential opportunities.

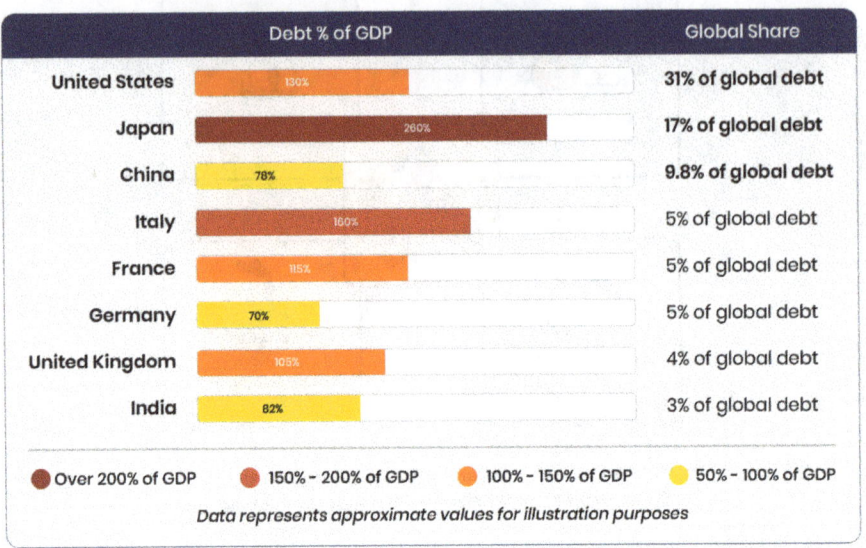

Figure 3: Leading Countries by National Debt

If you don't have expertise in any industry or situation, it's not a deal-breaker. But it means you'll need extra effort upfront to get up to speed. While distressed investing isn't rocket science, it's important to remember that no one will make it easy for you. At some point, you may be tempted to jump into a deal in an industry you know little about, but I strongly advise against it. This is a competitive and complex field, so be prepared to roll up your sleeves and do your homework.

Once you've identified a promising opportunity, the real work begins. To succeed in distressed investing, you must combine rigorous fundamental research, legal and financial creativity, and good old-fashioned hustle. As I spelled out in the preface, this is not a game for the timid. Distressed investing attracts some of the brightest and most ruthless people on the planet, all of them vying for the same deals. However, the rewards can be substantial for those willing to work hard and navigate the challenges.

The key is to stay focused, disciplined, and adaptable. As you gain more experience and build your network, you'll develop a sharper sense of which opportunities are worth pursuing and how to navigate the complexities of a situation. Success in distressed investing is a marathon, not a sprint, so pace yourself and never stop learning along the way.

The Six Rules for Distressed Investing (as Followed by Industry All-Stars)

God gave Moses the Ten Commandments, which have served mankind well for thousands of years. Distressed investing doesn't rise to the same level of importance in the grand scheme of life, but these six rules will serve distressed investors well. While they may not save your soul, they could very well save your capital.

Rule 1: Buy at the Right Price or Be Damned

The foundation of successful distressed investing begins with understanding liquidation value. No one embodies this principle better than Howard Marks, co-founder of Oaktree Capital Management, who famously advised, "The most important thing is knowing what you don't know." Marks built Oaktree into a $170 billion powerhouse by focusing relentlessly on entry price and downside protection. Similarly, Marc Lasry of Avenue Capital Group made his fortune by buying distressed debt at the right price.

During the 2008 financial crisis, Lasry purchased bank debt at 60 cents on the dollar that later recovered par (100%), thereby generating billions in profits. In the FTX case, early investors who purchased claims at 3 to 6 cents on the dollar created enormous downside protection, as the eventual recovery will turn out to be much higher than initially expected. These investors understand that no matter how compelling the turnaround story might seem, overpaying for distressed assets is the quickest path to failure.

Rule 2: Do Your Homework

As you'll learn, distressed investing demands more rigorous due diligence than almost any other investment strategy. Paul Singer of Elliott Management is legendary for his forensic approach to investment research; his team has been known to spend months analyzing a single distressed opportunity, leaving no document unread and no stone unturned. This meticulous approach helped Singer secure a remarkable victory in his 15-year battle with the Argentine government over sovereign debt.

Similarly, Cherokee Acquisition founder Vladimir Jelisavcic has built his reputation by reading every filing in bankruptcy cases that others deemed too complex or opaque. His exhaustive analysis of the FTX bankruptcy revealed value that less diligent investors missed entirely, earning him outsize returns from FTX claims he purchased for pennies on the dollar.

Another industry veteran with a successful 40-year track record is Jon Bauer of Contrarian Capital Management. His firm specializes in complex capital structures and "off-the-run" opportunities, investments that are often overlooked by larger funds due to their complexity or lack of liquidity. With a focus on deep fundamental research and legal expertise, Bauer and his team have built a reputation for navigating distressed and special situations across multiple market cycles, an approach that has made Contrarian Capital one of the more respected names in the industry.

These industry leaders understand that success requires understanding not just what went wrong but *why* it went wrong, whether due to temporary market conditions, poor management decisions, or fundamental flaws in a business model.

Rule 3: Debt Comes First

As we will cover at length in the next chapter, in bankruptcy, the capital structure hierarchy is sacred, with debt holders getting paid before equity holders. This is fundamental. When I first left the law to join Jay Goldsmith and Harry Freund at Balfour Investors in 1997, they practically laughed me out of the room when I showed them a distressed investment without a complete debt structure to invest in (meaning, holding positions in multiple priority levels of debt across the capital stack, to increase chances of a recovery). "Do you think we're venture capital investors? How are we getting in the front door?" they retorted. Bruce Richards and Louis Hanover of Marathon Asset Management have built their careers around this principle, strategically positioning their $23 billion fund in the debt structures of distressed companies to ensure priority in any recovery scenario. Even Sam Zell, best known for building a real estate empire in the 1980s and 1990s, made some of his most profitable investments by purchasing distressed debt rather than equity.

These investors understand that controlling debt often means controlling the company's fate, whether through reorganization or liquidation. Knowing where your claims sit in the priority hierarchy can mean the difference between significant returns and substantial losses.

Rule 4: Protect Yourself

The distressed investing landscape is filled with legal pitfalls and hidden liabilities. Jay Alix, founder of AlixPartners and advisor on some of the largest bankruptcy cases in history, built his reputation on identifying and mitigating risks in complex distressed situations. Similarly, Kenneth Moelis, who founded Moelis & Company after leading UBS's investment banking division, emphasizes structural protections in every distressed transaction his firm advises on. David Tepper of Appaloosa Management is known for his aggressive trading style but is equally meticulous about legal protections when entering distressed positions. As you will learn in the case study on Sears in a later chapter, preference liability can significantly impact the value of even seemingly straightforward claims.

These industry leaders understand that court-approved transactions provide crucial protection against future challenges or clawbacks, and they work closely with experienced bankruptcy counsel to structure transactions that minimize legal risks.

Rule 5: Bankruptcy Sales Offer Advantages

Section 363 sales in bankruptcy (another topic covered in later chapters) provide unique opportunities to acquire assets "free and clear" of liens and encumbrances. Wilbur Ross, often called the "King of Bankruptcy," built his fortune by using these provisions to acquire distressed assets in the steel, coal, and textile industries. By purchasing assets through bankruptcy proceedings, Ross was able to shed legacy liabilities like pension obligations and environmental costs. Similarly, Carl Icahn's successful turnaround of the Trump Taj Mahal casino in Atlantic City was facilitated by bankruptcy protections that allowed him to restructure the business without inheriting its troubled past. Jamie Salter of Authentic Brands Group has used this strategy repeatedly, most recently in the acquisitions of Brooks Brothers, Forever 21, and Barneys New York, allowing his company to acquire valuable brand assets without their accompanying retail liabilities.

These strategic investors recognize that bankruptcy creates a special environment where they can cherry-pick the best assets while leaving behind troubled liabilities.

Rule 6: Take Advantage of Uncertainty

The greatest opportunities in distressed investing emerge when information is scarce and uncertainty is high. Take John Paulson of Paulson & Co., who became a household name during the 2008 financial crisis by betting against subprime mortgage-backed securities, a notoriously opaque market that most investors failed to understand. His firm's calculated move at the height of uncertainty became one of the most profitable trades in Wall Street history.

Similarly, Jason Mudrick of Mudrick Capital Management has made his reputation by entering situations where uncertainty is highest, like his investment in FRONTEO (formerly UBIC), a Japanese data analytics company that was reeling from accounting irregularities. Andrew Herenstein and Jason Beckman of Monarch Alternative Capital likewise built their $9.4 billion firm on the principle that market overreactions to uncertainty create the best buying opportunities. These investors recognize that optimal entry points occur amid maximum uncertainty, while exit opportunities peak when information becomes plentiful.

Write these rules (see Fig. 4) down in red letters, commit them to memory, save them as wallpaper on your smartphone, or embroider them on a pillow. But do not forget them.

These six rules form the foundation of successful distressed investing. While markets evolve and specific strategies change, these principles have guided profitable investments through countless economic cycles. The all-stars of distressed investing, from Howard Marks to Marc Lasry to Paul Singer, have built multibillion dollar fortunes by adhering to these fundamentals. Like the Ten Commandments, they provide a framework that, if committed to memory and followed faithfully, will help investors avoid the most common and costly mistakes in the challenging world of distressed investing.

Bankruptcy in 2025: Things Are Heating Up

As I finish writing this book in early 2025, I can confidently say that the current distressed market environment is nothing short of explosive. In 2024, U.S. bankruptcy filings experienced a significant uptick. Total bankruptcy filings reached 508,758, a 14% increase from the 445,286 recorded in 2023. Commercial Chapter 11 filings rose by 20%, totaling 7,879 in 2024, up from

SIX RULES FOR DISTRESSED INVESTING

1. BUY AT THE RIGHT PRICE
A good investment starts with understanding liquidation value.

2. DO YOUR HOMEWORK
Investigate why the business failed and assess potential risks.

3. DEBT COMES FIRST
Debt holders get paid before equity. Controlling debt means controlling assets.

4. PROTECT YOURSELF
Ensure court-approved transactions to avoid legal risks.

5. BANKRUPTCY SALES OFFER ADVANTAGES
Assets can often be bought free and clear of liens.

6. TAKE ADVANTAGE OF UNCERTAINTY
The best opportunities arise when others lack full information.

Figure 4: Six Rules for Distressed Investing

6,583 the previous year. Small business filings under Subchapter V (more on this below) also increased by 32%, with 2,381 filings in 2024 compared to 1,808 in 2023.[1]

This bankruptcy surge stems from several economic factors, including rising interest rates, persistent inflation, and shifts in consumer spending habits. These challenges have particularly impacted overleveraged companies that previously thrived in a low-interest-rate environment. As their debts mature, many companies cannot meet their obligations, increasing restructurings and liquidations.

For distressed investors, this environment presents substantial opportunities. Bankruptcy cases are typically filed under Chapter 11 of the U.S. Bankruptcy Code, which allows companies to restructure their debt and continue operating while repaying creditors. Chapter 11 filings often involve larger companies, particularly in the real estate and energy sectors, which have been hard hit in recent years. Overleveraged property developers face high vacancy rates and falling rents, while energy producers are vulnerable to volatile commodity prices. Investors who understand local real estate markets, capital structures, and commodity dynamics can capitalize on these opportunities.

For small businesses, recent changes to bankruptcy laws have made it easier and faster to restructure through Subchapter V of Chapter 11, a provision introduced under the Small Business Reorganization Act. Subchapter V has streamlined the bankruptcy process by reducing costs, eliminating certain procedural hurdles, and allowing owners to maintain control of their businesses. This reform has opened up a new category of distressed investment opportunities, especially for investors who are willing to work closely with business owners to navigate the restructuring process.

Consider the tale of Twisted Root Burger Co., a Texas-based restaurant chain founded in 2006.[2] Under the ownership of entrepreneur Jason Boso, it grew rapidly from a single location to twenty-four, including several bars, a brewery, and a theater. The outbreak of the COVID-19 pandemic, however, forced the company to shut down operations in March 2020. While some locations briefly reopened in June, they soon closed again as coronavirus cases surged.

Facing mounting debts and an unpredictable future, Boso strategically filed for Chapter 11 bankruptcy for five of the restaurants, using the new provisions under Subchapter V. This move allowed him to keep control of his business, reduce its liabilities by $500,000, and continue operating under more favorable terms. As a pioneer in applying these new bankruptcy rules, Boso successfully restructured his business and ensured its long-term survival.

Apart from traditional bankruptcies, some of the most lucrative distressed investment opportunities arise from niche, idiosyncratic situations. These "special situations" can involve complex litigation, environmental liabilities, or corporate fraud: cases where traditional investors shy away due to uncertainty and legal complexity.

One of the more interesting and illuminating special situations includes claims from the Madoff Ponzi scheme. When Bernie Madoff's massive fraud was exposed in 2008, it triggered a complex web of bankruptcy proceedings and litigation. Distressed investors who purchased claims from defrauded investors were able to achieve significant returns once assets were recovered through legal settlements and asset sales. Debt purchased at 20 cents on the dollar ultimately paid off at 100 cents—a 5x return. This case illustrates the potential rewards of navigating high-risk, high-complexity situations where other investors fear to tread.

Before we move on, let's recap the key insights that will guide you as you explore the world of distressed investing.

KEY INSIGHTS

1. Distressed investing involves buying assets or companies at steep discounts when they experience financial difficulties, with the goal of profiting when their value rebounds.
2. Successful distressed investors must combine rigorous research, creativity, quick decision-making, and risk tolerance.
3. Three core principles define distressed investing: Buy Low/Sell High, Be Creative, and Move Fast.
4. Distressed investing requires understanding liquidation values and downside protection, as seen in the approach of industry leaders like Howard Marks and Marc Lasry.
5. Thorough due diligence is fundamental for identifying valuable claims and avoiding costly mistakes, as demonstrated by investors like Paul Singer and Vladimir Jelisavcic.

6. Bankruptcy asset sales under Section 363 provide opportunities to acquire valuable assets free of encumbrances, as used successfully by investors like Wilbur Ross and Jamie Salter.
7. Uncertainty and market inefficiencies create some of the best investment opportunities in distressed markets, as demonstrated by Seth Klarman and Jason Mudrick.
8. Chapter 11 of the U.S. Bankruptcy Code allows companies to restructure while continuing operations, while Subchapter V streamlines the process for small businesses.
9. Distressed assets span various types, including trade claims, real estate loans, operating businesses, and special situations involving litigation, regulation, or fraud.
10. The United States dominates the global distressed market, thanks to its transparent bankruptcy system and steady deal flow. However, opportunities also exist in international markets like Japan and China.
11. Small businesses are increasingly using Subchapter V to restructure, creating new opportunities for investors willing to engage with smaller, more hands-on deals.
12. Niche opportunities include "special situations" like corporate fraud (e.g., the Madoff scheme), complex litigation, and environmental liabilities.
13. Investors should focus on industries and situations they understand, leveraging their expertise to assess value and manage risk.
14. Distressed investing is competitive, requiring diligence, hustle, and the ability to navigate complex legal and financial processes.
15. The current economic environment, shaped by rising interest rates and looming debt maturities, is ripe with opportunities for those prepared to act.

CHAPTER 2

Bankruptcy 101

Every business has a birth story.

For most, though, the beginning is more bureaucracy than mythology: the owners file incorporation documents with state offices and obtain a tax identification number from the Internal Revenue Service. Then shareholders or members contribute capital, open bank accounts, and commence operations. Essentially all corporations have followed or will follow this path, from Amazon and Apple to the millions of other businesses launched each year.

At some point in a company's life cycle, however, extreme challenges may arise that jeopardize its continuity and force decision-makers to navigate uncertain waters. The U.S. bankruptcy system was developed to address these challenges. Unlike in many countries where business failure leads to permanent closure, the American system is designed to provide companies with tools to restructure and continue operating. The United States is a country of second chances.

Consider Apple, now one of the world's most valuable companies. In July 1997, it was reportedly just 90 days from bankruptcy, unable to raise even $1 million to file for Chapter 11 protection. Apple's near-collapse illustrates that not every distressed company ends up in bankruptcy; sometimes, strategic investment or leadership changes can provide a lifeline. I remember the moment vividly. At the time, I was working as a bankruptcy attorney. As the firm's top biller, I had been immersed in bankruptcy cases, working relentlessly long hours and moving quickly from one case to the next.

My boss called me into her office. "You're going to Menlo Park," she said, instructing me to handle Apple's potential bankruptcy filing at its headquarters. What struck me most at that moment was my reaction. I was disappointed that we hadn't been brought in earlier. By the time we *were* approached, Apple was already on the edge of insolvency (sometimes referred to as the "zone of insolvency").

I ended up not going. Luckily for Apple, they ultimately found a lifeline outside the bankruptcy system. Just weeks after we received that fateful phone call from Apple Headquarters, and with time running out, the company hired Steve Jobs as interim CEO and simultaneously secured a $150 million investment from their archrival Microsoft.

This situation underscored a pattern I've observed repeatedly: technology companies and manufacturers often have different options than businesses with heavy debt loads and few assets. Companies with valuable intellectual property or groundbreaking technology are, in my experience, more likely to attract strategic investments rather than require traditional debt restructuring.

Apple's near-collapse illustrates why the American approach to business failure is unique. Even iconic companies can face existential threats, and the U.S. bankruptcy system is designed to give them pathways to recovery rather than forcing them to shut down. Had Apple filed for bankruptcy, it likely would have survived, but the company emerging from that process would have been shaped by lawyers and restructuring advisors—not Steve Jobs. My guess is that Apple would look far different today.

The Bankruptcy Landscape: Fundamentals

Corporate bankruptcy in the United States is primarily governed by two key sections of the Bankruptcy Code: Chapter 7 liquidations and Chapter 11 reorganizations. These two paths represent fundamentally different outcomes, though liquidations can also occur within Chapter 11.

Chapter 7 liquidations are typically the end of the road for a company. When Chapter 7 is filed, a court-appointed trustee sells all the company's remaining assets and distributes the proceeds to creditors. While this can present opportunities for investors to acquire assets at significant discounts, it also marks the dissolution of the corporate entity. Sometimes, cases begin as Chapter 11 reorganizations but later convert to Chapter 7. Additionally, some large Chapter 11 cases end in liquidation despite never officially converting, which can confuse creditors and shareholders alike.

Chapter 11 reorganizations, by contrast, allow companies to restructure their debts and operations while continuing to function. This process gives companies a second chance to fix their problems, but the road from entry to exit is never straightforward. Chapter 11 is where much of the drama and opportunity in distressed investing unfolds, which is why it is the focus of this book. To navigate it successfully, investors must understand the priority scheme and leverage points.

From a historical perspective, Chapter 7 is more common than Chapter 11 because small businesses often have little recourse when business turns sour except to liquidate (see Fig. 1). Also, as you would expect, bankruptcy filings are highly cyclical. Most people remember the period between 2008 and 2011 as horrible, when the housing market imploded and businesses fell off a cliff. For many distressed investors, however, those years are fondly remembered as the best of times.

Bankruptcy operates according to specific rules, power dynamics, and strategic considerations that aren't immediately obvious to outsiders. Those who take the time to learn the applicable laws and procedures and develop the ability to negotiate effectively with stakeholders can generate outsized returns. Think of this as learning the rules of the game before placing your bets. With this foundation in place, you will have a much easier time navigating the opportunities and pitfalls within Chapter 11.

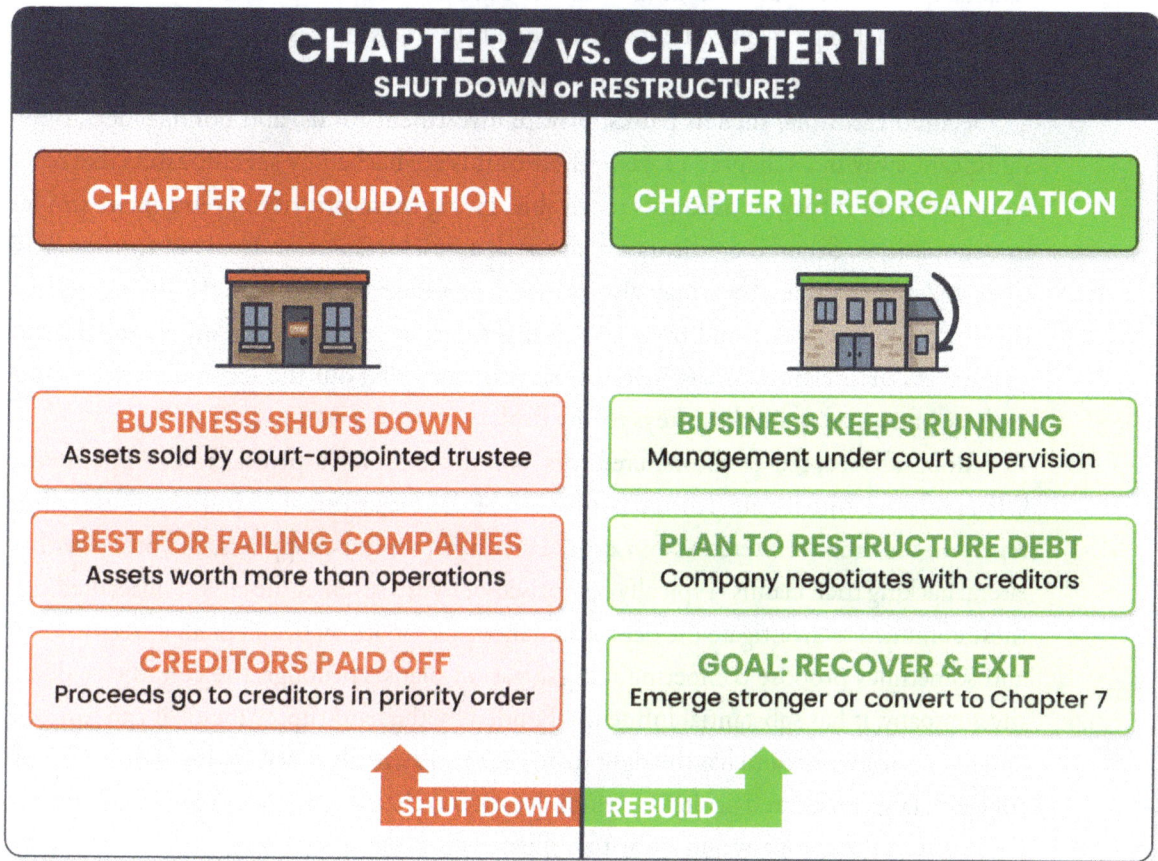

Figure 1: Chapter 7 vs. Chapter 11: Shut Down or Restructure?

Bankruptcy Parties

When a company becomes financially distressed, control often shifts from shareholders to creditors. The investor's role is to navigate this transition and seek the best recovery on their claims. This can involve gaining control of the company's assets, limiting the time spent in bankruptcy court, and reducing the total amount of creditor claims. Achieving these outcomes requires detailed involvement in the restructuring process, both legally and financially, and a clear view of who else is involved and what they seek to gain.

Chapter 11 brings together a diverse set of players, each with different interests and levels of influence over the process. Understanding who these parties are, and how they interact, is essential for anyone navigating a restructuring.

At the center of the process is the debtor, the company that has filed for bankruptcy. In most cases, the management team stays in place as the "debtor in possession (DIP)", continuing to run day-to-day operations and charged with developing a reorganization plan. The goal is to stabilize the business and emerge from bankruptcy as a viable entity, often requiring deep operational changes and debt restructuring. Although it may seem counterintuitive to leave management in control after a company has failed, the system recognizes the value of keeping leadership in place that is familiar with the business and its operations. That said, creditors sometimes challenge management's continued role. I've seen cases where creditors demanded new leadership as a condition for supporting a restructuring.

Secured creditors, such as banks, private investment funds, and bondholders, often hold significant sway in a Chapter 11 case. Their claims are backed by specific assets like real estate, equipment, inventory, or accounts receivable, giving them priority in repayment and leverage in negotiations. Secured creditors usually seek a quick resolution to avoid further erosion of their collateral's value. They may also provide, or refuse to provide, DIP financing (more on this in the next section), and their approval is typically necessary for any reorganization plan that affects their claims. Smart investors start by mapping out the secured creditor landscape, as these parties often hold the keys to any deal.

Alongside secured creditors, creditors' committees play a pivotal role. Appointed by the Office of the United State Trustee (a division of the Department of Justice), these committees represent the broader interests of unsecured creditors, vendors, suppliers, and others without collateral backing their claims. Typically comprised of five to seven of the largest unsecured creditors, these committees investigate the debtor's finances, negotiate on behalf of all unsecured creditors, and sometimes propose competing reorganization plans. Although the committee doesn't run the company, it has substantial influence. Funded by the bankruptcy estate, it can hire attorneys and financial advisors and has the right to be heard on virtually every matter in the case. For investors with large unsecured positions, winning a seat on the committee can provide direct input on the future of the company and a way to influence the terms of recovery.

The broader group of unsecured creditors, which includes many smaller vendors and suppliers, relies on the committee to advocate for their interests. Recoveries for unsecured creditors vary widely, depending on how much value remains after satisfying secured debts. In some cases, unsecured creditors might recover only pennies on the dollar; in others, they might receive meaningful recoveries in cash, new debt, or equity in the reorganized company. The difference often comes down to how much enterprise value is left and whether unsecured creditors can organize effectively to push for a fair share.

In some cases, labor unions also become a key part of the negotiations. In industries where unions represent a large share of the workforce, such as manufacturing, transportation, and hospitality, union agreements can make or break a restructuring. Although companies can attempt to reject union contracts under Section 1113 of the Bankruptcy Code, doing so requires a separate legal process with specific hurdles. I've seen cases where union negotiations became the focal point of the entire bankruptcy, with jobs, wages, and pensions hanging in the balance.

Government entities also play a role, sometimes behind the scenes and sometimes front and center. The U.S. Trustee oversees the administrative side of the case, making sure all parties follow bankruptcy procedures. Regulatory agencies may get involved, especially if the company operates in a highly regulated industry like healthcare or energy. Tax authorities, including federal, state, and local offices, may also have claims for unpaid taxes. And, of course, the bankruptcy court itself has to approve all major decisions. The judge's approach can shape the entire case. Some judges are very hands-on, actively managing negotiations, while others prefer to let the parties work things out on their own. For serious investors, understanding the particular court and judge is part of the diligence process.

All these parties—the debtor, secured and unsecured creditors, unions, government agencies, and the court—interact in ways that shape the course of a Chapter 11 case. Their competing interests create a mix of negotiation and conflict, but also opportunities for creative solutions. The bankruptcy process is, at its core, a structured negotiation that balances these different forces. The most successful investors know how to read the room, identifying where interests align, where they clash, and how to build coalitions that move the process forward.

One of the most powerful aspects of Chapter 11 is its flexibility. The process gives companies room to negotiate with creditors, reject or assume contracts, and develop a plan of reorganization tailored to their specific needs, all under the protection of the court. But as anyone familiar with distressed investing knows, no two Chapter 11 cases are alike. Timelines can vary from a few months to several years, depending on how much consensus can be built among stakeholders and what challenges emerge during the case (see Fig. 2). This flexibility is what makes Chapter 11 so useful—and potentially complex.

Exclusivity is another element of Chapter 11 that fundamentally shapes the dynamics of the case. The Bankruptcy Code grants the debtor the exclusive right to propose a reorganization plan for the first 120 days after filing. During this period, creditors cannot propose competing plans. Courts can extend this period up to 18 months, giving the debtor more time to develop a viable restructuring strategy.

For investors, exclusivity is a double-edged sword. It gives the debtor significant control over the reorganization process, potentially limiting creditors' influence. Yet it also provides

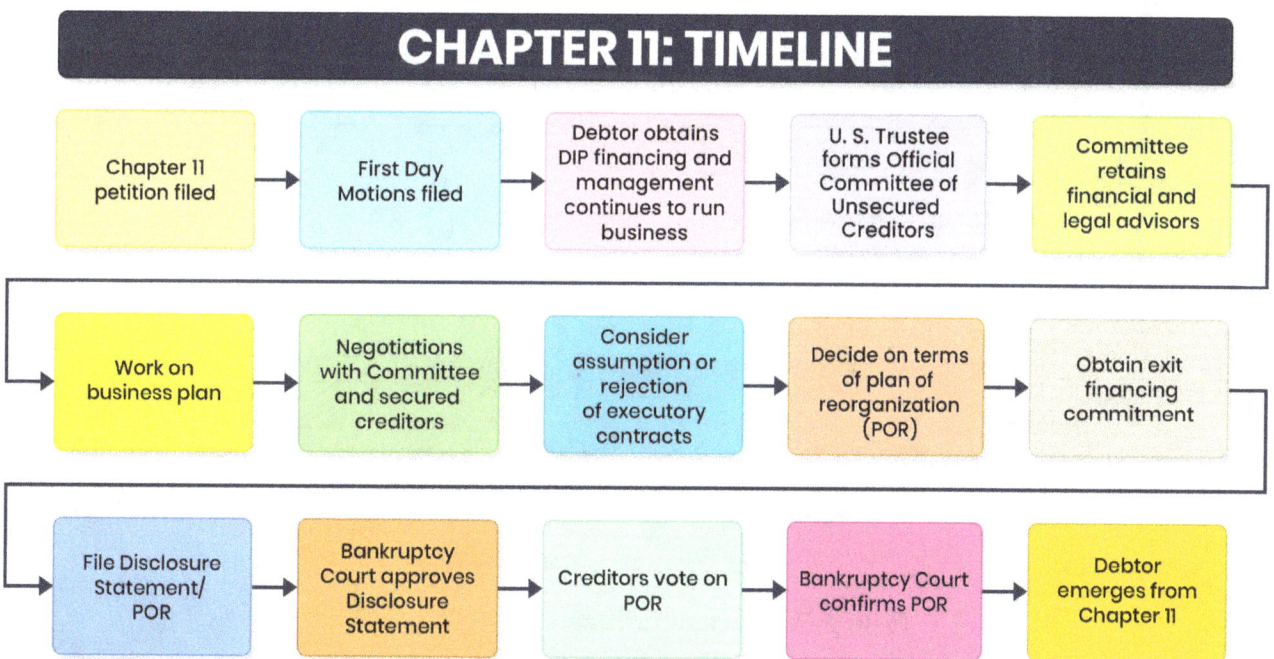

Figure 2: Chapter 11: Timeline

certainty, as investors know the debtor will initially drive the restructuring process. I've been involved in cases where the real negotiation was about the extension of exclusivity, because whoever controls the plan essentially controls the outcome (see Fig. 3).

The takeaway is that each party to a bankruptcy has their own agenda and negotiating position. As an investor, you must assess where you sit within the capital structure and how best to protect and improve your position.

Bankruptcy Levers

As we covered just above, each party's strategy is influenced by its unique position. But they must also take into account five essential components that govern the bankruptcy process: absolute priority, automatic stay, claim, Rule 3001(e), and liquidation value (see Fig. 4).

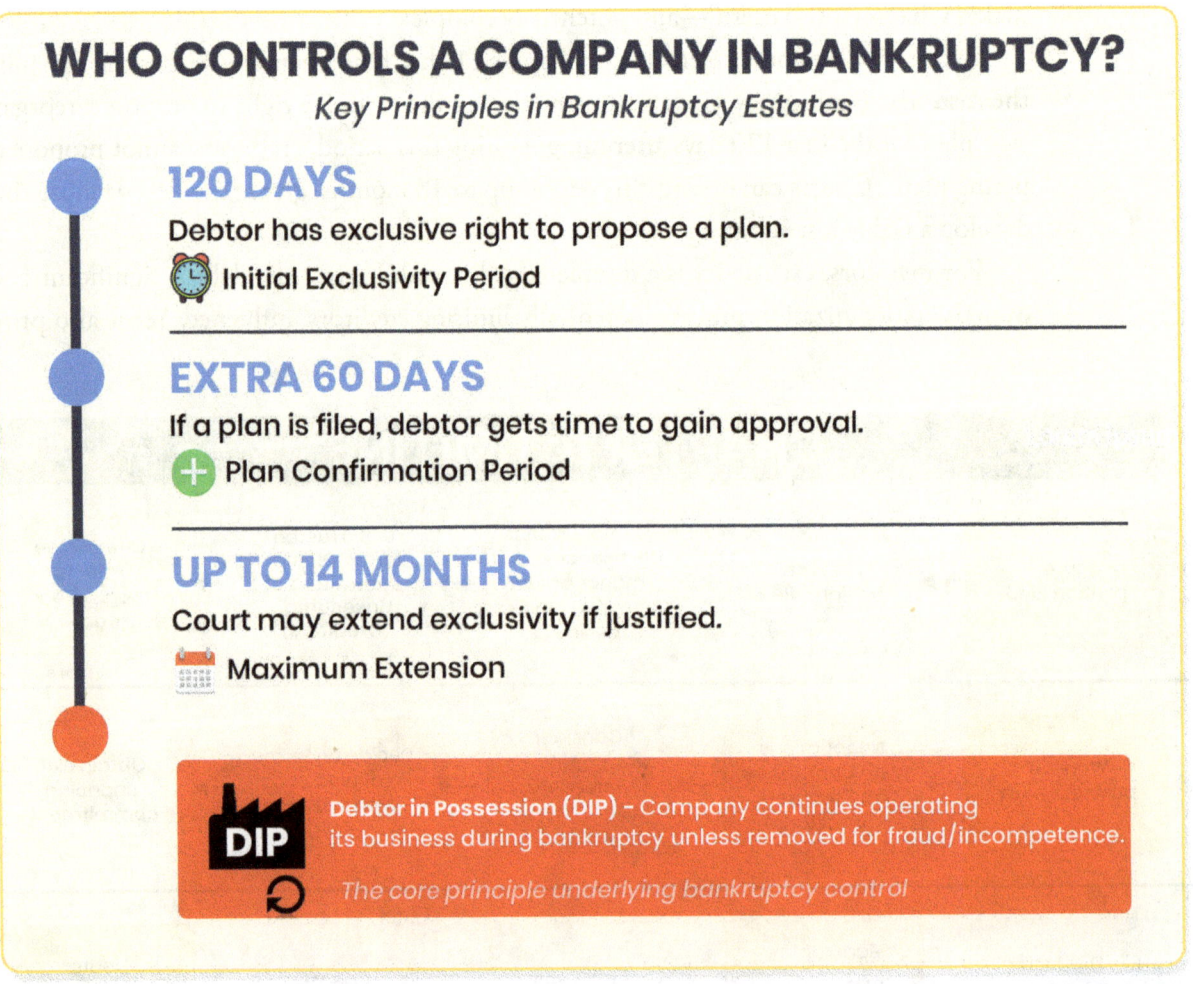

Figure 3: Who Controls a Company in Bankruptcy?

Figure 4: Bankruptcy: Key Concepts

Absolute priority, which appears in Section 507 of the U.S. Bankruptcy Code, sets the order in which creditors are paid when a company is liquidated. It establishes a clear hierarchy, starting with senior secured lenders and ending with shareholders. Think of it as a corporate caste system. Secured lenders, often banks or investment funds, are first in line to claim whatever assets remain. Unsecured creditors, such as suppliers and bondholders, follow behind and often receive less. Shareholders usually get nothing. Where you stand in this hierarchy shapes your negotiating leverage, the potential size of your recovery, and your approach to the investment. Senior secured debt may offer more protection but typically comes with lower returns. Junior claims or equity can offer greater upside, but only if you navigate the process well.

The **automatic stay**, which takes effect when a company files for Chapter 11 bankruptcy, pauses all collection efforts and lawsuits against the debtor. It gives the company breathing room to reorganize. For investors, an automatic stay can help protect value by preventing a rush to liquidate assets, but it can also delay resolution and drain resources. Investors who understand how to work within this pause may offer debtor-in-possession (DIP) financing to keep the company operating, often at attractive terms, or they may push management to sell assets before value deteriorates.

DIP financing is a specific type of funding provided to companies that have filed for Chapter 11 bankruptcy protection. In Chapter 11, the company's management is "the debtor in possession" in control of the company. DIP loans are unique because they take priority over existing debt, equity, and other claims. Despite the borrower's distressed state, this super-priority status makes DIP loans attractive to lenders.

These loans play an important role in bankruptcy cases by providing the working capital a company needs to continue operating while it restructures. Beyond covering day-to-day expenses, a DIP loan shows the bankruptcy court and other stakeholders that the company has the resources to execute a realistic business plan to move the case forward. In some cases, securing a DIP loan can even help bring in additional investors by signaling that lenders see value in the company's future and are willing to support it through the restructuring process. However, DIP loans often have high interest rates and strict covenants—legal agreements that impose specific conditions or restrictions on the borrower to protect the lender's interest—reflecting the risky nature of lending to a bankrupt company. For investors, DIP financing can offer attractive returns, but it requires deep pockets and a thorough understanding of bankruptcy law and corporate finance.

To influence the outcome of a restructuring, an investor must hold a **claim**. In bankruptcy, it is a right to payment based on a loan, bond, invoice, or other obligation. Claims are grouped into classes according to their seniority and security (see Fig. 5), and each class votes together as a bloc. An investor who controls a large enough share of a class may be able to shape the final deal.

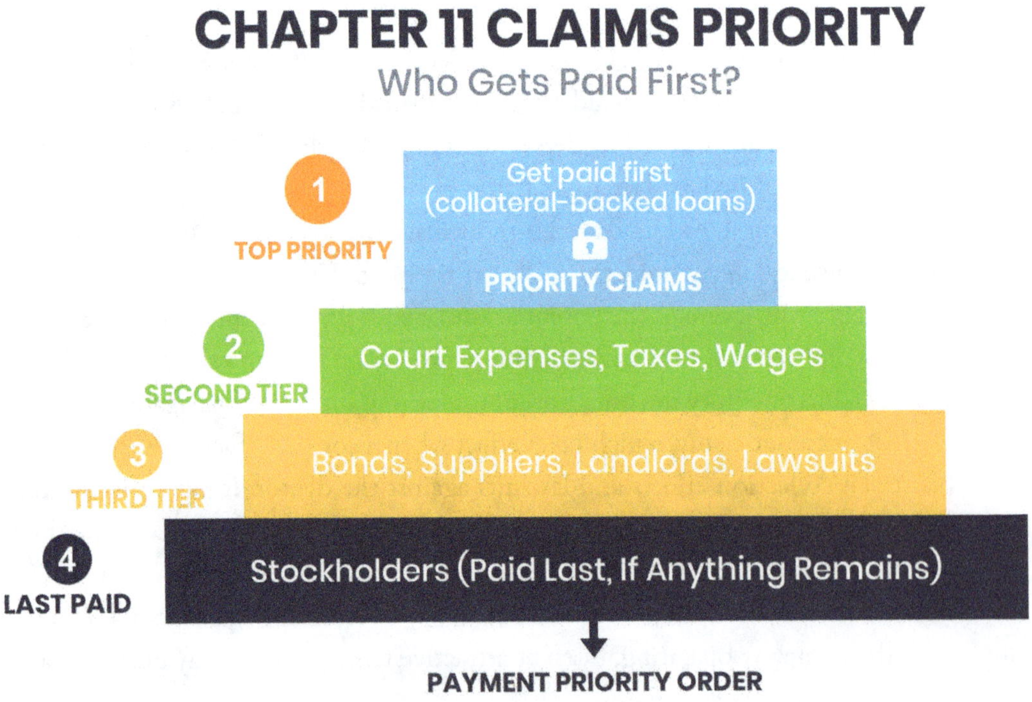

CHAPTER 11 CLAIMS PRIORITY
Who Gets Paid First?

1 TOP PRIORITY — Get paid first (collateral-backed loans) — PRIORITY CLAIMS

2 SECOND TIER — Court Expenses, Taxes, Wages

3 THIRD TIER — Bonds, Suppliers, Landlords, Lawsuits

4 LAST PAID — Stockholders (Paid Last, If Anything Remains)

PAYMENT PRIORITY ORDER

Figure 5: Chapter 11 Claims Priority: Who Gets Paid First?

Claims, however, do not always remain with the original creditor. A secondary market exists where claims are bought and sold, governed by **Rule 3001(e)** of the Federal Rules of Bankruptcy Procedure. This market allows creditors to sell claims for cash or to avoid the complexity of bankruptcy, while providing an entry point for new investors to gain influence. Claims may be transferred to others if the right documentation is filed and no one objects within 21 days. Later in this book, we will look more closely at how claims trading works, but for now, it is enough to understand that building a significant stake in the capital structure can give an investor real leverage in negotiations.

Whether you are providing DIP financing, encouraging a sale of assets, or accumulating claims, every strategy in distressed investing comes back to a single question: is the company worth more alive or dead? To answer this, consider the **liquidation value**, i.e., the price that could be achieved if the company's assets were sold off individually. Liquidation value sets a floor for what creditors might recover. If the assets are worth more sold off than operated, creditors may force a Chapter 7 liquidation. If there is greater value in keeping the company running, Chapter 11 reorganization becomes the focus. The investor's job is to evaluate these alternatives, identify the path that offers the greatest recovery, and help guide the outcome.

Professionals in Bankruptcy Cases

Beyond debtors, creditors, and government agencies, a wide range of bankruptcy professionals shapes the outcome of a Chapter 11 case. Attorneys, financial advisors, and restructuring specialists guide strategy, manage negotiations, and influence both the pace and direction of the process, all under court supervision. For investors and industry professionals, understanding who these players are and how they operate can open doors to valuable insights and opportunities.

Among the most influential are the debtor's attorneys, the legal team representing the company throughout the case. This is rarely a solo role; debtors are typically represented by a team from a specialized bankruptcy law firm, and the firm's retention must be approved by the court under strict guidelines. Although the court oversees their appointment and fees, debtor's counsel often wields enormous influence, including helping determine where to file the case, a choice that can shape everything from procedural speed to the applicable case law. Delaware, New York, and Texas are among the most common venues. For anyone seeking to operate in the bankruptcy world, whether as an investor or service provider, building relationships with debtor's counsel can be a key entry point.

On the other side of the table are the attorneys for the Official Committee of Unsecured Creditors, who represent the collective interests of unsecured creditors. Appointed by the U.S. Trustee, the creditors' committee selects its own counsel, and these lawyers play a central role in negotiating with the debtor and helping shape the reorganization or liquidation plan. They work to maximize recoveries for unsecured creditors and often act as a check on the debtor's proposals.

Increasingly common in larger Chapter 11 cases is the appointment of a chief restructuring officer (CRO), an experienced restructuring professional brought in to guide the company through the bankruptcy process. The CRO often takes the lead on financial and operational matters, oversees the company's budget during bankruptcy, and prepares key filings, including sworn statements explaining why the company needed to seek Chapter 11 protection. In many cases, the CRO effectively runs the business day-to-day while management focuses on restructuring.

Financial advisors are also integral to the process, typically hired by both the debtor and the creditors' committee. On the debtor side, financial advisors help assess the company's restructuring options, including debt negotiations and asset sales. On the committee side, they evaluate the company's finances, analyze proposed restructuring terms, and advise on the fairness of asset valuations and potential recoveries. In larger cases, multiple advisory firms may be involved, with specialists focused on particular issues such as lease renegotiation or asset disposition.

Although all these professionals are compensated from the bankruptcy estate, they must be approved by the court and are expected to act as disinterested parties, even as their fees grow with the length and complexity of the case. For investors, understanding how these professionals operate, and recognizing their incentives, can provide insight into how a case is likely to unfold. Developing relationships with these players can also create deal flow and open the door to investment opportunities that might not otherwise be visible.

The field of bankruptcy and restructuring advisory work remains an accessible pathway into distressed investing. Many professionals who work as attorneys, financial advisors, or CROs eventually transition into investing roles, including positions at large distressed-focused hedge funds and private equity firms. I often encourage my students at NYU to consider these roles as a starting point, since working on large Chapter 11 cases provides not only technical knowledge but also exposure to decision-makers in the distressed space.

Indeed, bankruptcy cases are some of the best training grounds for learning how to value distressed companies, structure deals, and negotiate under pressure. Unlike classroom exercises, these are real businesses with real stakes, often involving hundreds of millions of dollars. For students and early-career professionals, gaining experience in this environment can be a great stepping stone.

Restructuring Support Agreements (RSAs)

One of the most important developments in Chapter 11 practice over the past decade has been the widespread adoption of restructuring support agreements, or RSAs. These contracts, negotiated between a debtor and key creditors before a bankruptcy case is even filed, are now a common feature of large corporate restructurings. In effect, an RSA is a deal to make a deal, a way to lock in the key terms of a restructuring and avoid the delays, costs, and uncertainty of a fully contested case (see Fig. 6). While Chapter 11 was once a free-for-all that left outcomes wide open, RSAs reflect a shift towards negotiated solutions that seek to preserve value and minimize chaos.

BANKRUPTCY 101

WHAT IS A RESTRUCTURING SUPPORT AGREEMENT (RSA)?

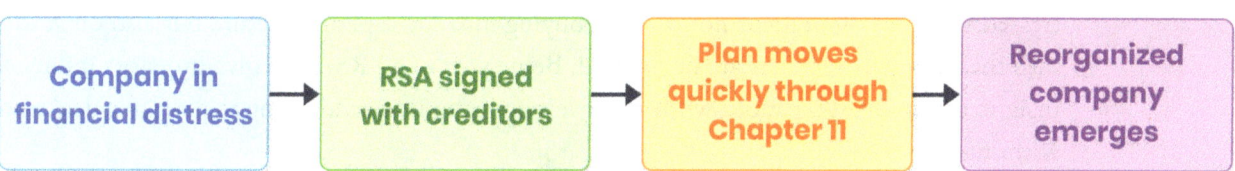

Figure 6: What Is a Restructuring Support Agreement (RSA)?

At their core, RSAs are about forging consensus among the most influential players in a restructuring. They outline the main terms of a proposed reorganization plan and bind creditors to support that plan once the bankruptcy case is underway. In doing so, RSAs seek to ensure that the debtor's plan can move through the bankruptcy court without being derailed by creditor opposition or endless rounds of litigation. For investors, this means that much of the real work, and many of the real decisions, are now made at the negotiating table long before the formal bankruptcy process begins.

Although no two RSAs are exactly alike, they tend to share common elements. A plan term sheet is usually attached, summarizing how each class of creditors will be treated, who will be paid in full, who will take a haircut, and who might receive equity in the reorganized company. RSAs also include support obligations, requiring signatory creditors to vote for the plan and to refrain from taking actions that would obstruct the process. To ensure momentum, RSAs set milestones and deadlines for key events, such as filing the plan, soliciting votes, and seeking confirmation from the court. To prevent the negotiated deal from unraveling, RSAs often impose transfer restrictions, limiting the ability of creditors to sell their claims unless the buyer agrees to be bound by the RSA. Recognizing that restructurings are inherently uncertain, most RSAs also include termination provisions, allowing creditors to walk away if certain conditions, such as court approval or financial performance benchmarks, aren't met.

For companies and supporting creditors, RSAs offer a way to impose structure and predictability on what might otherwise be a chaotic and value-destructive process. They can help ensure that a company doesn't lose momentum or value while parties argue over competing plans. From the debtor's perspective, RSAs can also signal to the market that key players are aligned, which may help stabilize operations and relationships with customers, vendors, and employees during a difficult time.

But RSAs are not without controversy. By locking in the terms of a deal before other creditors can weigh in, RSAs can tilt the playing field and limit options for nonparticipating stakeholders. Courts have become increasingly aware of these risks and are more likely to scrutinize RSAs that appear to unfairly predetermine the outcome of a case or disadvantage certain groups of creditors. Still, because of the value they can preserve, RSAs are often favored in large, complex cases where time and uncertainty can erode what's left for creditors.

For investors, RSAs present a double-edged sword. If you're at the negotiating table, they can be a powerful tool for shaping the deal, protecting your position, and securing commitments from other creditors. But if you're left out of the process, you may find yourself boxed into a restructuring plan that has already been largely decided. That's why sophisticated distressed investors often focus not only on buying into the capital structure but also on getting into the room where RSAs are negotiated. Being part of an RSA can give investors influence, insight, and a seat at the table, while being left out can mean scrambling to react to a deal made without you.

In the modern Chapter 11 landscape, RSAs have become more than just paperwork; they are where many of the most important decisions are made. Understanding how they work, how they are negotiated, and how they can impact your position is now a requirement for anyone serious about distressed investing.

CASE STUDY IN REORGANIZATION: J.CREW

Now that we've covered the framework of Chapter 11 and the key players in it, it's time to look at how these elements work in practice. Few cases illustrate the challenges and opportunities of a corporate restructuring better than J.Crew, whose saga has become almost legendary in distressed investing circles.

J.Crew's 2020 restructuring offers a textbook example of how Chapter 11 can be used strategically. Once one of the most recognizable brands in American retail, J.Crew had been struggling for years under a crushing debt load, worsened by declining sales and the broader turmoil in the retail sector. When the COVID-19 pandemic hit, it pushed the company over the edge, forcing J.Crew to file for Chapter 11 protection in May 2020. As the company acknowledged at the time, the pandemic accelerated problems that had been building for years.

Yet what makes J.Crew's case especially instructive is how the company and its investors used Chapter 11 not simply to survive but to reposition itself for long-term success. Unlike many retailers that succumbed to the so-called retail apocalypse during the COVID-19 pandemic, J.Crew approached bankruptcy not as a death sentence but as a strategic opportunity for comprehensive restructuring. I have seen many cases where companies wait too long to file, clinging to hope and draining resources, only to leave themselves with fewer options and more damage to repair. By contrast, companies that embrace restructuring with purpose tend to emerge stronger, and J.Crew is a clear example of this mindset in action.

The company's reorganization plan addressed both its financial and operational challenges by focusing on four main areas.

First, through a debt-for-equity swap, J.Crew converted $1.7 billion of debt into equity, effectively handing control to its lenders but reducing its debt burden to a level the business could sustain. This step alone cut interest payments by $150 million annually, freeing up cash flow to reinvest in operations and growth.

Second, J.Crew secured $400 million in DIP financing to ensure it could continue operating, pay employees, and keep stores stocked during the bankruptcy process. This financing was necessary to keep the business running and to avoid further harm to the brand.

Third, the company used Chapter 11 to renegotiate or reject unprofitable store leases, trimming its expensive brick-and-mortar footprint and reducing fixed costs. This effort to optimize its store network was central to repositioning the business for a retail environment that increasingly favors online shopping and selective physical locations.

Finally, and perhaps most significantly, J.Crew treated the restructuring as an opportunity for broader strategic reinvention. The company brought in new creative leadership, refocused on its core strengths in quality and style, and worked to rebuild customer trust. Bankruptcy gave J.Crew not only a financial reset but also a strategic one.

Taken together, these elements show that successful restructurings require more than just fixing a broken balance sheet. You can't simply swap debt for equity and expect a turnaround. The companies that thrive after bankruptcy are those that address operational and strategic issues at the same time. I've watched many companies go through bankruptcy only to falter again because they never dealt with the real underlying problems, whether flawed business models, bad management, or outdated strategies.

J.Crew's case also highlights how the legal and financial elements of Chapter 11 must work hand in hand. Its legal team structured a deal that significantly reduced debt while management tackled operational issues and repositioned the brand for a post-bankruptcy world. Not everyone was happy with the result. Some creditors were left holding painful losses. But from a restructuring standpoint, it was a textbook example of using Chapter 11 to solve a company's problems, not just paper over them (see Fig. 7).

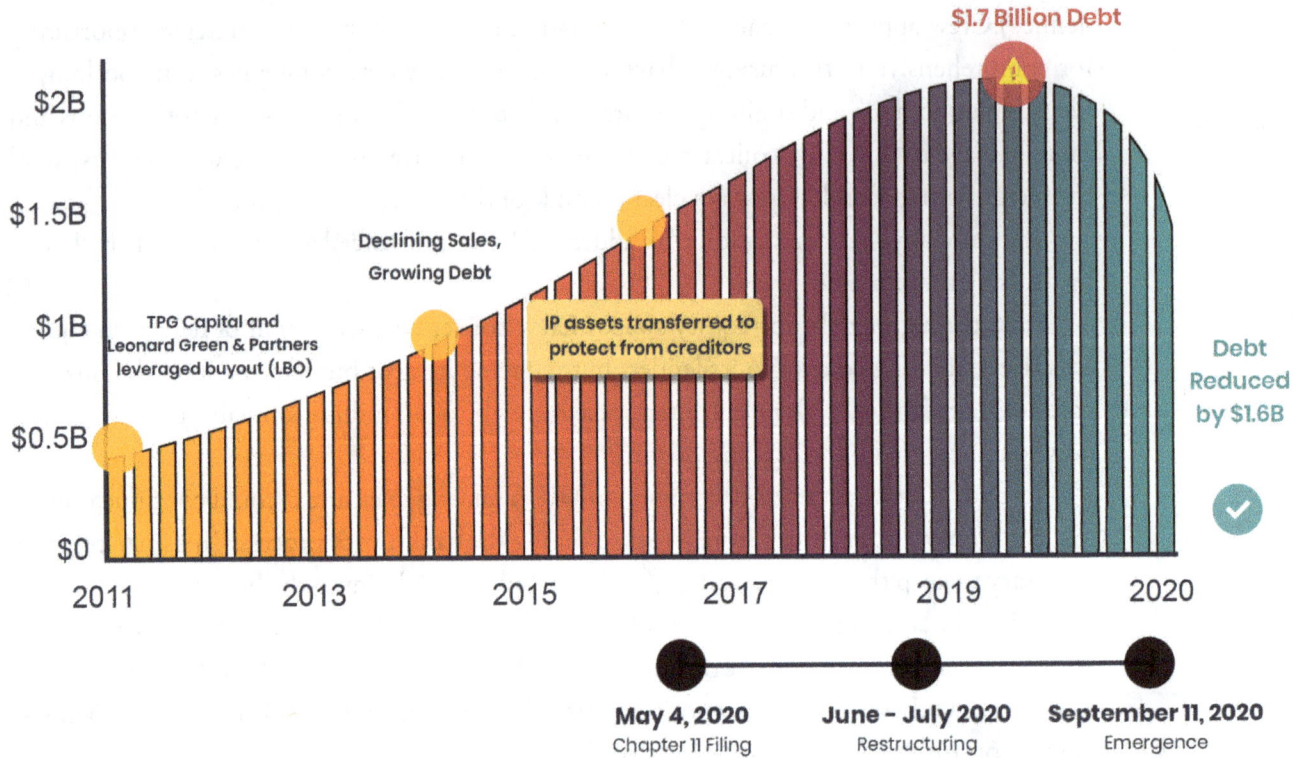

Figure 7: J.Crew: From Debt Crisis to Rebirth

These coordinated efforts resulted in a leaner, more agile J.Crew that emerged from bankruptcy in September 2020, just four months after filing. The speed and effectiveness of this turnaround underscore the potential of Chapter 11 as a tool for corporate renewal when leveraged with clear strategy and decisive action.

The four-month timeline is remarkably quick for a company of J.Crew's size and complexity. This efficiency was largely due to extensive pre-bankruptcy planning and negotiations. When you see a case move this quickly, it usually indicates that major stakeholders reached a consensus on the key terms before the filing. For investors, this highlights the importance of being involved in those pre-filing discussions whenever possible.

The company's successful reorganization was a testament to the power of the Chapter 11 process and the importance of having a clear vision and strategy for the future. In particular, taking steps to secure $400 million in DIP financing significantly helped its reorganization prospects (see Fig. 8).

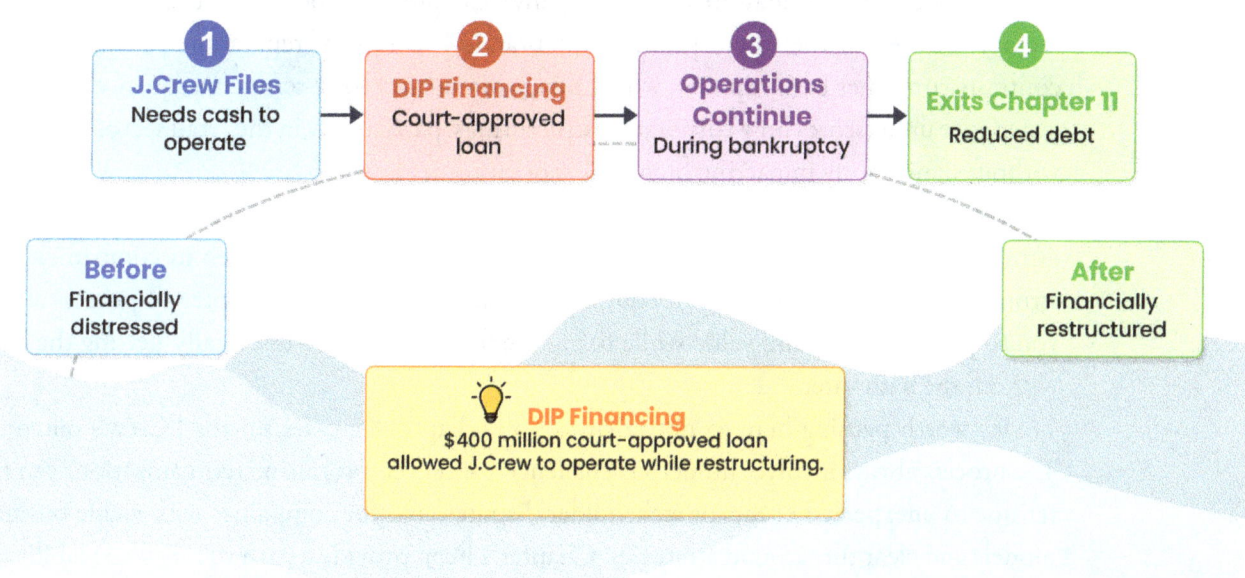

Figure 8: DIP Financing: How J.Crew Stayed Afloat

DIP financing deserves special attention from investors because it represents both a potential investment opportunity and a powerful control mechanism. The DIP lender often gains significant influence over the case through the covenants and milestones built into the loan agreements. I've seen DIP lenders effectively dictate the timeline and even the outcome of cases through these provisions.

This situation creates interesting dynamics for investors. Sometimes, the best strategy is to become the DIP lender, while in other situations, you might focus on ensuring the DIP terms don't unfairly disadvantage your position. What's critical is understanding that DIP financing isn't just about providing liquidity—it's about establishing leverage in the restructuring process.

For J.Crew, this financing kept its supply chain intact, stores open, and covered bankruptcy-related costs. Without it, J.Crew might have followed the path of so many retailers, who enter Chapter 11 only to end up in liquidation.

The company's story isn't one of unqualified success, however, as J.Crew continues to face ongoing challenges, including stiff competition and shifts in consumer behavior due to the pandemic. However, using Chapter 11's tools to restructure its balance sheet and operations, J.Crew has improved its chances in a difficult retail environment.

This point is worth emphasizing: bankruptcy is rarely a silver bullet that solves all problems. What it does is give companies a fighting chance by addressing acute financial distress and creating space for operational improvements. The best Chapter 11 outcomes occur when the company emerges with both a sustainable balance sheet and a credible plan for addressing market challenges.

Notably, J.Crew's bankruptcy filing carried little to no stigma among consumers. Most shoppers likely remain unaware of the company's Chapter 11 process, and those who do know seem unaffected in their perception of the brand. This lack of reputational damage starkly contrasts consumer bankruptcies, where filings often carry long-term consequences. J.Crew's experience underscores how corporate restructurings, particularly in the retail sector, can occur without significantly impacting brand value or customer loyalty.

This disconnect between financial restructuring and consumer perception creates interesting opportunities. Some of my most successful investments have been in companies with strong brands and customer loyalty but broken balance sheets. The Chapter 11 process allows you to preserve the brand value while fixing the financial issues—essentially, getting the baby without the bathwater.

It's worth pausing here to note that not all Chapter 11 cases mirror J.Crew's outcome. The process always involves numerous challenges, and even promising reorganizations can falter due to unexpected events or stakeholder disputes. Yet, for companies with viable business models and clear turnaround strategies, Chapter 11 can provide a path to renewed viability. A well-structured Chapter 11 reorganization can provide a struggling company with a second chance while allowing investors and creditors to recover value.

However, not all restructurings are created equal. Bankruptcy gives companies a second chance, but it doesn't guarantee success, nor does it always unfold in predictable ways. Increasingly, creditors and investors are pushing the boundaries of what's possible in restructurings, using advanced legal and financial maneuvers that can dramatically shift outcomes, sometimes in ways that leave other stakeholders behind.

In Chapter 7, we'll take a closer look at these emerging strategies and contentious deal structures, from liability management exercises and uptier transactions to drop-down deals and the much-debated "Texas Two-Step." We'll also explore how courts are responding to these innovations, how tax considerations shape deal outcomes, and how different industries bring their own sets of challenges and opportunities to the restructuring process.

In the next chapter, though, we'll continue to keep our focus on the fundamentals: the different types of distressed assets.

KEY INSIGHTS

1. The American bankruptcy system is unique in its focus on second chances and business continuity, allowing companies to recover rather than shutting down permanently.
2. Economic downturns increase bankruptcy filings, creating both risks for businesses and opportunities for distressed investors who understand the restructuring process.
3. The automatic stay provides immediate protection for debtors, preventing creditors from taking collection actions outside the bankruptcy process and allowing businesses time to reorganize.

4. The exclusivity period grants debtors control over the reorganization process for at least 120 days, shaping negotiations with creditors.
5. The Absolute Priority Rule dictates payment hierarchy in Chapter 11 cases, influencing how much each creditor class recovers and shaping negotiations.
6. Claims trading allows investors to enter bankruptcy cases by purchasing debt from creditors, but proper documentation and compliance with Rule 3001(e) are essential.
7. Liquidation value establishes a baseline for creditor recoveries in Chapter 11 cases, making it a critical factor in negotiations and plan confirmation.
8. DIP financing provides liquidity during bankruptcy and often gives lenders significant influence over the restructuring process through covenants and milestones.
9. The DIP structure allows management to remain in control, but creditors sometimes push for leadership changes if management is seen as responsible for the company's decline.
10. Creditors' committees represent unsecured creditors and wield significant influence in Chapter 11 cases, often shaping the reorganization process through negotiations and legal challenges.
11. RSAs pre-negotiate bankruptcy outcomes, reducing uncertainty but sometimes raising concerns about fairness for nonparticipating creditors.
12. Pre-bankruptcy negotiations often determine outcomes more than the formal bankruptcy process itself, making early engagement crucial for investors.
13. Successful restructurings address both financial and operational challenges; fixing balance sheets alone does not ensure long-term success.
14. The J.Crew case demonstrates how companies can use Chapter 11 strategically to shed debt, optimize operations, and reposition themselves for future growth.

CHAPTER 3

Types of Distressed Assets

Opportunity rarely arrives with a clear label.

More often than not, it appears as a messy, complicated situation that most investors would rather avoid. Imagine hearing that a once-profitable manufacturing company has filed for bankruptcy after a series of missteps, such as supply chain disruptions, rising interest rates, and a failed product launch. On the surface, the headlines scream "failure!" But for those who know where to look, the situation might hold hidden value: unpaid invoices that could be bought at a discount, equipment that could be resold, or a core business that could thrive with the right capital and leadership.

Distressed investing is about seeing what others miss. It's about recognizing that assets often become undervalued when fear and uncertainty take hold. Success comes not from chasing every troubled company but from identifying situations where the risk is mispriced and the potential upside is worth the challenge. Of course, not every deal is a home run. Sometimes, the win is simply getting on base, securing a trade claim at a discount, purchasing distressed real estate with hidden upside, or investing in a struggling business poised for a turnaround. Over time, these smaller wins can add up to significant profits.

In this chapter, I'll explore four primary categories of distressed assets: trade claims, special situation investments, distressed real estate notes, and operating businesses. Each presents unique risks and rewards, but they all share a common theme: the opportunity to generate strong returns by buying low when others are eager to sell.

We'll begin with trade claims, an asset class that frequently serves as a gateway into the world of distressed investing.

Trade Claims

Suppose you're a vendor, and a company you've been supplying goods to for years suddenly files for bankruptcy. You're left holding unpaid invoices, wondering if you'll ever see a dime. That's where the opportunity to purchase trade claims arises for investors. Simply put, a trade claim is the right to collect money owed by a company that has filed for bankruptcy, typically for goods or services provided before the bankruptcy filing. These claims are often sold at a discount because the outcome of the bankruptcy process is uncertain (see Fig. 1).

TRADE CLAIMS INVESTMENT FLOW

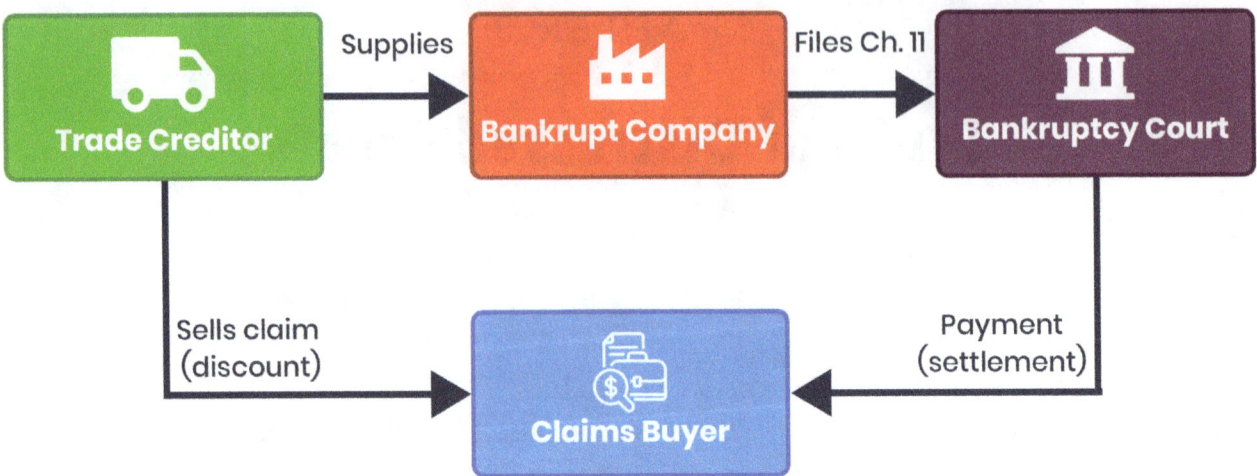

Figure 1: Trade Claims Investment Flow

You might wonder why anyone would want to buy a claim against a bankrupt company. Well, there are several reasons. First, buyers have an opportunity to profit by purchasing claims at a discount and recovering more from the bankruptcy process than they paid. Second, if an investor buys enough trade claims, they may actually be able to influence the bankruptcy process itself. Third, buying multiple trade claims in multiple bankruptcies can diversify risk, as returns may vary from one case to another. As for why vendors sell trade claims, it's because they want to "take the cash and run." It's a classic case of "one man's trash is another man's treasure."

Trade claims represent a large market, with billions of dollars in claims changing hands each year. In 2018, trade claims topped $25 billion, according to the leading online industry news source DailyDAC (Distressed Asset Central), not counting claims related to the Lehman Brothers bankruptcy.[3]

Investing in trade claims isn't without risk (but you know that). One big one is that, unless you resell a claim, you may have to wait years for the underlying legal case to be resolved before receiving any money. For example, suppose you buy a claim at 20 cents on the dollar and recover 25 cents. At first glance, that sounds like a 25% return (5 cents profit on a 20 cent investment). But if the process takes three years, the annualized return is much lower, approximately 7.5% per year. Factoring in the time, effort, inflation, and potential legal fees involved, the return might not seem as appealing, especially if the ultimate value of your claims isn't very much to begin with.

So when you purchase a claim, you are essentially betting on how the bankruptcy process will unfold. Key questions to consider include: Will there be enough money to pay creditors? Will the claim's validity be challenged in court? How long will the process take? These uncertainties can significantly impact the return on investment.

TYPES OF DISTRESSED ASSETS

JCPenney, Nortel Networks, Lehman Brothers: What Trade Claim Cases Reveal About Industry-Specific Risks and Opportunities

To understand how trade claims work, let's look at three recent real-life examples: a retail case, a technology case, and a financial services company case.

In May 2020, as the COVID-19 pandemic was ramping up, JCPenney filed for Chapter 11 bankruptcy. The company's first move was to immediately ask the court to let them pay their most important suppliers to maintain inventory, stabilize operations, and keep the business running, an action commonly referred to as a "critical vendor motion" in retail bankruptcies. At the time of filing, it owed millions to suppliers like Nike, Adidas, Lee, and Van Heusen. These companies were part of a class of 29,000 unsecured creditors whose claims amounted to approximately $40 million.

Despite its storied brand name, JCPenney did not present as an attractive opportunity for trade claim investors. In fact, most buyers avoided JCPenney trade claims because they knew from experience that when a retailer's business starts declining, they borrow against every available asset to help stay afloat, a business practice that leaves little value for unsecured creditors. In fact, most of the inventory you see when you visit a gleaming department store, whether neatly arranged on racks or stacked on tables, is totally leveraged. If you've ever been to a going-out-of-business sale, you know that inventory is worth pennies on the dollar if it doesn't sell in the store.

The only solution JCPenney could wrangle to stay in business was for its two largest landlords, Simon Property Group and Brookfield Asset Management, to form a venture with the retail behemoth Authentic Brands Group. While that might seem counterintuitive given Penney's financial struggles, the landlords had a clear incentive: saving JCPenney meant preserving occupancy in hundreds of shopping malls, whereas losing an anchor tenant would have triggered rent reductions or co-tenancy clauses with other retailers. Authentic, meanwhile, saw long-term brand value it could monetize through licensing. Together, the three parties formed a new ownership structure that kept JCPenney afloat, albeit in leaner form, and avoided a total liquidation of the chain. This deal allowed the landlords to continue having rent-paying tenants and vendors to sell goods. As for the trade claim debt: when the case was finalized, unsecured creditors received a total of $750,000, approximately two cents on the dollar. An investor who purchased claims for 10 cents on the dollar would have lost 80% of their investment.

In my experience, this is a common outcome when it comes to companies like JCPenney. Retail bankruptcies rarely deliver meaningful returns to unsecured claimants.

The same is not true, however, when companies with valuable intellectual property rights are involved, as was the case with telecommunications giant Nortel Networks in 2009. Because of Nortel's IP, it was clear from the beginning of its bankruptcy case that investors in its trade claims had the potential for earning outsized gains. Indeed, for those willing to roll up their sleeves and do their homework, Nortel's bankruptcy became one of the most successful trade claims investments in recent history.

THE DISTRESSED INVESTING PLAYBOOK

At its peak, the Canadian telecommunications firm had been valued at $300 *billion*. But in January 2009, after a series of accounting scandals and the bursting of the tech bubble, it faced financial collapse. Nonetheless, when it filed for bankruptcy, the company still held significant assets in its patents covering wireless, data networking, optical, voice, internet, and semiconductor technologies; its patents related to 4G mobile broadband and LTE standards were particularly valuable.

Nortel sold off its various business units first, for about $3.2 billion. But the real windfall came in 2011 when a consortium of six companies (Apple, Microsoft, Sony, BlackBerry, EMC, and Ericsson) acquired Nortel's patent portfolio for $4.5 billion after a competitive auction that started with Google's initial bid of $900 million. The final price far exceeded expectations, creating a deep pool of assets for distribution to creditors.

This windfall was an extraordinary outcome for early investors who purchased Nortel's debt at steep discounts. Combined with the earlier asset sales, the total recovery exceeded $7 billion, and some creditors reported near-full recovery on their claims. Investors who bought trade claims at 55 cents on the dollar in March 2010 and held them to final recovery would have earned returns of more than 80%. Not too shabby.

My third example is the Lehman Brothers bankruptcy, the largest bankruptcy of a financial institution in U.S. history. When it filed in the fall of 2008, kick-starting the 2008 market crash, Lehman listed a whopping $639 billion in assets. Beyond its financial holdings, Lehman owned a real estate portfolio spanning four continents, including office buildings in New York and London, apartment complexes in Florida, and hotels in Hawaii. On top of this, the company held billions in loans secured by commercial real estate. I'll have much more to say about this case in Chapter 6, but for now I will just consider the trade claims that resulted from the bankruptcy.

In investment banking, a time-honored belief is that when the partners and associates go home each night, the "assets" of the corporation essentially walk out the door because they possess the knowledge, relationships, and experience (the "intellectual capital") that makes the firm valuable. In other words, their primary assets are not hard assets. The 2008 market crash initially masked that Lehman Brothers was different, because it also owned significant commercial real estate in a portfolio that maintained positive cash flow despite plummeting valuations. Examples included 1301 Avenue of the Americas in New York, valued at over $900 million, and the International Financial Centre in Seoul, which sold for $768 million in 2010. Because of the financial crisis, so many other bankruptcies filed at the time were characterized by panic-driven fire sales that left most creditors in the dust. But because of Lehman's real estate cushion, their bankruptcy administrator was able to take a more methodical approach, selling off their assets as markets recovered rather than liquidating them at crisis prices.

During the proceedings, hundreds of Lehman claims changed hands over the life of the case, and investors purchased billions in claims with a recovery for unsecured creditors exceeding 40%. Investors who bought claims at 15–20 cents on the dollar during 2008–2009 eventually received 40+ cents, yielding 100%–166% returns. This outcome demonstrates an important principle in trade claims investing: those who took the time to analyze Lehman's underlying assets rather than reacting to market panic and making blind assumptions were well rewarded.

Of course, as they say in the automobile business, your mileage may vary. Precise success and recovery rates are difficult to pin down because outcomes depend so much on the nature of the bankruptcy and the specific assets involved. As a general rule, though, retail bankruptcies tend to offer fewer positive returns because retailers typically have limited tangible assets and high unsecured debt, making recoveries challenging. On the other hand, companies with substantial intellectual property, real estate, or other valuable assets may present more promising opportunities.

The reality is that no two cases are the same. Investors who succeed in trade claims learn how to spot the difference between a company with hidden value and one that's just a sinking ship. It takes more than just crunching numbers; it requires seeing past the obvious and understanding how the pieces might come together.

How to Buy Trade Claims

There are two primary ways to buy trade claims: negotiating directly with creditors or using a claims-trading platform. Each approach has its own advantages and challenges, depending on your level of experience, professional network, and willingness to invest time in the process.

One option is to purchase claims directly from creditors, which can sometimes offer better pricing since you'll avoid broker fees and middlemen. However, negotiating directly requires strong communication and negotiation skills, as well as a good understanding of the bankruptcy process. Typically, this process begins by identifying potential sellers. Creditors are listed in publicly available bankruptcy court filings and include suppliers, service providers, and other vendors owed money. Many of these creditors receive unsolicited offers from investors looking to buy claims at a discount.

Once you've identified a potential seller, the next step is to reach out directly, often to the company's CFO, accounts receivable manager, or even the bankruptcy attorney representing the creditor. It's important to be clear and professional when making initial contact, explaining that you are interested in purchasing their claim and offering immediate liquidity in exchange for a negotiated price.

The negotiation process itself is a key part of buying claims directly. Creditors may initially hold out for higher prices, especially if they are optimistic about recovering more through the bankruptcy process. To arrive at a deal, you'll want to emphasize the benefits of receiving cash upfront, particularly when the bankruptcy timeline is uncertain and could drag on for years. You should also be prepared to explain your offer in light of the company's financial condition, expected recovery rates, and the risks involved in waiting for the bankruptcy to conclude.

Before finalizing any agreement, make sure you've done enough due diligence. You'll need to verify the amount owed, confirm the claim is valid and properly documented, and assess the likelihood of objections or challenges during the bankruptcy process. This typically involves reviewing bankruptcy court filings, financial statements, and legal documents to make sure there are no red flags.

Once you are ready to move forward, a formal purchase agreement is required to transfer ownership of the claim. This contract should specify the purchase price and payment terms and include representations and warranties from the seller confirming the claim is valid. Although you could draft a basic agreement yourself, I highly recommend you work with a bankruptcy attorney to ensure the contract is legally sound and your interests are protected.

After the sale is completed, it's important to notify the bankruptcy court and submit any required documentation to update the creditor list. This step is crucial: failure to properly notify the court could mean missing distributions or payments down the line.

For investors who prefer a more streamlined process, online claims-trading platforms like Xclaim and Claims Market offer an alternative to negotiating directly. These platforms connect buyers and sellers of trade claims, providing greater transparency, standardized documentation, and faster transactions. While they do charge fees, many investors find the convenience and reduced administrative burden well worth the cost, especially if they are new to buying claims. Generally, if you use a platform like Xclaim or Claims Market, you may not need an attorney because these platforms are designed to simplify the process and ensure that documentation and procedures comply with bankruptcy court rules.

That said, there are still situations where legal counsel may be necessary. For higher-value transactions, or if any unusual issues arise (such as disputes over claim validity, challenges from other creditors, or compliance questions), it's wise to consult an attorney experienced in bankruptcy law. Legal support is particularly valuable when negotiating directly with creditors or dealing with large, complex claims. An attorney can help draft and review the purchase agreement, conduct due diligence, and assist in navigating any disputes that may emerge during the bankruptcy process.

Compliance with bankruptcy court procedures will make or break a deal. An attorney can ensure that all necessary filings are made correctly to formalize the claim transfer and secure your right to receive distributions. If you're new to the trade claims market, I strongly recommend seeking legal advice as part of your initial investment process. Mistakes in this area can be costly, and until you gain enough experience to handle the process on your own, it's better to consider legal support as part of the cost of doing business, an investment in protecting your interests and increasing the likelihood of a successful outcome.

Special Situation Investments

Special situation investments refer to unique, often time-sensitive opportunities involving distressed or undervalued assets. These opportunities can include providing rescue financing to a struggling company, taking advantage of a one-time event like a spin-off or merger, or purchasing assets from a bankruptcy estate. What ties these investments together is their complexity, the need for quick decision-making, and the potential for higher-than-average returns.

TYPES OF DISTRESSED ASSETS

While special situations can be highly profitable, they often require significant capital, sometimes tens of millions or even billions of dollars. However, investors with more modest resources can still participate, especially when they have specialized knowledge or access to niche markets. In fact, some investors have built successful careers by focusing on smaller, overlooked deals that larger firms tend to ignore.

One example of a special situation investment that's gained attention in recent years is litigation finance. In this type of investment, individuals or firms provide funding to plaintiffs or law firms in exchange for a share of any monetary award. Litigation finance can level the playing field, allowing individuals with strong legal cases to pursue justice even when facing well-funded opponents.

A famous example that brought litigation finance into the spotlight is the case of Hulk Hogan vs. Gawker Media. In 2012, the former professional wrestler sued the popular media and gossip blog for publishing a sex tape without his consent. Hogan's legal team was secretly funded by billionaire Peter Thiel, who had his own grudge against Gawker for outing him as gay in a 2007 article.

The case went to trial in 2016, with a jury awarding Hogan $140 million in damages. This massive judgment forced Gawker into bankruptcy, and the company was eventually sold to Univision. Securing a large judgment doesn't always translate to collecting the full amount, especially if the defendant lacks sufficient assets or goes bankrupt, as was the case with Gawker. Ultimately, Hogan received $31 million in the bankruptcy case, not $140 million. While Thiel's involvement was controversial, the case demonstrated how outside financing can dramatically influence legal outcomes, highlighting both the financial opportunities and ethical considerations involved in litigation funding.

Another common type of special situation investment is distressed debt investing, which involves purchasing the defaulted or bankruptcy debt of companies in financial distress or those that have already filed for bankruptcy, typically at a discount from face value. Investors then seek to restructure the debt, convert it to equity, or sell it at a profit once the company's financial situation improves.

This is what happened with Pacific Gas and Electric Company (PG&E), the California utility that filed for bankruptcy in 2019 due to billions in liabilities from wildfires caused by its equipment. Hedge funds like Elliott Management and the Pacific Investment Management Company (PIMCO) acquired PG&E's bonds at discounted prices, betting the company would eventually settle with wildfire victims and emerge from bankruptcy. Their gamble paid off when PG&E's restructuring plan was approved in 2020, resulting in what the company called a $5 billion "windfall" for bondholders.

Special situation investments can also involve providing rescue financing to companies in crisis. These investments often take the form of DIP loans.

Successfully identifying and executing special situation investments requires a combination of deep industry knowledge, strong professional networks, and the ability to move quickly when opportunities arise. Investors must thoroughly assess each opportunity's risks and potential rewards, often under tight deadlines, while conducting complex legal and financial analyses.

Patience and persistence are important traits to cultivate, as these investments can take years to yield results. Yet for those who master the process, special situation investing can deliver exceptional returns and provide a competitive advantage in the world of distressed assets.

Distressed Real Estate Notes

When most people think of investing in real estate, they picture buying physical properties like houses or apartment buildings. But there's another way to invest in real estate that doesn't involve dealing with tenants or fixing toilets: buying distressed real estate notes, which can often provide faster returns with less hands-on management.

A real estate note is essentially an IOU secured by a piece of property. When borrowers take out a mortgage to buy a house or commercial building, they sign a promissory note agreeing to repay the loan over time. If the borrower defaults on the loan, the lender can foreclose on the property and sell it to recoup their investment. However, foreclosure can be lengthy and expensive, so some lenders sell their non-performing notes to investors at a discount instead. For investors, the opportunity lies in purchasing these notes below the property's market value, creating a built-in margin of safety and potential for profit (see Fig. 2).

Investing in distressed real estate notes can offer several advantages over traditional property ownership. First, you're not responsible for property management, repairs, or ongoing expenses, as you hold the debt rather than the property itself. Second, because lenders often sell non-performing notes at a significant discount to the property's market value, investors can potentially achieve a higher return on investment. Third, note investing allows for greater diversification, as you can spread your capital across multiple properties and geographic regions.

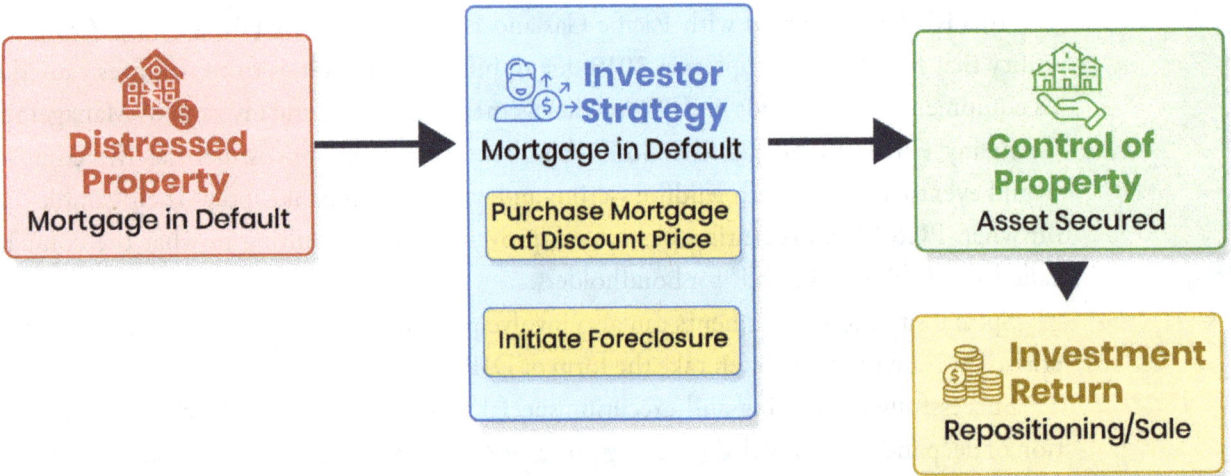

Figure 2: Real Estate Investment Strategy

TYPES OF DISTRESSED ASSETS

However, investing in real estate notes has significant risks, the most common of which is that the borrower may not resume payments even after you've purchased the note. In that case, you may have to foreclose on the property, which can be costly and time-consuming. Foreclosure laws also vary by state, impacting the timeline and complexity of repossessing a property. Moreover, there's a risk that the property's value declines, leaving you with a loss even after foreclosure.

Successful note investors conduct thorough due diligence on the borrower and the underlying property before purchasing to lessen these risks. This involves reviewing the borrower's credit history, income, and assets to assess their ability to repay the loan. It's essential to verify that the property has sufficient value to serve as collateral, which typically involves ordering an appraisal and conducting a title search to uncover any hidden liens or encumbrances. Skipping these steps can lead to costly surprises.

A real estate opportunity I brought to a group of investors several years ago offers an example of this strategy in action. The property in question was a 25,000-square-foot, ten-story condominium with retail space that was 95% complete. The controlling partnership had a $12 million mortgage that was in default. Determining the property's market value was straightforward because real estate comparables were readily available, showing the building was worth approximately $7 million at the time. The goal was to approach the bank and negotiate a purchase price as close to or below $7 million as possible.

What did the bank say? They pointed out that once the building was finished, its value could reach $12 million, $10 million, or at least $8 million, especially with a new subway station being built nearby and the neighborhood improving. As expected in distressed deals, the negotiation process became high pressure and time sensitive, with each side trying its best to outmaneuver the other.

During this process, principal decision-makers often create artificial deadlines, hint at competing offers from deep-pocketed investors, or suggest an imminent bidding war to push buyers into higher bids. Stay disciplined—and be prepared to walk away from the deal if the numbers no longer make sense. Additionally, when negotiating distressed assets, having cash in hand speaks volumes, as sellers often prioritize the certainty of closing over theoretically receiving the highest price.

It took a while, but my group bought the mortgage and secured a good deal close to our target price. Unfortunately, we were also the victims of Murphy's Law. Even though we owned the mortgage, we didn't own the building. The day after we signed the paperwork and wired the money, we arrived to inspect the property and discovered it had been flooded. A massive thunderstorm had hit the city the previous night, and the contractors had left the doors and windows open. The repair costs came out of our pocket, serving as a reminder that unexpected issues are common with distressed properties. Lesson learned: buy at a low enough price to leave room for contingencies.

A few weeks after we purchased the note, there was an additional twist: we decided to pursue a purchase of the property. To secure it, we paid the building's equity owner, the person who controlled the bankruptcy, $500,000 to transfer ownership to us. Although the bank would never have paid her half a million dollars, we recognized that gaining full control of both the mortgage and the property would maximize our long-term returns. At that point, we had already invested significantly in the project, including repairs, and controlling the property outright allowed us to better protect our investment and eliminate the risk of competing claims or legal obstacles.

While it took time to stabilize the asset and navigate the challenges, we eventually realized a solid profit on the overall investment.

How to Access Distressed Real Estate Notes

The market for distressed real estate notes is highly competitive, with hedge funds, private equity firms, and other institutional investors all vying for deals. As a result, individual investors may struggle to access the best opportunities without the right connections and resources. However, several strategies can help level the playing field.

One option is to work with an experienced note broker or investment firm specializing in distressed real estate debt. These intermediaries can help source off-market deals, conduct due diligence, and negotiate with borrowers on your behalf, typically in exchange for a fee or a share of the profits. Their industry relationships often provide access to deals that would otherwise be unavailable to individual investors.

Another option is to participate in online note investing platforms like Paperstac or Yieldstreet (see Fig. 3). These marketplaces allow accredited investors to browse and bid on fractional interests in pre-vetted note portfolios, with minimum investments as low as $5,000. While the returns may be lower than those achieved through direct investments, these platforms offer greater transparency, liquidity, and diversification, making them a practical entry point for investors new to the space.

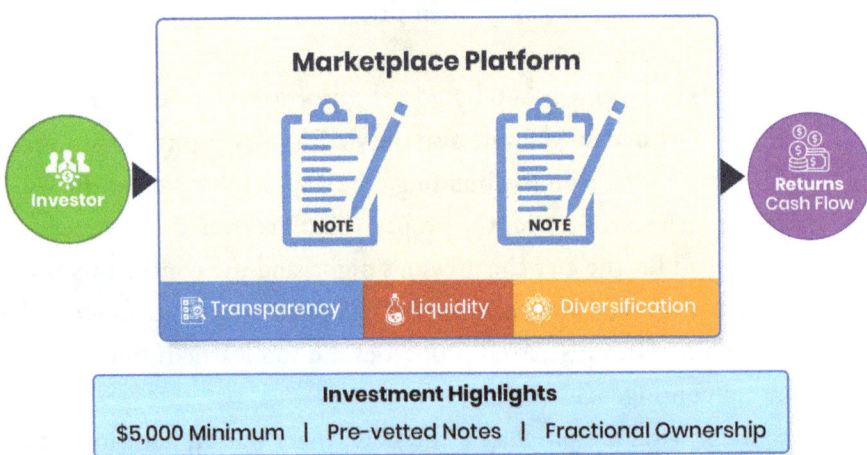

Figure 3: Online Note Investing Platform

Ultimately, succeeding as a real estate note investor requires a combination of financial acumen, legal knowledge, and people skills. You must be able to analyze loan documents and property values, assess the borrower's financial health, and navigate the foreclosure process if necessary. And you must know how to negotiate, whether dealing with borrowers, lenders, or competing investors.

Additionally, always have adequate cash reserves to cover unexpected expenses, whether it's repairing flood damage, paying legal fees, or covering holding costs during a prolonged foreclosure. The real estate market can be unpredictable, so having a financial buffer can make the difference between a profitable investment and a costly mistake. For those willing to put in the work and manage the risks, real estate note investing can offer the potential for double-digit returns and steady cash flow without the day-to-day responsibilities of property ownership.

Operating Businesses

The final type of distressed asset we'll cover in this chapter is operating businesses, companies that continue to generate revenue and maintain day-to-day operations despite financial or operational challenges.

In most countries outside the United States, when a company declares bankruptcy, the laws and courts focus primarily on liquidating the company's remaining assets. The U.S. bankruptcy system, on the other hand, encourages restructuring and rehabilitation. This approach, I'd argue, has significantly contributed to the dynamism of the U.S. economy, by providing new opportunities for investors and companies that would otherwise be forced to close.

Many of our financial titans, including Wilbur Ross, a former U.S. Secretary of Commerce and founder of WL Ross & Co., a private equity firm specializing in distressed investments, have made similar points. On a recent appearance on the popular business and entrepreneurship podcast *The James Altucher Show*, Ross said:

> The American bankruptcy system is relatively unique in the world in that our system is organized to facilitate the conversion of debt to equity and the rehabilitation of a business....Our bankruptcy code is very well-written; it's very effective, and it lets you take care of the worst of the problem.[4]

Investing in distressed operating businesses allows investors to acquire assets at a steep discount to their intrinsic value. Financial pressure often forces owners to sell for less than what the business would be worth in a stable market. This creates opportunities to buy low, enhance the company's operations and profitability, and ultimately sell it at a higher valuation.

Operating businesses frequently possess tangible assets, such as real estate, equipment, and inventory, that can be used as collateral for financing or sold to generate cash. They may also hold valuable intangible assets, including patents, trademarks, and customer relationships, which can be monetized or leveraged to attract strategic buyers. However, success hinges on the investor's ability to stabilize the business, improve cash flow, and navigate the unique challenges associated with distressed companies.

Unlike trade claims or notes on distressed real estate, investing in operating businesses requires ongoing management and oversight. Distressed companies often face issues such as declining revenues, high debt levels, and inefficient operations. To unlock value, investors must have the expertise and resources to implement strategic changes, optimize performance, and restore profitability. This process may involve cutting costs, restructuring debt, improving operational efficiency, and repositioning the company within its market. Additionally, investors must be prepared to inject additional capital to support working capital needs, fund growth initiatives, and cover unexpected expenses.

Reputation and legal risks are also considerations. Distressed companies may face negative media coverage, customer complaints, and legal challenges that can damage their brand and limit growth opportunities. Investors must proactively manage these risks, maintain clear communication with stakeholders, and ensure compliance with all legal and regulatory requirements. Having a skilled legal team is essential to navigate potential lawsuits, regulatory investigations, and other liabilities that may arise during the turnaround process.

Turnaround Strategies

When investing in distressed operating businesses, investors generally pursue one of two approaches, depending on their strategy, risk tolerance, and desired level of involvement.

One approach is to make a control investment, which involves acquiring a controlling stake in the company, either by purchasing equity or by converting debt into equity as part of a restructuring. By taking control, investors can implement comprehensive turnaround plans, restructure operations, and guide the company's strategic direction. The eventual goal is to stabilize the business, improve cash flow and profitability, and eventually exit the investment through a sale, IPO, or strategic merger. Control investments often require significant time and expertise but can offer substantial upside if the turnaround is successful.

In contrast, some investors prefer to make non-control investments, typically by acquiring a minority stake. This often happens through purchasing distressed debt that may later be converted into equity if the company undergoes restructuring. While this approach allows investors to participate in potential upside without directly managing the business, it limits their ability to influence the turnaround process. Non-control investments are generally better suited for investors seeking passive exposure to distressed opportunities, with less day-to-day involvement.

To illustrate the complexities and opportunities involved in investing in distressed operating businesses, consider the following real-life examples, all drawn from my own career or projects I've advised others on. Although certain details have been adjusted to maintain confidentiality, they highlight the kinds of situations investors encounter in the industry and the range of challenges and outcomes investors may face.

TYPES OF DISTRESSED ASSETS

CASE STUDY A: MANUFACTURING BUSINESS WITH HIGH DEBT AND LOW MARGINS

The first case involved a manufacturing business with approximately $150 million in annual revenue and $15 million in senior debt. Despite its sizable revenue, the company struggled with cash flow due to high debt payments and poorly managed accounts receivable. With an interest rate of 10%, the company needed at least $1.5 million annually just to cover interest expenses, excluding principal repayments. Additionally, it had stretched its vendors significantly, accruing $28 million in accounts payable and only generating $15 million in accounts receivable, most of which was owed by customers with poor credit and limited ability to pay (see Fig. 4).

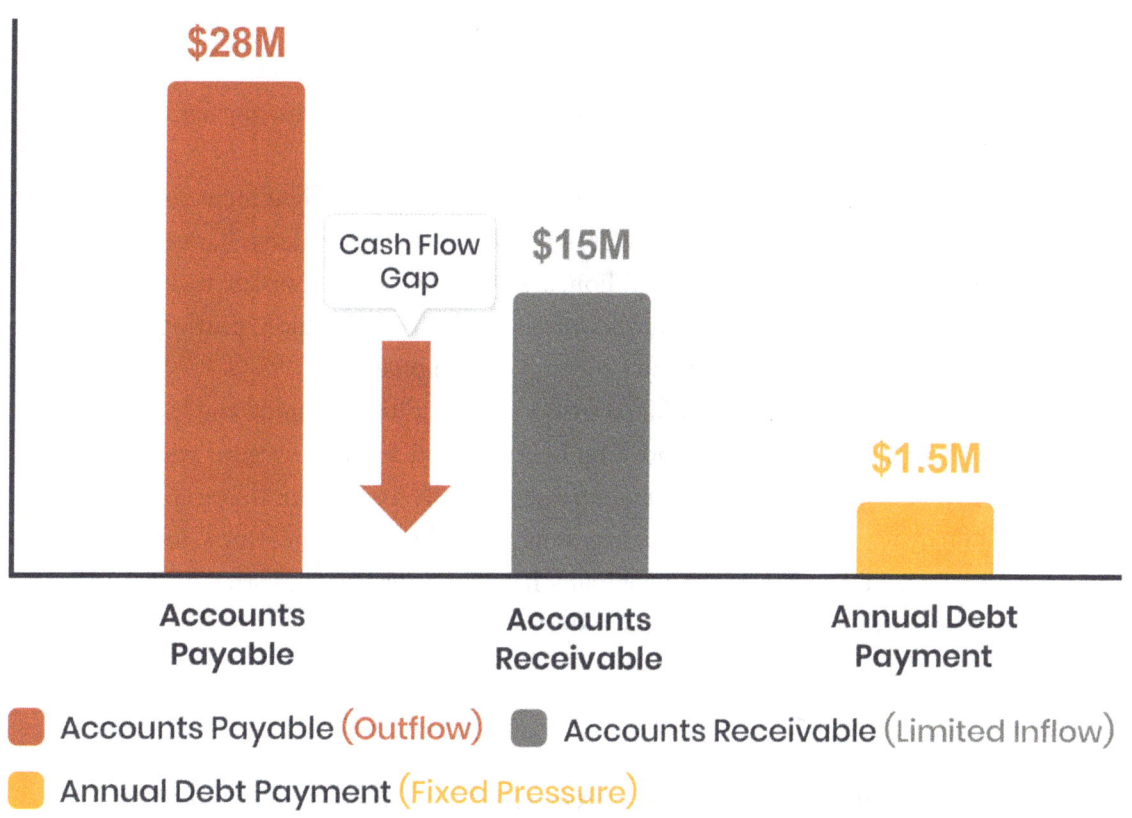

Figure 4: Financial Distress Snapshot

While a turnaround was possible through cost reductions, operational improvements, and better credit management, the challenges to implement it were significant. Success would require not only substantial capital to support the company during the turnaround period but also a skilled management team capable of executing the restructuring plan. Finding experienced executives willing to lead a distressed company is often difficult, and even if they are highly talented, the existing management team may lack the expertise or vision needed to implement their strategy and restore profitability. An investment opportunity in this company was going to require an investor to take out the secured creditor, $15 million, invest another $10 million to pay vendors to purchase new inventory, and provide the company some runway for a turnaround.

Given that the company's profit margins were relatively low, less than 5%, the turnaround opportunity was not as attractive as it might have appeared on the surface. If an investor puts $25 million into a company through a combination of debt and equity, they need to evaluate whether the company's cash flow is sufficient to support that level of investment.

In this case, the company was generating less than $7.5 million in annual cash flow. This means that for every dollar invested, the company was producing only about 30 cents in cash flow ($7.5 million divided by $25 million = 0.30). That's a 3x cash flow-to-investment ratio, which may sound acceptable at first, but it's important to remember that distressed businesses typically require significant additional investment in operations, management, and restructuring, and there is often little room for error.

More concerning, with profit margins under 5%, even a slight increase in costs or decline in revenue could wipe out what little profit the company was making. For example, if the company's annual revenue were $150 million, a 5% margin would translate to $7.5 million in profit, but if margins slipped to 3%, profits would drop to $4.5 million, putting even more pressure on the ability to service debt and generate a return on equity.

Ultimately, this company failed to secure the additional capital and leadership required for a successful turnaround and ended up in liquidation, leaving investors with substantial losses.

This example underscores the need to carefully assess both financial viability (whether a company can realistically generate enough cash flow to support new investment) and operational viability (whether the company has the leadership and strategy needed to execute a turnaround). Without both, even a seemingly low-priced investment in a distressed business can quickly turn into a costly mistake.

CASE STUDY B: CABINET MANUFACTURER WITH HIGH MARGINS AND STRONG MANAGEMENT

In contrast, let's look at a case involving a cabinet manufacturer that had $10 million in annual sales, $1 million in secured debt, $500,000 in accounts payable, and $750,000 in accounts receivable. Despite facing financial challenges, the company had strong profit margins of 15%, a capable management team, and a loyal customer base.

TYPES OF DISTRESSED ASSETS

For a business generating $10 million in annual revenue with 15% margins, stabilized cash flow would be around $1.5 million. At a reasonable multiple—say, four times cash flow—the company's enterprise value would likely be about $6 million. This meant that if investors could stabilize the business with a $1 million investment and secure operating control, they would effectively create a $6 million asset, a highly attractive return on capital. Most investors would consider it a compelling proposition to invest $1 million to create $6 million of value, provided the turnaround can be achieved within a reasonable time frame.

This is exactly what happened. Investors secured a new loan backed by its property, plant, and equipment, providing the manufacturer with the working capital needed to fulfill customer orders, stabilize cash flow, and restore profitability. Over time, the company regained its financial footing and delivered strong returns to investors.

These cases illustrate that even small businesses can present excellent investment opportunities when they combine operational strength, market demand, and the right financial support. It also shows why maintaining perspective when evaluating distressed investing opportunities is so crucial.

Risky Business

Regardless of the approach, investing in distressed operating businesses requires a high level of due diligence and risk management. Investors must thoroughly analyze the company's financial statements, assess its competitive position, and evaluate the management team's capabilities. Identifying turnaround opportunities involves understanding the root causes of the company's distress, developing a realistic plan to address those issues, and ensuring that sufficient capital and resources are available to execute the plan.

Having a clear monetization strategy is also a must, whether the goal is to keep the business and enjoy positive cash flow, sell the company to a strategic buyer, take it public through an IPO, or liquidate its assets for a profit (see Fig. 5). Timing is critical; exiting too early may leave

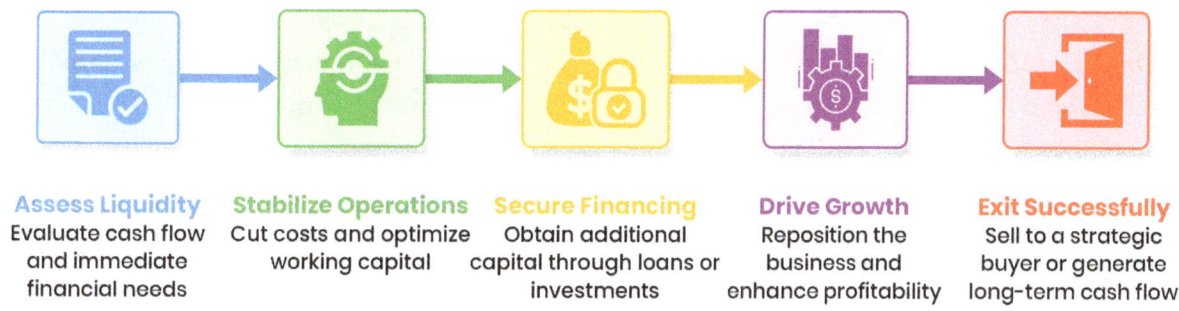

A successful turnaround requires both financial restructuring and operational improvements.

Figure 5: Turnaround Process: Stabilizing a Distressed Business

value on the table, while waiting too long can expose investors to additional risks if market conditions or the company's performance deteriorate. Successful investors know when to capitalize on improved performance and when to cut their losses if the turnaround proves unachievable.

Despite the inherent challenges, distressed operating businesses can offer some of the most attractive returns in the distressed investing landscape. By acquiring companies at a discount, implementing effective turnaround strategies, and leveraging both tangible and intangible assets, investors can generate substantial profits while revitalizing businesses and preserving jobs. However, success requires a combination of financial expertise, operational know-how, and strategic vision, making it a field best suited for experienced investors with the skills and resources to navigate the complexities of distressed investing.

KEY INSIGHTS

1. Trade claims offer potential profits by purchasing unpaid invoices from bankrupt companies at a discount, though success depends on the timing, recovery rates, and the bankruptcy's duration.
2. Negotiating directly with creditors can yield better pricing, but using claims-trading platforms, like Xclaim and Claims Market, simplifies the process, often without requiring an attorney.
3. Special situation investments include litigation finance, distressed debt investing, and DIP loans, all of which demand quick decision-making, financial acumen, and strong industry networks.
4. DIP financing, with its granting of super-priority status, provides lenders with a higher chance of repayment but comes with elevated risks and requires deep knowledge of bankruptcy law.
5. Distressed real estate notes allow investors to profit from properties without direct ownership, but due diligence on both the borrower and property is essential to avoid costly surprises.
6. Negotiation skills are especially critical in real estate note investing, as success often hinges on securing assets below market value while maintaining enough of a financial buffer for unexpected expenses.
7. Operating businesses present some of the most challenging but rewarding opportunities in distressed investing, with success relying on operational improvements, debt restructuring, and strategic management.
8. Investing in operating businesses requires ongoing oversight, additional capital injections, and expertise in both financial restructuring and day-to-day operations.
9. Control investments provide the greatest opportunity to drive a turnaround, while non-control investments offer less influence but can still yield profits if the company recovers.
10. Due diligence is essential across all asset classes and should include a thorough analysis of financial statements, legal risks, market conditions, and the company's competitive position.
11. Timing and liquidity are critical. Investors must be prepared to hold positions for extended periods and know when to exit to maximize returns.
12. Patience, discipline, and the ability to see value where others see risk are essential traits for success, as both bankruptcy processes and business turnarounds can take years to yield results.

CHAPTER 4

Getting on First Base: Sourcing Distressed Opportunities

I get calls about potential new investment opportunities every day of the week.

Many of them lead nowhere, but once in a while I'll discover one that piques my interest and seems worth pursuing. One of the most important lessons I've learned in distressed investing is that the best opportunities don't necessarily come from cold calls or random tips; they come from being plugged into the right networks and having a reputation for acting quickly. Let me tell you about an especially memorable example.

In December 2022, I got a call from a lawyer representing a client with $1 million invested in a company that had just declared bankruptcy: FTX, the Bahamian-based cryptocurrency exchange. The filing was shocking to many, and it generated an enormous amount of media attention thanks in large part to the company's enigmatic CEO, Sam Bankman-Fried. When I spoke with this attorney, Bankman-Fried had just appeared on CNBC to discuss the bankruptcy, but it hardly reassured anyone. Confusion and unanswered questions still swirled through the investment community.

"Joe, what do you think my client's claim is worth?" the lawyer asked. "He got a bid for nine cents from a claims trader, but that seems really low."

At that moment, even with no information beyond the identity of the professionals handling the case and the involvement of government authorities, I made a quick decision: "We'll pay ten cents." Why? My gut instinct told me two things: (1) there would be some recovery in this case, and (2) the most my firm could lose was ten cents on the dollar, or $100,000. It was a calculated risk based on limited information, but it was the kind of opportunity that comes from being in the right networks and having a reputation for acting quickly.

This story isn't just about making a fast decision, but about being the person who gets the call in the first place. In distressed investing, cultivating strong relationships and a reputation for decisive action means you're more likely to be informed when unique opportunities arise.

The best deals in distressed investing aren't due to luck or being in the right place at the right time. In reality, they're the result of consistent effort and strategic networking. After decades of working with some of the shrewdest players in the industry, I've found that the most successful distressed investors are those who cultivate large networks and employ a wide range of strategies and resources. They're constantly in touch with people who are deep in the flow of dealmaking, diligently monitor public information sources, leverage specialized databases, and will sometimes even make cold calls to potential sellers or intermediaries in pursuit of a must-have deal.

When you boil it down, sourcing deals comes down to four essentials: network, communication, public information, and online searches (see Fig. 1).

As a newly minted investor in distressed assets, you must outline a game plan to build your network, all with the goal of finding an investible deal. No one is going to hand you a deal, especially the self-styled alpha dogs who make up the distressed investing industry. If this sounds intimidating, it really isn't. I can assure you that by following the strategy I outline below, you will find those first deal opportunities.

HOW TO SOURCE DEALS

Network
What you know,
Who you know,
Industry expertise

Communication
In Person, Referrals,
Email, LinkedIn,
Professional Networks
(attorneys, accountants, bankers)

Public Information
Trade Publications,
Court Dockets
Claims Agents,
PACER, ABI, TMA

Online Searches
Google Keywords:
Defaults,
Bankruptcy

Effective deal sourcing requires multiple channels and consistent effort.

Figure 1: How to Source Deals

The "Getting on First Base" Approach

At the core of this process is what I call the "Getting on First Base" approach, a foundational starting point of a successful distressed investing strategy. In baseball, there are multiple steps to scoring a run—but it all starts with getting on base. The same is true in distressed investing. Getting on first base in baseball positions you to advance and eventually score; similarly, in distressed investing, you must first position yourself advantageously to capitalize on opportunities.

The "Getting on First Base" approach combines three elements: what you know, who you know, and the industry you know (see Fig. 2). Think of these elements as analogous to a batter's technical skills (what you know), relationships with coaches and teammates (who you know), and understanding of the opposing team's strategies (the industry you know). Let's dig into the details.

GETTING ON FIRST BASE: SOURCING DISTRESSED OPPORTUNITIES

GETTING ON FIRST BASE
The Starting Point for Every Successful Distressed Investment

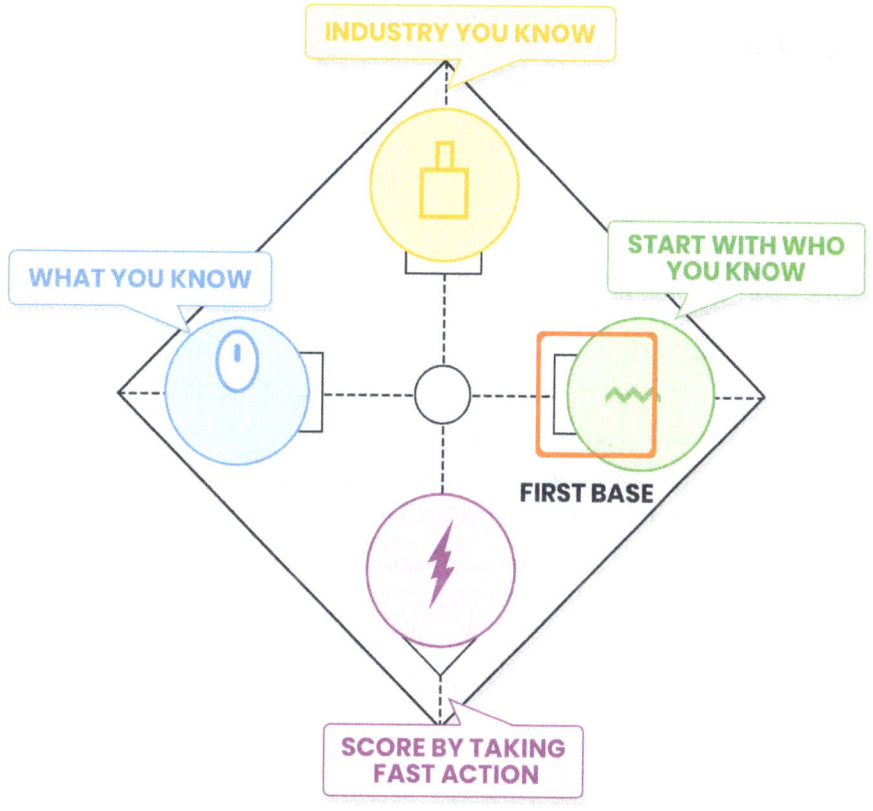

Figure 2: Getting on First Base

Who You Know: Leveraging Your Network

In distressed investing, your network isn't just an asset; it's your competitive advantage. While public information is essential, the best opportunities often come from personal connections. Everyone with a bank account knows a banker, and bankers often know which companies are struggling. Lawyers, accountants, and brokers are usually the first to spot financial trouble. Building relationships with these professionals can lead you to off-market deals before they become public.

Consider the careers of William ("Bill") Brandt and Jeffrey ("Jeff") Hecktman, two distressed investing pioneers who built their success restructuring businesses by leveraging extensive networks and seizing opportunities others overlooked.

Brandt, who recently passed away, didn't plan to become a turnaround advisor. His entry into the field began unexpectedly when his family's business faced financial difficulties. Through that experience, he developed a talent for corporate restructuring and founded Development Specialists Inc. (DSI), a firm that became a leader in advising distressed companies. Brandt's success wasn't just because of his financial expertise; it was also because he established strong personal relationships. Over his career he built a network that spanned beyond the business world, coming to include hugely influential figures like former President Bill Clinton, as well as leading lawyers, accountants, and fellow restructuring professionals. His reputation for solving complex cases meant that when businesses ran into trouble, Brandt often received the first call.

Jeff Hecktman followed a similarly unexpected path into the restructuring world. After his family's industrial supply business went bankrupt, he founded Hilco Trading Company (now Hilco Global), transforming it into one of the world's leading firms specializing in asset valuation, monetization, and advisory services. Like Brandt, Hecktman's success was rooted in relationships. By developing a vast network of relationships with financial institutions that lent to troubled businesses, Hecktman positioned Hilco as the go-to advisor to firms trying to capitalize on distressed opportunities in sectors ranging from retail and manufacturing to real estate and intellectual property. Initially, he provided appraisal and liquidation services but ultimately offered every service possible to distressed companies, including investment capital.

Both Brandt and Hecktman illustrate a central truth about the restructuring world: success often comes from knowing the right people, hearing about opportunities before they become public, and having the confidence to act when others hesitate. Yet, building a strong network takes far more than collecting business cards. It requires participation, contribution, transparency, and sustained engagement. Joining organizations such as the Turnaround Management Association (TMA), led by Scott Stuart, or the American Bankruptcy Institute (ABI), led by Karim Guirguis, is a good starting point. These groups are not just industry trade organizations; they are led by people who are accessible to members and who can open doors if approached thoughtfully. Active participation in events, committees, and discussion groups offers a way to meet others who work on distressed transactions and to stay informed on emerging developments.

Sharing insights and analysis is another way to build meaningful connections. Offering thoughtful perspectives on restructuring strategies or distressed cases, especially if supported by sound reasoning and good research, will get you noticed. If you have specialized knowledge, present it professionally, following the approach outlined in this book, and send it to restructuring advisors, investors, or lawyers who work on relevant cases. People remember those who bring value, especially when it comes without being asked.

Openness about your own approach to investing also helps. By being transparent about your criteria, timeline, and available resources, you allow others to assess whether you are a good fit for specific opportunities. Trust is earned when people know where you stand and what you bring to the table.

But even after making that first connection, relationships require maintenance. Regular contact, whether through email, phone calls, or in-person meetings, keeps you on people's radar. Many distressed situations move quickly, and the investor who gets the first call is often the one who has stayed in touch.

Although lawyers, bankers, and turnaround professionals are often the most obvious contacts in this world, many of the most valuable relationships come from less-expected places.

GETTING ON FIRST BASE: SOURCING DISTRESSED OPPORTUNITIES

Academics, for example, can be a valuable resource. Professors who specialize in bankruptcy law or corporate restructuring often advise on complex cases and can offer insight into broader trends and strategies. Journalists can also provide valuable context and insights. They often have a strong grasp of industry developments and emerging trends, and by following their reporting and understanding the stories they cover, investors can gain early insight into which companies may be facing difficulties.

Former executives may be the most underappreciated resource of all. People who have lived through a restructuring understand where the real bottlenecks and opportunities are. In fact, this realization helped create the booming "expert network" industry, where firms like Gerson Lehrman Group (GLG) are paid six-figure retainers to maintain relationships with current and former executives willing to speak with investors. If you know anyone who has worked in an industry you are watching, take them to lunch. They may give you insight no public filing ever could.

Every relationship adds a new way of looking at a situation, a different lens that can help you understand where value might emerge, sharpen your analysis, and improve your results.

Industry You Know: Using Sector Expertise to Spot Opportunities

Start by focusing on industries where you have deep knowledge or a strong interest. Casual research won't cut it when competing with industry veterans. Success comes from combining an outsider's perspective with insider-level knowledge, allowing you to spot signs of distress before they become public.

Having deep industry knowledge allows you to recognize when a company's challenges are temporary rather than terminal. For example, understanding seasonal cash flow patterns in retail can help you distinguish between short-term liquidity issues and fundamental operational problems. Similarly, knowing which competitors are thriving and why can help you assess whether a struggling company has a realistic path to recovery. Early on in my career, I often teamed up with a senior executive in the meat industry, whom I called Meat Man. Meat Man and I profited greatly from his knowledge of the meat industry and my expertise in the restructuring field.

It's equally important to know the key players within your industry. By maintaining relationships with suppliers, lenders, and trade associations, you position yourself to hear about distressed companies before their problems become public. These connections can provide critical insights into a company's financial health, competitive position, and management team.

While industry knowledge helps you identify opportunities, it also prevents you from pursuing deals that look promising on the surface but have little chance of success. By understanding the nuances of an industry, you can quickly assess whether a distressed company's challenges are fixable or whether its best days are behind it.

What You Know: Using Public Information to Gain an Edge

If I had to come up with a single trait that defines all successful distressed investors, I'd have to say it is their obsession with details. I say this with the deepest respect: they work over the minutiae of investment opportunities like a dog gnawing on a bone. If you aren't prepared to obsess over the details, you will lose much more often than you win.

To compete with the best, you need the stamina and persistence to learn every nuance about what might go wrong and to keep digging even when you think you've already mined every scrap of information worth extracting. This isn't about reading a few industry reports; it's about knowing the subtleties others miss, understanding which companies are vulnerable, and recognizing when an operational misstep or liquidity crunch presents a buying opportunity. Staying ahead of the curve requires constantly staying updated on industry trends, legal and regulatory developments, and best practices in turnaround management and restructuring (see Fig. 3). Here are three of the most important resources for doing so.

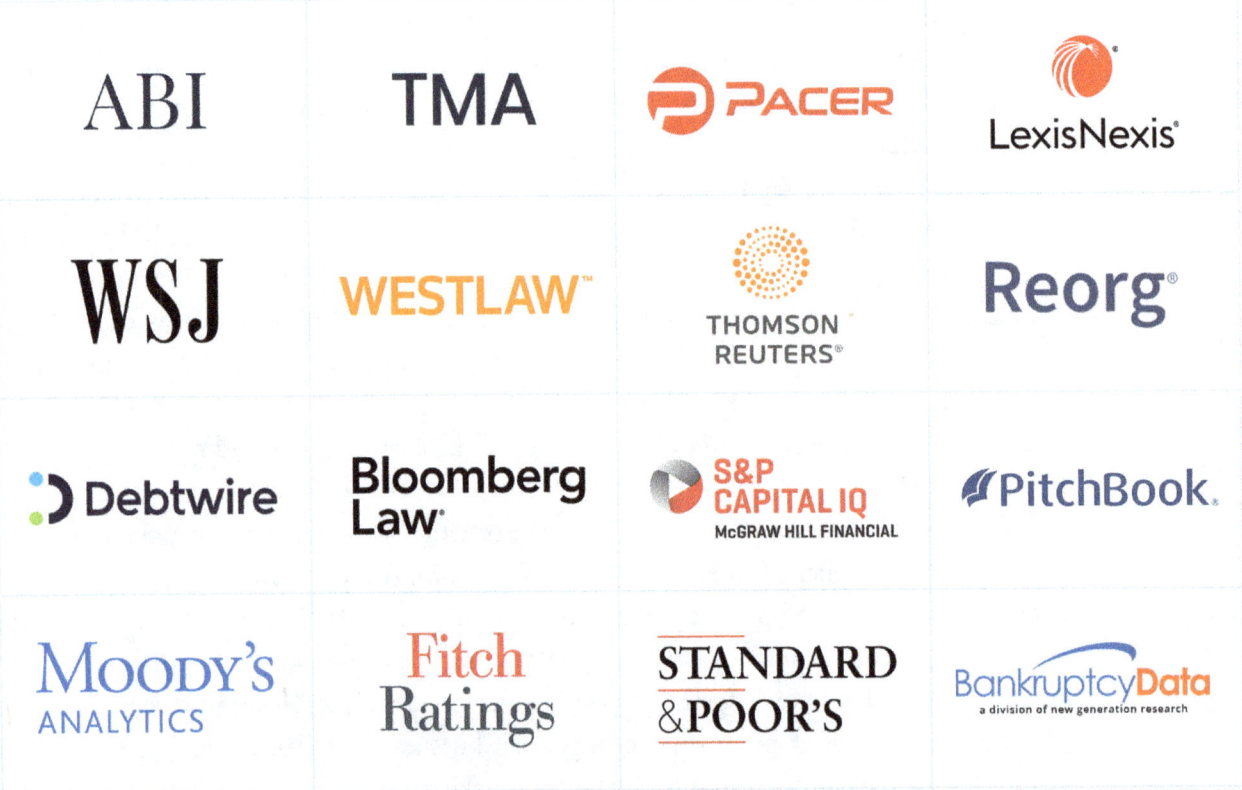

Figure 3: Sources of Information

GETTING ON FIRST BASE: SOURCING DISTRESSED OPPORTUNITIES

Trade Publications and Industry News Sources

Decades ago, I routinely spent hours in law libraries hunting for a few bits of information or journal articles that were often in a volume that had been checked out or left haphazardly on the wrong shelf. For that reason, I deeply appreciate today's instant online access to vast information resources. The contrast between past limitations and current abundance is remarkable.

While information has become plentiful, time remains our scarcest resource. This reality makes time-saving information particularly valuable, sometimes worth paying for. Premium services like LexisNexis offer comprehensive data but at costs that can challenge even midsized law firms. For those serious about distressed investing, alternatives exist: public law libraries typically provide PACER terminal access (more on that below), while university law libraries may offer LexisNexis. Making an effort to locate these resources is important—investors with superior information access gain a significant competitive advantage that's difficult to overcome.

Attending industry events is also an excellent investment in relationships and time. ABI's annual conference, held each spring in Washington, DC, brings together some of the sharpest minds in restructuring, from bankruptcy judges to turnaround consultants. Likewise, the TMA, where professionals populate panels on hot topics in the restructuring field, offers unmatched networking opportunities (more on it shortly). Even if you're just starting out, these events provide a chance to hear directly from the people shaping the industry, and if you make the right connections, you might hear about a new deal before anyone else.

Google and AI Keywords

This may sound elementary and obvious, but conducting targeted Google searches or AI chats using keywords like "defaults" and "bankruptcy" can sometimes yield surprisingly good information. Don't dismiss simple tools. Sometimes a well-timed search can reveal a local news article or court filing that hasn't hit industry databases yet. AI platforms are worth investigating, but be cautious of fictitious information. If you can't verify something through a targeted search, assume it's not real. In this industry, bad information is worse than no information.

A Digital Gold Mine: Public Information Sources

Your network of contacts can provide invaluable insights, but public information sources will always be the bedrock of your research. These digital repositories are teeming with clues about potential opportunities if you know where to look and how to interpret what you find.

Bankruptcy filings in particular are treasure troves of information. When a company files for Chapter 11, it must divulge information that most companies go to great lengths to keep private. Detailed balance sheets, creditor lists, restructuring plans—it's all there, waiting for savvy investors to uncover hidden value or potential pitfalls. Five major, free bankruptcy claims services host the documents of all the major bankruptcy cases: Stretto, Verita, Kroll, Donlin Recano, and BMC.

The Public Access to Court Electronic Records (PACER) is a U.S. government-run online system that will become your portal to a vast universe of federal court documents, including bankruptcy cases. With PACER, you can track filings in real time, search by company name or case number, and dive deep into the nitty-gritty details of each case.

Imagine seeing a company's complete list of assets and liabilities or reading its restructuring strategy before it hits the news. That's the power PACER puts in your hands. Surprisingly, even though this information is public, relatively few investors take the time to dig into it. This oversight creates opportunities for those willing to do the legwork.

But PACER is just the tip of the iceberg. SEC filings, news reports, and industry-specific publications can all provide early warning signs of distress (see Fig. 3). Success in the distressed investing arena hinges on a methodical approach to monitoring these sources. If you're systematic, you can spot patterns and anomalies.

The "First-Day Declaration" in Chapter 11 cases is a gold mine of information for distressed investors. Typically running between 30 and 50 pages, this document is filed by a senior executive of the debtor company at the beginning of the bankruptcy process. It serves as a comprehensive dossier on the company's condition and future prospects, offering a concise explanation of how the business unraveled and what assets or value may remain.

Anyone willing to study one of these declarations, which I encourage you to do, will find a detailed account of the company's history, business model, and financial profile, including recent performance data and debt structure. It walks through the events leading up to the bankruptcy filing, giving insight into whether the company's challenges are rooted in broader market shifts or isolated incidents. The declaration also identifies the key stakeholders, describes the proposed restructuring path, and outlines motions submitted to the court that need urgent attention, such as requests that address immediate risks to operations.

A close reading of the declaration allows investors to form an initial view of the company's prospects, pinpoint possible investment angles, and detect warning signs that may not be visible in standard financial filings. For most serious distressed investors, this document is the logical starting point for deeper analysis, laying the groundwork for any further investigation.

Although bankruptcy filings like the First-Day Declaration provide a wealth of information, they are not the only public signals of distress. Litigation filings, for example, may offer early warnings about a company's financial or operational troubles. By reviewing court dockets and legal databases, investors can learn about lawsuits that may affect a company's stability or future cash flows. Regulatory filings, especially those required of public companies, are another source. Documents submitted to agencies such as the SEC, particularly annual reports (10-K), quarterly updates (10-Q), and current event disclosures (8-K), contain valuable details on a company's financial condition, risks, and potential liabilities.

Press releases and news articles also play a role, shedding light on a company's market position and strategic choices. Earnings reports, which may reflect declining revenue, margin pressure, or unsustainable debt levels, can offer clear signals of distress before a bankruptcy filing.

In addition, industry publications and trade journals often highlight sector-specific trends, emerging risks, or competitive shifts that could push a company into trouble. These sources may offer insight into not just individual companies but also broader patterns affecting entire industries.

To make the most of these resources, investors should adopt a regular system for monitoring and gathering information. Setting up alerts through databases that track bankruptcies, regulatory filings, and material news events allows investors to stay informed without constant manual searching. Alerts tied to specific companies, industries, or keywords can surface timely updates that may reveal emerging opportunities. Social media monitoring tools, which scan for mentions of companies or financial terms, can also identify early signs of trouble that have yet to appear in formal filings.

Building a structured routine for analyzing public data is a practical way to avoid missing opportunities. One approach is to set aside dedicated times during the week to review bankruptcy dockets like PACER, corporate filings with the SEC, and news from specialized industry outlets. Keeping a running log—whether in a spreadsheet, note-taking app, or project management tool—can help organize this flow of information and highlight patterns over time. Subscribing to newsletters or research services that focus on sectors of interest can also save time by consolidating relevant updates.

Finally, investors may benefit from using technology to handle large volumes of data and detect patterns that aren't immediately visible. AI-driven tools can sift through legal, regulatory, and market data to highlight inconsistencies, emerging risks, or opportunities that may otherwise be overlooked. While effort and discipline remain necessary, combining those habits with the smart use of technology can give investors an edge in spotting distressed situations before they become obvious to the wider market.

Networking and Cold Outreach

It is easy to forget that distressed investing is, at its core, a human business. Databases and online resources play an important role, but there is no substitute for personal connections.

The TMA Distressed Investing Conference, held each year in Las Vegas the week before the Super Bowl, is perhaps the single most concentrated gathering of people active in this space. Hundreds of turnaround professionals, bankruptcy attorneys, and investment bankers come together under one roof, creating an unmatched environment for connecting with others in the field. What makes it valuable is not just the formal programming but the informal conversations that happen throughout the event. Sitting in on roundtable discussions, sharing experiences at evening receptions, and getting to know people who work on distressed deals every day can lead to relationships that open up real opportunities. Approach these events as a chance to listen, learn, and engage meaningfully, rather than simply to accumulate business cards.

Local chapters of groups like TMA and ABI also offer ongoing opportunities to meet people in the field. These smaller, more regular gatherings provide a window into regional trends and transactions that may not make national headlines. Because you are likely to see the same participants repeatedly, these meetings can foster longer-term relationships and trust.

In addition to events specifically focused on distressed investing, conferences across various industries can provide valuable intelligence. For example, real estate investment forums, energy sector symposiums, or technology innovation summits often attract industry insiders who may have insight into struggling companies or sectors. Coming to these gatherings prepared with a solid understanding of who will be attending and why they might be relevant to your work can turn a casual meeting into a productive exchange.

Cold outreach can be another effective way to build connections, though it requires thought and effort. A well-written email that shows you have taken the time to understand the recipient's work and interests will always stand out from a generic message. Similarly, a physical letter can leave an impression in a world where inboxes are overcrowded and messages are easily missed. Even picking up the phone still has its place. A short, well-prepared call that clarifies why you are reaching out and what you bring to the table can sometimes open doors that email cannot.

Crowdsourced platforms are another way to extend your reach and keep you plugged into the flow of distressed opportunities. Seeking Alpha, for example, offers more than stock commentary. By following companies and sectors under pressure, you may spot signs of distress early and identify where deeper digging might be warranted.

Brokers and Firms

It is also worth cultivating relationships with brokers and firms active in selling distressed assets. Firms such as Northgate, Auction Advisors, Keen-Summit Capital Partners, A&G Real Estate Partners, Hilco, and Gordon Brothers are active in this space (see Fig. 4). Regular contact with brokers like these can keep you informed of assets coming to market. Likewise, banks such as PNC, based in Pittsburgh, frequently publish lists of loans for sale, offering another channel for sourcing deals.

Taken together, a thoughtful approach to networking and outreach, one that combines personal connection, strategic outreach, and ongoing engagement with platforms, can create a steady pipeline of opportunities in distressed investing.

Being persistent is the only way you'll make progress. Your next great opportunity might be hiding in plain sight, maybe even in your backyard. Keep your eyes open open and your network active, and never stop exploring. In distressed investing, spotting trouble before others do is your secret weapon.

Navigating Ethical Considerations

Bankruptcy proceedings are public, which might suggest that everyone has equal access to information. But in practice, distressed investing resembles a private marketplace more than an efficient stock exchange. Some insiders have deeper insight or a better understanding of a case,

MAJOR LOAN SALE ADVISORY FIRMS AND PLATFORMS

debtx.com

MountainSeed.com

ffncorp.com

cbre.com

us.jll.com

jackhenry.com

nmrk.com

loan-street.com

debticate.com

cushmanwakefield.com

Figure 4: Major Loan Sale Advisory Firms and Platforms

and they can share that knowledge selectively without making it broadly available. Relationships, therefore, provide a real advantage.

For example, a bankruptcy attorney might offer a perspective on complex court filings that help clarify a company's future prospects. A turnaround consultant could share operational challenges that would never be obvious from financial statements. This gap in access to information is part of what makes distressed investing both rewarding and difficult. It underscores the need to build a strong network and raises serious ethical questions.

Although this kind of information sharing is not insider trading in the traditional sense, you must be mindful of how you use what you learn. It is worth asking whether the information you act on is publicly available, even if it is buried in court filings or difficult to locate, or whether it is material that has not been disclosed to the court or creditors. The line is not always clear, so maintaining a steady ethical compass matters. If gaining access to non-public information requires signing a non-disclosure agreement (NDA), doing so is often worthwhile. But once you sign, you must respect that agreement. No deal is worth putting your reputation at risk. If there is ever doubt, consulting with legal counsel is a prudent step. In this industry, reputation is as valuable as any deal on the table. (*To view a sample NDA, please refer to the appendix.*)

Navigating these challenges requires a thoughtful approach. It is always better to act on public information, even if few others have recognized its value. Be upfront with partners and stakeholders about the sources of your information. Avoid any conduct that could be viewed as manipulative or misleading. If unsure of where the line is, seek legal guidance rather than guessing and potentially crossing into unethical (and possibly illegal) territory.

Distressed investing is a surprisingly small industry. Reputation travels fast, and once lost, trust is difficult to recover. Integrity must come first. Conducting yourself with honesty will ensure that people continue to share valuable insights and opportunities with you. Cutting corners may bring a short-term gain, but over time, the best opportunities will pass you by.

The "Getting on First Base" Approach in Action

Suppose you're a distressed investor specializing in the retail sector, specifically men's shoes. You've spent years studying the industry, tracking trends in consumer behavior, supply chain disruptions, and shifts in retail financing. You know which companies are struggling, which suppliers are nervous, and which landlords are growing impatient. You've built this expertise by attending industry conferences, participating in retail trade groups, and maintaining relationships with bankers, factors, and other stakeholders who have their fingers on the pulse of the business.

One day, a supplier to a midsized regional shoe retailer mentions that the retailer owes them money, and not just a little. Payments are late, orders are smaller, and the supplier is starting to worry. Separately, you speak with bankers who lend to retailers and hear murmurs that this particular chain is behind on its loans. You even contact a few landlords who lease space to the retailer and learn that rent payments have been delayed more than once. You're considering

GETTING ON FIRST BASE: SOURCING DISTRESSED OPPORTUNITIES

calling the retailer's president or CFO to get a sense of the situation, but before you do, you spot the news: the retailer has just filed for bankruptcy, citing declining foot traffic, online competition, and unsustainable debt levels.

This is the moment you've been preparing for. Within minutes, you review court dockets and public filings to understand the company's financials and bankruptcy proceedings. Your network kicks into high gear; you reconnect with bankers, investment bankers, and real estate professionals who know the retailer's situation. Drawing on your industry knowledge, you quickly sketch out a business plan to address the retailer's fundamental issues: cutting unprofitable locations, renegotiating vendor contracts, and strengthening the online sales channel.

Recognizing that speed is fundamental to success, you contact a bankruptcy attorney to understand the mechanics of purchasing the company's assets. Time is of the essence; bankruptcies often move faster than people realize, and good assets get snapped up quickly. Within days, you're negotiating directly with the company and its creditors, exploring options to acquire inventory, real estate leases, and intellectual property at a fraction of their original value.

Fall in Love with Making Money, Not Your Hobbies

Before we move onto the next chapter, one final and important bit of advice.

In my experience, often the hardest part of distressed investing isn't spotting a deal. There are plenty of deals available for anyone willing to spend the time combing through Chapter 11 filings. The *real* challenge is avoiding the temptation to chase deals that look exciting but lack solid fundamentals. It's easy to be swayed by personal interests or compelling narratives, but so often the best opportunities are the ones others overlook, what some might call the "ugly" deals. These opportunities are attractive precisely because most investors shy away from them.

Years ago, I found myself eyeing Cannondale, the iconic bicycle company, as it navigated bankruptcy. I've been an avid cyclist for years, and Cannondale had always been one of my favorite brands. The idea of turning around such a well-known and respected company appealed to me not just as an investor, but as a cycling enthusiast.

Renowned for its innovative bicycles, the company faced significant challenges when it ventured into the motorsports industry in the late 1990s. The company invested heavily (approximately $80 million) into developing off-road motorcycles and all-terrain vehicles (ATVs). This ambitious expansion aimed to capitalize on a new market but ultimately led to Cannondale's financial downfall. Despite its struggles, I believed the company's strong brand and industry reputation offered turnaround potential.

The primary issue stemmed from Cannondale's inexperience with engine manufacturing. The company tried to create proprietary engines for its motorcycles, a complex endeavor that led to engineering delays and cost overruns. The initial motorcycle model, the MX400, faced multiple redesigns and did not reach the market until 2001, well behind schedule. Early reviews highlighted problems such as excessive weight, approximately 20 pounds heavier than competitors; unreliable performance; and maintenance difficulties. These issues resulted in poor sales and damaged the company's reputation in the motorsports sector.

Financially, the motorsports division's losses were substantial and unsustainable. Cannondale reported a loss of $46.6 million due to the underperforming motorcycle and ATV lines, which contributed to eleven consecutive quarterly losses. The company's stock price plummeted by 83% in the year before its Chapter 11 bankruptcy filing in January 2003.

Still, I couldn't ignore the potential upside. I pitched the idea to my partners, confident that Cannondale's core bicycle business could recover with the right strategy. Their response was swift and brutally honest: "What are you even thinking, Joe? Don't fall in love with your hobbies. Fall in love with making money." Their scrutiny was intense. Every flaw in the deal was exposed, from the capital required to restructure the motorsports division to the risks of reviving consumer confidence. In the end, we passed, and it was the right call.

That experience left a mark. In distressed investing, passion can blind you. Discipline is essential. The first goal isn't hitting a home run; it's getting on first base. You need to focus on deals where the fundamentals are solid, the risks are manageable, and the upside is clear. That lesson I learned from the would-be Cannondale deal has guided my approach ever since: prioritize opportunities with a clear path to profitability, even if they don't capture your imagination at first glance.

Conclusion: The Harder You Work, The Luckier You Get

Sourcing distressed deals requires persistence, preparation, discretion, and quick decision-making. Success doesn't come from luck; it comes from consistently applying the "Getting on First Base" approach. By building strong relationships, developing industry expertise, and leveraging public information, you can position yourself to recognize opportunities that others overlook.

I cannot stress enough how important it is to be proactive. Maintain regular contact with your network, stay informed about industry trends, and monitor public filings for signs of distress. When the right opportunity arises, act decisively. The best deals often go to those who move quickly and have the confidence to seize the moment. The more you work at sourcing deals, the more opportunities you'll uncover and the luckier you'll become.

KEY INSIGHTS

1. Success in distressed investing comes from combining three core elements: who you know, the industry you know, and what you know, summarized as the "Getting on First Base" approach.
2. Building relationships with bankers, lawyers, accountants, turnaround consultants, and industry professionals provides early access to off-market deals and insights into distressed companies.
3. Unexpected sources like academics, journalists, and former executives can offer unique perspectives that others may overlook.
4. Networking requires more than exchanging business cards. It involves active participation in organizations like TMA and ABI, as well as sharing your knowledge to build trust and credibility.
5. Cold outreach through personalized emails, letters, and phone calls can lead to valuable connections,

GETTING ON FIRST BASE: SOURCING DISTRESSED OPPORTUNITIES

especially when combined with industry expertise.

6. Monitoring loan sales platforms like DebtX, Newmark, First Financial Network, JLL, Debticate, and others can help identify distressed assets before they hit the open market.
7. Industry expertise is essential for identifying opportunities and distinguishing between temporary setbacks and structural problems. Understanding the nuances of an industry helps investors recognize when a company's challenges are fixable.
8. Case studies like the Cannondale one illustrate the importance of assessing the underlying causes of financial distress and avoiding deals driven by passion rather than financial fundamentals.
9. Public information is a powerful tool; investors can use bankruptcy filings, PACER, SEC reports, and industry publications to verify information and assess opportunities.
10. The First-Day Declaration in Chapter 11 cases offers detailed insights into a company's financial health, restructuring plan, and key stakeholders.
11. Google searches and alerts for keywords like "defaults" and "bankruptcy" can uncover valuable information that others might miss.
12. Staying ahead of the competition requires monitoring litigation filings, regulatory reports, press releases, and news articles for early signs of distress.
13. Ethical considerations are critical; investors must ensure they act only on publicly available information and maintain the highest standards of integrity.
14. NDAs are often necessary to access confidential information, and honoring their terms is essential for maintaining credibility and trust.
15. Combining insights from relationships, industry expertise, and public information allows investors to move quickly and confidently when opportunities arise.
16. The "Getting on First Base" approach focuses on securing deals with limited downside and strong upside, positioning investors for long-term success.
17. Persistence and preparation are keys to success. Building a strong network, developing industry expertise, and consistently monitoring information sources increase the likelihood of finding and capitalizing on distressed opportunities.

CHAPTER 5

Analyzing and Valuing Distressed Assets

For millennia, distressed asset marketplaces have existed in one kind or another all over the world in the form of the humble pawnshop. According to the National Pawnbrokers Association, they can be dated as far back as 3,000 years ago in China, and they thrived in ancient Greece and Rome.[5] Clothing was the earliest type of collateral people used to secure loans, which is how the term "pawn" came into being. It's derived from the Latin word *patinum*, which means "cloth" or "clothing."

Whether you visit a pawnshop or watch a reality TV show about the daily life of pawnbrokers, the experience will undoubtedly teach you an important lesson: namely, that asset valuation is often more subjective than people think, shaped by urgent negotiations between sellers in need and buyers looking for a bargain. These shops tend to thrive in areas where financial strain is common, making them natural hubs for quick transactions where the prices paid are often well below what an item would fetch if the market were more competitive and efficient.

Pawnshops are where perceived value meets reality, often in unexpected ways. You might think that a rare or valuable item would automatically fetch a high price, but that's not always the case. The interaction between a customer and a broker can reveal just how wildly different their perceptions of value can be.

Here's a fictionalized example that could easily take place in real life:

A well-dressed man walks into a shop, clutching a rare 1929 Indian Head $5 gold coin.
"How much can I get for this?" he asks.
"Are you selling or getting a loan?"
"It's much too valuable to sell. I just need a loan."
"How much do you need?"
After a pause, he says, "Ten thousand."
The broker examines the coin with an eyepiece and then takes it to the back office for further scrutiny. He returns after several minutes and places the coin on a velvet pad atop the store's glass case.
"We can loan you $289," he states firmly.

The customer stares in disbelief. "Are you serious? This coin is an incredibly rare 1929 Indian Head gold piece. It's easily worth $100,000."

"We're aware," says the pawnbroker.

"Then why offer only $289?"

"First, I don't know anyone who would pay $100,000 for the coin. Second, a $5 gold coin contains about 3 grams of gold. At $96.41 per gram, that's $289—the melt value."

This scene offers a valuable primer in valuing distressed assets, whether it takes place in a board room among men and women in expensive suits or between two people separated by thick bulletproof glass in a cramped store.

To start, the pawnbroker's approach exemplifies the strategy of "protecting downside risk." It's safe to say that everyone who walks into a pawn shop with an item to sell or borrow against is in distress, willing to let go of valuable items at "fire-sale prices." Equally certain is that the shop will only agree to purchase or lend against distressed assets if the broker can get a breathtakingly good deal.

While someone with a valuable gold coin might hope to get "market value" for the item, the reality is that secondary markets are thin, and it could take a very long time to find a counterparty willing to pay the price quoted on eBay. The pawnbroker knows this, which is why he can start the negotiation with a lowball offer. A customer might haggle and get the broker to lend him $500, but it's still a no-lose proposition.

Suppose the customer takes the loan and doesn't retrieve the item. In that case, the broker gets to sell the coin to some other broker for $10,000, who gets to sell it to another for $20,000, who sells it to another for $30,000 as it moves up the food chain, before it ends up in someone's Madison Avenue shop with a $100,000 price tag waiting for the retail customer with deep pockets to show up. Alternatively, should the customer return three months later to retrieve his gold coin, the broker still makes a 40% APR profit on the loan.

Sadly, desperate people make unfortunate and desperate choices when in great financial distress. In 2014, thieves broke into a museum and stole ten diamond and gold World Series rings owned by the legendary New York Yankee Yogi Berra. Even though each ring was probably worth hundreds of thousands of dollars, it would have been impossible to sell them, which the thieves knew. History, *shmistory*. Accordingly, they made the rational but tragic decision to cut up the rings, remove the gemstones, and melt the gold. When they were caught five years later, it came out that a dealer in Manhattan's Diamond District paid $12,000 for the lot, no questions asked.[6]

Corporate assets are subject to similar valuation challenges. How do you know if you are overpaying or missing out on potentially lucrative investments? In this chapter, we'll look at the methods and strategies experienced distressed investors use to value troubled companies and assets.

Just as the pawnbroker must assess both the immediate resale value and the underlying worth of an item, distressed investors rely on structured valuation techniques to determine whether an asset is truly a bargain. To that end, we'll discuss liquidation analysis, a fundamental tool for estimating recovery value in worst-case scenarios. From there, we'll explore discounted cash flow models and comparable company assessments, methods that help investors look beyond distress to uncover long-term potential. Finally, we'll examine how collateral, liens, and legal risks shape the true value of a distressed asset. Whether you're a seasoned distressed investor or just starting to explore the market, the concepts and strategies covered in this chapter will provide you with a solid foundation for success.

Before we dive in, though, let's pause for a moment to discuss something even more fundamental: how to tell the difference between healthy and unhealthy companies.

Understanding the Distressed Company Structure

If you take the time to look carefully, the signs that a company is under distress are almost always evident. For retail companies, when you're a customer, you'll notice obvious issues. You might notice poorly maintained inventory, understaffed stores, or deferred maintenance issues like broken shelves and worn carpeting. However, for other types of companies, the signs aren't always so apparent. Vendors might not get paid as quickly, or staff turnover might be unusually high. To uncover these less visible signs of trouble, the balance sheet is often the best place to start.

Healthy vs. Distressed Balance Sheets

In the NYU class I teach, I've found that comparing healthy companies to distressed ones is hugely valuable for my students. To bring this analysis to life, I turn to one of the sharpest young minds in distressed analytics, Richard Falk-Wallace, who guest lectures on how to build a financial model for distressed situations. What makes him so effective is his ability to break down complex issues into simple, intuitive models.

Falk-Wallace begins by suggesting that we examine two versions of the same company: one healthy, one distressed. In the healthy scenario, the company's assets exceed its liabilities, leaving positive equity for shareholders. By contrast, in the distressed version, liabilities exceed assets, effectively wiping out the equity value.

This comparison highlights a key principle in distressed investing: as a company's finances deteriorate, value shifts from equity holders to creditors. Recognizing this shift is essential for identifying investment opportunities and evaluating risks in distressed situations.

To illustrate this concept further, we can look at the "BoxCo" example from Stephen G. Moyer's 2004 book, *Distressed Debt Analysis*. Moyer, a portfolio manager and analyst in the distressed credit group at PIMCO, is one of the leading authorities in high-yield and distressed securities analysis. His BoxCo analysis, summarized in simplified form below, shows how a company's capital structure evolves as it moves from health to distress (see Fig. 1).

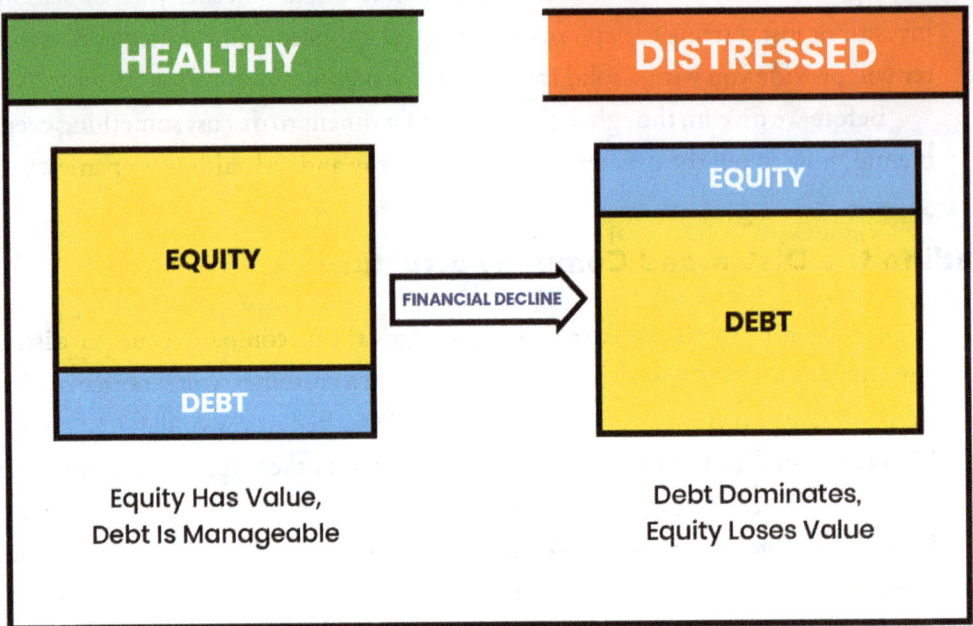

Figure 1: How Capital Structure Shifts as a Company Deteriorates

In BoxCo's healthy state, equity makes up a large part of the company's value. As the company becomes distressed, equity value shrinks to almost nothing, while debt becomes a larger portion of the company's total value. This highlights an important point for distressed investors: in many cases, a distressed company's equity may be nearly worthless, with the real value lying in its debt.

As a company's financial troubles worsen, equity value usually falls faster than the overall company value. This happens because equity holders are last in line to be paid, after all the creditors. In severe cases, equity can become worthless even if the company still has valuable assets.

This recurring pattern creates opportunities for distressed debt investors. By buying a company's debt at a discount, they might gain control of the business. If the company's performance improves, these investors could see significant returns, either through debt repayment or by converting their debt to equity in a restructured company.

However, to fully understand the nuances of this process, investors must grasp the concept of the distressed investing waterfall, which details the priority of debt claims. We touched briefly on this in Chapter 1, in the section on parties and absolute priority, but it's important to take a deeper look.

The Distressed Investing Waterfall

In distressed investing, understanding how different claims are prioritized is absolutely essential. This prioritization is often referred to as a "waterfall" because it illustrates how value flows through a company's capital structure, much like water cascading down a series of pools (see Fig. 2).

The waterfall concept is grounded in the principle of absolute priority, which dictates the order in which claims are paid in a distressed situation. At the top of the waterfall are the most senior claims, typically secured debt with a first lien on the company's assets. As we move down the waterfall, we encounter second-lien debt, unsecured debt, and finally, at the bottom, equity.

In a distressed scenario, the available value "flows" down this waterfall. Senior claims are paid in full before junior claims receive anything. This means that in severe cases, lower-ranking claims may receive little or no recovery. For instance, if a company's value is only sufficient to repay its first-lien debt, all other claimants—including second-lien creditors, unsecured creditors, and equity holders—may be left empty-handed.

The form of payment, or "currency," in these situations can vary. Claimants might receive cash, new debt instruments, or equity in a restructured company as settlements. The type of currency often depends on the company's liquidity, future prospects, and the negotiations between various stakeholder groups.

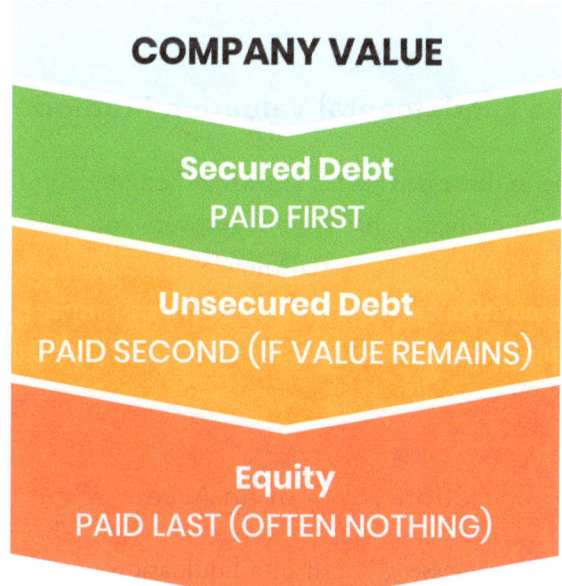

Figure 2: Bankruptcy Value Waterfall

While this waterfall concept seems straightforward in theory, real-world situations often introduce complexities. For instance, companies may have complicated corporate structures with multiple entities (HoldCo/OpCo structures), each with their own set of creditors. In these cases, questions about lien perfection can arise, potentially altering the priority of certain claims. Also, valuation disputes can significantly impact recovery for different classes of creditors.

Understanding this waterfall concept helps investors assess where they stand in the capital structure and what their potential recovery might be under various scenarios. This knowledge, combined with a thorough liquidation analysis, forms the foundation for making informed investment decisions in distressed situations.

Building a Financial Model

Financial modeling is a cornerstone of distressed investing, particularly when the goal is to take control of a company. In my NYU class, Rich Falk-Wallace helps students build a simple model from the ground up. Although this book focuses more on trading strategies and straightforward recovery scenarios than on complex modeling, learning how to break a company apart and reconstruct it on paper is an essential skill for anyone serious about distressed investing. So that's what we'll do in the rest of this chapter.

(For those who want to dive deeper into the craft, I recommend *The Credit Investor's Handbook* by Michael Gatto, head of private credit at Silver Point Capital. Gatto has shaped a generation of investors through his approach to modeling and memo writing. His book cuts through the noise and gets to the heart of credit analysis. For my money, Gatto's work does for credit and distressed debt what Benjamin Graham and David Dodd's *Security Analysis* did for equity investors.)

Liquidation Analysis: The Fundamental Valuation Method

When investing in distressed assets, knowing the liquidation value helps you determine your downside risk and estimate what kind of recovery you might expect in a worst-case scenario (see Fig. 3). This is absolutely essential knowledge; negotiating a deal without knowing it is like flying an airplane without an altimeter. In both cases, you're probably going to crash.

Let's examine the three main rules for an accurate liquidation analysis, also known as "buying right."

Rule #1: Determine the Liquidation Value of an Asset

Begin by assessing the asset's worth in a liquidation scenario. Examine appraisal values and market comparables to see what similar assets have sold for recently. Consider both the "fire-sale" liquidation value (what you could get for the asset if you had to sell it today) and the "orderly" liquidation value (what you could get with more time to shop the asset around).

LIQUIDATION VALUE

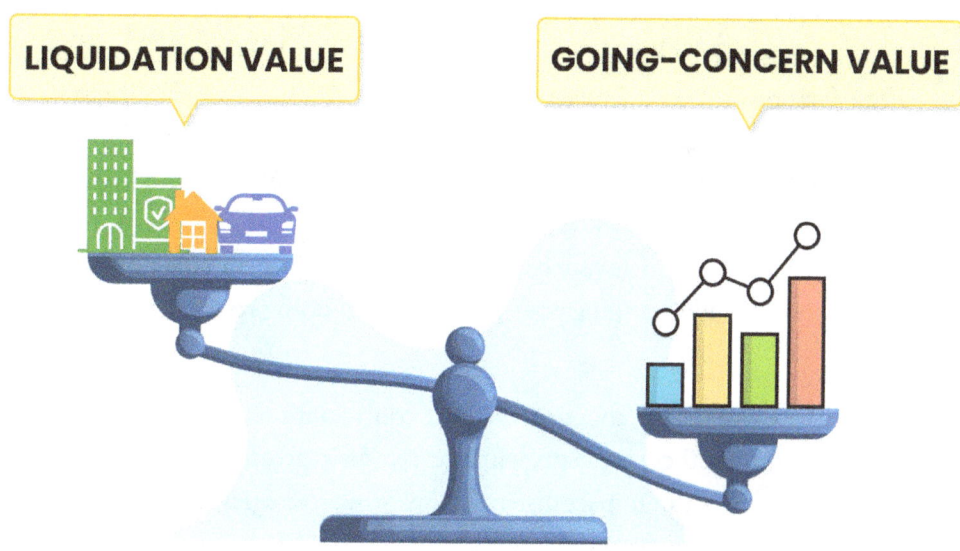

CORE RULES:

- Liquidation Value = total asset value if sold off
- If Liquidation Value > Going-Concern Value → company isn't worth saving

Figure 3: Liquidation Value

For operating businesses, closely analyze the company's balance sheet, focusing on cash, accounts receivable, inventory, and property, plant, and equipment (PP&E). Also, evaluate the company's earnings before interest, taxes, depreciation, and amortization (EBITDA), as it provides a clearer picture of operating performance by excluding nonoperational expenses, making it easier to compare profitability across companies and industries. Additionally, consider what multiple of EBITDA you're paying for the business.

Rule #2: Anticipate Changes to the Balance Sheet

Next, project how the company's balance sheet might change during bankruptcy. For example, the company may take on new liabilities through DIP financing to keep the business running.

As we touched on earlier in this chapter, the priority of creditors' claims may shift based on factors like expenses that are incurred by a bankruptcy debtor after the filing of the bankruptcy or causes of action that are asserted against certain creditors in the bankruptcy case. Additionally, some assets may be clawed back through preference or fraudulent conveyance claims. Always assume the worst-case scenario due to uncertainties.

Rule #3: Do Your Due Diligence

Lastly, investigate why the asset is troubled. Is it simply because of excessive debt, or are there deeper issues like bad management, significant legal liabilities, or environmental problems? These factors can greatly impact the asset's long-term value and ability to secure financing.

Fair warning: gathering this information may be challenging. Knowledgeable individuals may be reluctant to talk, while those without information won't be able to offer any useful insights.

In sum, the steps to any successful distressed investment come down to knowing the value of the asset(s), understanding your downside, and doing your homework (see Fig. 4).

While we've briefly touched on legal considerations such as fraudulent conveyance and preference claims, these concepts will be explored in greater depth in later chapters, where we'll examine how they can impact distressed investing strategies and outcomes.

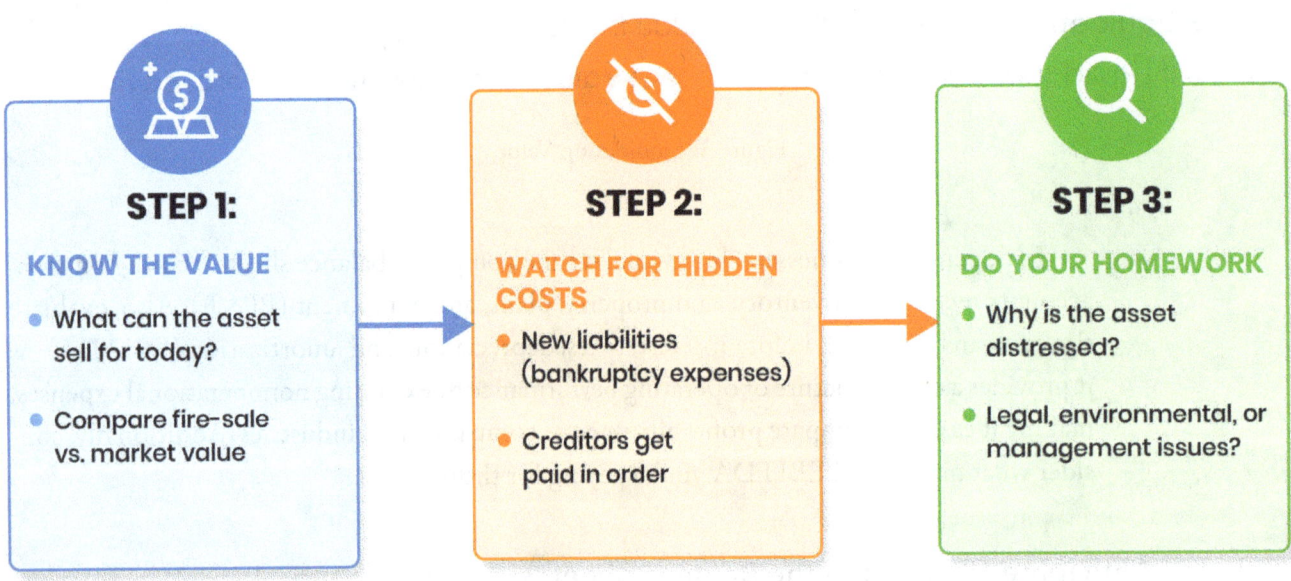

Follow these three steps to protect your downside risk in distressed investing

Figure 4: Buying Right: Liquidation Value

American Airlines Liquidation Analysis

To help you better understand the role of liquidation analysis and buying right, let's look at a real-world example.

In 2011, the airline industry faced significant challenges, including rising fuel costs, intense competition from low-cost carriers, and the economic downturn following the 2008 financial crisis. Unlike its major competitors, American Airlines avoided bankruptcy in the early 2000s, leaving it with higher labor costs and less flexible operations. Eventually, following years of financial struggles, American Airlines filed for Chapter 11 bankruptcy protection in November 2011.

If the lay investor had performed a liquidation analysis at the outset of the bankruptcy case, they would have seen tremendous opportunity in purchasing unsecured claims and equity. Here's why:

The company entered bankruptcy with over $4 billion in unrestricted cash, a strategic move that gave it significant leverage in negotiations with creditors and unions. This cash position allowed it to pursue a restructuring strategy without relying on DIP financing, which often comes with stringent conditions.

The liquidation analysis filed with the court in bankruptcy documents estimated recovery values for American Airlines' assets in forced, orderly, and going-concern liquidation scenarios. In Chapter 11 cases, the debtor company itself prepares a liquidation analysis as part of the court filings, often with assistance from financial advisors or restructuring professionals. This analysis is intended to provide a realistic estimate of how much creditors might recover under different scenarios. Even though debtor companies typically provide this analysis, potential investors and creditors still perform independent assessments to verify assumptions and conclusions.

To illustrate how asset recovery can vary across different scenarios, consider the case of cash: it was expected to recover 61% of its net book value in a forced liquidation, while in an orderly liquidation, it would recover 79%. Other asset types showed even greater variation. For instance, routes, airport slots, and gate costs were estimated to recover 368% of their book value in a forced liquidation, and up to 421% in an orderly liquidation, reflecting their high strategic value. In contrast, operating flight equipment was projected to recover only 39% to 53% of its book value, depending on the liquidation scenario.

The analysis also presented a priority waterfall for distributing proceeds from liquidated assets. Administrative and priority claims were given precedence, with an estimated recovery of 100% under both forced and orderly liquidation scenarios. Secured claims had a recovery rate ranging from 75% to 88%, depending on the liquidation process. However, unsecured claims, including pension liabilities and intercompany claims, faced significantly lower recoveries. For example, unsecured creditors were projected to recover as little as 0.14% in a forced liquidation scenario and up to 1.55% in an orderly liquidation.

An important consideration for American Airlines during its restructuring was the Section 1113 process, which allows a debtor to reject collective bargaining agreements under certain conditions. This process enabled American Airlines to reduce its labor costs and align them with industry standards. The company negotiated with its unions, including the Allied Pilots Association, the Association of Professional Flight Attendants, and the Transport Workers Union, to modify existing labor agreements. Negotiations were contentious but ultimately resulted in new agreements that significantly reduced the airline's labor costs.

As the restructuring progressed, it became clear that a merger could provide additional benefits and value for stakeholders. US Airways, which had long been interested in consolidation, saw an opportunity to create a stronger, more competitive airline. The idea of a merger gained traction among American's creditors, particularly the Unsecured Creditors' Committee, who believed it could maximize the value of their claims. American's management, initially resistant to the idea, eventually agreed to explore the merger option.

The restructuring process culminated in a merger agreement with US Airways, which was incorporated into American's reorganization plan, creating the world's largest airline at the time. By combining American's strong domestic network with US Airways's international presence, the merger allowed the two airlines to compete more effectively with other recently merged carriers like Delta and United. However, the plan faced an unexpected challenge when the Department of Justice (DOJ) filed an antitrust lawsuit, citing concerns about reduced competition and higher fares. After another round of intense negotiations and some concessions, the merger was ultimately approved, including divesting certain airport slots and gates to low-cost carriers.

Ultimately, unsecured creditors recovered 100%-plus interest on their claims, and equity also returned a healthy multiple. The bottom line is that American Airlines was never going to be liquidated, and reasonable investors knew that to be the case. There would either be a standalone reorganization or a merger with a competitor like US Airways. Accordingly, the general unsecured claims presented an enticing investment from the outset for investors.

The American Airlines liquidation analysis provides a clear view of the relative recovery prospects for different creditors classes, highlighting the importance of understanding asset values and the potential outcomes of various liquidation scenarios. While the goal for the company and its stakeholders is usually to avoid liquidation altogether and either restructure the company's debts or sell its assets as a going concern, liquidation analysis remains a valuable tool for assessing downside risks and negotiating with other stakeholders in bankruptcy.

Most of us will never perform a liquidation analysis on companies as large as American Airlines, but we will encounter similar situations with smaller businesses. To that end, let's look at a liquidation analysis for Titan Solar, a once-popular solar panel installation business that closed in 2024. After our analysis, we'll consider how its fortunes may have changed if it had been given a $2 million loan.

Titan Solar Liquidation Analysis

After its founding in 2013, Titan Solar quickly became a rising star in the solar panel installation industry, expanding its operations across sixteen states and developing a significant footprint in the country's residential solar market over the next few years. Despite its rapid growth, however, the company faced numerous operational challenges by 2019 that led to financial instability. Its reliance on third-party dealers for sales, combined with aggressive pricing models and a strained relationship with its customers, created a fragile financial structure. On top of this, the company faced increasing working capital costs, legal disputes, and negative public perception.

Taken together, all these challenges proved too much, and in June 2024 Titan Solar closed down.

This situation is typical of many fast-growing companies, especially in niche sectors like solar, where aggressive expansion can outpace financial and operational controls.

The starting point for any liquidation analysis is the company's balance sheet, and looking at Titan's before its closure reveals a company struggling to maintain liquidity and manage its obligations. As of September 2022, Titan Solar had total liabilities of $13.073 million against total assets of $9.477 million, resulting in negative shareholder equity of $3.596 million. The company faced mounting liabilities, including substantial deferred revenues (customer deposits) and payables, which reflected its operational difficulties and cash flow problems. Without an immediate infusion of capital, Titan was on the brink of insolvency, unable to cover its short-term obligations or fund ongoing operations (see Fig. 5).

But suppose an investor or investor group had given them a $2 million cash infusion. If Titan Solar were to secure such a loan, it could immediately address some of its cash flow issues, covering payables and stabilizing operations in the short term. The additional funds might allow the company to invest in more inventory, streamline its supply chain, or restructure its dealer program to improve margins and customer satisfaction.

Whether or not to inject new capital into a distressed company like Titan Solar depends on a complex interplay of assumptions about future market conditions, operations, and the effectiveness of management's strategy. Nevertheless, I recommend that distressed investors do such analyses because the exercise offers valuable insights into what went wrong and what might go right if the company were given a second chance.

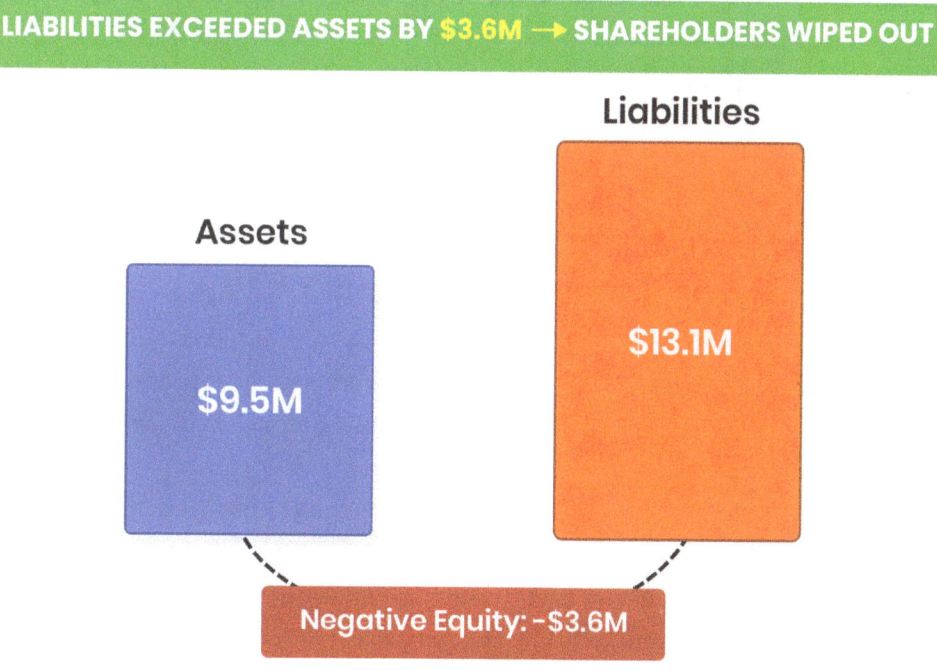

Figure 5: Titan Solar Financial Position

Important Features of Liquidation Analyses

As discussed earlier, the goal of a liquidation analysis is to estimate how much value can realistically be recovered from a company's assets if operations cease. Several factors shape that outcome, especially the type and quality of assets. Real estate, inventory, and equipment are treated differently in a liquidation, and each comes with its own set of challenges. Some assets, like general-purpose machinery, may be easier to sell, while specialized equipment might sit on the market for months or only sell at deep discounts.

Market conditions also affect recovery values. Broader economic trends and industry-specific cycles influence demand for assets. In a downturn, buyers may be scarce, forcing sales at lower prices. In stronger markets, there may be more competition for assets, improving potential recoveries.

The time available to sell assets can also affect outcomes. Quick sales often result in lower prices, while allowing more time might help attract better offers. Of course, waiting longer also means incurring additional costs, such as storage, security, and insurance, and comes with the risk that asset values could decline further. Some assets, like perishable inventory, lose value quickly, while others, like real estate, may hold or even gain value if properly managed.

Liquidation costs, including legal fees, professional fees, and other expenses, must be accounted for as well. These costs reduce the amount available to creditors. In cases where disputes arise over who owns which assets, or where there are questions about liens and creditor priorities, these costs can be substantial.

Investors typically perform a liquidation analysis when they believe a company cannot survive as a going concern. If the estimated value of liquidating assets exceeds what the business might be worth if it keeps operating, selling off assets becomes the logical choice. Although liquidation analysis focuses on downside protection, it's only one part of evaluating a distressed company. To assess whether a business might recover and generate value over time, investors often turn to a discounted cash flow (DCF) analysis, which models future cash flows and potential value if the company restructures and returns to profitability.

Discounted Cash Flow (DCF) Analysis

This valuation method estimates a company's intrinsic value based on its projected future cash flows. The basic idea behind DCF is that the value of a business today is equal to the sum of all its future cash flows, discounted back to the present at an appropriate rate. This rate, known as the discount rate, accounts for the time value of money and the risk associated with those future cash flows.

Here's a simplified overview of the mechanical steps involved in the DCF process:

- Project the company's future cash flows over a certain period (usually 5 to 10 years).
- Estimate a terminal value for the company at the end of the projection period.
- Choose an appropriate discount rate based on the risk profile of the company and the cost of capital.

ANALYZING AND VALUING DISTRESSED ASSETS

- Discount the projected cash flows and terminal value back to the present using the discount rate.
- Sum up the discounted cash flows to determine the company's present value.

There are mathematical formulas and spreadsheets you can use to calculate the present value of cash flows, based on many different assumptions, but the fundamental takeaway is that *money today is worth more than the same amount in the future* (see Fig. 6).

While DCF sounds straightforward, building a DCF model can be complex and time-consuming. It requires a deep understanding of the company's operations, industry dynamics, and financial statements, as well as the ability to make reasonable assumptions about future growth, profitability, and risk. For many distressed investors, building a full-blown DCF model from scratch may be impractical or beyond their technical capabilities. However, various online tools and resources can now help simplify the DCF process and make it more accessible to investors.

One such tool is the DCF calculator provided by the Corporate Finance Institute.[7] This free online calculator lets users input basic assumptions about a company's financials and growth prospects and generates a simple DCF valuation based on those inputs.

Another option is to use AI-powered financial analysis tools like FinChat (https://finchat.io/). These tools can automatically pull data from a company's financial statements, generate projections based on historical trends and user-defined assumptions, and calculate key

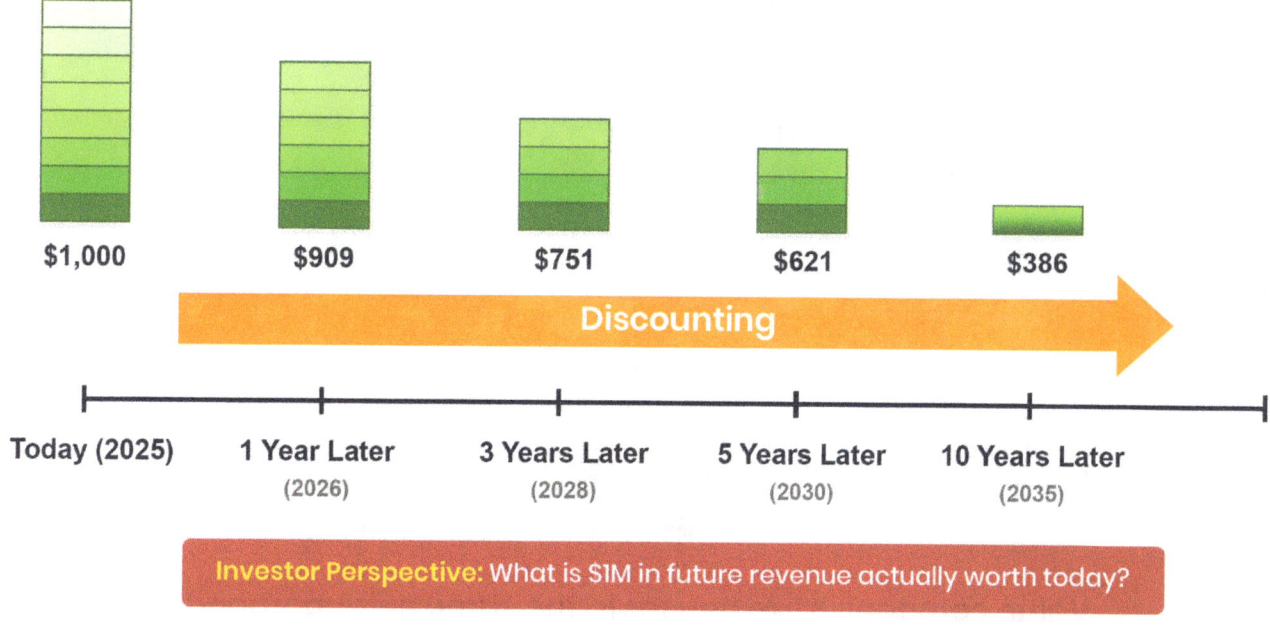

Figure 6: Discounted Cash Flow: The Time Value of Money

valuation metrics like the DCF. One of my colleagues at the NYU Stern School of Business, Aswath Damodaran, put together a definitive overview of DCF valuations in distressed investing.[8] If you're good at math and finance, you may find it especially useful.

While these tools can help streamline the DCF process, remember that they are only as good as the assumptions and inputs provided by the user. Distressed investors still need to have a solid grasp of the fundamentals and be able to make informed judgments about a company's prospects.

Despite its complexity, DCF analysis remains a powerful tool for assessing the intrinsic value of a distressed company and identifying potential investment opportunities. By projecting future cash flows and discounting them back to the present, investors can get a good sense of what a company might be worth if it can successfully turn around its operations and meet its financial obligations.

Assessing a company's value based on its own projected cash flows isn't always enough, however. To gain a broader market perspective, it's helpful to compare the distressed company against its peers using a comparable company analysis.

Comparable Company Analysis

Comparable company analysis, also known as "comps" or "peer group analysis," is another widely used valuation technique in distressed investing. The basic idea behind comps is to value a company based on how similar companies are valued in the market.

The premise is that companies in the same industry, with similar business models, growth prospects, and risk profiles, should trade at similar valuation multiples. By looking at the valuation of comparable public companies, investors can understand what a distressed company might be worth if it were healthy and trading in the public markets (see Fig. 7).

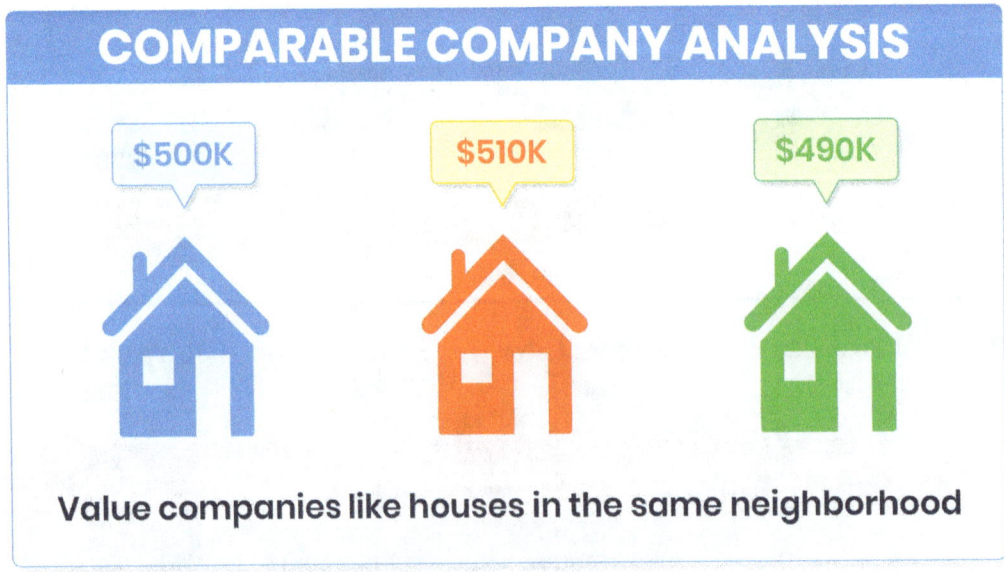

Figure 7: Comparable Company Analysis

ANALYZING AND VALUING DISTRESSED ASSETS

Here's a simplified overview of the comps process:

1. Identify a group of public companies that are like the target company in terms of industry, size, growth, and profitability.
2. Gather financial data and trading multiples for the peer group, such as revenue, EBITDA, earnings, and market capitalization.
3. Calculate the average or median valuation multiples for the peer group, such as EV/Sales, EV/EBITDA, and P/E.
4. Apply the peer group multiples to the target company's financials to arrive at a range of implied valuations.

Like all valuation methods, comps have their limitations and challenges. Choosing comparable companies is often easier said than done, as no two companies are exactly alike. Differences in size, growth rates, profitability, and other factors can skew the results. Additionally, distressed companies often have negative or volatile financial metrics, making applying healthy company multiples challenging.

Despite these challenges, comps remain useful for distressed investors looking to quickly assess a troubled company's potential value. And just as with DCF analyses, various online tools and resources can now help streamline the comps process.

For those with substantial resources, CapitalIQ from S&P is an excellent online tool with almost as much horsepower as a Bloomberg terminal. Finbox, an AI-powered financial analysis platform offering a user-friendly interface for comparable company analysis, is a less expensive option. Finbox lets users easily search for and select peer groups, customize valuation metrics, and generate detailed comps reports with just a few clicks.

While these tools can help simplify the comps process, they are no substitute for careful analysis and judgment. Distressed investors still need to deeply understand the industry, business model, and unique circumstances of the target company to identify truly comparable peers and draw meaningful conclusions from the data.

When used with other valuation techniques like liquidation analysis and DCF, comparable company analysis can provide valuable insights into the potential upside of a distressed investment opportunity. By understanding how the market values similar companies, investors can make more informed decisions about the risks and rewards of a given situation.

All valuation techniques can provide insights into a distressed company's potential value, but they don't capture all the risks. To understand the complete picture, a distressed investor must also evaluate collateral liens and recovery risks.

Evaluating Collateral, Liens, and Risks to Recovery

In many distressed situations, certain creditors may have claims secured by specific assets, such as real estate, equipment, or intellectual property. These secured creditors generally have priority over unsecured creditors in the event of a liquidation or restructuring, meaning they are more likely to recover a larger portion of their investment. As a distressed investor, you must understand a given situation's collateral and lien structure. So let's review some key considerations and strategies for evaluating them.

First, as discussed earlier, you must conduct thorough due diligence on the assets that secure the various creditor claims. To do that, you'll need to review legal documents, such as security agreements and Uniform Commercial Code (UCC) filings, which provide public notice of a lender's interest in a debtor's collateral, helping you understand the scope and priority of each lien. It also means assessing the value and liquidity of the underlying collateral, considering factors such as market conditions, physical conditions, and any potential legal or regulatory issues that could impact the ability to sell or transfer the assets.

One common strategy for distressed investors is to focus on senior secured debt, which typically has the highest priority claim on a company's assets. Investing in senior secured bonds or loans can often achieve higher recovery rates in the event of a default or restructuring, as they are first in line to be repaid from the proceeds of any asset sales or liquidation.

However, it's not always that simple. In some cases, the value of the collateral may be insufficient to fully cover the senior secured claims, leaving junior creditors and equity holders with little or no recovery. Also, competing liens or legal challenges may complicate the recovery process and impact the ultimate distribution of value.

Distressed investors often employ various strategies and legal tactics to mitigate these risks. For example, they may seek to challenge the validity or priority of certain liens or negotiate with other creditors to reach a consensual restructuring plan that maximizes value for all stakeholders. They may also look for opportunities to provide DIP financing or other forms of capital that can help the company continue operating and preserve the value of its assets. I'll have much more to say about this use of DIP financing in Chapter 8, when we look at managing bankruptcy cases. For now, all you need to know is that DIP financing can be a tool sophisticated investors use to keep companies going long enough to extract maximum value (see Fig. 8).

DIP FINANCING: EMERGENCY FUNDING FOR BANKRUPT COMPANIES

Figure 8: DIP Financing: Emergency Funding for Bankrupt Companies

ANALYZING AND VALUING DISTRESSED ASSETS

While these established methods of financial analysis and asset valuation are important to understand, distressed investing often requires thinking outside the box. Advanced strategies, such as those employed by innovative investors, can open up new opportunities beyond traditional valuation techniques.

Advanced Strategies in Distressed Investing: Beyond Traditional Valuation

Buying distressed assets is a gripping experience, and I hope you will have the chance to experience it someday. But when an opportunity presents itself, don't rush in blindly. Take a step back, assess the fundamentals, and make sure the potential reward justifies the risk. Even when the deal seems too good to pass up, you need discipline and careful evaluation.

You may be tempted to do a valuation analysis, give the number you come up with a slight haircut, put in your bid, and call it a day. There are several reasons why proceeding in such an automatic way might not be a great idea, starting with how claims are adjudicated. For example, a bankruptcy trustee can claw back assets you thought you owned, all perfectly legal, for reasons you might not have appreciated when you agreed to buy them.

Successful distressed investing demands a combination of legal, financial, and strategic thinking to navigate situations with multiple competing interests and, crucially, adequately protect your downside.

I opened this chapter with a discussion about pawnbrokers because they are distressed investors who know how to protect their downside risk. They assume worst-case scenarios as a matter of course, or they wouldn't stay in business. If the tools of this kind of investing were just a spreadsheet, meaning that investment decisions were based solely on quantitative data without considering the impact a bankruptcy court might have on the process or various parties competing for limited recoveries can have in the legal process, the market would be so efficient that there would be no upside. But reality is never that simple. A spreadsheet can never tell you what the potential downside is, and what it takes to cover it. Only you can figure this out.

It all comes back to valuation: more specifically, using the right tool in your toolkit to make an accurate one. For some investors, the usual tools aren't good enough.

A March 2024 *Bloomberg* article about Jefferies Financial Group's distressed debt team provides a fascinating example of how investors can find opportunities in unconventional places.[9] The seventeen-person group, led by former Navy SEAL Joe Femenia, focuses on relatively small investments, often in obscure corners of the market, using the firm's capital. These investments could include anything from tax-receivable agreements and insurance claims to litigation rights—assets that can be difficult to value and structure but offer the potential for significant returns.

While the traditional methods of distressed investing, such as liquidation analysis, DCF, and the priority waterfall, focus on valuing distressed companies as a whole, Jefferies's approach highlights an alternative strategy: identifying overlooked or niche assets that may be undervalued due to their complexity. This approach requires not only financial expertise but also deep legal and structural analysis to assess enforceability, potential recovery, and risk factors.

The team's success is a testament to the value of creative thinking and specialized expertise in distressed investing. By diving deep into unconventional assets and leveraging their unique skills and resources, investors like Femenia and his team consistently find deals others weren't even willing to consider.

This strategy parallels some of the themes discussed earlier in this chapter. Just as liquidation analysis helps investors understand the downside risk of a distressed asset, and DCF can uncover long-term intrinsic value, Jefferies's focus on niche opportunities highlights the importance of strategic positioning. Rather than waiting for a distressed company to emerge from bankruptcy, their team proactively identifies under-the-radar claims and assets that may have strong legal protections or future cash flow potential.

For individual distressed investors, Jefferies's success offers an important takeaway: there are multiple ways to approach distressed investing beyond traditional company valuation. Whether through acquiring debt that may convert to equity, providing DIP financing, or purchasing niche claims that others overlook, flexibility and creativity can be key differentiators in achieving outsized returns.

Distressed investing is not merely a matter of playing around with numbers on a balance sheet; it's a disciplined approach that requires a comprehensive understanding of value and risk. We explored various techniques for valuing distressed assets, from liquidation analysis to discounted cash flow modeling, and examined how these methods' interplay can offer insights beyond conventional assessments. But more than just crunching numbers, successful distressed investors recognize that these techniques are only as valuable as the broader context in which they are applied.

Valuation is a tool, not an answer. It's a starting point for a deeper investigation into the dynamics of a troubled company, its market environment, and the potential for creative solutions that others might overlook. As we move into the next chapter, we'll explore various ways to acquire distressed assets, including asset deals, stock acquisitions, UCC Article 9 sales, bankruptcy 363 sales, and receiverships. We'll examine how the valuation techniques discussed earlier can help you choose the most effective strategy for each situation. Understanding the right acquisition approach will allow you to maximize recovery potential and minimize risks.

I am often approached by companies or investors involved in new ventures that are running out of money and seeking further capital infusion. One of the first questions I ask is: What kind of business are we dealing with? Is it an established company with tangible assets, like real estate, inventory, or equipment, or is it an asset-light startup? While valuations of the latter may have used DCF or comparable company analysis at the outset, once these companies are out of cash, the only thing that counts is the liquidation value. In other words, what would a distressed investor pay now?

CASE STUDIES FROM INDUSTRY: HIGHLIGHTING THE VALUE OF BOTTOM-UP RESEARCH

Revlon's Bankruptcy Case

Revlon's journey to bankruptcy in 2022 offers a good example of how to use bottom-up industry research for distressed investing. With this approach, a combined analysis of the company within a broader industry trend could have identified Revlon's mounting troubles well before its Chapter 11 filing.

Founded in 1932 by Charles Revson, Revlon innovated and disrupted the cosmetics industry of the day with transformative products like lacquered nail polishes and matching lipsticks. However, the beauty industry shifted dramatically in the years leading up to Revlon's bankruptcy. Consumer preferences shifted towards "clean" beauty and niche brands, while social media influencers disrupted traditional marketing channels. Revlon, a century-old company, struggled to keep pace with these changes. By 2017, after multiple acquisitions and operational missteps, the company was losing $60–$80 million per quarter.

Revlon's financial statements also revealed clear signs of strain. By the end of 2019, the company's long-term debt stood at $2.9 billion, outstripping its annual revenue of $2.4 billion. This high leverage ratio was a red flag, indicating potential future liquidity issues. Moreover, Revlon's repeated refinancing efforts in the years leading up to bankruptcy, often at higher interest rates, pointed to growing financial distress.

The COVID-19 pandemic intensified Revlon's problems. The company's once-advantageous global supply chain became a liability as lockdowns and shipping delays increased costs and reduced inventory availability. Lockdowns, event cancellations, and the massive shift to working from home dealt another blow to makeup sales, particularly lipstick, a Revlon staple. Nielsen data indicated a 15% decline in prestige makeup sales in 2020, directly impacting Revlon's core business.

On-the-ground research would have provided further evidence of Revlon's declining position. Store visits and retail data would have shown Revlon losing valuable shelf space to newer, trendier brands. Major retailers like CVS and Walmart were allocating more space to private labels and emerging brands, directly impacting Revlon's visibility and sales potential.

For decades, Revlon competed with established players like L'Oreal and Estée Lauder, but online sales from direct-to-consumer brands like Glossier, Fenty, and Kylie Cosmetics, backed by clever social media marketing, posed a new threat for which Revlon was unprepared. These new competitors, unburdened by legacy costs and more attuned to millennial and Gen Z consumer tastes, had better-targeted marketing and pricing.

Five Forces Analysis

A Five Forces analysis provides a clear picture of Revlon's competitive pressures. Named for the framework developed by Harvard Business School professor Michael Porter, it offers a structured approach for analyzing industry dynamics and competitive pressures (see Fig. 9). The model examines the factors that shape an industry's competitive landscape: the threat of new entrants, bargaining power of both suppliers and buyers, threat of substitute products, and rivalry among existing competitors. It assesses how easily new competitors can enter the market, the ability of suppliers and customers to influence prices and terms, the availability of alternative products, and the intensity of competition within the industry.

Figure 9: Five Key Market Forces That Impact Competition

As it pertains to Revlon, here is what a Five Forces analysis might have revealed:

1. **Threat of New Entrants**: The cosmetics industry has relatively low entry barriers, especially with the rise of e-commerce and social media marketing. New brands like Glossier, Fenty, and Kylie Cosmetics were able to enter the market quickly and gain traction by appealing directly to consumers. These brands did not have Revlon's legacy costs and could focus more effectively on emerging trends, like clean beauty and sustainability. Revlon struggled to compete with these new entrants, who were often more agile and better positioned to respond to shifting consumer preferences.

2. **Bargaining Power of Suppliers**: Revlon's global supply chain became a significant liability during the COVID-19 pandemic, as supply disruptions and increased costs hit hard. Due to shortages and delays, suppliers had greater bargaining power, forcing Revlon to pay higher prices for raw materials and transportation. Additionally, with a declining financial position, Revlon may not have been the preferred customer for many suppliers, who might have prioritized more financially stable companies.
3. **Bargaining Power of Buyers**: The bargaining power of buyers (retailers and consumers) increased over time. Large retailers like CVS and Walmart began to allocate more shelf space to private label and niche brands, reducing Revlon's visibility and sales potential. Consumers also shifted their preferences towards clean beauty and indie brands promising more transparency and sustainability, which pressured Revlon to adapt quickly or lose market share.
4. **Threat of Substitute Products**: Substitute products were a significant threat to Revlon. Consumers could easily switch to other brands offering similar products with perceived better quality or more alignment with current trends, like cruelty-free or vegan cosmetics. Moreover, during the pandemic, a decline in social outings and events reduced the demand for makeup, particularly lipstick, a core product for Revlon.
5. **Rivalry Among Existing Competitors**: The cosmetics industry is fiercely competitive, with well-established players like L'Oreal, Estée Lauder, and Coty and new direct-to-consumer brands competing aggressively for market share. Revlon faced intense competition from traditional rivals and new entrants that were more agile and responsive to market trends. The company struggled to differentiate itself in an increasingly crowded market, particularly with its slower adoption of digital marketing and e-commerce strategies compared to newer brands.

Using this framework, distressed investors can identify potential sources of stress and opportunity. For example, an industry with low entry barriers or high rivalry might be more prone to disruption and financial distress among incumbent players. This analysis can help reveal which companies are most vulnerable to competitive pressures and better positioned to weather challenges.

In distressed investing, successful investigation extends well beyond surface-level financial analysis. Footnotes and disclosures in financial filings often contain information about potential risks and liabilities that are not immediately apparent in the main statements. Can you guess which legendary investor is renowned for reading footnotes in corporate reports?

You don't have to be Warren Buffett, though, to take advantage. Modern technology has democratized the intelligence-gathering process in many ways. Advancements in AI and financial software have made sophisticated financial analysis more accessible, even to those without extensive backgrounds in finance or accounting. Such tools can help investors quickly identify trends and anomalies that might signal impending distress.

By applying the research strategies we discussed earlier in this chapter, a distressed investor could have spotted Revlon's weaknesses long before its bankruptcy filing. For example, monitoring public financial data and court filings would have highlighted the company's high debt levels and frequent refinancing, a clear sign of financial distress. Everything that happened to Revlon was in the public domain; any distressed investor could have put the pieces together and turned a profit.

PG&E's 2019 Bankruptcy Filing

The PG&E bankruptcy of 2019 exemplifies how bottom-up research and careful analysis of company disclosures can reveal potential distressed situations and their likely outcomes. In November 2018, the Camp Fire wildfire devastated the town of Paradise, California, killing eighty-five people and destroying over 18,800 structures. Investigations quickly pointed to PG&E's electrical transmission lines as the cause. This catastrophe wasn't an isolated incident; PG&E, an investor-owned utility, had been implicated in numerous California wildfires over the previous years. In other words, the PG&E debacle had happened before, and the outcome of the bankruptcy case was somewhat predictable. This is an important lesson about distressed investing: history often repeats itself, and the successful investor should be a good student of history.

A thorough review of PG&E's financial disclosures in the months leading up to the bankruptcy would have revealed mounting liabilities related to these wildfires. The company's quarterly reports and investor presentations increasingly highlighted the potential for significant financial impacts from wildfire-related claims. By December 2018, PG&E estimated its potential liability for the 2017 and 2018 wildfires could exceed $30 billion, far surpassing its insurance coverage.

Analyzing California's regulatory environment would have provided helpful context. The state's "inverse condemnation" doctrine held utilities liable for wildfire damages caused by their equipment, regardless of negligence. This policy, and the increasing frequency and severity of wildfires due to climate change, created a perfect storm of financial risk for PG&E.

When PG&E filed for Chapter 11 bankruptcy in January 2019, it listed $71.4 billion in assets and $51.7 billion in debts. However, a closer examination of the company's financial structure would have revealed that much of its debt was secured or related to its regulated utility operations, which needed to continue functioning to maintain essential services.

The insight for distressed investors lay in understanding that despite the bankruptcy, PG&E remained a vital utility provider for millions of Californians. One way or another, the state was going to ensure the company's continued operations and financial viability. This political reality, coupled with PG&E's substantial assets and ongoing revenue streams, made it all but certain that the company would emerge from bankruptcy as a going concern. Buying claims against PG&E was like buying claims against the State of California.

Furthermore, PG&E's disclosures indicated significant unencumbered assets and the potential for rate increases to cover wildfire-related costs. These factors, along with creating a state wildfire fund to help utilities pay for future wildfire damages, pointed to a high likelihood of full recovery for general unsecured creditors.

ANALYZING AND VALUING DISTRESSED ASSETS

When PG&E emerged from bankruptcy in July 2020, the reorganization plan provided for payment in full to unsecured creditors, plus interest. While perhaps surprising to casual observers given the scale of the wildfire damages, this outcome was predictable for investors who had conducted thorough bottom-up research.

This pattern of utility-related environmental disasters continues to create distressed investing opportunities. In early 2025, Southern California Edison faced potential liability from devastating wildfires that swept through Los Angeles County. Similarly, Hawaiian Electric faced massive claims following the 2023 Maui wildfires that destroyed the historic town of Lahaina. In both cases, the same fundamental analysis applies: these are essential service providers with significant assets and revenue streams operating in states where regulators must balance accountability with maintaining vital infrastructure. The astute distressed investor recognizes that despite headline-grabbing liability figures, the political and economic realities often lead to outcomes where creditors recover more than initial estimates might suggest.

The PG&E case shows how combining detailed financial analysis, industry knowledge, and an understanding of the regulatory environment can reveal valuable distressed investment opportunities. Your ability to dig deep, connect the dots, and anticipate outcomes before they unfold in the market will set you apart and position you for success.

Successful distressed investing is both a science and an art. The science involves conducting rigorous analysis and thorough research. The art involves recognizing patterns, synthesizing information, and acting when others hesitate.

KEY INSIGHTS

1. Liquidation analysis provides a baseline for understanding the potential recovery value of a distressed company's assets, helping to assess downside risk in a worst-case scenario.
2. Richard Falk-Wallace's method of comparing healthy and distressed balance sheets reveals how value shifts from equity holders to creditors as a company's financial health deteriorates, forming a foundational principle for identifying distressed investment opportunities.
3. The BoxCo example illustrates how a company's capital structure evolves from health to distress, highlighting that in many distressed cases, the true investment potential often lies in debt instruments rather than equity.
4. The distressed investing waterfall illustrates how value flows through a company's capital structure based on the principle of absolute priority, with senior claims paid before junior claims.
5. Real-world complexities such as HoldCo/OpCo structures, lien perfection issues, and valuation disputes can complicate the application of the waterfall concept, requiring thorough due diligence.
6. Closely analyzing a distressed company's balance sheet, including cash, accounts receivable, inventory, and PP&E, helps identify the value of assets available for recovery.
7. EBITDA is a metric for assessing operational performance and comparing profitability across companies, especially in distressed situations where earnings are volatile.

8. Evaluating potential legal risks, such as fraudulent conveyance, preference claims, and the structure of collateral and liens, helps protect investments and ensure priority in recoveries.
9. DCF analysis helps estimate a company's intrinsic value based on its projected future cash flows, providing insight into whether a distressed investment has the potential to generate long-term returns.
10. Comparing a distressed company to its peers offers insights into the market's valuation of similar businesses, allowing investors to adjust their expectations accordingly.
11. Assessing the value and enforceability of collateral and understanding the lien structure helps determine the likely recovery in a distressed scenario, particularly for secured creditors.
12. The American Airlines case demonstrates how thorough liquidation analysis can guide restructuring decisions, highlighting the value of strategic negotiation and asset preservation in achieving favorable outcomes.
13. Innovative approaches, such as seeking unconventional assets or niche opportunities, can offer significant returns in distressed investing beyond traditional valuation techniques.
14. Successful distressed investing combines financial analysis, legal understanding, strategic thinking, and strong professional relationships.
15. A comprehensive approach to assessing and mitigating risks, including understanding market conditions, asset liquidity, and potential legal challenges, maximizes recovery and minimizes losses.
16. Distressed investing extends beyond number crunching, requiring an understanding of the broader context, including the company's market environment, management, and potential for restructuring or turnaround.
17. Integrating valuation techniques with the appropriate acquisition strategy, such as asset deals, stock acquisitions, or bankruptcy sales, enables investors to optimize recovery potential.
18. When evaluating turnarounds, there is a critical distinction between established businesses with hard assets and asset-light startups, with liquidation value becoming the primary consideration for cash-strapped ventures.
19. Bottom-up industry research, as shown in the Revlon and PG&E cases, can reveal distressed investment opportunities before they become widely recognized, giving insightful investors a significant advantage.

CHAPTER 6

Acquisition Mechanisms and Strategy

One of the absolute best things about bankruptcy for distressed investors is that you can purchase the assets you want and leave behind the assets you don't want. Through the mechanics of the U.S. Bankruptcy Code, you can strip a company of its assets and leave its liabilities behind. There's no better example of how this works than the Lehman Brothers bankruptcy and aftermath.

In 2008, as the global financial crisis unfolded, one of the most dramatic corporate collapses in history was taking place: Lehman Brothers, a storied investment bank, was on the verge of bankruptcy. The firm had been severely impacted by the subprime mortgage crisis, and its failure threatened to destabilize the entire financial system. In the midst of this turmoil, Barclays swooped in to buy Lehman's North American investment banking and trading divisions. The entire $250 million deal closed in just five days, a stunning feat given the scale of Lehman's operations, including not only trading desks but also its iconic headquarters at 745 Seventh Avenue and thousands of employees who would show up to work under a new owner the following Monday.

How did Barclays pull off such a complex acquisition so quickly? The answer lies in one of the most frequently used provisions of the U.S. Bankruptcy Code: Section 363. By leveraging the guidelines in this section, Barclays was able to move faster than other potential buyers, avoiding many of the delays and liabilities that would have come with a traditional acquisition. The good news for you is that the same techniques used to acquire pieces of a fallen giant apply to much smaller, everyday distressed assets, whether it's a multifamily residential building or a small manufacturing business.

This chapter explores the four fundamental mechanisms distressed investors use to acquire troubled assets: asset and stock deals, UCC Article 9 sales, Section 363 sale agreements like the one used by Barclays in Lehman, and receiverships (see Fig. 1). We'll examine real examples of each, dissecting what worked, what didn't, and why. Although these tools can be complex, they are accessible to investors who understand the process and work with experienced counsel.

THE DISTRESSED INVESTING PLAYBOOK

FOUR WAYS TO BUY DISTRESSED ASSETS – PROS & CONS

Compare these four methods to determine the best approach for your distressed investment situation.

Figure 1: Four Ways to Buy Distressed Assets – Pros and Cons

Knowing how to navigate these mechanisms is another key to taking control of distressed assets. You can use your knowledge to spot opportunities others miss—and avoid the pitfalls that can sink even the most promising deals.

Asset vs. Stock Acquisitions: The First Fork in the Road

The Barclays-Lehman deal is often remembered as a headline-grabbing Section 363 sale, but it also highlights one of the most basic and consequential choices in distressed investing: whether to buy assets or stock. That decision shaped how Barclays approached the acquisition, allowing them to move quickly and avoid many of Lehman's liabilities. By the time Lehman Brothers filed for bankruptcy protection, the advisors involved in the case had already conducted a sale process, determining that the best way to preserve value for creditors and to preserve jobs for thousands of employees was to have Barclays acquire Lehman's North American investment banking and trading divisions. Clearly Barclays was not going to assume all of Lehman's Brothers liabilities, since doing so would have them inheriting the same woes that caused the company's downfall. So, by utilizing Section 363 Barclays had a path to buy just the valuable assets without taking on the full weight of Lehman's debts and obligations.

When considering the purchase of any distressed company, investors face this same choice. Asset deals involve buying specific pieces of a business, such as property, equipment, or contracts, and often allow buyers to leave behind unwanted debts and obligations. Stock deals, by contrast, involve purchasing the company itself, including all of its assets and liabilities, offering a path to control the entire business, but one with greater risks attached.

In the Lehman case, Barclays focused on acquiring a targeted set of assets, its U.S. investment banking and trading operations, rather than taking on the entire company, which was burdened with enormous liabilities. This asset-focused approach not only shaped the transaction's structure but also determined what risks Barclays would assume and how quickly they could close the deal.

Every distressed acquisition starts with this basic decision: whether to buy the company whole or pick and choose what parts to acquire. Far from being a mere legal distinction, this choice influences everything from pricing to liability exposure to the speed and complexity of the transaction.

Asset Deals

An asset deal allows investors to selectively acquire specific assets, such as inventory, equipment, or intellectual property, without assuming the seller's broader liabilities unless explicitly agreed upon. This approach provides flexibility and risk management, making it a preferred option in many Chapter 11 bankruptcies. The primary advantage of asset deals is the ability to cherry-pick the most valuable components of a business while leaving behind unwanted obligations. Unlike stock acquisitions, which transfer all liabilities along with ownership, asset sales typically protect buyers from legacy legal and financial burdens.

However, asset deals can be more complex and expensive due to the need for detailed agreements outlining exactly what is being purchased. Additionally, certain assets, like licenses and permits, may have transfer restrictions that add further complications. There is also the challenge of retaining employees and maintaining business continuity, as an asset sale can disrupt existing relationships with customers, vendors, and workers.

Stock Deals

In contrast, a stock deal involves purchasing the entire company, including both its assets and liabilities. This approach is often simpler in terms of transaction structure because it does not require individual asset transfers or renegotiation of contracts. When a buyer acquires stock, they step directly into the shoes of the previous owner, inheriting all rights, obligations, and liabilities of the company. This continuity can be an advantage when maintaining existing contracts, licenses, and customer relationships is critical to the business's ongoing operations.

However, stock deals carry significant risks, particularly in a distressed context. One of the biggest dangers is inheriting undisclosed liabilities, such as pending lawsuits, environmental claims, or tax obligations. This heightened legal exposure highlights how important it is to identify any hidden risks before completing the acquisition. This is one reason why stock purchases are far less common in a bankruptcy setting, unless they are part of a larger reorganization plan, such as a debt-for-equity swap where creditors receive ownership in exchange for debt forgiveness. Nine times out of ten, asset purchases are the preferred route because they allow buyers to acquire valuable assets while mitigating exposure to legacy liabilities.

Stock deals are more frequently used in healthy acquisitions outside of bankruptcy. On the other hand, while asset deals offer a cleaner separation from a distressed company's past obligations, stock acquisitions provide a streamlined path to ownership with fewer immediate transaction hurdles. And in cases where high-profile investors or strategic buyers seek to maintain continuity and avoid operational disruptions, stock purchases may present unique opportunities, particularly when structured as part of a broader turnaround strategy.

The right approach depends on the buyer's risk tolerance, strategic goals, and ability to conduct comprehensive due diligence.

Pacific Ethanol: Stock Acquisition, Asset Deal, or Funding a Stand-Alone Reorganization?

When evaluating distressed companies, investors typically consider three options: asset deals, stock acquisitions, or funding a plan of reorganization. This third possibility happens when no one buys the assets or stock and the company restructures internally to continue operating. This outcome is particularly likely when potential buyers perceive the company as having greater value as a reorganized entity rather than as a collection of assets. To understand why this path is chosen, let's look at the story of Pacific Ethanol and how distressed investors evaluated their options.

Founded in 2005 when the demand for ethanol was quickly rising, Pacific grew rapidly to become one of the leading ethanol producers on the West Coast. This was due in no small part to having its headquarters in the politically strategic city of Sacramento, California's capital. The company's stock gained significant attention in 2006 when Microsoft co-founder Bill Gates invested, indicating its potential as a major player in the renewable energy industry. Its commitment to producing low-carbon renewable fuels captured the attention of many beyond Gates, and it continued to grow rapidly. However, it soon faced a perfect storm of challenges that undercut its financial stability: a combination of volatile corn prices, declining demand for ethanol, and the global credit crunch of 2008–2009.

In 2010, Pacific Ethanol Inc. filed for Chapter 11 and submitted a reorganization plan to the U.S. Bankruptcy Court in Delaware. The central feature of the company's plan was to reduce its debt and resume operations at Pacific Ethanol's Madera and Stockton facilities in California. The company hoped to continue as a going concern while serving its customer base and maintaining production with more liquidity and debt reduction.

Unfortunately, the business plan failed. Pacific's business model relied heavily on global ethanol pricing, leaving it vulnerable to industry-specific downturns. While the plan enabled the company to continue operating its production facilities, the unstable demand for ethanol and high production costs remained. The company tried to diversify into specialty alcohol products and other ventures, like hand sanitizers and mouthwash, but those opportunities weren't big enough to offset the broader challenges in the ethanol market. In 2017, Pacific Ethanol was back in court with a second Chapter 11 bankruptcy filing. In bankruptcy slang, this is known as a Chapter 22 (Chapter 11 x 2).

Investors evaluating Pacific Ethanol in 2017 now had a choice whether to bid for the company's assets or the entire company. What would they choose?

The Pros and Cons of Each

Pacific Ethanol's assets included production facilities, intellectual property, and customer contracts. Given its ongoing financial struggles and high debt levels, an asset deal may have been a cleaner way to acquire valuable parts of the business while minimizing risk.

On the other hand, a stock deal would have appealed to investors with the resources to manage the company's existing debt and legal obligations. Presumably, a larger player in the specialty chemicals industry might have considered buying the company's stock as an inexpensive way to enter the market. This approach could be attractive if the investor saw potential in Pacific Ethanol's existing contracts, customer relationships, and business model.

The Outcome

In the end, no one came to Pacific Ethanol's rescue, and no one made any compelling offers for the company's assets. Instead, the management chose the third option: internal reorganization. They shed more debt, streamlined operations, and eventually rebranded the company as Alto Ingredients in 2021. The new name reflected a broader focus on specialty alcohol products, including those used in cosmetics, disinfectants, and hand sanitizers. This shift allowed Alto Ingredients to diversify its revenue streams and reduce reliance on ethanol production.

This scenario highlights an important takeaway for distressed investors: sometimes, despite bankruptcy, no one steps in to acquire the distressed assets or stock, and the company instead restructures internally to continue operating. Being prepared for this outcome can help investors make more informed decisions when evaluating distressed opportunities.

UCC Article 9 Sales

Bankruptcy proceedings can be lengthy, complex, and expensive. In contrast, UCC Article 9 sales offer a more streamlined process that can often be completed in a matter of weeks. Investors typically think of distressed asset purchases as involving companies that are still operational but require restructuring or reorganization. However, when a borrower defaults on its loans, and the company's financial condition deteriorates beyond repair, traditional acquisition methods may no longer be feasible. This is where UCC Article 9 comes into play, giving secured creditors a legal pathway to recover collateral and facilitate the sale of assets in a way that is both fast and commercially reasonable.

Article 9 sales are particularly common in transactions involving real property and secured equipment. Governed by the Uniform Commercial Code (UCC), a set of laws adopted by most U.S. states to standardize commercial transactions, Article 9 specifically outlines the rights of secured creditors to foreclose on collateral when a borrower defaults. Through this process, creditors can sell the collateral through public or private sales to recover their losses, as long as the sale is conducted in a "commercially reasonable" manner. This standard gives creditors and buyers some flexibility in structuring a deal while still providing safeguards to ensure fairness.

For investors, UCC Article 9 sales offer several advantages. First, they are fast. Unlike a bankruptcy process that might take months or even years, an Article 9 sale can often close in a matter of weeks. Second, transaction and legal costs are generally lower, making this route more cost-effective. Third, the flexibility provided by the "commercially reasonable" standard allows for creative deal structuring that might not be possible in a court-supervised sale. When done properly, an Article 9 sale can also deliver a relatively clean title, cutting off the rights of junior lienholders in the collateral.

Like anything else, however, Article 9 sales are not without risks. One of the main limitations is that only assets subject to a valid security agreement can be sold. This means buyers cannot cherry-pick from the company's entire pool of assets; sales usually involve a specific asset or set of assets tied to the secured loan. Moreover, the process is lender-driven, meaning the secured lender controls both the timeline and structure of the sale, while buyers have relatively little influence compared to a Chapter 11 sale. Another potential drawback is that UCC Article 9 sales do not automatically eliminate successor liability claims, as bankruptcy sales typically do, and buyers may remain exposed to certain obligations tied to the borrower. Finally, the due diligence process can be challenging. Since distressed borrowers are often uncooperative or have limited records, buyers may have to make decisions based on incomplete information and under tight time constraints.

When Article 9 sales proceed smoothly, they are sometimes called "friendly foreclosures" because both the creditor and debtor may work together to facilitate the sale. Unlike a bankruptcy filing, an Article 9 sale is generally not public, so there is usually little to no publicity around the company's distress. Customers and vendors typically remain unaware, since only parties directly involved in the asset are notified.

Still, not all Article 9 sales go smoothly. A case in point is N&N Partners, LLC a company that financed commercial equipment purchases in 2007 and 2008 but defaulted on its obligations in 2009 during the Great Recession. Following N&N's default, the lender repossessed and liquidated the equipment in an Article 9 sale for the best price they could get under the circumstances. But, as is often the case with fire sales, the proceeds didn't cover the full amount N&N owed. What had started as a "friendly foreclosure" soon turned adversarial. The lender filed a lawsuit against N&N Partners to recover the remaining balance—and won.[10]

Another point worth noting is that many Article 9 sales are conducted privately, often out of reach for the typical investor. So unless you have an existing relationship with a finance company or lender, you may not be able to participate. These sales tend to be tightly controlled processes, with assets often sold to buyers known to the lender rather than to the general public.

However, for distressed investors who can access them, Article 9 sales can present valuable opportunities, offering speed, simplicity, and, in some cases, attractive pricing. As with any distressed transaction, they require careful analysis of the underlying risks, particularly regarding liability exposure and the quality of the assets on offer.

Section 363 Sales

A Section 363 sale, named after Section 363 of the U.S. Bankruptcy Code, allows a company in Chapter 11 to sell its assets during bankruptcy. Unlike typical Chapter 11 bankruptcies, where the company must submit a reorganization plan and gain court approval before restructuring its assets and liabilities—a process that can take months—a 363 sale provides a faster way for companies to raise cash or shed assets to facilitate restructuring. These sales are overseen by the bankruptcy court, which ensures the process is fair, transparent, and properly noticed to all interested parties. One of the primary advantages for buyers is that assets can be sold "free and clear" of liens and other claims, making them more attractive than purchasing assets in a traditional transaction where liabilities may follow the sale.

For distressed investors, 363 sales can present valuable opportunities to acquire assets such as real estate, equipment, intellectual property, or entire business units, often at a discount. Because of the urgency inherent in many bankruptcy situations, sellers may be motivated to move quickly, and buyers can avoid many liabilities that would otherwise attach to the assets. In effect, a court-approved 363 sale provides a "cleansed" title, shielding buyers from successor liability and competing claims.

The bankruptcy court's involvement also brings legitimacy and structure to the process. By supervising the sale, the court provides a level of transparency that gives comfort to buyers, who can be confident that their acquisition will be protected against future challenges. Another advantage is speed: while Chapter 11 cases often take months or years to resolve, a 363 sale can often be completed in a fraction of that time. Additionally, unlike a plan of reorganization, which requires creditor voting and other procedural hurdles, 363 sales allow debtors to sell some or all their assets without a vote. This flexibility makes 363 sales a useful tool in complex restructurings where a quick sale may be the best way to preserve value.

However, the foregoing should not convey the impression that 363 sales have no drawbacks. Since these sales typically involve an auction process, buyers risk being outbid. While stalking horse protections, such as breakup fees or expense reimbursements, are often negotiated to protect the initial bidder, there's no guarantee that a buyer will win the final auction. Another challenge is due diligence. Because bankrupt companies are often in disarray, with incomplete records or limited cooperation from management, buyers may struggle to get the information they need to properly assess the assets. The compressed timeline for 363 sales only adds to this challenge, making it difficult to conduct a thorough review before the sale closes.

Buyers must also address potential objections from creditors. Creditors can challenge the sale price, argue that the process is unfair, or demand changes to the sale terms. These disputes can delay the closing or force buyers to adjust their offers.

Finally, arranging financing can be more complicated in the context of a distressed asset sale. Lenders may hesitate to provide acquisition financing for assets coming out of bankruptcy, especially if time constraints make underwriting difficult.

Despite these challenges, 363 sales remain one of the most powerful tools in distressed investing, offering opportunities to acquire assets quickly, often at attractive prices, and with the added protection of a court order that can cut through much of the legal complexity associated with distressed situations.

A Balloon Maker Goes Pop

Within the past few years there has been a spate of retail bankruptcy filings resolved via Section 363 sales: Party City, Big Lots, and Joann Stores, to name just a few. As you can imagine, these shakeups have had many repercussions downstream, particularly with suppliers. Here's an example.

When Party City filed for bankruptcy for the first time in January 2023, Anagram International, a Minnesota-based foil balloon manufacturer established in 1977 that had become a major supplier to the party supply store, found itself in a challenging position. The loss of one of its biggest retail clients forced the manufacturer, a 100% wholly owned subsidiary, into its own bankruptcy that November (see Fig. 2).

Its strategy was to seek a 363 sale to restructure its operations and secure new ownership. Celebration Bidco LLC, a group of pre-bankruptcy investors, served as the stalking horse bidder, setting the initial price for the assets. This group included funds managed by Barings LLC, JPMorgan, Neuberger Berman Investment Advisers LLC, and Littlejohn & Co. LLC. The process ensured that the new owners would retain all of Anagram's employees and assume trade payables, maintaining business continuity throughout the transition.

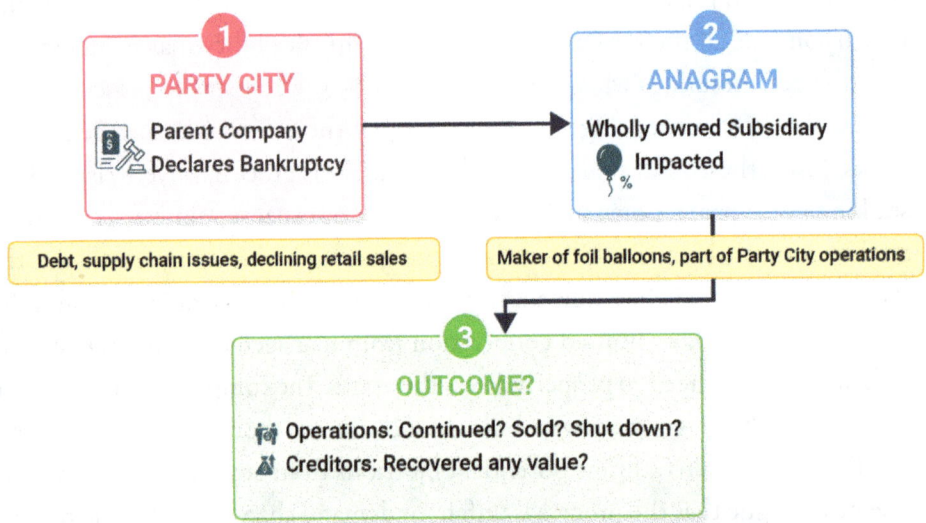

Figure 2: Party City Bankruptcy and Anagram Outcome

ACQUISITION MECHANISMS AND STRATEGY

The 363 sale concluded with Celebration Bidco acquiring Anagram's assets, providing a pathway for the balloon manufacturer to emerge from bankruptcy with a stronger balance sheet and continued operations. The restructuring also allowed Anagram to maintain its relationships with key clients, including Party City, and to focus on regaining stability in its market position.

Anagram's story highlights why 363 sales are popular in Chapter 11 filings. They provide a mechanism for companies to transition quickly while at the same time preserving business operations. In this case, because all the pieces lined up quickly and because the company had a long history of success, Anagram got to party on.

Receiverships

Receivership is a court-supervised process where a neutral third party (the "receiver") takes control of a distressed company's assets. This process is often used when mismanagement, fraud, or legal disputes threaten the company's stability. Receivers manage the company's assets, operate the business (if applicable), and may sell assets to repay creditors.

Receiverships can be more flexible than bankruptcy, with a faster timeline and lower costs. They can be governed by state or federal law, offering more control to the receiver. However, they also have risks, including less oversight, unclear priority rules, and the possibility of piecemeal asset sales. Although creditors might have fewer protections in receivership, the process can be attractive for distressed investors seeking quick asset acquisition.

Consider a recent case involving Heritage Village Assisted Living in Mesa, Arizona, which became subject to receivership. (see Fig. 3).

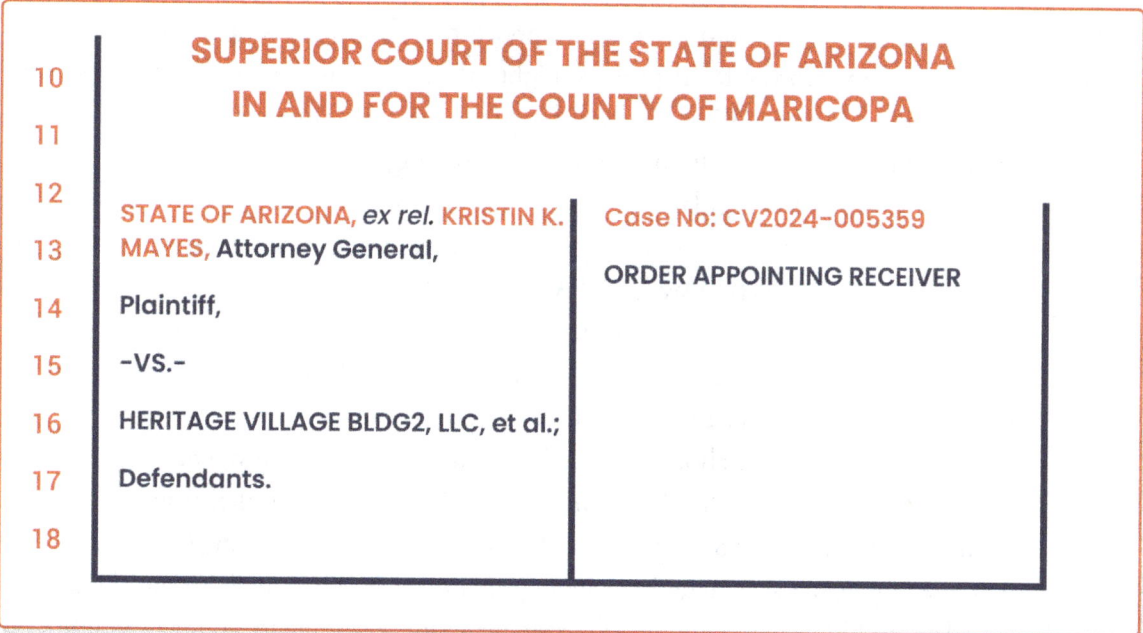

Figure 3: State of Arizona vs. Heritage Village Bldg2 LLC

On April 23, 2024, Arizona's attorney general, Kris Mayes, filed a lawsuit accusing Heritage Village Assisted Living and its owners of elder abuse and consumer fraud. Given the severity of the allegations, the facility was at real risk of losing its license. Had this happened, however, it wouldn't just be the owners who would be penalized—the residents would have to find another facility. So the attorney general asked the Maricopa County Superior Court to appoint a receiver to manage the facility and safeguard the vulnerable residents. Although a sale of the Heritage Village facility in Mesa was approved by the court in February 2025, the lawsuit itself remains ongoing, as the state continues to seek the removal of the current owners from control. The goal is to ensure that a new, competent management structure is in place to provide proper care and services.

The court appointed Peter S. Davis of J.S. Held LLC, as the receiver to oversee the operation and management of the facility's assets. Davis's role includes taking control of the facility, ensuring its assets don't disappear, and implementing necessary changes to improve its operation. His most important mission is to ensure that current residents continue to receive proper care while the lawsuit is pending.[11]

As the receiver, Davis can enter into contracts, hire or dismiss employees, and manage financial transactions to stabilize the business. He can also seek court approval for any sale or disposal of assets. While in his position, Davis must maintain accurate records and submit reports to the court within 90 days of appointment. The court has also allowed Davis to keep defendants and others from interfering with his duties or the facility's assets.

Given the severity of the allegations, the attorney general has indicated that the goal is to find new ownership for Heritage Village Assisted Living and permanently prevent the current owners from having any future contact with vulnerable adults in Arizona.

Is this an opportunity for a distressed investor? Yes, in theory. Depending on court approval and other legal considerations, the receiver might ultimately be tasked with facilitating the sale of the facility, which could present an opportunity for an investor to purchase the assisted living company. However, the process might take time, and the company or entity that may eventually buy Heritage Village will have to prove that it is competent to run a licensed assisted living company, an obviously complicated undertaking.

Receivership cases regularly occur, and for investors with the right background and skill set they can be significant opportunities. That said, receivers are generally shrewd and seasoned businesspeople. Will Peter Davis, a CPA, a certified fraud examiner, certified turnaround professional, certified insolvency and restructuring advisor, and not to mention a business valuation expert, sell something for cheap? Let's just say it's unlikely that the eventual new owner of Heritage Village will get a screaming deal.

One final comment about receiverships. They are highly prevalent when the Securities and Exchange Commission (SEC) is involved and has filed a complaint against a company for securities violations. The SEC has a list of approved, non-government-employed receivers. So, if you're looking to see where there are opportunities, look no further than the press releases issued by the SEC when there's an enforcement action. By doing so, you may be able to identify a company or assets that are subject to a receiver's control.

ACQUISITION MECHANISMS AND STRATEGY

Summary of Mechanisms

Distressed investing involves using a range of legal tools to acquire assets or entire companies experiencing financial distress or legal complications at discounted prices. Knowing how these different approaches work helps investors navigate the risks and opportunities in this space.

Asset and stock deals are some of the most common methods. Asset deals allow investors to buy specific parts of a business while leaving behind unwanted liabilities. These deals can offer tax advantages and more control over what components of the business are acquired. Stock deals, on the other hand, involve taking over the company as a whole, including its contracts, relationships, and obligations. This approach can simplify the transfer of business operations but may also expose buyers to more risks (and, of course, potentially more rewards).

UCC Article 9 sales give secured lenders a way to recover collateral when a borrower defaults. These are typically fast, private sales focused on the assets tied to a loan. Because Article 9 sales happen outside bankruptcy, they are often quicker and less costly than court processes. But buyers must be careful. These sales can involve risks around title, successor liability, and lack of transparency.

Section 363 sales take place in bankruptcy under court supervision. Though usually slower and more involved than Article 9 sales, 363 sales give buyers added protections. The court's approval clears away most liens and claims, giving buyers a cleaner path to ownership. Because these sales often involve public auctions, they can also draw competitive bids, which helps ensure that the assets are sold for fair value.

Receiverships offer another option. In these cases, a court appoints a neutral party, a receiver, to take control of the company or its assets. Receiverships are flexible and can allow a business to keep operating while its assets are sold. They can also be cost-effective, though court oversight often means the process takes longer than a private sale.

Choosing the Right Mechanism

Which path to take depends on what the buyer is trying to achieve. If speed is the goal, UCC Article 9 sales are often the fastest, while receiverships and 363 sales take longer because of court involvement. Cost is another factor: Article 9 sales and receiverships tend to be less expensive, while 363 sales require more legal work and public procedures.

Buyers also need to think about legal risks. Asset deals and 363 sales usually offer better protection against liabilities, while stock deals and Article 9 sales may leave some exposure. Finally, buyers should consider what kind of recovery they are looking for. Public 363 sales may bring the highest price because of competitive bidding, but Article 9 sales and receiverships offer more flexibility in structuring a deal. Asset and stock deals can be tailored to specific needs but require careful diligence and negotiation.

Final Thoughts

Each of these options comes with trade-offs. The right choice depends on timing, cost, risk, and the investor's end goal. But no matter which approach is used, these deals sit within a broader legal system that shapes how distressed assets are bought and sold.

The next chapter looks at that legal framework, as well as the rules and processes that govern business distress and recovery. Whether an investor is looking at a 363 sale, a receivership, or an asset deal, understanding this broader system is the only way to make good decisions and avoid costly mistakes.

KEY INSIGHTS

1. Distressed investors have four primary mechanisms for acquiring troubled assets: asset deals, stock deals, UCC Article 9 sales, and Section 363 sales.
2. The acquisition mechanism investors choose significantly impacts deal speed, cost, legal risk, and potential returns.
3. In asset deals, investors can selectively acquire specific assets without inheriting all of a company's liabilities, offering flexibility but potentially increasing complexity and costs.
4. Stock deals involve purchasing the entire company, providing continuity but exposing the buyer to all existing and potential liabilities.
5. Asset deals are generally preferred in distressed situations due to their flexibility and ability to limit liability exposure.
6. Stock deals in Chapter 11 are less common and typically involve larger restructuring plans or debt-for-equity swaps.
7. UCC Article 9 sales offer a faster, less costly option for secured creditors to recover collateral but are limited to assets covered by the security agreement.
8. UCC Article 9 sales are often private, limiting opportunities for outside investors but offering speed and lower costs for secured creditors.
9. Section 363 sales, exemplified by the Barclays-Lehman deal, allow for quick asset sales with court oversight, potentially cleansing assets of liabilities.
10. Section 363 sales can offer better protection against successor liability claims but may involve a more complex and public process.
11. Receiverships provide flexibility in managing distressed assets but may offer less protection than formal bankruptcy proceedings.
12. Receiverships can be an effective tool for managing and potentially selling distressed assets, especially in cases of fraud or mismanagement.

ACQUISITION MECHANISMS AND STRATEGY

13. Each acquisition mechanism requires different levels of due diligence and risk assessment, emphasizing the importance of thorough analysis in distressed investing.
14. The effectiveness of each mechanism can vary based on the specific circumstances of the distressed company, market conditions, and the investor's goals.
15. Understanding the nuances of each acquisition mechanism allows investors to strategically approach different distressed situations and potentially uncover overlooked opportunities.

CHAPTER 7

Advanced Bankruptcy Strategies and Industry Case Studies

For decades, investors and lenders relied on a simple rule: first in line meant having the strongest claim on a company's assets. But over the last decade, that assumption has been flipped on its head. Modern corporate restructuring is no longer just about priority of payment—it's about financial maneuvering. With aggressive legal strategies and contract loopholes, companies have found ways to strip assets, shift liabilities, and push favored lenders ahead of others. The result? A high-stakes battleground where even senior creditors can be left powerless.

Getting J-Screwed

In Chapter 2, we learned how J.Crew's early and aggressive embrace of bankruptcy helped them get on the path of solvency, and within an impressively quick time period.

That's not the whole story, however. J.Crew's path to solvency was not without controversy. As part of their reorganization, they also relied on a loophole in their loan agreements to transfer valuable intellectual property to a separate subsidiary, effectively shielding those assets from creditors. They then used these assets to raise new debt.

This maneuver sent shockwaves through the lending community. I remember when it happened; suddenly, every credit agreement was being scrutinized for similar loopholes. The move underscores how creative legal strategies can dramatically alter recovery expectations. For investors, it highlights the importance of understanding not just the written terms of debt documents but how those terms might be interpreted or manipulated under pressure.

What's particularly interesting about the transaction is that it occurred before bankruptcy but became a central issue in the company's Chapter 11 case. This illustrates how the pre-bankruptcy period is often when the most consequential decisions are made—another reason why distressed investors need to engage early when they see a company heading towards restructuring.

By shifting valuable intellectual property assets to an unrestricted subsidiary, thus placing them beyond the reach of existing creditors, the company secured new financing at the expense of its original lenders. The ploy created a whole new terminology. J.Crew's creditors complained about being "J-Screwed," while the strategy became known throughout the distressed investing industry as the "J.Crew Trap."

What followed was escalation across the industry. Debt contracts evolved to include stricter covenants, yet companies continued to test the boundaries, fueling an arms race in liability management exercises (LMEs). As corporate borrowers and their lawyers now push for greater flexibility, creditors scramble to defend their rights, setting the stage for the next evolution in restructuring tactics.

That being the case, this chapter explores the most controversial maneuvers shaping today's bankruptcy landscape, from "drop-down" transactions to uptier exchanges. For better or for worse, you will see how companies continue to exploit legal and financial loopholes to pursue strategic advantage.

Liability Management Exercises (LMEs): The New Battleground

I've watched with fascination as LMEs have transformed the distressed landscape over the past decade. These transactions represent a new frontier in the constant chess match between companies and their creditors. For investors, understanding these maneuvers isn't optional—it's essential.

LMEs, are strategies companies use to restructure their debt outside formal bankruptcy proceedings. These transactions have become increasingly common and controversial as companies find creative ways to manage their liabilities while avoiding or preparing for Chapter 11.

One reason LMEs have gained traction is their ability to provide breathing room for distressed companies without the costs and uncertainties of a bankruptcy filing. Companies leverage these transactions to extend maturities, swap debt for equity, or adjust payment terms while maintaining control over the restructuring process. However, these strategies often come at the expense of certain creditors, leading to disputes over fairness and legal challenges that test the boundaries of existing debt agreements.

Uptier Transactions: The Art of Leapfrogging Creditors

An uptier transaction is perhaps the most contentious LME I've encountered. In simple terms, it's a way for a company to work with a subset of its lenders (who are typically hedge funds that focus on distressed investments) to create new debt that jumps ahead of other lenders in payment priority. Picture it as changing the rules of the game while the game is in progress.

Here's how it typically works: A company with an existing credit agreement approaches some of its lenders (the "included lenders") with a proposal. These lenders will provide new money, and, in exchange, both their new and existing loans will move to a more senior position in the capital structure. The other lenders (the "excluded lenders") are left behind in a junior position without their consent.

I was involved in a case where the excluded lenders woke up one morning to discover their formerly first-lien position had effectively become third-lien. They went from expecting near-full recovery to potentially pennies on the dollar, all without a vote or even advance notice. The shock and outrage were palpable.

Companies execute these transactions through amendments to their credit agreements. The included lenders, holding enough debt to approve amendments, change the agreement to permit the new senior debt. They might also strip covenants and other protections to ensure the new senior debt controls any future default scenarios.

But why would any other creditor allow themselves to be put in this position? In many cases, they may not even realize the potential risk when they first enter into the credit agreement. Often, the original agreement contains vague or loosely worded provisions that don't explicitly prohibit such maneuvers. Additionally, creditors may underestimate the likelihood of the company exploiting these loopholes. By the time the issue arises, the controlling lenders have typically amassed enough voting power to push through amendments that protect their new senior debt, leaving other creditors with little recourse.

What makes these transactions so controversial is that they often rely on creative interpretations of provisions never intended for this purpose. The most common example is using "open market purchase" exceptions, which are originally designed to allow companies to buy back their own debt at a discount directly from the market. However, some distressed companies have used this clause to selectively retire debt from friendly lenders while excluding others, effectively bypassing the pro-rata requirements that ensure equal treatment among creditors.

Drop-Down Transactions: The Shell Game

If uptier transactions are about changing priority through contractual means, drop-down transactions achieve similar results through structural means. I think of these as corporate shell games: moving valuable assets to places where only certain creditors can reach them.

In a drop-down transaction, a company transfers valuable assets from entities that have guaranteed its existing debt to subsidiaries that haven't. These subsidiaries, often called "unrestricted" or "excluded" subsidiaries, then pledge these assets to secure new debt. The original lenders effectively lose their claim on these assets, as they're now structurally subordinated to the new lenders.

As seen in the J.Crew restructuring, drop-down transactions have become a widely adopted LME. The company moved its valuable intellectual property, arguably its most important asset, to an unrestricted subsidiary. This maneuver eventually became known as "J-Screwing," a term no lender ever wants to hear in connection with their loan.

Drop-downs can sometimes be executed without lender consent if the credit agreement has enough flexibility in its covenants. More often, they require amendments similar to uptier transactions, which means working with a group of cooperative lenders while excluding others.

The Serta Mattress Decision: Courts Draw a Line

As LMEs became more aggressive, it was inevitable that courts would eventually weigh in. The watershed moment came with the Serta Mattress case, which fundamentally changed the landscape for uptier transactions, especially with regard to the interpretation of "open market purchases" in credit agreements.

In 2020, Serta Simmons Bedding executed a controversial uptier transaction, collaborating with a select group of lenders to amend its credit agreement and create new super-priority debt. This move effectively relegated certain lenders to a junior position without their consent, triggering a legal battle that ultimately reached the U.S. Court of Appeals for the Fifth Circuit.

On December 31, 2024, the Fifth Circuit issued a landmark ruling that further restricted LMEs. The court invalidated Serta's 2020 uptier transaction, holding that it did not qualify as a true "open market purchase" under the company's 2016 credit agreement. The ruling emphasized that an open market purchase must occur in a public or widely accessible market, not through private negotiations. This decision reversed earlier rulings by the bankruptcy court and set a precedent limiting the flexibility of future LMEs.

For excluded lenders such as Apollo Global Management, this ruling reopened the door for damage claims, potentially reshaping the dynamics of creditor negotiations in distressed debt markets. Furthermore, the Fifth Circuit invalidated indemnities granted to participating lenders in Serta's Chapter 11 plan, citing their impermissibility under the Bankruptcy Code. As a result, as of March 2025, the case remains active, with the bankruptcy court now tasked with determining damages and other remedies for excluded lenders.

For distressed investors, this ruling underscores the risks of assuming that contractual loopholes will hold up in court. In the wake of Serta's legal setback, companies are reassessing how they structure liability management transactions, with many now emphasizing broader creditor participation to mitigate litigation risks.

Investment Implications: Navigating the New Landscape

As noted, LMEs create both risks and opportunities for investors. For those on the wrong side of an LME, the impact can be severe; investments can lose significant value overnight as more senior tranches are created or collateral is moved out of reach. But for investors who understand how these transactions work and position themselves strategically, LMEs can offer opportunities for outsized returns.

Navigating this landscape requires careful due diligence on credit agreements before committing capital. It's no longer enough to understand the company's balance sheet; you must know how flexible the credit documents are and what tools management and other creditors might use against you. That means digging into the fine print to assess how much room the company has to amend its agreements, what exceptions exist to pro-rata treatment among lenders, what limits, if any, apply to transferring assets to unrestricted subsidiaries, and what voting thresholds are needed for different types of amendments.

I've seen investors make substantial profits by identifying weak points in credit agreements, buying in at distressed levels to participate in a forthcoming LME or shorting debt they expect to be pushed down the capital structure. On the other hand, I've also watched funds build blocking positions to prevent LMEs or to ensure they are included in any deal that might otherwise leave them behind.

Since the Serta case, this field has continued to evolve. Companies and their advisors are already crafting new ways to structure deals that fit within the boundaries set by recent court decisions. It's natural to question how companies can seemingly sidestep their own agreements without legal repercussions. Doesn't this contradict basic principles of contract law? In reality, these LMEs typically don't break contracts. Instead, they leverage ambiguities or loosely worded clauses that leave room for interpretation. Courts have often upheld these maneuvers when the language in the agreements allows flexibility.

As always, I strongly suggest that investors take the time to understand not just the letter of these agreements but also how courts are likely to interpret them. Those who do so will have a distinct advantage in navigating the next wave of complex restructurings. Perhaps this restates the obvious, but it bears repeating: always read the fine print.

Tax Considerations: The Hidden Value Drivers

While legal strategies like LMEs often grab headlines, tax considerations can be equally important in Chapter 11 cases. I've seen numerous situations where tax assets or liabilities dramatically altered the economics of a restructuring. Yet many investors overlook these factors, creating opportunities for those who understand their significance.

Net Operating Losses (NOLs): The Valuable Tax Asset

Net operating losses (NOLs) are one of the most valuable tax attributes a distressed company can possess. In simple terms, NOLs are tax losses from prior years that can be carried forward to offset future taxable income. For a company emerging from bankruptcy with prospects for future profitability, these NOLs can significantly enhance value by reducing or eliminating tax liabilities for years to come.

The math is straightforward: each dollar of NOL can potentially save up to 21 cents in federal corporate income tax (at current rates). A company with $100 million in NOLs has a potential tax shield worth up to $21 million in future tax savings. For investors acquiring a company through Chapter 11, this represents real economic value.

I've been involved in cases where the NOLs were worth more than the operating business itself. In one situation, we structured the entire reorganization around preserving these tax attributes, which significantly increased recoveries for creditors. However, preserving NOLs through bankruptcy requires careful planning. The Bankruptcy Code and tax law contain provisions that can limit the use of NOLs after a change in ownership, which often occurs in Chapter 11 reorganizations. Section 382 of the Internal Revenue Code is particularly important, as it can severely restrict the rate at which NOLs can be used after an "ownership change."

Sophisticated distressed investors always model the impact of Section 382 limitations and work with tax experts to develop strategies for maximizing NOL preservation. These might include special provisions in the reorganization plan, careful timing of transactions, or strategic structuring of the post-emergence equity. While NOLs can provide significant tax advantages, restructuring also presents risks, most notably the potential for massive taxable income through debt cancellation.

Cancellation of Debt (COD) Income: The Bankruptcy Exception

When debt is forgiven or discharged for less than full payment, the amount forgiven is generally considered taxable income to the debtor. This is called cancellation of debt (COD) income, and it can create significant tax liabilities. Imagine a company restructuring $500 million of debt to $200 million. The $300 million difference would normally be taxable income, potentially triggering a $63 million tax bill (at 21%).

Fortunately for distressed companies, the Bankruptcy Code provides a crucial exception. Under Section 108 of the Internal Revenue Code, COD income is excluded from taxable income when the discharge occurs in a bankruptcy case or when the debtor is insolvent. This exception is one of the most significant advantages of restructuring through Chapter 11 rather than out of court. I've advised companies that chose bankruptcy specifically for this tax benefit, even when they had the support for an out-of-court restructuring.

There's a trade-off, however. While the COD income isn't taxed, the company must reduce certain tax attributes, including those valuable NOLs, by the amount of excluded income. While the COD exclusion prevents immediate taxation, it reduces the debtors' NOLs, limiting long-term tax benefits. This trade-off forces companies to carefully structure Chapter 11 plans to balance short-term tax relief with long-term value preservation.

Strategic Implications for Investors

For those who take the time, understanding these tax dynamics can unlock significant value, often where many others fail to look. In fact, I've seen investments where the numbers on the surface didn't add up—where the enterprise value seemed too low to justify the risk—until tax benefits, like preserved NOLs and COD income exclusions, were factored into the equation. Once those were considered, the deal suddenly made much more sense, sometimes turning into an outsized return.

This is why integrating tax analysis into your investment thesis from the outset is not just nice to have; it's often a decisive factor. Before committing capital to any distressed situation, investors need to look hard at the company's tax attributes, including NOLs and other carryforwards that may survive a restructuring. They should also model how much COD income might arise under various restructuring scenarios, and, more importantly, how that COD income will affect other valuable tax assets. Not all restructuring paths are equal from a tax perspective, and understanding those trade-offs in advance can dramatically shift your view of the opportunity.

Equally important is thinking through how the structure and timing of a deal might impact the company's ability to use these tax attributes down the line. A company that emerges with preserved NOLs but no path to profitability won't be able to take advantage of them, so modeling expected future earnings is just as important as analyzing the immediate tax consequences of the restructuring itself.

Too often, investors leave these questions to tax experts and focus only on capital structure mechanics. But some of the best investors I know are those who understand tax value just as well as they understand debt terms and creditor negotiations. They know how to identify tax benefits buried in complex situations and how to ensure those benefits are preserved and used to their full potential. Deals that look mediocre on a simple EV-to-EBITDA basis can become highly attractive once tax considerations are layered in.

Of course, tax laws are not static. Major shifts like the Tax Cuts and Jobs Act of 2017 have changed how bankruptcies are taxed, and future legislation may alter the landscape again. What worked in 2025 may not work in 2027, so be cognizant that your playbook must evolve as laws change.

Finally, keep in mind that tax considerations often create unexpected alignments among stakeholders. In many cases, preserving tax attributes benefits both the reorganized company and its new owners, providing a shared incentive to structure a deal that works for everyone. I've seen situations where otherwise opposing creditor groups found common ground around preserving NOLs, unlocking solutions that improved recoveries across the capital structure.

In short: tax is not an afterthought in distressed investing; it's a core part of value creation. The investors who understand this have an edge beyond simply buying cheap debt; they know how to unlock hidden value others overlook.

The "Texas Two-Step" and Mass Tort Liabilities

The case of LTL Management LLC, a Johnson & Johnson (J&J) subsidiary, is another illustration of how companies have attempted to use Chapter 11 in unconventional ways to manage liabilities. So far the novel maneuver has not panned out, and given the court's unfavorable rulings, similar strategies are unlikely to succeed in the future. But I think it's worth examining, even if only to give you a sense of the landscape.

In October 2021, J&J executed a corporate restructuring known as the "Texas Two-Step." This maneuver involved creating LTL Management as a new subsidiary and transferring the liabilities of J&J's talc-based products, such as baby powder, to this entity (see Fig. 1).

JOHNSON & JOHNSON'S "TEXAS TWO-STEP" BANKRUPTCY STRATEGY

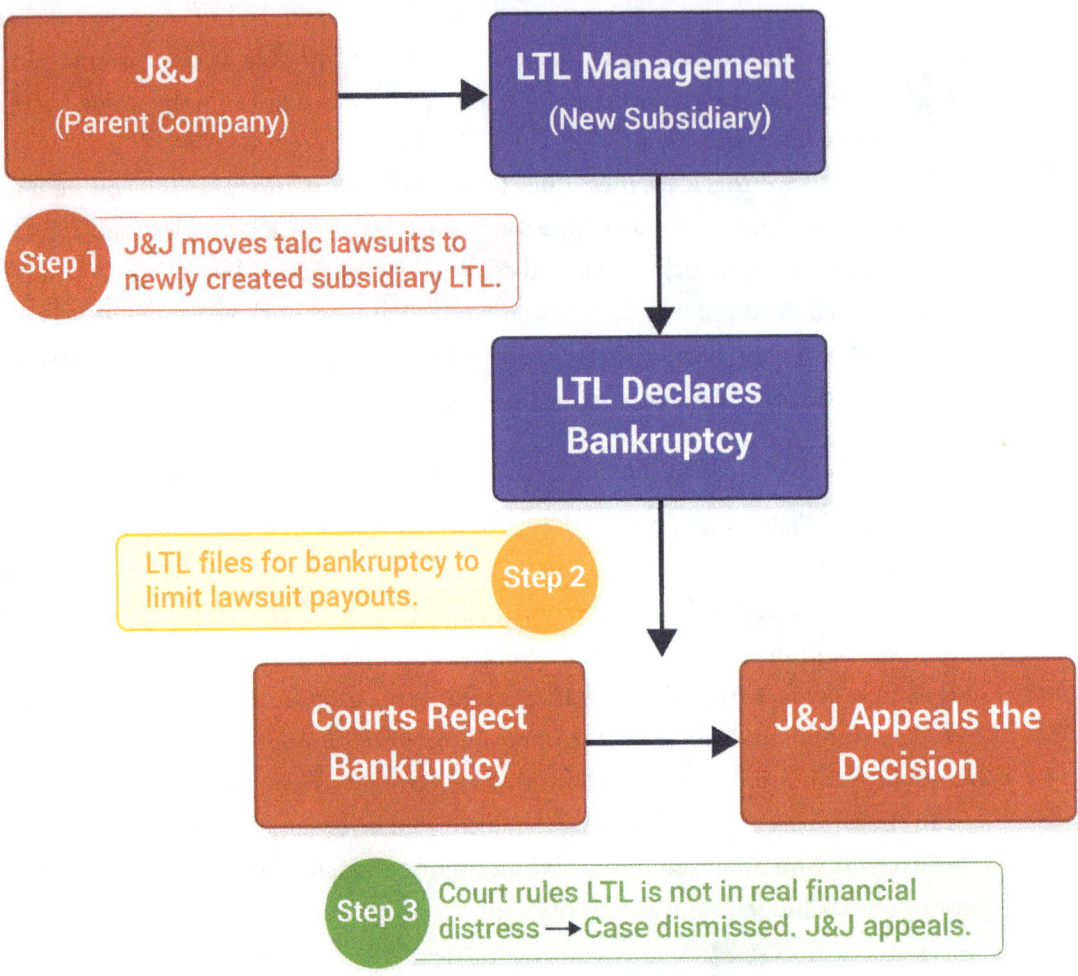

Figure 1: Johnson & Johnson's "Texas Two-Step" Bankruptcy Strategy

The strategy gets its name from a "divisive merger" under Texas law, which allows a company to split into two separate entities. This tactic became widely discussed after Texas passed the Texas Business Organizations Code in 2006, which explicitly permits companies to divide their assets and liabilities among newly formed entities. While Texas is the most prominent state to allow such a maneuver, other states, including Delaware, have similar provisions, though they are less frequently used in this context. LTL Management, the new entity with all the talc-related liabilities on its books, promptly filed for Chapter 11 bankruptcy, initially in North Carolina, before moving to New Jersey.

This strategy aimed to address tens of thousands of lawsuits alleging that J&J's talcum powder products caused cancer. Plaintiffs claimed that J&J had known about these risks for decades but failed to warn consumers. By isolating these liabilities in a separate entity, J&J sought to shield its other assets from these claims.

In the bankruptcy proceedings, J&J proposed that LTL Management pay $8.9 billion to resolve all talcum powder claims, with payments being made over 25 years through a bankruptcy trust. J&J has claimed that 83% of claimants approve of the settlement.[12]

However, the strategy faced significant legal challenges. In July 2023, a bankruptcy court dismissed the case, ruling that LTL Management wasn't in "imminent or immediate financial distress." Because of this, the judge determined that LTL Management's bankruptcy filing lacked good faith, viewing it as a tactic to limit J&J's exposure to mass tort claims rather than a legitimate restructuring need.

Undeterred, J&J continued to push for the settlement. Yet in March 2025, a U.S. bankruptcy judge rejected the revised $8.9 billion settlement, citing problems with the voting process and the inclusion of legal claim releases for non-bankrupt entities. This ruling reinforced the courts' increasing willingness to scrutinize bankruptcy filings they perceive as manipulative or designed to circumvent the system.

The LTL Management case underscores the complex relationship between Chapter 11, mass tort liabilities, and corporate restructuring strategies. Courts have shown a growing reluctance to approve bankruptcy maneuvers seen as bad faith, particularly those using the Texas Two-Step strategy. If the court's rejection holds, J&J may face renewed individual lawsuits, potentially leading to prolonged litigation and greater financial exposure.

For distressed investors, the LTL Management case serves as both a cautionary tale and a potential opportunity. Investors who buy claims at a discount could profit if the settlement is approved and structured payouts are secured. On the other hand, those seeking to challenge or block bad-faith bankruptcy filings must conduct thorough due diligence, particularly in cases involving mass tort liabilities. The LTL case reminds us, yet again, how important it is to understand not just the financials but also the legal and regulatory landscape when assessing distressed investment opportunities.

The Scrub Island Case: Navigating Complex Restructurings

The 2013 bankruptcy of Scrub Island, a beautiful 230-acre resort in Tortola, British Virgin Islands, revealed how Chapter 11 can be used not just to restructure debt but also as a strategy to counter aggressive creditor actions. Let's run through the chain of events.

It all started when the resort's primary lender, FirstBank Puerto Rico, filed for receivership in the courts in the British Virgin Islands due to unpaid debts. While Scrub Island had accumulated over $100 million in debt, the receivership was unexpected, especially because it threatened the resort's ability to continue operations. Faced with the possibility of losing control, the company turned to bankruptcy court for relief. In November 2013, it filed for bankruptcy in Tampa, Florida. Why there? It was where the principal owner and manager of the resort was located.

Scrub Island's strategy was multifaceted. First, filing for Chapter 11 allowed the principals to maintain ownership of the resort and protect it from being seized or sold off by FirstBank Puerto Rico. Second, it challenged the legality of the receivership and permitted the principal to restructure the debt on more favorable terms. Third, it allowed Scrub Island to attack its lender for allegedly engaging in improper conduct and challenge its mortgage.

This third prong became a major focus of the case as Scrub Island filed a lender liability lawsuit against FirstBank. The resort asserted that FirstBank had a forbearance agreement with it and went behind the debtor's back in trying to negotiate a sale of the property; ultimately, Scrub Island sought to subordinate the bank's mortgage. For its part, FirstBank argued that the receivership was justified due to the resort's financial instability. A complete trial of all the facts and issues wound its way through bankruptcy court, further prolonging the case.

Throughout the bankruptcy process, Scrub Island continued to operate as a functioning luxury resort. This proved to be an advantage, since its ability to generate cash flow during the proceedings helped support its case for reorganization. The resort's continued operations preserved the underlying value of the asset, making it more appealing to potential investors. This included distressed investors who, drawn in by the combination of asset quality and litigation upside, began acquiring claims and providing capital to support the reorganization. It also gave Scrub Island additional time to attract a new investor group that ultimately became the plan sponsor, infusing the business with fresh capital in exchange for equity and upside participation.

Scrub Island ultimately prevailed at trial and in the appeals in its suit against FirstBank. The momentum it gained from this greatly assisted the resort. As with most successful bankruptcy cases, Scrub Island cut a deal with FirstBank and emerged from Chapter 11 with a restructured debt plan and new capital infusion. The court agreed to terminate the receivership, allowing the company to retain control of the resort. With its financial situation stabilized, Scrub Island continued to operate, benefiting from its premium location and ongoing revenue generation (see Fig 2).

For distressed investors, the takeaway is that bankruptcy can sometimes preserve the value of an ongoing operation, especially when the business remains functional throughout the process.

Chapter 11 is never without risk; court battles, extended timelines, and unexpected challenges are common. But Scrub Island showed how strategic use of bankruptcy law, combined with targeted capital from opportunistic investors, can turn a troubled real estate asset into a long-term recovery story. Those who invested in Scrub Island's plan saw their investment appreciate as the business regained stability.

Special Considerations

I know I've thrown a lot at you in this chapter. But before we can move on, it's essential that we discuss several special considerations that can significantly impact bankruptcy cases and investment opportunities.

The bankruptcy process isn't one-size-fits-all. It varies dramatically based on company size, industry, and specific circumstances. Understanding these nuances can mean the difference between success and failure for distressed investors.

SCRUB ISLAND: A CASE STUDY

Bankruptcy Case Timeline

STEP 1 — Initial Investment & Development

STEP 2 — Financial Struggles Leading to Bankruptcy

STEP 3 — Emergence from Bankruptcy and Restructuring

STEP 4 — Current Operational Status

Key Selling Points

1. **Fully Entitled** — All permits and government approvals secured
2. **Unique Development** — The only major development in BVI in 20 years
3. **Prime Location** — Accessible by ferry and near other popular destinations
4. **Environmentally Friendly** — Built with sustainability in mind
5. **Financial Strength** — Strong investor backing and recovery from bankruptcy

Figure 2: Scrub Island: A Case Study

Small Business Bankruptcies: Subchapter V

In my decades of bankruptcy experience, I have long observed that the traditional Chapter 11 process is too costly and cumbersome for smaller businesses to make use of. Fortunately, in 2019 Congress finally addressed this issue with the creation of Subchapter V, a streamlined version of Chapter 11 specifically designed for small businesses. This new option has changed the landscape dramatically for companies with debt under $3,024,725. (Before June 2024 this amount was set at $7.5 million, and it may soon be raised again to that level.)

Subchapter V maintains many of the benefits of standard Chapter 11 while eliminating several costly and time-consuming requirements. Most notably, it removes the requirement to file a disclosure statement, eliminates quarterly U.S. Trustee fees, and doesn't require the formation of a creditors' committee. It also streamlines the plan confirmation process and creates more favorable rules for business owners who want to retain equity.

I remember working with a manufacturing business with $6 million in debt that would have faced prohibitive costs in a traditional Chapter 11. Under Subchapter V, they completed their restructuring in just four months, and at about a third of the cost they would have incurred otherwise. The owners retained control, creditors received better recoveries than they would have in liquidation, and jobs were preserved.

For investors, Subchapter V creates distinct dynamics and opportunities. These cases move much faster than traditional Chapter 11s, often concluding within three to six months. The compressed timeline forces investors to act quickly when identifying potential opportunities, as waiting too long can mean missing out entirely. Additionally, the reduced administrative costs in Subchapter V preserve more value for distribution to creditors, increasing the potential for improved recoveries across the board.

Another important aspect is the more favorable treatment of equity, frequently allowing existing owners to remain involved in the business. Depending on their leadership abilities and the root causes of the distress, this can be either a stabilizing force or a significant risk. Investors must assess not only the financial structure of a Subchapter V case but also the competence and motivations of the existing ownership to determine whether the restructuring is likely to lead to long-term success or simply delay an inevitable failure.

One particularly interesting aspect of Subchapter V is the role of the trustee. Unlike a Chapter 7 trustee who takes control of assets, the Subchapter V trustee serves more as a mediator and facilitator. I've seen cases where skilled trustees helped bridge seemingly insurmountable gaps between debtors and creditors, creating value for all parties.

For investors considering opportunities in Subchapter V cases, I recommend focusing on businesses with strong underlying fundamentals but temporary financial challenges. The streamlined process works best when operational issues are limited and the primary need is financial restructuring. Due diligence should emphasize core business viability, as these cases typically don't provide the runway for major operational turnarounds.

ADVANCED BANKRUPTCY STRATEGIES AND INDUSTRY CASE STUDIES

Industry-Specific Factors in Bankruptcy: Challenges and Opportunities for Investors

Bankruptcy does not happen in isolation; it unfolds within industries that each have unique challenges, regulatory obstacles, and market dynamics. While the legal framework of Chapter 11 remains consistent, how it is applied varies significantly across sectors. For distressed investors, understanding these industry-specific nuances is essential to identifying risks and opportunities. Let's take a look at some of the most common industries for distressed investing.

Retail: Adapting to a Changing Consumer Landscape

Retail bankruptcies have been among the most visible in recent years, driven by the relentless rise of e-commerce, shifting consumer preferences, and oversized brick-and-mortar footprints. The ability to shed unprofitable stores through lease rejections is one of the most valuable tools in retail cases. Under Section 365 of the Bankruptcy Code, retailers can walk away from costly leases, with landlords receiving only an unsecured claim, often capped at one year's rent. Retailers have used this provision to close hundreds of locations in a single filing, dramatically reducing their cost structures.

Inventory management is another critical aspect of retail restructurings. Many retailers file for bankruptcy at precise points in their inventory cycle, after securing seasonal merchandise but before paying suppliers. This timing creates complex disputes over ownership, consignment agreements, and reclamation rights, requiring careful navigation. Even in cases where some stores continue operating, going-out-of-business sales play a key role in maximizing asset recovery. The execution of these sales can mean the difference between a successful restructuring and a failed liquidation.

For investors, retail bankruptcies offer both risks and opportunities. The most successful retail turnarounds involve more than just store closures; they require strategic reinvestment in e-commerce, logistics, and digital branding. Simply reducing physical footprint without addressing long-term customer engagement is rarely a path to sustainable success.

Energy: The Volatility of Commodities and Asset Valuation

Energy bankruptcies present a different set of challenges, shaped by commodity price cycles, complex reserve valuations, and regulatory burdens. Unlike retail, where demand fluctuations are tied to consumer behavior, the energy sector's financial health is directly impacted by oil and gas price swings. This volatility makes timing a crucial factor in energy bankruptcies. Cases filed during downturns often provide the greatest returns if prices recover during or shortly after the restructuring process.

One of the most contentious aspects of energy restructurings involves reserve valuations. The PV-10 metric, which calculates the present value of future cash flows from proven reserves, can be the focal point of intense disputes. Even minor adjustments in production forecasts or discount rates can result in valuation swings worth hundreds of millions of dollars.

Beyond valuation, regulatory obligations add another layer of complexity. Upstream energy companies often face significant plugging and abandonment liabilities, which may receive priority treatment over other creditor claims. Additionally, joint operating agreements can create entanglements between multiple stakeholders, influencing whether assets can be sold or how reorganized companies can operate post-bankruptcy.

For investors, the key to profiting from energy bankruptcies lies in understanding asset valuation dynamics and commodity cycles. Acquiring distressed reserves at the bottom of a market downturn can generate massive returns, but this requires both financial patience and a strategic exit plan.

Healthcare: Navigating Regulation and Patient-Centered Restructuring

Healthcare bankruptcies introduce a layer of complexity that extends beyond financial concerns. Unlike most industries, where creditor recoveries drive restructuring decisions, courts overseeing healthcare cases must prioritize the continuity of patient care. Hospitals and healthcare providers facing bankruptcy often receive special allowances to continue paying physicians and suppliers to avoid service disruption.

The regulatory environment is a dominant factor in these cases. Government agencies such as the Centers for Medicare and Medicaid Services (CMS) play a central role, as licensing, certifications, and provider agreements must remain intact for a hospital to continue operations. Bankruptcy courts routinely grant exceptions to typical priority rules to ensure uninterrupted patient care. At the same time, reimbursement structures in healthcare, particularly the delay between service provision and insurance payments, create unique cash flow challenges, making DIP financing essential for survival.

For distressed investors, healthcare bankruptcies require an understanding of both financial restructuring and regulatory compliance. The most successful restructurings involve close coordination with regulators, strategic partnerships with healthcare operators, and careful attention to reimbursement structures that affect post-bankruptcy viability.

Hospitality: Balancing Real Estate Value and Brand Strength

Hospitality bankruptcies sit at the intersection of real estate, branding, and operational performance. Unlike energy companies, which derive value from their reserves, or retailers, which must balance inventory and store leases, hotel operators rely on a mix of physical assets and brand strength. While a hotel property itself may carry significant value, its success post-bankruptcy often depends on whether it retains key management and franchise agreements.

Ownership structures in the hospitality sector further complicate bankruptcies. Many hotels are owned by one entity but operate under a licensing agreement with a major brand. In Chapter 11, the ability to assume or reject management contracts can dramatically alter a property's valuation. A hotel that loses its flag may struggle to maintain revenue, while a well-negotiated agreement during restructuring can preserve brand recognition and guest loyalty.

Timing also plays a critical role. Filing during the low season may provide breathing room for restructuring, but it also means reduced cash flow. Conversely, emerging from bankruptcy before a peak season can provide crucial liquidity. Another major consideration is property improvement plans, capital investments required by franchisors to maintain brand standards. Successfully negotiating these obligations in bankruptcy can significantly ease financial burdens for the reorganized entity.

For investors, the key to hospitality bankruptcies lies in recognizing the balance between real estate value and operational performance. A distressed hotel with strong management in a prime location may recover quickly post-restructuring, while a property with weak operations, even in a valuable market, could continue struggling. Distressed investors must analyze not just the asset value but also the competitive positioning and management quality of the underlying business.

The Bigger Picture: Industry-Specific Knowledge Is a Competitive Advantage

Bankruptcy laws may be universal, but their application varies widely by industry. Retailers must navigate lease rejections and inventory challenges, energy companies grapple with volatile valuations and regulatory burdens, healthcare providers face intense oversight and unique cash flow constraints, and hospitality businesses balance real estate with branding concerns.

For distressed investors, understanding these nuances is critical. Industry-specific knowledge can mean the difference between identifying a lucrative restructuring opportunity and walking into a high-risk scenario with limited upside. Those who can navigate these complexities, anticipating how bankruptcy strategies play out in different sectors, will position themselves to capitalize on distressed investments more effectively than the competition.

Conclusion: The Investor's Mindset

If there's one thing that separates successful distressed investors from everyone else, it's mindset. Bankruptcy and restructuring are not just about understanding legal tools or analyzing financial statements. They're about navigating uncertainty, reading people, and making decisions when the path forward is anything but clear. In a world where companies are fighting for survival and creditors are battling for a piece of what's left, the investors who consistently succeed are those who can think several moves ahead, adapt as conditions shift, and negotiate effectively with parties whose interests may conflict with their own. They understand that bankruptcy is a negotiation first and a legal process second, and that every negotiation is shaped by power, leverage, and timing.

The best investors I've worked with approach each situation with intellectual honesty and discipline. They don't fall in love with their trade, and they don't rely on hope as a strategy.

Instead, they focus on realistic outcomes, what can be achieved given the company's business prospects, creditor dynamics, and the practical limits of the law. They also know when to walk away, recognizing that not every distressed opportunity is worth the risk, no matter how tempting the price.

Another defining trait of the successful investor mindset is flexibility. No matter how much due diligence you do or how well you map out a strategy, something will change. A judge might issue an unexpected ruling. A key creditor may shift their position. A surprise bidder might emerge. Successful distressed investors don't just tolerate these surprises; they expect them and adjust accordingly.

Patience also matters. Some of the best returns in distressed investing come from waiting for the right moment to strike, not from chasing every deal. Sometimes that means sitting on cash until the market turns. Other times, it means buying early when everyone else is running for the exits. Above all, the right mindset means understanding what you're really investing in. You're not just buying a piece of paper or a claim in a bankruptcy; you're investing in a business, in a set of people, and in a process that can take years to play out. Distressed investing rewards those who approach it with a long view, a strong stomach, and a deep understanding of both value and risk.

In the chapters ahead, we'll shift from examining the legal and structural side of Chapter 11 to analyzing how investors put these concepts to work in real cases. We'll explore the hands-on realities of managing bankruptcy situations, buying trade claims, navigating fraud cases, and investing in emerging areas like crypto distress. Each of these topics requires not only technical knowledge but also the right mindset, one that balances analysis, negotiation, and judgment in situations where there are no easy answers.

KEY INSIGHTS

1. LMEs, such as uptier and drop-down transactions, have altered the distressed investing landscape, sometimes creating conflicts between lenders.
2. The Serta Mattress decision imposed new legal limitations on certain LME strategies, requiring companies to adapt their liability management tactics.
3. Tax considerations, including NOLs and COD income, can significantly impact the financial benefits of restructuring.
4. The Texas Two-Step strategy, used by J&J's LTL Management, highlights how companies attempt to isolate mass tort liabilities; though courts have increasingly scrutinized such maneuvers.
5. Bankruptcies in different industries present unique challenges: retail involves lease rejections and inventory management, energy hinges on commodity cycles, healthcare requires regulatory compliance, and hospitality depends on branding and real estate value.
6. Subchapter V streamlines the bankruptcy process for small businesses with debts under $7.5 million, offering a faster and more cost-effective restructuring alternative.

7. Timing is crucial in distressed investing, both in acquiring positions and determining the best moment to exit.
8. Relationships with key stakeholders, including creditors, financial advisors, and bankruptcy attorneys, can provide critical insights and influence case outcomes.
9. Understanding both the legal framework and the underlying business fundamentals is essential. No legal strategy can salvage a company with a fatally flawed business model.
10. While bankruptcy can seem technical, at its core, it is about negotiating among competing interests to maximize value and provide viable businesses with a second chance.

CHAPTER 8

Managing Bankruptcy Cases

In business, as in filmmaking, success hinges on knowing when to take a creative risk and when to walk away. Few understood this better than Ismail Merchant, the legendary producer behind Merchant Ivory Productions. His films, elegant, richly detailed period dramas, were celebrated for their artistry and meticulous craftsmanship. Yet behind the genteel veneer of his literary adaptations and impeccable costume design, Merchant was, at heart, a businessman.

I once found myself in a room with him in the early 1990s. I was representing a bankruptcy debtor by the name of Cinecom, an independent film distributor that had collapsed into bankruptcy. Cinecom had played a critical role in the art-house film boom of the time, handling distribution for several Merchant Ivory films, including the Oscar-winning *A Room with a View*. But despite distributing some of the most celebrated independent films of its era, Cinecom had overextended itself and was now in bankruptcy proceedings.

Merchant was there because he had a financial stake in Cinecom's assets, i.e., residual rights from past and future distribution deals. At the heart of his concern was his contract for *A Room with a View*, an executory contract that still carried obligations for both parties. I, on the other hand, was a young associate at the law firm representing Cinecom, eager to talk to him about filmmaking, his creative process, and what the future of independent cinema might look like. I had admired his work for years and thought this was a rare opportunity to hear his thoughts.

I was wrong.

When I broached the subject, Merchant barely acknowledged my question before brushing me off. "Ah, yes, yes," he said, waving his hand dismissively. Then, without missing a beat, he turned to the group and asked, "But how much do I get?"

Being at the start of my business and legal career, I found his question to be a jarring wake-up call. Under other circumstances, Merchant might have been more friendly and willing to make small talk, like at a cocktail party or film event, but in a bankruptcy proceeding, his attitude was the same as everyone else's: what's my cut?

At one point, someone else in the room tried to steer the conversation to the broader financial issues of moviemaking, throwing out examples of recent box office successes. Merchant didn't even let them finish. "Yes, yes," he said impatiently, "but how much did they actually make?"

Someone rattled off a film's astronomical box office numbers, but he shook his head. "No, no. How much did they make? The people who put up the money? After the agents, the distributors, the marketing, and everyone else took their cut?"

The room fell silent. It was a fair question, one that investors in any industry, whether films or distressed assets, often forget to ask.

The collapse of Cinecom, despite its prestigious catalog, along with Merchant's blunt questions, underscored a critical point. The company had been responsible for distributing some of the most critically acclaimed films of its time, but that hadn't saved it from bankruptcy. Investors who were drawn in by its association with award-winning films assumed success would translate to financial returns, but they were wrong. Prestige doesn't pay the bills.

What did pay the bills? Well, after Cinecom ultimately emerged from bankruptcy, its library served as collateral for a successor company that made *The Blair Witch Project*. The cult horror movie was reportedly made on a bare-bones budget of $60,000...before grossing around $250 million worldwide.[13]

It's a lesson that applies just as well to bankruptcy investing as it does to the film industry. A struggling business, like an ambitious independent film, might have all the right elements for a big comeback: brand recognition, valuable assets, and a devoted customer base. But if the structure of the deal doesn't allow investors to benefit, it doesn't matter how much money it generates on paper. In distressed investing, as in filmmaking, the winning formula isn't just finding a good story; it's ensuring you're positioned to get paid when the credits roll.

With this perspective in mind, let's look at another example where brand strength and strategic positioning played an important role: the bankruptcy of Brooks Brothers.

Brooks Brothers: The Ripple Effects of Retail Collapse

Merchant's brand of business pragmatism is always on display in corporate bankruptcies, where the fallout extends far beyond the boardroom. In each negotiation, there are typically clear winners and losers. Those who say the wrong thing or unwittingly give up rights they didn't realize they have can end up handing millions of dollars to someone else. While bankruptcy cases offer investors opportunities to acquire assets, restructure businesses, and unlock hidden value, they also come with complexities that can trap the unwary. Financial distress doesn't just affect creditors and shareholders; it ripples outward, often leaving a trail of unexpected victims in its wake.

For an illuminating example of these dynamics we can look to the 2020 bankruptcy of Brooks Brothers, a brand that, for more than 200 years, stood as a symbol of American menswear. Like Merchant Ivory, Brooks Brothers carried prestige. It had dressed nearly every U.S. president since Abraham Lincoln, and its name evoked a time when tailored suits and silk ties were the uniform of success. As a young man, I used to raid my father's closet, taking his classic Brooks Brothers Oxford button-down shirts to project an air of legitimacy. However, prestige doesn't guarantee profitability, and in July 2020, after years of declining sales and shifting consumer habits, the company filed for Chapter 11 bankruptcy protection. The pandemic had accelerated its demise, and though it was ultimately sold for $325 million, its restructuring left a wide swath of collateral damage.

The headlines focused on store closures and new ownership, but the lesser-known consequences of the bankruptcy were unfolding in a warehouse in Enfield, Connecticut. There, in a 375,000-square-foot facility, remnants of the Brooks Brothers empire sat abandoned. It was a retail graveyard, with racks of mannequins standing motionless, circular tables where silk ties once sat neatly folded, and framed posters of gentlemen on horseback, evoking a bygone era of corporate America. A massive pile of artificial Christmas trees surrounded by gold-painted sheep ornaments, the brand's iconic Golden Fleece symbol since 1850, stood collecting dust.

For Chip and Rosanna LaBonte, the warehouse owners, Brooks Brothers' bankruptcy wasn't just a headline—it was a personal financial disaster. The company had been leasing the space for $20,000 per month, using it to store the aforementioned assortment of display fixtures, promotional materials, and seasonal decorations from closing stores. But after filing for bankruptcy, Brooks Brothers walked away from the lease, abandoning the property and leaving behind an estimated $240,000 cleanup bill, a sum so large that it threatened to force the LaBontes to sell their home. To make matters worse, the warehouse and its contents were not included in the acquisition deal, meaning the new owners of Brooks Brothers had no legal obligation to take responsibility for the abandoned inventory or the lease.[14]

This situation illustrates a hard truth: bankruptcy is not just about numbers. It has real-world consequences that extend far beyond a company's immediate stakeholders. The LaBontes, who had no role in Brooks Brothers's financial struggles, found themselves among its casualties. And they weren't alone. Landlords, suppliers, and small business owners across the country were left holding the bag when the company collapsed, a reminder that the ripple effects of corporate distress can be unpredictable and far-reaching.

For distressed investors, the Brooks Brothers case provides more than just a cautionary tale. It reminds them that bankruptcies reshape businesses and entire ecosystems. Successful investors in this space don't just evaluate balance sheets; they dig deeper, uncovering hidden liabilities, potential risks, and the broader impact of a bankruptcy beyond the immediate financials. The warehouse in Enfield is a stark illustration of what happens when a company collapses. Sometimes, the physical remnants are as revealing as the financial statements.

The Anatomy of a Bankruptcy

To help you get a better understanding of how the bankruptcy process plays out, and how and when key decision points arrive, we'll briefly walk through the first days of a bankruptcy proceeding.

As you'll see, the actions a party takes in the first days and weeks after a company files set the tone for everything that follows and can significantly impact the outcomes for all stakeholders involved. Investors who understand these steps can position themselves to identify opportunities, mitigate risks, and, as Ismail Merchant would have put it, make sure they're the ones getting paid when the dust settles.

First-Day Motions: Setting the Stage

When a company files for Chapter 11 bankruptcy, the initial days shape the course of the restructuring. During this period, the debtor files a series of "first-day motions" seeking court approval for various actions to maintain operations, preserve value, and set the stage for reorganization.

These motions serve multiple purposes but are primarily aimed at maintaining business continuity and preserving relationships with stakeholders. The debtor may seek permission to pay employee wages, continue customer programs, and honor existing utility agreements. Often, they request approval to only pay critical vendors, as we saw in the Brooks Brothers case.

The request to pay critical vendors is frequently one of the most contentious first-day motions. Brooks Brothers sought approval to pay over $30 million in pre-petition claims to suppliers of raw materials, finished goods, and logistics services. Such payments are justified when the vendor's support is essential to the debtor's reorganization, and the benefit to the estate outweighs any harm to other creditors.

However, vendor payment motions can face objections from other creditors who argue that such payments unfairly favor certain parties or deplete the estate's resources without adequate justification. Courts may deny or limit these payments, forcing the debtor to find alternative ways to maintain vendor relationships. This tension between maintaining operational stability and ensuring fairness to all creditors is a recurring theme in bankruptcy proceedings.

Beyond vendor payments, first-day motions often address a wide range of operational and financial issues. Debtors frequently file motions to use cash collateral or obtain DIP financing, which can provide liquidity during the restructuring process. They may also seek to streamline administrative processes by consolidating multiple cases, extending deadlines for filing schedules and statements, or establishing procedures for handling claims.

For distressed investors, these first-day motions provide a wealth of valuable information. By analyzing these filings, investors can gain insights into the debtor's operations, relationships, and overall restructuring strategy. The motions often telegraph the debtor's intentions and can significantly influence the case's trajectory.

Consider a motion to retain certain executives or employees. Such a motion can signal which individuals the debtor considers necessary for its turnaround efforts. Similarly, motions related to asset sales or lease rejections can offer early clues about the debtor's plans to streamline operations or raise capital. The specific motions filed in each case depend on the circumstances of the debtor and its industry. A retailer like Brooks Brothers might prioritize motions related to inventory and store operations, while a manufacturing company might focus more on supplier relationships and equipment leases.

As investors examine these first-day motions, they're not just looking at the immediate requests. They're also assessing the likelihood of a successful reorganization, identifying potential risks and opportunities, and gauging the level of support (or opposition) from various stakeholder groups. This information can prove invaluable in making decisions about whether and how to participate in the case, whether through buying claims, providing financing, or even acquiring assets.

If the investor does decide to get involved, there's a good chance they will seek to arrange DIP financing. We've covered this type of financing earlier in the book, but it's important enough to revisit it in greater detail in the next section. This tool can provide a lifeline for companies in bankruptcy, but it also presents its own set of complexities and strategic considerations for all parties involved. Understanding the nuances of DIP financing is essential for any investor looking to navigate the unpredictable waters of distressed investing.

Debtor-in-Possession (DIP) Financing: A Lifeline for Debtors

When a company files for Chapter 11, one of its first and most urgent tasks is to secure the money it needs to keep operating. After all, a bankruptcy filing doesn't stop payroll, rent, or the need to stock shelves and pay vendors. Without immediate access to cash, even companies with viable restructuring plans can collapse before those plans ever take shape. That's where DIP financing comes in. As we discussed in earlier chapters, it's a specialized form of funding designed to give companies in bankruptcy the liquidity they need to survive the process and reorganize.

DIP financing is often described as a lifeline, but it's also a high-stakes negotiation and a key battlefield in modern Chapter 11 cases. Lenders who provide DIP loans typically receive extraordinary protections under Section 364 of the Bankruptcy Code, and the deals struck over DIP financing can shape the entire trajectory of a case.

The process of obtaining DIP financing typically unfolds in a number of stages. First, before filing for bankruptcy, a company will contact known providers of financing to discuss the terms of a DIP loan. Next, right after filing, the company will seek interim approval of the loan from bankruptcy court through what are called "first-day motions." Earning this approval is crucial, since it will give the company immediate access to a portion of the loan. This interim funding covers urgent expenses, like making payroll, keeping suppliers on board, and reassuring customers that it's business as usual. Then, after notice and a court hearing, and at least twenty days (as outlined in the Bankruptcy Code), the DIP loan facility is approved on a final basis, locking in the terms that will govern the company's access to capital throughout the reorganization.

What makes DIP loans so powerful, and controversial, is their super-priority status. In bankruptcy, DIP lenders sit at the very top of the capital structure. Their loans are repaid before virtually all other claims, including pre-bankruptcy secured debt. And if unsecured credit isn't available, the court can authorize increasingly stronger protections for DIP lenders: first, treating the loan as an administrative expense; then securing it with unencumbered assets; and finally, granting priming liens that leapfrog existing liens and effectively put DIP lenders in control of the collateral. This is why DIP financing is sometimes called the "King of the Case," because the lender holding the DIP note often holds the power to dictate what happens next.

For investors, DIP loans can be highly attractive, offering high interest rates and fees in exchange for their top-priority position. Often, existing lenders will step up to provide DIP financing, both to protect their pre-bankruptcy claims and to maintain influence over the restructuring process. Other times, new investors see an opportunity to inject capital and gain a strategic foothold in a company's future. Either way, DIP financing isn't just about funding operations. It's about controlling the case.

That control comes in the form of strict loan covenants and milestones that the debtor must meet to keep access to the funds. DIP lenders may require the company to meet specific cash flow targets, stick to an agreed budget, file a reorganization plan by a set date, complete asset sales on a defined timeline, and maintain minimum liquidity levels. These milestones give DIP lenders ongoing leverage to push the company in the direction they prefer, whether that's a sale, a restructuring, or something else. DIP loan documents also provide investors a great deal of information about the trajectory of the company and case.

But DIP financing isn't automatic. The bankruptcy court must approve both the need for the financing and the terms offered. Judges scrutinize whether the loan is necessary to preserve value for creditors, whether the terms are fair, and whether the company made a real effort to find better options. Fees, interest rates, and control provisions all get reviewed, and courts are careful to balance the debtor's need for funding with the rights of other creditors. In many cases, other creditors may object to the DIP deal, arguing that its terms are too favorable to the DIP lender or that the financing unfairly skews the case in one group's favor.

For pre-bankruptcy secured creditors, DIP financing can create difficult choices. They may object to having their liens primed by a new lender, but if the company doesn't get DIP financing, there may eventually be *nothing* left to recover. Sometimes, these creditors resolve this tension by providing DIP financing themselves, converting part of their pre-bankruptcy claims into DIP loans, which allows them to stay at the center of the case and avoid being pushed aside.

Of course, DIP financing comes at a price. In addition to high interest rates, DIP facilities often carry commitment fees, unused line fees, exit fees, and other charges that add up quickly. While these costs can strain the debtor's finances, they are usually seen as the price of survival, the necessary cost of buying time to restructure.

DIP financing isn't just a lifeline for the debtor. It often determines who holds real power in a bankruptcy case. The terms of a DIP loan can reveal the direction of the restructuring, whether the company is headed for a sale, reorganization, or liquidation, and show which creditors have the leverage to drive that outcome. Because DIP lenders sit at the top of the priority ladder, they often control the timeline, set milestones, and influence the shape of any final deal.

If you want to know who's running a bankruptcy case, follow the DIP financing.

Brooks Brothers's Zero-Interest DIP Financing

In July 2020, amid the COVID-19 pandemic, Brooks Brothers secured an $80 million DIP loan from ABG-BB LLC, a joint venture between Authentic Brands Group and Simon Property Group. The terms were unprecedented in bankruptcy financing: a zero-interest rate and no closing fees (see Fig. 1).

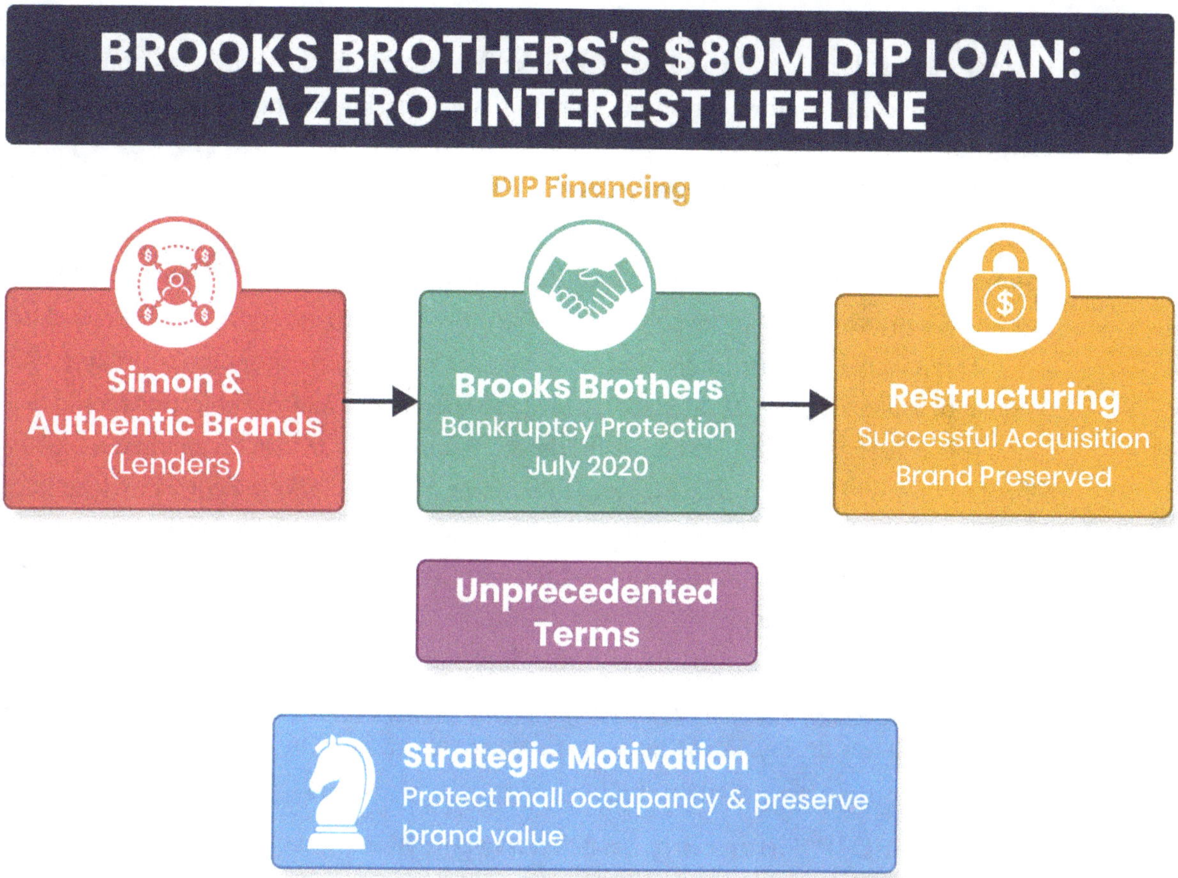

BROOKS BROTHERS'S $80M DIP LOAN: A ZERO-INTEREST LIFELINE

DIP Financing

- **Simon & Authentic Brands** (Lenders)
- **Brooks Brothers** Bankruptcy Protection July 2020
- **Restructuring** Successful Acquisition Brand Preserved

Unprecedented Terms

Strategic Motivation Protect mall occupancy & preserve brand value

Figure 1: Brooks Brothers's $80M DIP Loan: A Zero-Interest Lifeline

The irony wasn't lost on many observers. While Brooks Brothers had left the LaBontes with a warehouse full of abandoned fixtures and a $240,000 cleanup bill, they themselves benefited from extraordinarily favorable financing terms during their bankruptcy. This remarkable arrangement emerged from intense competition among potential lenders and investors, all vying to acquire the iconic retailer.

Typically, DIP loans carry higher interest rates than conventional loans, reflecting the inherent risk of lending to bankrupt companies. But in this case, the strategic interests of the lenders, who were positioning themselves as potential buyers, fundamentally altered the traditional DIP lending dynamics. ABG-BB LLC used the DIP financing as a tool to gain an advantage in the eventual acquisition of the company.

This case reveals how market conditions and competitive pressure among potential buyers can reshape standard bankruptcy financing practices. More broadly, it demonstrates how companies in bankruptcy can leverage their assets and situation to negotiate favorable terms, particularly when multiple parties see value in the distressed business beyond its immediate financial condition.

For investors and creditors, the case adds a new dimension to evaluating DIP financing arrangements. The terms of DIP loans can signal not just the availability of working capital but also the broader strategic interests at play in a bankruptcy proceeding. While providing a zero-interest DIP loan in a case like Brooks Brothers is not something any purely financial lender would do, a more common opportunity is offering financing to small businesses in distress.

Years ago, I made such a loan to a paper mill in Texas that had been spun off from a larger business. With $10 million in sales but no existing lenders, the company owed $2 million to suppliers and needed an emergency cash infusion to keep running. I provided a $100,000 loan at an 18% interest rate, approved by the bankruptcy court, to cover payroll and raw materials.

As with any DIP financing, the process required notice to creditors and court approval. This meant that all existing creditors were aware of the transaction, and any objections could be raised before the funds were advanced. Initially, the court approved the loan on an interim basis, with a final hearing scheduled twenty days later to confirm the terms. This structure provided necessary protections for both the debtor and the lender, ensuring that the financing was properly authorized and that repayment priority was secured within the bankruptcy framework.

The case took some unexpected turns, leading to hard-earned lessons on my behalf about working capital, market volatility, and the challenges of turning around struggling manufacturers. While the investment was ultimately repaid, the time and effort required far exceeded the financial upside. I explore this case, and what went wrong, in greater detail in Chapter 14.

GWG Holdings Case: DIP Financing and Strategic Maneuvers in Bankruptcy

While the Brooks Brothers bankruptcy illustrates how DIP financing can benefit a debtor, the 2022 bankruptcy of GWG Holdings demonstrates how DIP financing can be used as a strategic tool by lenders to gain control of valuable assets. This case also reveals the human cost of bankruptcy, showing how financial deterioration can cascade through a system, affecting everyone from sophisticated investors to retirees who thought they were making safe investments. The complexity of GWG's business model and the mechanics of its DIP financing provide important lessons for distressed investors about both opportunities and risks in bankruptcy cases.

GWG Holdings was a Dallas-based financial services company specializing in life insurance policies on the secondary market. A few years ago, it faced significant challenges that culminated in its Chapter 11 bankruptcy filing in April 2022. Its business model involved purchasing life insurance policies at a discount from policyholders and later profiting from the death benefits. This strategy relied heavily on precise actuarial forecasts and robust financial management, elements that proved problematic for GWG over time.

One of the critical warning signs for investors was the regulatory scrutiny GWG faced. The SEC launched an investigation into GWG and its subsidiary, Beneficient, due to concerns about accounting practices and asset valuation. When the SEC began requesting detailed information in late 2020, it was a clear red flag. As the saying goes, "Where there's smoke, there's fire"—and for investors, an SEC investigation often signals looming financial distress.

In this case, the deeper the investigation went, the worse the situation became. Internal reviews revealed misappropriated funds, flawed accounting, and signs of financial mismanagement, including substantial sums diverted to executives' personal expenses.

This led to a catastrophic liquidity crunch when GWG was forced to halt sales of its high-yield L bonds. These L bonds,, designed to provide funding for GWG's life settlement investments, were the company's primary source of capital. Without new bond sales, GWG couldn't meet its obligations, and bankruptcy became inevitable (see Fig. 2).

By April 2022, GWG had filed for Chapter 11, listing over $2 billion in liabilities, including $1.3 billion in L bonds, which were held by individual investors, many of them retirees who believed they had purchased safe, income-generating securities.

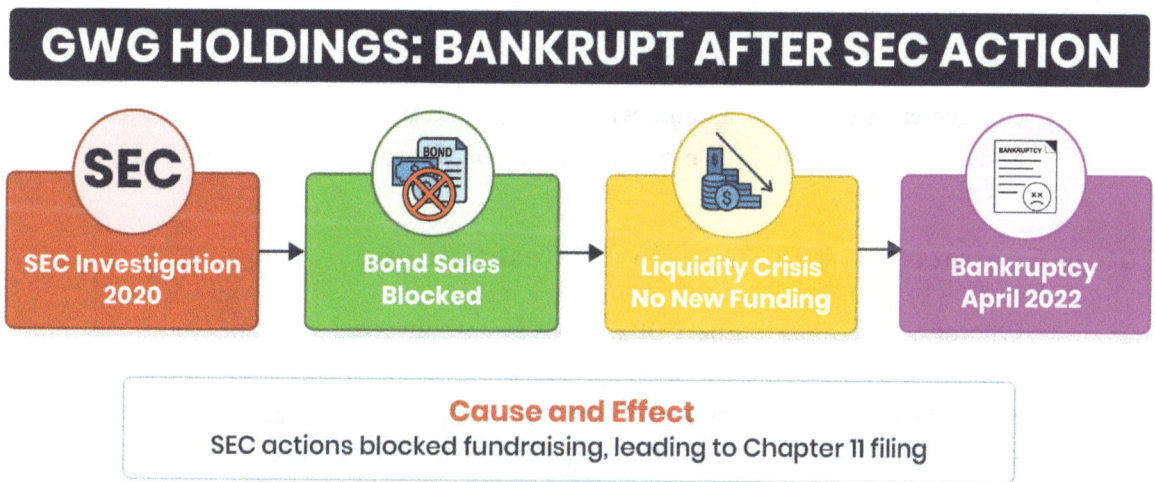

Figure 2: GWG Holdings: Bankrupt After SEC Action

DIP Financing and the Battle for Control

To maintain operations while restructuring, GWG secured DIP financing from Obra Capital, which structured the loan through Vida Insurance Credit Opportunity Fund III. The financing package included a $564 million term loan and a $40 million revolving credit facility, both secured by GWG's life settlements portfolio.

However, this was not just a lifeline; it was a strategic maneuver. The DIP financing included super-priority claims, allowing Obra to jump ahead of existing creditors. Additionally, it contained a roll-up provision, which converted pre-bankruptcy claims into higher-priority DIP loans, effectively strengthening Obra's control over the restructuring process. The agreement also outsourced the servicing of GWG's life settlements portfolio to Magna Servicing LLC, a subsidiary of Obra, meaning Obra had operational control over the assets even before GWG exited bankruptcy.

As an investor with extensive bankruptcy experience, I wanted to see firsthand how the process would unfold. To gain insight into the restructuring, I purchased $10,000 worth of L bonds at par (meaning face value), believing this would give me a seat at the table. (They were called "L bonds" because they were investments in life insurance.) My thought was that owning a bond would allow me to participate in discussions, potentially influence the process, and stay informed about the developments through firsthand experience.

However, despite being a bondholder, I quickly discovered that my influence was limited. The court-appointed restructuring team and major creditors had already established control over the process, and smaller stakeholders, like individual bondholders, had little leverage. Even writing a letter to assert my position didn't change the reality: the main players had already shaped the restructuring in a way that benefited institutional investors over smaller creditors.

For other distressed investors like me, this was an important lesson: owning a piece of a debt does not automatically mean you'll influence the bankruptcy proceedings. The rules of engagement are set early, and unless you have significant capital at stake, or the ability to form a strong creditor group, you may find yourself on the outside looking in.

Executory Contracts and Their Role in the Restructuring

One often overlooked aspect of the GWG case involved executory contracts, agreements where both sides still have ongoing obligations, such as servicing contracts and financing arrangements. Under Section 365 of the Bankruptcy Code, a debtor in Chapter 11 has the right to assume or reject these contracts, a decision that can directly shape the outcome of a restructuring.

For GWG, how these contracts were handled became a major part of its asset restructuring strategy. Some agreements were rejected, allowing the company to shed obligations it could no longer afford. Others were assumed and renegotiated, including key servicing agreements tied to its life settlements portfolio, the contracts essential to maintaining value for creditors and investors.

For investors evaluating distressed situations, watching which contracts are kept and which are discarded offers insight into what matters most to the debtor. Contracts the company fights to keep often point to core business operations, while rejected agreements may highlight areas of weakness or create openings for competitors and new entrants. Understanding these choices is a window into the real value drivers in a restructuring.

Outcome: Who Won and Who Lost?

Despite DIP financing and an aggressive restructuring effort, GWG ultimately did not survive as an operating company. On August 1, 2023, it emerged from Chapter 11, but not as a going concern. Instead, the company transitioned into a liquidation vehicle, the GWG Wind Down Trust, tasked with selling off assets and distributing the proceeds to creditors.

The centerpiece of GWG's business, its life settlements portfolio, was sold in October 2023 for $605 million, enough to cover debt obligations to Obra, the DIP lender. For Obra and other DIP participants, this was a partial win, as they recovered their investments through priority repayment. But for many others, including retail bondholders, the picture was far less clear. I count myself among them. As a GWG L bondholder, I'm still unsure how much, if anything, I will ultimately recover. I remain hopeful that I'll see my initial investment returned, but I'm realistic about the timeline and outcome. If the funds come back in a few years, it will be a hard-earned lesson that those dollars could have been put to better use elsewhere. Still, I don't consider it a failure; it is just a costly education on how these cases play out.

Others were hit even harder. Individual investors like Ronald J. Inlow, a retiree who had placed his life savings in GWG's L bonds, suffered devastating losses.[15] Inlow had been advised by his financial advisor to treat L bonds as a safe, income-producing investment. When GWG collapsed, he was left with nothing. His case went to Financial Industry Regulatory Authority (FINRA) arbitration, where he was awarded $1 million in damages, revealing the deep misrepresentations and negligence behind the marketing of GWG's products. His experience highlights a harsh reality in distressed investing: while large institutional players maneuver for position and influence, retail investors are often left without meaningful protection or recourse.

Looking back at GWG's bankruptcy, I see several hard but valuable lessons for anyone involved in distressed investing. First, DIP financing is more than just a way for companies to survive bankruptcy; it's a tool of control. Obra structured its DIP loan to ensure it would be repaid first, while also steering the course of the case. Second, owning debt is not the same as having influence. As a smaller creditor, I had no ability to shape negotiations or outcomes, and neither did many other individual investors. Third, the treatment of executory contracts can determine the fate of a company's assets. Watching which contracts GWG kept or rejected offered insight into which parts of the business had lasting value. Finally, and perhaps most sobering, retail investors often suffer the most. While sophisticated funds and strategic creditors protect themselves, individuals like Inlow bear the full brunt of these failures.

GWG's bankruptcy was a contest for control. Ultimately, the players with leverage and strategy, DIP lenders and large creditors, walked away with the best outcomes. The smaller investors were left trying to recover what they could from the remnants.

With that backdrop, we'll now turn to another powerful concept in bankruptcy investing: cash collateral. As we'll see, cash collateral often works hand in hand with DIP financing to shape the course of a Chapter 11 case. Understanding how it's used can offer further insight into who holds power and how value is preserved or lost.

The QualTek Case: Using Cash Collateral to Access Working Capital

After examining DIP financing through the GWG case, we turn to another aspect of bankruptcy: the use of cash collateral. While DIP financing provides new money to fund operations, cash collateral involves a company's existing cash and receivables, often the lifeblood of daily operations. QualTek Services Inc.'s 2023 bankruptcy offers a clear illustration of how cash collateral works in practice and why it matters to distressed investors.

Founded in the early 2010s, QualTek Services Inc. grew to become a leading provider of telecommunications infrastructure services in North America, including installation and maintenance services for telecom and renewable energy sectors. By May 2023, however, it faced significant financial distress, culminating in a Chapter 11 filing. The company's financial troubles were compounded by rapid expansion fueled by debt, adverse market conditions, and operational challenges. These difficulties culminated in a liquidity crisis that made reorganization under Chapter 11 of the Bankruptcy Code necessary.

The company had grown quickly through strategic acquisitions financed largely by substantial debt obligations. It operated in a highly competitive industry, where cash flow management was crucial due to the project-based nature of the business and the necessity of investing in equipment and manpower continually. As the telecommunications sector evolved, with increasing demands for upgraded infrastructure to support 5G technology and renewable energy initiatives, QualTek needed to adapt swiftly (i.e., required more capital). But a downturn in project volumes and delays in receivables severely impacted its liquidity.

On May 24, 2023, QualTek filed for Chapter 11 bankruptcy protection to restructure its debts and secure the necessary funding to continue operations. With more than $600 million in debt, the company had been deeply impacted by interest rate hikes instituted by the Federal Reserve in March 2022 to get inflation under control. By the third quarter of 2022, QualTek's interest payments ballooned to nearly $60 million, up 33% from a year earlier. It wasn't all bad news, though; the company generated revenues of $750 million in 2022, giving it money in the bank. But interest payments were eating the company alive.

At the heart of QualTek's restructuring strategy was using cash collateral. Cash collateral refers to any cash or cash equivalents subject to a creditor's security interest. In the context of Chapter 11, cash collateral typically includes a debtor's cash on hand, bank accounts, accounts receivable, and any other cash generated from the debtor's operations or assets (see Fig. 3).

In this case, cash collateral allowed QualTek to maintain its business operations, including meeting payroll, supplier payments, and other operational costs. Without access to these funds, QualTek risked losing its ability to operate, which would diminish the company's value for all stakeholders and potentially lead to liquidation.

Under the U.S. Bankruptcy Code, a debtor in possession, like QualTek, is required to obtain permission to use cash collateral either through the consent of secured creditors or by court approval. In legal parlance, this mandate is called "adequate protection." Essentially it requires the debtor to protect the value of the creditor's collateral and compensate the creditor for any decrease in value that may occur during the bankruptcy case.

Forms of adequate protection can vary depending on the case's specific circumstances. They may include periodic cash payments to the creditor, replacement liens on other assets, or other measures designed to preserve the value of the collateral. The specific terms of adequate protection are often heavily negotiated between the debtor and the secured creditor and can significantly impact the overall restructuring plan.

CASH COLLATERAL: WHAT IT IS & WHY IT MATTERS IN BANKRUPTCY

Figure 3: Cash Collateral: What It Is and Why It Matters in Bankruptcy

In QualTek's scenario, the strategic use of cash collateral gave the company a path forward. Through it, the company was able to access the funds needed to sustain its daily operations and fund restructuring activities by negotiating with creditors and obtaining court approval. The court's approval included stipulations to protect the creditors adequately, ensuring their interests were safeguarded. These measures typically included granting additional or replacement liens and offering periodic cash payments based on the ongoing valuation of the collateral.

The strategic management of cash collateral fundamentally shapes a company's path through Chapter 11. While cash collateral provides access to existing funds, many companies find they need both cash collateral and DIP financing to successfully reorganize. QualTek's case illustrates this interplay: the company needed access to its cash collateral for daily operations while seeking additional financing to fund its longer-term restructuring.

This dual approach to bankruptcy financing, using existing cash collateral and securing new DIP loans, creates opportunities for strategic investors. Some may provide DIP financing to companies already managing cash collateral arrangements, gaining influence over the restructuring process while securing superior liens. Others might offer exit financing, helping companies transition from reliance on cash collateral to more flexible post-bankruptcy arrangements. Each strategy requires careful analysis of the company's collateral position, cash flow projections, and existing creditor rights.

Understanding this relationship helps investors identify opportunities throughout the bankruptcy process, from initial filing through eventual emergence or sale. As we'll see in the next section, on executory contracts, these financing decisions influence every aspect of a company's restructuring options.

Treatment of Executory Contracts: Assuming or Rejecting Ongoing Agreements

At the beginning of this chapter, I discussed the Cinecom case and my conversation with Ismail Merchant about his contract for *A Room with a View*. That contract was an executory contract, meaning both parties still had obligations to fulfill. Merchant, who was well aware of his rights, understood that Cinecom would have to make him whole on any unpaid amounts if it wanted to assume the contract. A fundamental rule of the Bankruptcy Code is that in order to assume and assign an executory contract, a company must cure (resolve or compensate for) any outstanding defaults or negotiate an alternative treatment with the counterparty. Because of this legal imperative, Merchant had the upper hand in negotiations.

This same issue arises frequently in bankruptcy cases and is governed by Section 365 of the Bankruptcy Code, which allows debtors to either assume or reject ongoing agreements. The decision to keep or discard such contracts can shape a company's restructuring strategy, financial position, and ability to attract financing. We saw this when we looked at Brooks Brothers, which faced a pivotal decision regarding its 200+ store leases after entering Chapter 11. The company ultimately rejected over 50 underperforming locations, while keeping 125 stores that supported its business. The ability to selectively retain beneficial agreements while shedding costly ones is one of the most powerful tools in bankruptcy.

Executory contracts encompass a broad range of agreements, including real estate leases, supplier agreements, licensing arrangements, and employment contracts. Under Section 365, a debtor can assume or reject each contract, subject to court approval. If a debtor chooses to assume a contract, it means committing to continue meeting the contractual obligations. To do so, the debtor must resolve any past default, for example, by paying overdue rent or settling missed payments to vendors. Once assumed, the contract becomes a post-petition obligation, meaning it takes priority over most unsecured claims. On the other hand, if a debtor rejects a contract, it effectively walks away from its obligations, leaving the counterparty with a pre-petition unsecured claim, which is often worth far less than the contract's full value.

This process plays a major role in corporate restructurings, particularly in industries with extensive contractual obligations. Retail bankruptcies, for example, frequently use Chapter 11 as a tool to "right-size" operations, assuming profitable leases while rejecting unprofitable ones. By leveraging this ability, debtors can emerge from bankruptcy with a leaner, more sustainable cost structure, improving their chances of long-term viability.

These decisions also play a central role in DIP financing. A debtor that rejects contracts can significantly reduce its cash burn and operating costs, potentially decreasing the amount of financing it needs to sustain operations. On the other hand, assuming contracts may require substantial cure payments, meaning the company needs even more liquidity during the bankruptcy process. In some cases, creditors and DIP lenders will use contract assumptions and rejections as leverage to shape the terms of a restructuring.

The impact of these decisions extends beyond the debtor itself. Counterparties often object to the debtor's choices, triggering litigation over cure amounts, assurances of future performance, or the financial impact of rejection. These disputes can become major conflicts within the bankruptcy case, affecting its timeline and ultimate outcome. For investors, a company's treatment of its contracts offers valuable insight into its restructuring priorities and the viability of its business model. Contracts that a debtor fights to keep signal areas where management sees the most long-term value. Rejected contracts, on the other hand, may indicate fundamental shifts in the company's business strategy or opportunities for competitors to step in.

The Cinecom case illustrates how these dynamics can play out in unexpected ways. Merchant wasn't just concerned about how much money he would receive; he needed to understand who would control the film rights to *A Room with a View* after Cinecom's bankruptcy. If the contract was assumed, he might have been dealing with a new distributor or facing new financial terms. If it was rejected, he could potentially regain control over the rights but might have to fight for financial compensation. These are the same questions creditors, landlords, suppliers, and investors must ask in any bankruptcy case. The ability to read between the lines of contract assumptions and rejections can reveal opportunities and risks that aren't always obvious at first glance.

For sophisticated investors, rejected contracts can create openings to acquire valuable assets, while cure payments required for assumed contracts may present financing opportunities. Some investors purchase claims from rejected contract counterparties at a discount, betting on better-than-expected recoveries. Others structure financing deals to help fund cure payments in exchange for favorable terms in the reorganized business. The bottom line is that executory contracts aren't just legal technicalities. They shape the outcome of a bankruptcy case and determine which parts of a business survive reorganization.

Plans of Reorganization: Charting a Path Forward

A Chapter 11 reorganization resembles a complex puzzle where each piece—DIP financing, cash collateral, and executory contracts—must fit together perfectly. The plan of reorganization represents the final picture, showing creditors, the court, and other stakeholders how these elements combine to create a viable business. The plan serves as a comprehensive roadmap for the debtor's emergence from bankruptcy, outlining how claims will be treated, how assets will be restructured, and how the reorganized company will operate.

Developing and confirming a reorganization plan typically involves extensive negotiations among the debtor, its creditors, and other key stakeholders. These negotiations often take place through formal creditor committees, as well as through informal discussions and mediation sessions. As we've discussed earlier, one of the important features of a reorganization plan is the classification and treatment of claims. Under the Bankruptcy Code, claims must be divided into classes based on their legal and economic characteristics, and each class must receive fair and equitable treatment relative to other classes. Fair treatment means that senior claims, such as secured debt, must generally be paid in full before junior classes, such as unsecured debt or equity, can recover.

The plan must also specify how it will be implemented, which may involve a variety of restructuring transactions. These can include the sale or liquidation of certain business lines, the merger or acquisition of the debtor by a strategic buyer, the spin-off of valuable assets into a new entity, or the issuance of new debt or equity securities. The specific transactions contemplated by a plan will depend on each case's unique circumstances and the goals of the various stakeholders involved.

Once a plan of reorganization has been proposed, it must be submitted to a vote of the debtor's creditors. To be confirmed, the plan must meet several statutory requirements. The court must determine that the plan is feasible, meaning it is unlikely to be followed by another liquidation or further reorganization unless such an outcome is explicitly part of the plan. Additionally, it must satisfy the Best Interests of Creditors Test, a legal requirement ensuring that each creditor will receive at least as much under the plan as they would in a Chapter 7 liquidation. The plan must also be proposed in good faith, meaning it has been put forth with honest intent and without violating any provisions of bankruptcy law.

Even if one or more creditor classes reject the plan, it may still be confirmed under the "cramdown" provisions of Section 1129(b) of the Bankruptcy Code. This allows the court to approve the plan despite objections, provided it does not unfairly discriminate against dissenting creditors and remains fair and equitable in its treatment of all stakeholders (see Fig. 4).

The GWG Holdings case illustrates these principles in action. GWG's plan converted L bonds into a combination of cash, new secured notes, and equity in Beneficient Company Group, a newly structured entity that had been deeply entangled with GWG before its bankruptcy. Beneficient was initially designed to provide liquidity for investors trapped in illiquid alternative assets. However, its business model struggled to deliver cash liquidity, instead offering other illiquid securities. The company was formally separated from GWG before its bankruptcy, but its financial ties and governance structure remained murky.

Controversy followed Beneficient as creditors accused its leadership of fraud and self-dealing. Specifically, GWG bond sales allegedly funded Beneficient's operations, misleading investors about both companies' financial health. The SEC launched multiple investigations, and some creditors argued that Beneficient's strategy of getting listed on NASDAQ was an attempt to generate artificial value for a financially unstable company. Additionally, Beneficient secured a special financial charter in Kansas (a TEFFI), allowing it to operate under different regulatory conditions. This raised further questions about its governance and long-term viability.

Despite these uncertainties, Beneficient played a critical role in shaping creditor recoveries. The $564 million DIP financing from Obra Capital, which included the roll-up of preexisting debt, positioned Obra as a dominant force in the restructuring process. Through its DIP position and control over GWG's life settlements portfolio, Obra gained significant influence over the final plan terms.

While Obra Capital did not take full ownership of GWG's life insurance portfolio as initially intended, it still secured a strong recovery through its DIP financing strategy. Instead, GWG exited Chapter 11 on August 1, 2023, and the company ceased to be a going concern. The GWG Wind Down Trust was established to liquidate assets and distribute proceeds to

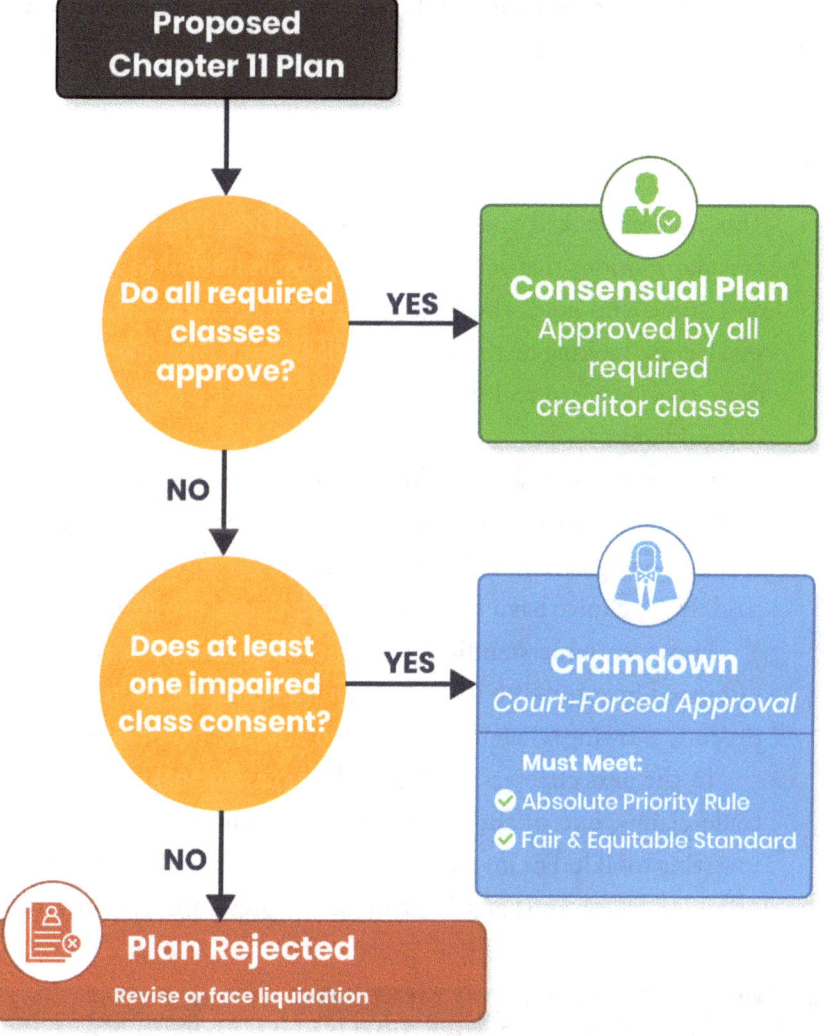

Figure 4: Bankruptcy Plan Approval Paths

creditors and bondholders. This sale ensured that Obra was repaid in full, while any remaining proceeds were distributed to other creditors according to the bankruptcy plan. While the exact profit is undisclosed, Obra's position as a secured DIP lender ensured it recovered its full investment and achieved a meaningful return.

Every bankruptcy case is unique, but for investors, the reorganization plan is perhaps the most important aspect of a Chapter 11 case. By understanding the proposed classification and treatment of claims, the feasibility of the restructuring transactions, and the potential risks and objections to the plan, investors can make informed decisions about whether to support or oppose the debtor's reorganization efforts.

Ultimately, a successful reorganization plan can unlock significant value for investors, while a failure can lead to further losses and uncertainty. As such, active engagement in the plan-development process, whether through direct participation on a creditor committee or through close monitoring of the case, is a requirement for investors seeking to maximize their returns in Chapter 11.

Wrapping Up

This chapter walked you through the building blocks of managing a bankruptcy case, from first-day motions that stabilize a company in freefall to DIP financing and cash collateral that determine who holds the reins to executory contracts that define what pieces of the business survive. By looking at the examples of Brooks Brothers and GWG, we were able to see how these tools work in real life, sometimes creating a path to reorganization, other times leading to liquidation.

If there's one lesson to take from these cases, it's that bankruptcy is a connected system. Every motion, financing term, and contract decision influences the next move. A fight over DIP financing isn't just about loan terms; it's about who controls the process and who gets paid. Every choice has a ripple effect that shapes the entire case.

However, understanding how cases are managed is only part of what makes a successful distressed investor. The real opportunities often lie in how you position yourself within that process, knowing when to buy, what to buy, and how to structure a trade.

In the next chapters, we'll shift from case management to investor strategy, starting with trade claims, one of the most overlooked but potentially profitable tools in the distressed investing toolkit. For investors who know where to look and how to price risk, trade claims can offer unique ways to participate in bankruptcies and turn complexity into opportunity.

KEY INSIGHTS

1. First-day motions help stabilize a company after filing for bankruptcy, with vendor payments often determining whether operations continue uninterrupted.
2. DIP financing offers more than just liquidity; it can be a strategic tool influencing control over the restructuring process, as seen in the GWG Holdings case.
3. Cash collateral arrangements require careful negotiations between debtors and secured creditors, as demonstrated in QualTek's bankruptcy, where interest payments became a central issue.
4. Executory contracts allow debtors to reshape their business by keeping valuable agreements and shedding burdensome ones, illustrated by Brooks Brothers's lease decisions.
5. Early bankruptcy decisions regarding financing, cash management, and contract obligations set the course for an entire case and affect the likelihood of a successful reorganization.

6. Secured creditors often use DIP financing and cash collateral agreements to strengthen their position, which can directly impact recoveries for other stakeholders.
7. Retail bankruptcies frequently involve rethinking lease portfolios, with contract rejections playing a major role in restructuring efforts.
8. Smaller creditors and business partners can suffer collateral damage in a bankruptcy, as seen in the LaBontes' struggle with abandoned Brooks Brothers inventory.
9. Reorganization plans must satisfy legal requirements while balancing competing creditor interests, leading to complex negotiations and shifting priorities.
10. Individual investors in distressed companies, such as GWG's L bondholders, face distinct risks, especially when dealing with intricate financial structures.
11. The interplay between DIP financing, cash collateral, and executory contracts is key to evaluating distressed investment opportunities.
12. Successful bankruptcy investing requires understanding both the mechanics of the process and the strategies employed by different stakeholders.
13. The timing of bankruptcy events, such as financing approvals, contract rejections, and creditor negotiations, can significantly shape investment outcomes.

CHAPTER 9

The Trade Claims Playbook: Rules, Risks, and Rewards

When cryptocurrency exchange FTX filed for bankruptcy in November 2022, over a million customers wondered if they would ever recover their funds. Among these customers were people like Bhagamshi Kannegundla, who had more than $170,000 worth of cryptocurrency stuck on the platform.[16] But as the bankruptcy proceedings began, a group of specialized distressed asset investors started circling, looking to buy up claims from FTX customers at a discount.

One early investor and broker of FTX claims was Vladimir Jelisavcic, who I first introduced in Chapter 1. The seasoned distressed investor has over 30 years of experience and a background in both law (JD) and accounting (CPA) from NYU Stern, the school where I teach. Early on, the founder of Cherokee Acquisition saw the FTX bankruptcy as a prime example of an inefficient market where information was scarce, and the true value of assets was unknown. Shortly after FTX filed, bidding on FTX claims was at just 3 to 6 cents on the dollar. There weren't a lot of buyers, but there also weren't a lot of sellers. Jelisavcic, who is one of the most thorough distressed debt analysts in the world, wasn't deterred. As part of his process he read every document filed in the case.

As he dug deeper into the company's assets, he became convinced that FTX creditors could eventually recover a meaningful portion of what they were owed. Throughout 2023, Jelisavcic's bet started to pay off. The FTX estate kept uncovering assets, settling claims, and recovering funds. By early 2024, FTX announced that it could repay creditors in full. For early investors and traders like Jelisavcic, who had bought claims at a steep discount, this news represented the potential for returns as high as thirty times their initial investment.

But while distressed asset investors stand to profit handsomely from the FTX bankruptcy, the process has been far more painful for the actual customers of the exchange. Many, like Kannegundla, sold their claims early on for a fraction of their value, forever locking in their losses.

There's a pointed question that many distressed investors ask when evaluating whether to purchase distressed debt: "What is the most I can lose if I'm wrong?" Well, if you pay 10 cents or less, then 10 cents is the most you can lose. Typically, the most you can make is 100 cents, but that's not the case when it comes to FTX, where it appears that investors will be paid between

120% and 150%. Such a windfall is extremely rare, but in this case, it was due to a rebound in crypto prices and FTX's investments in private companies like Anthropic that turned out to be worth a fortune.

On the other side, most distressed sellers have their own critical question: "If someone is offering me less than 20 cents, why should I sell?" Indeed, in most distressed situations, it is highly unusual for distressed debt to sell for less than 20 cents. Unless a distressed seller is desperate for cash, they would rather take their chances that the claim will eventually be paid off closer to their basis in the claim.

The FTX case illustrates the stark divide between sophisticated investors who can navigate the complexities of the bankruptcy process and ordinary individuals who are often left holding the bag when a company fails. It also highlights the unique nature of the trade claim market, where a lack of transparency and an established marketplace can create significant inefficiencies and opportunities for those with the right expertise.

For traders like Vladimir Jelisavcic, these market inefficiencies are precisely what make trade claims an attractive investment. With his background in distressed investing and his roots in the bankruptcy world, Jelisavcic has made a career out of finding value where others see only chaos and uncertainty.

To truly appreciate the appeal and the risks of investing in trade claims, we need to look at what these claims are, how they arise, and why they can be so lucrative for investors who know how to navigate this niche corner of the financial world. In the following sections, we'll dive deep into the mechanics and strategies behind trade claim investing, using real-world examples to illustrate this unique asset class's potential rewards and pitfalls.

Understanding Trade Claims

Simply put, trade claims are unpaid bills or invoices that a company owes to its suppliers or service providers. When a company enters financial distress and files for bankruptcy, these unpaid obligations become unsecured claims against the bankrupt estate. Unlike secured claims, which are backed by collateral such as real estate or equipment, trade claims hold no priority in the bankruptcy process. This means trade creditors, such as suppliers, vendors, and service providers, are often last in line when it comes to recovering what they are owed.

Before investing in trade claims, remember that the Absolute Priority Rule in Section 507 of the Bankruptcy Code is nonnegotiable. This rule determines whether creditors recover 100% of their claim or nothing at all (see Fig. 1). Investors who overlook this principle risk making decisions that could leave them with little to no return.

The life cycle of a trade claim often begins months before bankruptcy. As a company's cash flow deteriorates, it typically extends payment terms or misses payments altogether. A manufacturer might push a 30-day invoice to 60 days, then 90 days, prioritizing payments to essential suppliers while delaying others. A real-world example of this strategy occurred during the pandemic when Macy's, though avoiding bankruptcy, extended vendor payment terms to 105 days. By the time a company files for bankruptcy, some suppliers may be owed for multiple

THE TRADE CLAIMS PLAYBOOK: RULES, RISKS, AND REWARDS

Figure 1: Absolute Priority Rule

unpaid invoices spanning several months. These claims can range from thousands of dollars for small service providers to millions for major suppliers of raw materials or logistics services.

The collapse of FTX provides a clear example of this pattern. In the months leading up to its bankruptcy, FTX began selectively delaying payments and withdrawals. Some customers and vendors were paid, while others faced increasing delays. When the company ultimately filed for bankruptcy, these unpaid invoices and promises to pay turned into trade claims, leaving creditors to navigate the bankruptcy process for potential recovery.

Trade claims don't always emerge at the moment of bankruptcy. If a company is clearly struggling, failing to meet payment obligations, and showing signs of financial distress, suppliers may start selling their claims to investors at a discount rather than waiting for a prolonged bankruptcy process. However, not all trade claims hold the same value. In the next section, we will explore why some trade claims are more valuable than others and how the Absolute Priority Rule affects their potential recovery.

Types of Trade Claims

For investors, trade claims often represent opportunities to buy claims at a discount and profit on eventual recoveries. But not all trade claims are the same; the value of each depends on how they are classified under the Bankruptcy Code and where they sit in the capital structure. Some are straightforward unsecured debts, while others benefit from special protections that increase their chances of getting paid.

One of the most common examples is a contract rejection damage claim, which arises when a debtor rejects or terminates an executory contract under Section 365 of the Bankruptcy Code. The counterparty is entitled to damages, but these claims are usually treated as general unsecured claims. This means they often recover only a fraction of their face value, depending on how much money is left in the estate.

Deficiency claims are another major source of trade claims. These occur when a secured lender's collateral is not sufficient to cover the full debt owed. Under Section 506 of the Bankruptcy Code, the unsecured portion of that debt becomes a deficiency claim. Like other unsecured creditors, holders of deficiency claims share in whatever assets remain after higher-priority claims are satisfied.

In many large corporate bankruptcies, pension and other post-employment benefits (OPEB) claims are some of the largest claims in the case. These claims arise when debtors terminate collective bargaining agreements, cancel defined benefit pension plans, or eliminate retiree healthcare obligations under Sections 1113 and 1114 of the Bankruptcy Code. Cases like United Airlines, Delphi, and American Airlines are classic examples where pension and retiree claims shaped the entire restructuring process.

Another important category is contingent claims, which are based on potential future obligations such as lawsuits, environmental liabilities, or product liability claims. These types of claims have played major roles in cases like Owens Corning, W.R. Grace, and Armstrong World Industries, which involved asbestos-related liabilities. Similarly, Asarco and Tronox faced enormous environmental cleanup obligations. Whether these claims get paid and in what amount often depends on how the court evaluates the likelihood and size of the underlying liability. Even if payment is uncertain, contingent claims can have a huge impact on the case.

Priority claims hold a senior position over general unsecured creditors and must be paid in full before any unsecured claims receive distributions. These include unpaid employee wages and benefits, certain tax debts, and what are known as "gap claims." Gap claims are trade debts that arise during the period between the filing of an involuntary bankruptcy petition and the court's official order for relief. Lease deposits, which are capped at $2,452 under Section 507 of the Bankruptcy Code, also qualify as priority claims. Because of their higher rank in the priority waterfall, these claims are often considered safer investments and can be attractive for investors looking for lower-risk options in a bankruptcy case.

Reclamation claims add another layer of complexity. These claims allow creditors to reclaim goods delivered to a debtor shortly before the bankruptcy filing. Although the right to reclaim goods arises under state law through Section 2-702(2) of the UCC, it is protected in bankruptcy under Section 546(c). The Bankruptcy Abuse Prevention and Consumer Protection Act of 2005 (BAPCPA) extended the window for asserting reclamation claims; creditors now have up to 45 days before the bankruptcy filing and 20 days after to assert these rights. However, these claims are often contested, and debtors regularly argue that the goods are subject to preexisting liens that prevent reclamation. Even when valid, creditors must comply with strict notice requirements to preserve their rights.

Finally, 503(b)(9) claims are among the most attractive for investors because they are granted administrative expense priority, meaning they must be paid in full if the estate has sufficient funds. These claims apply to goods received by the debtor within 20 days before the bankruptcy filing. Because of their higher priority, 503(b)(9) claims usually recover at a much higher rate than ordinary trade claims. In fact, in recent retail bankruptcies such as Toys "R" Us, Sears, and JCPenney, 503(b)(9) claims were sometimes the only trade claims that received meaningful payment. For that reason, they tend to draw significant interest from distressed investors, especially in cases where the outlook for general unsecured creditors is bleak.

Although trade claims may seem like a broad category of unpaid bills, their type and legal status make all the difference in how they are treated in bankruptcy. For distressed investors, understanding these differences is essential to identifying which claims offer a real opportunity for recovery and which may be virtually worthless.

In the next section, we will explore why trade claims attract investors, how the market for these claims operates, and what risks and rewards investors should expect when buying into these positions.

The Rationale Behind Investing in Trade Claims

The primary appeal of investing in trade claims is the potential for outsized returns. Because trade claims are unsecured and often seen as a low priority in the bankruptcy process, they can frequently be purchased at a significant discount to their face value. For example, an investor might be able to buy a $100,000 trade claim for $20,000 or $30,000. If the bankruptcy process ultimately results in a distribution to unsecured creditors of 50 cents on the dollar, the investor would double their money or more.

In some cases, the potential returns can be even higher. In the FTX bankruptcy, early investors could buy claims at just a few cents on the dollar. If FTX can fully repay its creditors, as now seems possible, these investors could see returns of ten times their initial investment or more.

In addition to the potential for high returns, trade claims can offer investors diversification benefits. Because the performance of trade claims is tied to the specifics of individual bankruptcy cases, they tend to have a low correlation with broader market movements. In practice, a low correlation means that investing in trade claims can help reduce overall portfolio risk, especially during economic uncertainty or market volatility. While other assets may be losing value, a well-selected portfolio of trade claims can provide a steady source of uncorrelated returns.

Finally, the trade claim market is characterized by significant inefficiencies that can create opportunities for shrewd investors. Unlike stocks or bonds, which trade on public exchanges with transparent pricing, trade claims are bought and sold in a fragmented, opaque market. Without a centralized exchange or readily available pricing information, wide spreads emerge between what buyers will pay and what sellers will accept. For investors who can navigate this complexity, these inefficiencies create profit opportunities. By doing the legwork to find and value attractive claims, investors can often buy at prices well below what the claims are ultimately worth.

Of course, don't misconstrue what I just said to mean that investing in trade claims is without risk. Bankruptcy proceedings can be lengthy and complex, and there is always the possibility that the ultimate recovery for unsecured creditors will be less than expected and, in some cases, zero.

The Trade Claim Market Landscape

The trade claim market is a vast and largely uncharted territory in finance. While it's difficult to pinpoint the exact size of the market, estimates suggest that it represents a significant portion of the $1 trillion in bankruptcy claims traded each year. Despite its size, the trade claim market operates largely in the shadows. There is no centralized exchange or clearinghouse for trade claims, and much of the trading activity takes place through private, bilateral negotiations between buyers and sellers. This opacity makes it challenging to get a clear picture of the overall market landscape. However, bankruptcy filings and court documents can provide insight into the scale and scope of trade claim activity in specific cases.

The trade claim market is populated by diverse characters, each with their own motivations and strategies. On the sell side, the most common participants are the suppliers, vendors, and service providers owed money by the bankrupt company. These can range from small mom-and-pop businesses to large multinational corporations. For these trade creditors, selling their claims can be a way to recoup some of what they are owed and avoid the bankruptcy process's uncertainty and delay. In many cases, they may be willing to accept a significant discount on their claims to get cash in hand quickly.

On the buy side, the players are typically specialized distressed debt investors. These can include hedge funds, private equity firms, and other institutional investors with the expertise and risk tolerance to navigate the complexities of the bankruptcy process. Some of the most active buyers in the trade claim market are dedicated claims-trading firms, like my firm, SLAQ LLC, as well as Cherokee, Contrarian, Farallon Capital, Silverpoint Capital, Argo Partners, and TR Capital. Such firms focus exclusively on buying and selling bankruptcy claims and often have deep expertise in specific industries or types of claims. In addition to buyers and sellers, the trade claim market includes a range of intermediaries who help facilitate transactions. These can include brokers, who match buyers and sellers and help negotiate prices, and claims agents, who manage the administrative process of filing and transferring claims.

Multiple factors influence the trade claim market's supply and demand dynamics. Economic conditions play a primary role; during downturns, bankruptcy filings typically increase, expanding the supply of available claims. Industry-specific disruptions can also trigger waves of bankruptcies, as seen in retail and energy sectors during various cycles. Each bankruptcy case's unique characteristics shape claim values, from available assets to creditor priorities to reorganization prospects.

The appetite of distressed debt investors significantly impacts market dynamics. When these specialized funds have ample capital and seek opportunities, competition intensifies, and claim prices often rise. Conversely, when distressed investors pull back, claims may trade at deeper discounts. These market forces create a constantly shifting landscape of opportunities and risks.

By monitoring economic trends, industry developments, and specific bankruptcy cases, investors can position themselves to capitalize on emerging opportunities. To that end, in the next chapter we'll explore strategies that successful trade claim investors use to identify attractive opportunities and maximize their returns.

Final Thoughts

Trade claims investing isn't about luck or waiting for the perfect deal—it's about making decisions in the face of uncertainty. Whether buying into a high-profile bankruptcy like FTX, where claim values shift wildly, or navigating an obscure corporate failure with few buyers in sight, the best opportunities often come when the information is incomplete, but the risk is understood. The true skill in this market isn't just finding undervalued claims: it's knowing when the price reflects enough misjudgment by others to make the bet worth taking.

The hardest part isn't getting in—it's knowing when to get out. Some claims rise as confidence grows, while others prove that the market's skepticism was justified. The real profit in trade claims doesn't come from endless patience, but from recognizing when the upside has been realized and the unknowns are gone. Every distressed investor eventually learns that the moment certainty arrives is often the moment to move on.

KEY INSIGHTS

1. The FTX bankruptcy case highlighted the inefficiencies and opportunities in trade claims, showing how distressed asset investors profited while ordinary creditors often lost out.
2. In bankruptcy, debt holders take precedence over equity holders, making debt investments more secure than equity positions in distressed situations.
3. Trade claims represent unsecured obligations in bankruptcy, often ranking low in the payment hierarchy unless they fall under special provisions like 503(b)(9) claims.
4. Understanding the Absolute Priority Rule in Section 507 of the Bankruptcy Code is necessary for trade claim investors, as it determines recovery potential.

5. Trade claims often arise before a bankruptcy filing, with companies delaying payments as they experience financial distress.
6. Different types of trade claims carry varying levels of recovery potential, including contract rejection claims, deficiency claims, pension-related claims, contingent claims, priority claims, reclamation claims, and 503(b)(9) claims.
7. Investing in trade claims can yield high returns due to their discounted purchase prices, but assessing the debtor's financial position and industry conditions is critical.
8. Trade claims are traded in an opaque market without centralized pricing, creating opportunities for knowledgeable investors to capitalize on inefficiencies.

CHAPTER 10

Trade Claims Investing Strategies

You've heard me say it before, but it's worth repeating again and again: when it comes to distressed investing, timing is everything. For proof, look no further than the legendary distressed investor Carl Icahn.

In Las Vegas, fortunes are won and lost at the tables every day. But few players have gamed the booms and busts of the city itself as masterfully as Icahn. While high rollers bet on roulette wheels and blackjack hands, Icahn has spent decades making far more calculated wagers on bankrupt casinos, distressed assets, and overlooked opportunities that others deemed worthless.

One of his greatest bets was made in 1997, when the Stratosphere, an ambitious but deeply troubled new Las Vegas casino, collapsed into bankruptcy barely a year after opening. At a time when other investors saw nothing but financial wreckage, Icahn recognized an opportunity buried within the debt structure itself. He began quietly buying up the Stratosphere's debt for pennies on the dollar, positioning himself as the casino's largest creditor. By the time the company emerged from bankruptcy in 1998, Icahn had taken full control, not just of the casino, but of seventeen additional acres of surrounding land that many had written off as worthless.

For years, industry insiders dismissed Icahn's Las Vegas play as a long shot. The Stratosphere was located in a neglected, economically depressed part of the Strip, far removed from the glitzy action of the Bellagio and the Venetian. Some real estate analysts thought he had overpaid for land that might never appreciate. But Icahn wasn't interested in short-term speculation; he was playing a longer game. He waited for the inevitable upturn in the market, and in 2007, just before the financial crisis hit, he sold the Stratosphere and surrounding assets to Goldman Sachs for $1.3 billion, locking in a billion-dollar profit.

When the economy crashed a year later, and Las Vegas real estate values plummeted, Goldman's investment became a disaster. Icahn had once again timed the cycle perfectly. But his most famous Las Vegas bet was yet to come. In 2009, as the financial crisis devastated commercial real estate markets, an even bigger opportunity appeared: the Fontainebleau Las Vegas, a massive but unfinished $2.9 billion luxury resort. Originally developed by Jeffrey Soffer, the Fontainebleau was 70% complete when its financing collapsed. With its lead lender, Bank of America, halting an $800 million loan, the entire project was thrown into bankruptcy.

Icahn saw what others missed. While the Fontainebleau was an unfinished, dust-covered shell sitting empty on the Strip, it wasn't worthless. The developers had already spent billions bringing it close to completion, and Icahn knew the value was there; it just needed the right timing.

When the Fontainebleau went up for bankruptcy auction in 2010, Icahn was the only bidder who qualified, winning the project for just $148 million, a tiny fraction of its original price. His first move? Selling off every last rug, mattress, and piece of furniture for quick cash. Then, he waited.

For years, the Fontainebleau sat untouched, an eerie monument to the financial crisis. But Icahn wasn't in a rush. He knew that eventually, Las Vegas would recover and developers would once again be looking for prime Strip real estate. That moment came in 2017 when Steve Witkoff and Howard Lorber agreed to buy the Fontainebleau for $600 million, handing Icahn a $450 million profit on a property he never even finished.

The Trade Claim Investor's Mindset

Carl Icahn's success in Las Vegas wasn't just about buying distressed casinos or real estate. It was about understanding the hidden value within financial distress itself. He wasn't afraid to buy assets others had abandoned, wait for the right moment, and exit before the market turned.

This approach applies just as much to investing in trade claims. Just like bankrupt casinos, trade claims often look worthless at first glance. But to investors who understand how to source them, analyze the debtor's financials, and position themselves correctly in the capital structure, they can represent huge opportunities.

Unlike traditional stocks or bonds, trade claims don't have regulated centralized exchanges or transparent pricing mechanisms. They require deep research, strategic timing, and the ability to buy when others are desperate to sell. In this chapter, we'll explore exactly how investors find, evaluate, and execute trade claim investments, leveraging inefficiencies, navigating legal complexities, and capitalizing on opportunities that most of the market overlooks.

Uncovering Trade Claims

Given the lack of exchanges and limited public information about claims, investors must be proactive and creative in sourcing them. For many trade claim investors, the process begins with closely monitoring bankruptcy filings and court dockets. When a company files for Chapter 11, it must disclose a list of its creditors, including the nature and amount of each claim. By reviewing these filings, investors can get a sense of the size and scope of potential trade claim opportunities. They can also identify the largest and most influential creditors, who may be more likely to sell their claims because they are the most exposed and may want to reduce their risk or improve liquidity. Many filings are available through public access systems such as PACER.

TRADE CLAIMS INVESTING STRATEGIES

In addition to the initial bankruptcy filing, investors will also want to keep a close eye on subsequent court filings and docket entries. These can provide valuable information on the progress of the case, the assets available for distribution, and the likelihood of a meaningful recovery for trade creditors. Some investors may use specialized legal research tools or hire attorneys to help them navigate the complex world of bankruptcy dockets. Others will look at similar bankruptcies within the same industry and review their lists of creditors to identify vendors in the industry. For instance, Boeing and Bombardier are common vendors in airline industry bankruptcies.

Another strategy is to leverage relationships with bankruptcy professionals, such as attorneys, financial advisors, and claims agents. These professionals often have direct relationships with creditors and can provide valuable insights into the claims-trading market. They may also know claim holders looking to sell, offering investors an inside track of potential opportunities. Bankruptcy professionals can also help investors navigate the legal and procedural complexities of the claims-trading process, from conducting due diligence to negotiating purchase agreements and filing transfer notices with the court. Some investors may work with a handful of trusted professionals on an ongoing basis, relying on them as a source of deal flow and market intelligence. Others may take a more transactional approach, engaging professionals on a case-by-case basis as opportunities arise.

Organizations like the TMA and ABI, which I introduced in Chapter 4, host regular events that bring together investors, attorneys, and other professionals in the restructuring space. These events can provide valuable opportunities to learn about new cases, share market intelligence, and build relationships with potential counterparties.

It bears repeating that finding deals requires effort. Unless and/or until you become an established distressed investor, the deals will not find you (see Fig. 1).

Some of the most successful trade claim investors are known for their active presence on the conference circuit, using these events to stay on top of market trends and identify potential investment opportunities.

Online Marketplaces and Platforms

In recent years, several online marketplaces have emerged to facilitate the buying and selling of bankruptcy claims. These platforms aim to bring greater transparency and efficiency to what has traditionally been an opaque and fragmented market. One of the leading platforms in this space is Xclaim, which connects buyers and sellers of claims in major bankruptcy cases. The platform provides a centralized database of claims and tools for conducting due diligence and executing trades electronically.

Other notable platforms include Claims Market, which specializes in trading claims in middle-market bankruptcies, and Bankruptcy Claim Exchange, which offers various claim types across multiple industries. These platforms can be a valuable resource for investors looking to source and trade claims more efficiently. By aggregating claims data and providing standardized transaction documentation, they can help streamline the claims-trading process and

THE DISTRESSED INVESTING PLAYBOOK

FINDING DEALS IN DISTRESSED INVESTING

Banks & Financial Institutions — Offloading distressed assets

Bankruptcy Professionals — Lawyers, accountants, specialists

Brokers & Media — Market trends & opportunities

Personal Networks — Relationships drive best deals

Entrepreneurs & Business Owners

→ DISTRESSED DEALS

Figure 1: Finding Deals in Distressed Investing

reduce transaction costs.

Online platforms offer investors access to a broader pool of potential claims than they might source independently. The platforms aggregate claims from multiple sellers and typically provide pricing data and transaction history, helping investors assess market trends and benchmark valuations. Many platforms also offer standardized purchase agreements and electronic signing capabilities, speeding up documentation and closing processes.

However, these platforms come with trade-offs. Most charge transaction fees, either as a percentage of the claim amount or as flat fees per trade, which can erode returns. Trading through platforms may also limit investors' ability to negotiate deal terms or conduct extensive due diligence on individual claims. While platforms may perform some seller vetting, investors remain responsible for assessing counterparty creditworthiness and claim validity.

The emergence of these platforms marks an evolution in trade claim investing, potentially democratizing access to what has historically been an insider's market. So far, however, they should be seen as a supplement to rather than a replacement for traditional sourcing methods.

Many sophisticated investors use platforms selectively, using their efficiency to conduct standard transactions while still relying on direct relationships for more complex or sensitive deals. Investors must weigh these considerations when deciding how platforms fit into their broader sourcing and investment strategy.

Conducting Due Diligence

When evaluating a potential trade claim investment, a thorough documentation review determines both validity and enforceability. Start with the proof of claim, i.e., the official form filed with the bankruptcy court (see sample in the appendix). This document outlines the claim amount and its basis (goods sold, services provided) and includes supporting documentation. Missing or incomplete proofs of claim should immediately raise a red flag.

Next, examine invoices and purchase orders that evidence the underlying transaction. These documents should show that goods or services were actually provided and that claim amounts match. Discrepancies between invoiced amounts and filed claims warrant investigation. If the claim stems from a contractual relationship, review those agreements to understand payment terms and potential debtor defenses or setoffs, which allow a debtor to reduce what it owes by the amount it claims is owed back to it by the creditor.

The broader context matters, too. Analyze potential preference or fraudulent transfer risks, which could allow the debtor or trustee to claw back pre-bankruptcy payments. In addition to setoffs, consider recoupments, or counterclaims from the debtor that might reduce recovery. The FTX bankruptcy illustrates this complexity. Claims based on cryptocurrency deposits face questions about ownership rights and potential setoffs against margin loans or other obligations.

Beyond document review, investigate the claim's history. Have there been prior disputes about payment? Did the creditor continue delivering goods or services as the debtor's financial condition deteriorated? Understanding these dynamics helps assess both claim validity and potential recovery challenges.

Smart investors also examine the seller's authority to transfer the claim. This includes verifying corporate authority for business sellers and checking for any claim transfer restrictions in underlying contracts. Prior assigned or pledged claims can derail even otherwise attractive investments.

Assessing the Debtor's Financial Condition and Prospects

Beyond analyzing specific claims, investors must understand the debtor company's overall financial condition and prospects. This evaluation starts with a deep dive into bankruptcy filings: schedules of assets and liabilities, statements of financial affairs, and proposed restructuring or liquidation plans.

Asset value analysis forms the foundation of any recovery assessment. A thorough review catalogs not just obvious assets like real estate and inventory but also potential hidden value in intellectual property, tax attributes, or litigation claims. The FTX bankruptcy demonstrated how initial asset estimates can be deceptive; additional cryptocurrency holdings and recoverable transfers emerged months after filing, significantly improving potential recoveries.

Understanding the debtor's liability structure reveals where trade claims stand in the payment hierarchy. Total debt, secured creditor claims, priority claims, and other obligations all affect ultimate recoveries. Smart investors map out various scenarios, from full reorganization to liquidation, to gauge potential outcomes for their claims.

Cash flow analysis can prove particularly revealing. A debtor's ability to maintain operations through bankruptcy directly impacts asset values and recovery prospects. Strong cash flow can support reorganization and potentially higher recoveries, while weak liquidity might force quick asset sales at distressed prices.

Industry dynamics also often determine bankruptcy outcomes. A retailer filing amid broader sector disruption faces different challenges than a manufacturer dealing with temporary supply chain issues. Successful investors understand these industry-specific factors and how they affect reorganization prospects. Some industries, like telecommunications infrastructure, may offer better recovery prospects due to underlying asset value, while others might face permanent disruption that limits reorganization options.

Analyzing the Bankruptcy Case and Potential Outcomes

If you're a passive investor in the stock market, you can buy an ETF or mutual fund, check your statement once a month, and get on with your life. If you want to invest in trade claims successfully, however, you'll need to monitor the bankruptcy case's progression daily. By monitoring, I mean tracking court filings and rulings and any restructuring or liquidation plans proposed by the debtor or other parties in interest. Again, we can look to the FTX bankruptcy to see why this monitoring is essential. As court filings revealed previously unknown assets and successful recovery efforts, initial pessimism about recoveries gave way to increasing optimism. Had initial claims holders waited a bit for the dust to settle, they would have found themselves in a much better position.

Active participation can dramatically affect outcomes. In some cases, trade creditors may be able to play an active role in shaping the outcome of the bankruptcy case. For example, they may be able to serve on the Official Committee of Unsecured Creditors, which acts as a fiduciary for all unsecured creditors in the case and has the power to investigate the debtor's conduct and negotiate the terms of any restructuring plans. These committees often drive key decisions about asset sales, claim investigations, and reorganization strategies.

Investors may also influence case outcomes through strategic claim purchases or sales. Building a significant position, like acquiring 25% or more of outstanding claims, can provide blocking rights in plan voting or force consideration of alternative restructuring approaches. Some investors accumulate claims specifically to gain negotiating leverage or control particular assets in the reorganization. However, this strategy requires substantial capital and expertise. The

Lehman Brothers bankruptcy saw several hedge funds successfully employ this approach, but others faced losses when their strategic positions didn't yield the influence they expected.

That said, predicting the outcome of a bankruptcy case is never an exact science. Many factors can impact the ultimate recoveries for trade creditors, from the success of the debtor's reorganization efforts to the actions of other creditors and stakeholders in the case. The best approach is to maintain flexibility while monitoring developments that could shift recovery prospects.

Investing Strategies for Trade Claims

The most straightforward strategy for investing in trade claims is to buy them at a discount to their face value, which is precisely what numerous investment firms have been doing in the FTX bankruptcy case. As the FTX story illustrates, the early stages of bankruptcy can be chaotic, with little clarity on how much creditors will ultimately recover. This uncertainty often prompts claim holders to sell at steep discounts, creating opportunities for investors willing to take on the risk. Recall my anecdote about receiving a call from an attorney for an FTX creditor weeks after it filed for bankruptcy. That creditor wanted a bid for its claim, and fast—which is why I was contacted.

Another approach is to focus on specific industries or debtors where investors have built expertise through experience. Contrarian Capital Management, a hedge fund with years of investing in trade claims, has targeted bankruptcies of broker-dealers, including Lehman Brothers, MF Global, and Refco. Specializing like this lets investors better understand industry-specific factors that affect recoveries and value claims, giving them a leg up over generalist investors.

Some investors spot opportunities by tracking market dislocations. When entire sectors face distress, like retail during the COVID-19 pandemic or energy companies during oil price crashes, claims often trade at deeper discounts than warranted by the underlying assets. These situations reward investors who grasp both industry dynamics and bankruptcy processes.

Scale and aggregation offer another path for sophisticated investors. By building significant positions in specific bankruptcy cases, investors can influence creditor negotiations and reorganization outcomes. This strategy demands substantial capital and expertise but can generate outsized returns.

Timing Considerations

Timing shapes investment decisions throughout bankruptcy cases. To be clear, though, having "good timing" doesn't just mean buying early. Early-stage purchases offer steeper discounts but carry more risk.

Bankruptcy cases can stretch for years, locking up capital and creating hidden costs. And as cases progress and recovery prospects become clearer, claim prices typically rise. Smart investors weigh the potential upside of early entry against these holding costs. Some choose to trade actively throughout the process, responding to shifting information and market sentiment. Others may wait for specific milestones, like the filing of asset schedules or announcement of a reorganization plan, before investing, accepting higher prices for greater clarity.

Executing and Managing Trade Claim Investments

Once an investor has identified an attractive trade claim opportunity, conducted thorough due diligence, and decided the time is right to take action, the next step is to negotiate and document the claim purchase.

The process starts with price and term negotiations. Buyers and sellers must agree not just on the purchase price but also on the timing of payment, treatment of post-petition interest or fees, and representations and warranties from each party. These negotiations often reflect market conditions and case-specific factors that could affect claim value. Some buyers employ a strategy where they try to tie up a seller in a trade confirmation and wait to pay until they have greater certainty. Most sellers want to be paid immediately. In the Madoff case and FTX cases, this wait-and-see strategy led to many broken trades and litigation.

Before proceeding with any transaction, buyers must conduct know-your-customer and anti-money laundering checks on the seller. Particularly in the crypto bankruptcy cases, Russian-owned claims were of no interest to buyers because they were perceived as risky due to potential links to sanctioned entities, including the Russian government or organized crime outfits. These compliance requirements, while sometimes seemingly bureaucratic, protect against fraud and ensure regulatory compliance. They become particularly important in large bankruptcy cases where claims might change hands multiple times.

The purchase agreement documents all transaction terms. Sometimes, this document is called an Assignment Agreement or Assignment of Claim Agreement. A sample is shown and available for download in the appendix. This critical document states the purchase price, payment terms, and any closing conditions. It also addresses potential issues like claim objections or disputes that might arise during the bankruptcy process. Experienced investors often develop standardized agreements to streamline the process while protecting their interests.

Finally, buyers must file a transfer notice with the bankruptcy court to formally record the change in claim ownership. This step ensures proper distribution of any recoveries and establishes the buyer's standing in the bankruptcy case.

Even if you feel like you don't need any outside help, I strongly encourage you to work closely with experienced bankruptcy counsel throughout this process. Legal expertise helps you navigate procedural requirements and protects against potential pitfalls that could compromise claim value or validity. Consider it an inexpensive insurance policy, if you like. Trust me: it's worth the peace of mind.

TRADE CLAIMS INVESTING STRATEGIES

Monitoring the Bankruptcy Case and Claim Status

After purchasing a trade claim, investors must actively monitor the bankruptcy case to track their claim status and developments affecting recovery prospects. Regular review of court filings and docket entries provides essential updates on case progression. Key documents include proposed restructuring plans, disclosure statements, and orders approving asset sales or other transactions. The timing and substance of these filings often signal how recoveries might unfold.

Court hearings offer direct insight into case dynamics. While not every hearing warrants attendance, significant proceedings, like plan confirmation hearings or contested matters, can reveal crucial information about recovery prospects. Many investors participate by telephone to stay informed while managing time and travel costs.

Building relationships with other creditors and stakeholders creates valuable information networks. Regular communication with trade creditors, the official creditors' committee (a separate entity that represents the interests of all unsecured creditors), and other parties can surface early warnings about potential issues or opportunities. These relationships sometimes lead to coordinated strategies that enhance recoveries for all claim holders.

Financial reports and debtor disclosures demand careful analysis. Monthly operating reports, claims registers, and other periodic filings reveal trends in the debtor's performance and potential changes in claim values. Smart investors track these metrics systematically, looking for early indicators of whether recoveries might exceed or fall short of expectations. Changes in business performance, unexpected liabilities, or shifts in restructuring strategy can dramatically affect claim values. Successful investors maintain vigilance until their claims are fully resolved.

Exit Strategies

When is the right time to sell? Exit strategies will depend on various factors, including an investor's overall investment objectives, the status of the bankruptcy case, and market conditions for trade claims at the time.

Some investors choose to hold their claims throughout the bankruptcy case, expecting to receive distributions once a restructuring plan becomes effective. This approach suits investors with longer-term horizons and confidence in ultimate recovery prospects. But in many cases they are traded numerous times before a plan of reorganization is even approved; this is what happened with claims in the Madoff, Lehman, FTX, and Sears (covered in the next section) bankruptcies. In Madoff, some claims traders bought claims at 30%, sold them at 60%, and bought more when the market softened at 50%..

This approach makes sense when new information suggests peaked recovery values or when other opportunities offer better returns. Experienced investors recognize that claim values often plateau once major case uncertainties are resolved. At this point, holding longer rarely produces additional value. Formal auction processes sometimes provide structured exit opportunities. Another common strategy in claims trading is aggregating smaller claims, which typically sell for less money, and selling them as part of a package.

I advise clients with bankruptcy claims that the time to exit is when information is plentiful, meaning the process has provided full transparency. What's the point of holding an asset that is highly unlikely to appreciate further in value? At that moment, you know what you'll get, and you know you probably won't be getting much more. It's time to cash in and move on.

CASE STUDY: SEARS BANKRUPTCY

To see how a strategy for investing in bankruptcy trade claims can work, let's explore the Sears bankruptcy.

When Sears filed for Chapter 11 bankruptcy on October 15, 2018, it owed vendors over $2 billion. At the time of its bankruptcy filing it had 700 stores, 68,000 employees, and $16 billion in sales. At its peak, the company, which had been in business for over 100 years, boasted over 5,000 stores. But even in its diminished state it was still a significant player in retail, so it's not surprising that it owed so much to vendors. It was an attractive customer for large manufacturers who made good money by mass-producing products.

One Chinese vendor, ShoeMe, which manufactured girls' shoes, was owed over $1 million by Sears. The amount owed was not from a single invoice but a series of invoices over different time periods. From a bankruptcy perspective, these invoices constituted different types of claims, some of which were more valuable than others. At the same time, as a result of receiving payments from Sears within the ninety-day period before the bankruptcy filing, ShoeMe also had a significant liability to Sears. The most valuable claim ShoeMe held was for goods that Sears received within twenty days of the filing. Let me explain.

According to Section 503(b)(9) of the Bankruptcy Code, any goods delivered to Sears within the twenty days before its bankruptcy filing—that is, between September 26, 2018, and October 15, 2018—were entitled to administrative expense priority treatment. This provision exists because vendors who continue to supply goods to a financially distressed company help keep the business operational, rather than cutting off supply and forcing liquidation. As a result, these vendors are given higher repayment priority over general unsecured creditors, in recognition of their role in preserving the company's value, which in turn, benefits both the debtor and its secured lenders.

ShoeMe sent, and Sears received, $500,000 in goods after September 26, but ShoeMe was still owed $500,000 for goods received before that date. However, ShoeMe also had its own liability to Sears. Under Section 547 of the Bankruptcy Code, if a vendor receives payments within ninety days of a bankruptcy (in this case, between July 15 and October 15), they could have the liability to pay back the bankruptcy estate.

The reasoning is that bankruptcy is supposed to be a fair and equitable process for all similarly situated creditors. If one creditor is demanding payment when the company is insolvent, they should not receive better treatment than another vendor who isn't demanding payment. In fact, ShoeMe received $250,000 on August 15, 2018, as payment for goods shipped. Like all vendors, ShoeMe wasn't looking to sell goods to Sears and not be paid. The terms of its vendor agreements with Sears were for it to be paid in 30 days. Sears had been a great customer for ShoeMe, one of its largest, and typically, Sears paid ShoeMe, but it was often late in payment.

When Sears filed bankruptcy in October 2018, shortly before the period between Thanksgiving and Christmas, ShoeMe was caught off guard. Most retailers file bankruptcy after the New Year because that's when they have the most cash on hand. However, Sears could not get goods into its stores and needed a DIP loan to provide comfort to vendors, and the only way to do that was through bankruptcy. ShoeMe, on the other hand, needed money to pay its suppliers. By late January 2019, when it became clear that the only buyer for Sears was its current owner, Eddie Lampert, and that cash was still extremely tight, ShoeMe sought to sell its bankruptcy claims.

Buyers reviewing their bankruptcy claims learned the following:

ShoeMe had a combined $1 million unsecured claim composed of:

1. a $500,000 503(b)(9) claim, which should be ultimately worth 100% on the dollar because a bankruptcy debtor cannot emerge from bankruptcy without paying its administrative creditors 100% unless otherwise agreed
2. a $500,000 general unsecured claim, which is virtually worthless
3. a $500,000 potential preference liability to the debtor that the bankruptcy estate could sue for

What do you think buyers of bankruptcy trade claims offered ShoeMe?

Buyers were prepared to pay ShoeMe 80% for the $500,000 503(b)(9) claim, or $400,000. However, they weren't willing to pay them anything for the $500,000 general unsecured claim. Recovery here was highly unlikely. But wait: buyers also wanted a massive discount on ShoeMe's 503(b)(9) claim because ShoeMe had a $250,000 potential liability. Buyers also wanted an indemnification from ShoeMe in the event ShoeMe was sued for bankruptcy preference.

This was extremely unappealing to ShoeMe, so they didn't sell. They couldn't stomach that for a $1 million claim, someone was only offering them $250,000 and requiring indemnification.

Here's what happened next. In February 2019, Lampert finalized his bid to buy back Sears, but rather than paying the full purchase price in cash, he became embroiled in protracted litigation with the bankruptcy estate over the terms of the acquisition. This prolonged uncertainty had a ripple effect on creditors, delaying payments and increasing financial risk for vendors like ShoeMe.

By spring 2019, ShoeMe was sued by the Sears Creditors' Committee, which sought to claw back $500,000 under Bankruptcy Code Section 547, arguing that payments made to ShoeMe within 90 days of the bankruptcy filing constituted preferential transfers.

Before the lawsuit, ShoeMe had received an interim distribution of 10% ($50,000) on its 503(b)(9) claim, a partial payout from the bankruptcy estate. However, shortly afterward, ShoeMe received a formal demand letter from the bankruptcy estate, asserting that it owed $500,000 in clawback payments. After several months of legal negotiations, ShoeMe successfully reduced its clawback liability to $100,000, largely by offsetting part of the demand against its outstanding 503(b)(9) claim. This meant that, rather than forfeiting the full $500,000, ShoeMe's 503(b)(9) claim was reduced to $350,000.

Further complicating matters, Sears filed a bankruptcy plan of reorganization that outlined partial payments for 503(b)(9) claims while litigation against Lampert remained unresolved. The plan specified that creditors would receive 80% of their 503(b)(9) claims on an interim basis, as the estate generated proceeds from litigation, or 100% recovery upon full resolution, but with no set timeline for final payments.

Given the uncertainty surrounding the litigation outcome and payment timing, at this point buyers of bankruptcy claims were only willing to pay 20% of the face value of ShoeMe's remaining claim, or $70,000. However, ShoeMe faced severe financial pressure during the pandemic and badly needed liquidity.

In March 2021, nearly two and a half years after Sears's bankruptcy filing, ShoeMe opted to sell the remainder of its claims for $70,000. This meant that ShoeMe's total recovery on its original $1 million claim was $120,000 (12%).

Now, let's look at how the buyer of ShoeMe's claim made out.

The buyer acquired ShoeMe's claim for $70,000 in April 2021, with a maximum possible recovery of $350,000 if the full 503(b)(9) payout materialized. In early June 2021, the buyer received an interim distribution of 10% ($35,000) on the claim, immediately recovering half of their investment. By the fall of 2022, the litigation against Lampert was resolved, nearly four years after Sears' bankruptcy began. In early winter 2023, the buyer received the final payout on their claim, bringing their total proceeds to $350,000. In the end, the buyer turned a $70,000 investment into $350,000, a 5x return (see Fig. 2).

So, what are the lessons from the Sears bankruptcy for claims traders? First, at the outset, it appeared certain that 503(b)(9) claims would be paid swiftly and in full. Some claims traders paid 80% for these claims and made no money while waiting nearly four years to be paid. Second, you have to know the potential liabilities associated with claims before buying them. Vendors who received funds during the ninety-day preference period had claims that were worth less than those who did not.

Furthermore, chasing after foreign vendors is never an easy exercise, and even with indemnification provisions, it rarely makes for a good trade. Third, you have to know the players involved in a bankruptcy case. Eddie Lampert is a smart businessman and has the resources to conduct a protracted fight with the bankruptcy estate.

In most claims-trading situations, the best opportunities arise well before clarity emerges. However, in extremely rare cases, such as with Sears, prolonged litigation and unique circumstances can create opportunities for those who wait. But these situations are the exception. The rule still applies.

As I've noted earlier, but it bears repeating, successful trade claim investing requires a combination of deep industry knowledge, legal and financial expertise, and a healthy risk appetite. Investors can unlock significant value in this niche market by carefully selecting claims, timing investments, and managing the bankruptcy process.

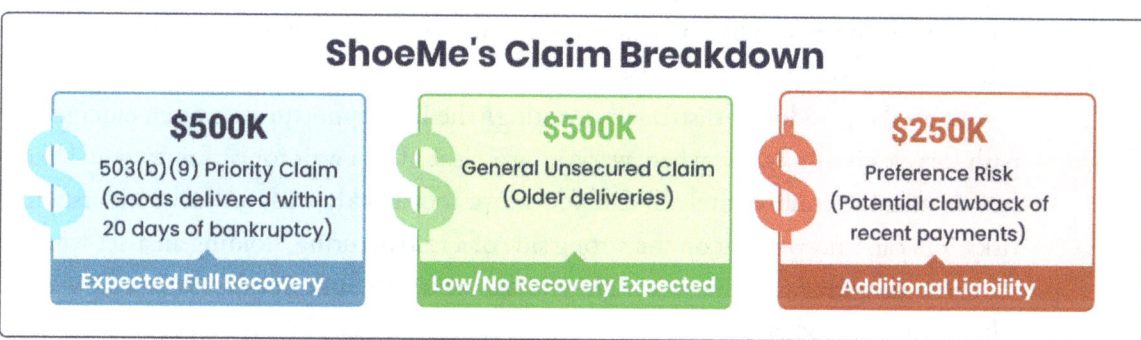
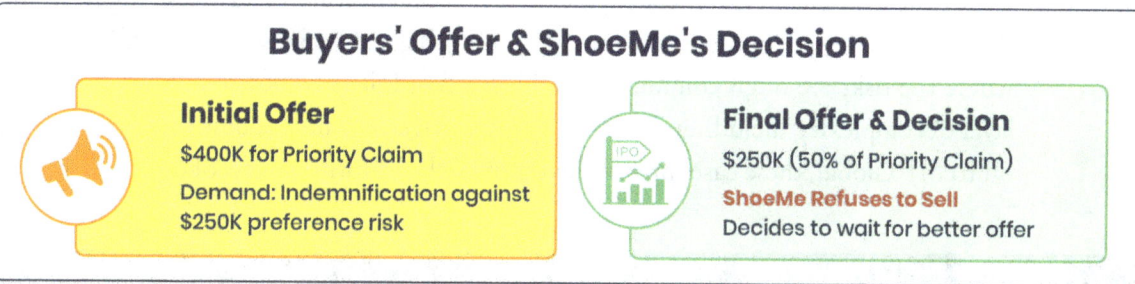
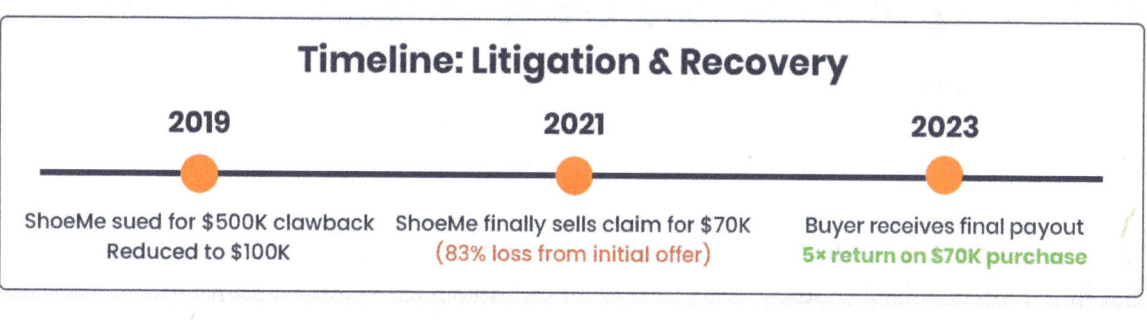
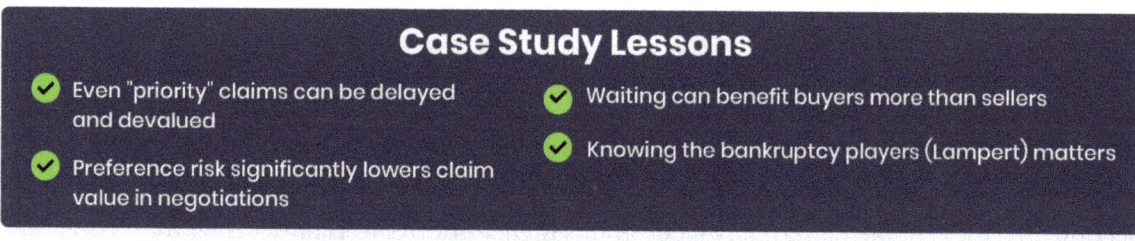

Figure 2: Sears Bankruptcy: ShoeMe Trade Claim Case Study

Final Thoughts

Throughout this chapter, we've explored trade claims investing and how it requires more than just financial analysis. It demands an understanding of legal complexities, market psychology, and, most importantly, timing. Carl Icahn's Las Vegas bets were not just about scooping up distressed assets; they were about recognizing when fear had driven prices too low and also when optimism had taken hold.

The ShoeMe case in the Sears bankruptcy reinforces this lesson. What seemed like a straightforward priority claim ended up entangled in litigation delays, preference risk, and unpredictable court rulings. Investors who rushed in too early paid a steep price for their certainty, while those who had patience, and the ability to withstand volatility, walked away with substantial gains.

That's the paradox of distressed investing. The best opportunities often emerge when the path forward is murky, not when everything is clear. If you wait for certainty, you'll likely overpay or miss the trade entirely. But if you move too quickly without fully understanding the risks, you can find yourself on the wrong side of a restructuring, holding an asset worth far less than you imagined. It's always a high-wire balancing act split between knowing what to buy, when to act, and when to walk away.

In the next chapter, we will explore a very different kind of distressed opportunity, one that involves navigating fraud, misconduct, and collapsed Ponzi schemes. Unlike trade claims, where the risks are often commercial and legal, fraudulent bankruptcies add an entirely new layer of complexity, including clawbacks, trustee litigation, and reputational issues. From Madoff to MF Global, these cases present investors with the ultimate test of diligence and strategy.

KEY INSIGHTS

1. Carl Icahn's success in distressed investing wasn't just about buying undervalued assets; it was about understanding market cycles, timing, and the psychology of financial distress.
2. Trade claim investing operates in an opaque and inefficient market where those with better information and execution skills gain a significant advantage.
3. There is no formal centralized exchange for trade claims, so investors must actively source opportunities by monitoring bankruptcy filings, leveraging industry relationships, and navigating complex legal landscapes.
4. Understanding a debtor's financial position, capital structure, and creditor hierarchy is critical to assessing the potential recovery value of a claim.
5. Bankruptcy court dockets provide key insights into creditor lists, asset distributions, and the likelihood of a successful recovery, but interpreting these filings requires both experience and legal knowledge.
6. Section 503(b)(9) of the Bankruptcy Code grants higher priority to claims arising from goods delivered within twenty days before a bankruptcy filing, offering trade claim investors an opportunity to target claims with a greater chance of recovery.

7. Timing matters as much as pricing; buying a claim too early can mean facing unnecessary litigation risk, while waiting too long can result in missing the best entry point.
8. Preference risk is a significant factor in trade claim investing, as payments made within ninety days of a bankruptcy filing can be clawed back, impacting the true value of a claim.
9. Successful investors in this space know that legal arguments and procedural delays can significantly impact the recovery timeline and final payout.
10. The Sears bankruptcy and the ShoeMe case illustrate how even priority claims can be entangled in litigation, preference actions, and unexpected court decisions, challenging initial expectations of value.
11. Patience and volatility tolerance often separate the best trade claim investors from those who exit too soon or take on excessive risk without sufficient due diligence.
12. Distressed investing is a paradox. The best opportunities emerge when uncertainty is high, but the greatest risks come from acting too quickly or waiting too long.
13. Recognizing when fear has driven prices too low and when optimism has taken hold is the key to maximizing returns and avoiding costly mistakes.
14. The ultimate skill in trade claim investing isn't just finding undervalued claims; it's knowing what matters, when to act, and when to walk away.

CHAPTER 11

Investing in Fraudulent Bankruptcies

The collapse of Bernard Madoff's investment empire stands as one of the most shocking financial scandals in history. What appeared to be a stable and successful business was, in reality, the largest Ponzi scheme ever uncovered, unraveling amid the chaos of the 2008 financial crisis.

It was a phone call that changed everything. On December 10, 2008, Bernie Madoff's sons, Mark and Andrew, reported to federal authorities that their father had made a confession: His entire investment advisory business was "all just one big lie." Madoff admitted to running a massive Ponzi scheme, an estimated $50 billion fraud, the largest in history.

The financial markets were already reeling from the mortgage loan crisis and the collapse of Bear Stearns and Lehman Brothers, which in part was what led to Madoff being uncovered. The news sent additional shockwaves through the financial world. Madoff, a former chairman of the NASDAQ stock exchange, had long been respected on Wall Street. His firm, Bernard L. Madoff Investment Securities LLC (BLMIS), had operated for decades, delivering high annual returns of about 12% and boasting profitable months 96% of the time. Among his clients were wealthy individuals, celebrities, and charitable organizations.

Investigators soon uncovered that Madoff's success was nearly a complete illusion. The scheme was simple: he created a fake fund and used money from new investors to pay returns to existing ones, the classic definition of a Ponzi scheme (see Fig. 1). When the global financial crisis hit in 2008, many clients rushed to withdraw their funds, and the scheme crumbled under its own weight. Ironically, Madoff had also founded a legitimate (and successful) trading desk years before, which he ran in parallel to his bogus fund. While there is no evidence that the trading desk was explicitly created as a cover, its success and credibility likely made the overall operation appear more legitimate, helping him avoid scrutiny.

THE DISTRESSED INVESTING PLAYBOOK

HOW A PONZI SCHEME WORKS
Cycle repeats until collapse

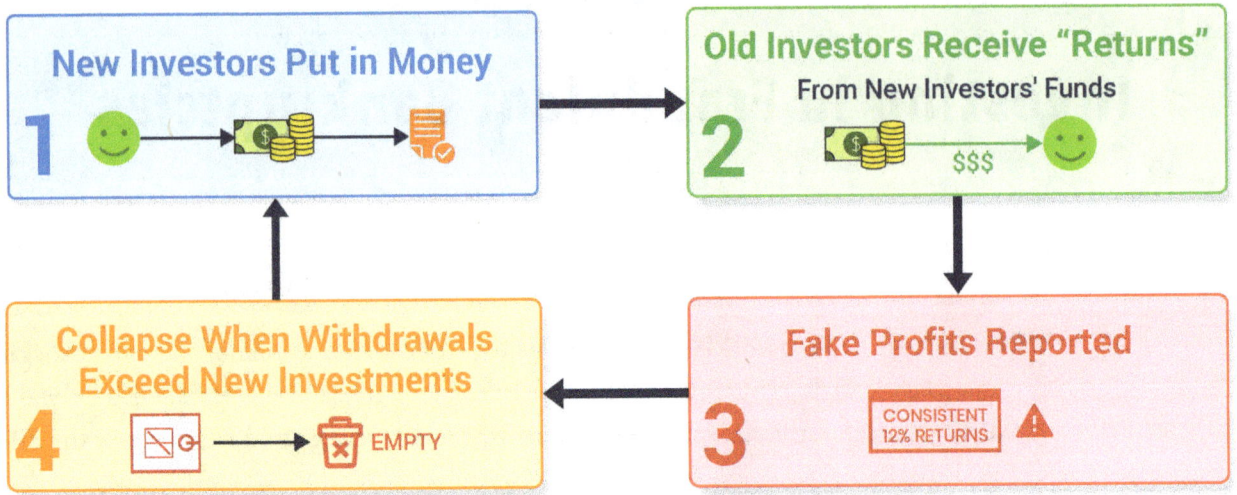

Ponzi schemes collapse when new investment inflows can't keep up with promised returns.

Figure 1: How a Ponzi Scheme Works

The fallout was devastating. Thousands of investors lost billions of dollars, with some losing their entire life savings. Charitable organizations invested with Madoff were forced to shut down and could not continue their work. The impact was felt globally, with investors from Europe, Latin America, and Asia also falling victim to the scheme.

As the details of Madoff's fraud began to emerge, questions arose about how he had avoided detection for so long. Red flags about Madoff's operations had been raised for years, with some investors and financial experts expressing skepticism about his consistently high returns. Yet, despite multiple investigations by the SEC, Madoff's ploy continued unabated. It was later revealed that Madoff had cultivated a reputation as a skilled and trustworthy investor, which he leveraged to consistently attract new clients and evade scrutiny. He was known for his philanthropy and was active in the Jewish community, using his standing to build a network of loyal investors. Madoff also used his position on Wall Street to deflect attention, serving on various industry committees and even advising the SEC on market structure issues.

The Madoff case highlighted significant gaps in financial regulation and oversight. The SEC faced intense criticism for its failure to uncover the fraud despite receiving numerous tips and conducting multiple investigations over the years. The agency's Office of Inspector General would later issue a scathing report detailing the missteps and missed opportunities that allowed Madoff's scheme to continue for so long.

The case also raised questions about the role of feeder funds, i.e., investment vehicles that channeled money to Madoff's firm and the due diligence (or lack thereof) performed by these funds and their managers. Many investors entrusted their money to these feeder funds, believing they were diversifying their investments and reducing risk. Instead, they had unwittingly concentrated their investments with a single, fraudulent manager.

Since Madoff, there have been numerous other high-profile Ponzi schemes and financial frauds, each with their own unique twists and red flags. From Allen Stanford's $7 billion scheme that centered on fraudulent certificates of deposit to the Fyre Festival fiasco, where a supposed luxury music festival turned out to be a complete sham, these cases highlight the enduring allure of "too good to be true" investment opportunities and the importance of investor vigilance. In the following sections, we'll delve into each of these cases in more detail, examining the red flags, the fallout, the lessons learned, and the opportunities for investors.

Investing in Fraud Cases: The Madoff Payoff

The idea of investing in a fraud case like the Madoff Ponzi scheme may seem counterintuitive at first. After all, the very nature of a Ponzi scheme is based on deception, and most of its "investors" end up losing money. However, some investors and institutions specifically seek out opportunities to invest in the aftermath of a fraud case, intending to profit from the recovery process.

In general, investing in fraud cases involves buying claims from the scheme's victims at a discount, with the expectation that the eventual recoveries from the liquidation process will exceed the claims' purchase price. This type of investment carries significant risks, as the outcome of the recovery process is often uncertain and can take years to resolve. However, for investors with a high risk tolerance and a deep understanding of the legal and financial complexities involved, fraud cases can offer the potential for substantial returns.

In the Madoff case, multiple investment opportunities emerged following the fraud's exposure. A secondary market developed for BLMIS claims as the Securities Investor Protection Act (SIPA) liquidation process progressed. Investors assessed the likely payouts and bought and sold claims accordingly. Irving Picard, the Madoff trustee, established an orderly transfer process that enabled this market to function.

Beyond direct Madoff claims, another secondary market emerged for claims tied to feeder funds, investment funds that had pooled client capital and placed it with Madoff. Since many of these funds went through separate insolvency proceedings, their claims were also actively traded, often at substantial discounts.

Litigation financing presented yet another avenue for investors. Some specialized firms provided funding to support legal efforts by fiduciaries pursuing clawback lawsuits, actions aimed at recovering funds from investors who withdrew more money than they had contributed. In exchange for financing these lawsuits, litigation financiers earned a share of the recoveries, turning legal action into an investment vehicle. A separate fund, the Madoff Victim Fund (MVF), was created by the DOJ to distribute forfeited assets to victims. It was administered by former SEC Chairman Richard Breeden. Some investors sought to acquire claims eligible for MVF distributions, betting on steady payouts from the government-managed fund.

Investing in fraud cases like the Madoff scandal requires significant due diligence, legal expertise, and a willingness to lock up capital for an extended period with an uncertain outcome. There are also ethical considerations, as some critics argue that profiting from the misfortune of fraud victims is morally questionable. While investors profit, victims may feel further exploited as their misfortune becomes a speculative opportunity.

However, proponents of this type of investing say that it can benefit victims by providing them with much-needed liquidity and shifting the risk of uncertain recovery to investors who are better equipped to bear it. In the Madoff case, the active involvement of institutional investors and litigation financiers may have contributed to the relatively high recovery rate compared to other Ponzi schemes.

In the aftermath of Madoff's confession, the Securities Investor Protection Corporation (SIPC) initiated a liquidation proceeding for BLMIS under the SIPA. The court then appointed Picard as the SIPA trustee to oversee the liquidation and recover funds for Madoff's victims. Picard's task was monumental, as he had to untangle a complex web of transactions and identify the true victims of the fraud.

A SIPA liquidation process involves several steps. First, all customer-related assets are put into a comingled fund of customer property, which is then allocated based on the trustee's motion and the court's approval. The trustee must then determine the allowed claimants and the total net equity of their claims before making any distributions. To speed up financial relief to victims, the SIPC can provide cash advances to the trustee for distribution, up to a maximum of $500,000 per allowed claim.

More than 15 years after Madoff was arrested and Picard was appointed SIPA trustee, recovery efforts continue. As of April 19, 2024, the SIPC had committed approximately $850.4 million to the BLMIS liquidation, with $592.2 million still outstanding after reimbursements from the Customer Fund. As of May 17, 2024, the trustee had received 16,521 claims from Madoff's investors. Of these, 2,656 claims, or ~16.1%, were allowed, representing a total value of $19.6 billion. Another 2,692 claims were denied, while 10,734 claims were denied because the claimants did not have an account *under their name* with BLMIS.

In this case, the liquidation process differs from most fraudulent bankruptcy proceedings because it involves two separate (dual) restitution bodies. A dual restitution structure ensures that both direct and indirect victims have paths to potential recovery, though through separate processes. Direct investors who had accounts with BLMIS could file claims in the main bankruptcy proceeding overseen by Trustee Picard. Indirect investors who invested through feeder funds cannot participate in this proceeding; they must file claims against the feeder funds or the MVF instead.

As of April 19, 2024, Trustee Picard had recovered or reached agreements to recover approximately $14.7 billion, an unprecedented sum for a Ponzi scheme recovery effort (see Fig. 2). These recoveries have come from various sources, including settlement agreements with feeder funds, banks, and other entities that facilitated Madoff's fraud.

MADOFF TOTAL RECOVERIES BY YEAR

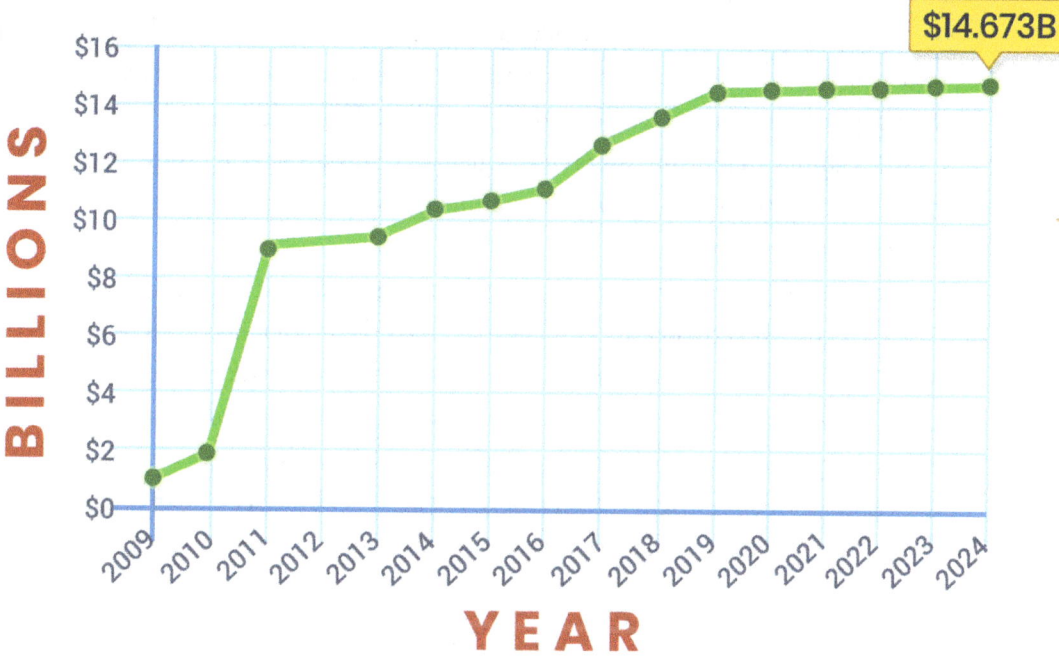

Figure 2: Madoff Total Recoveries by Year (2009–2024)

Some notable recoveries included:

- $860 million from Kingate Global Fund and Kingate Euro Fund (2019)
- $687 million from Thema International Fund (2017)
- $1 billion from the Tremont Group (2011)
- $5 billion from the estate of Jeffry Picower (2011)
- $326 million from the U.S. Internal Revenue Service (2011)
- $543 million from JPMorgan Chase (2014)

These recoveries have allowed the trustee to make significant distributions to Madoff's victims over the years. As of early 2025, the trustee had distributed $14.5 billion from the Customer Fund to allowed claimants, and a good majority of the victims have recovered substantially all their money.

Courting Controversy: Clawback and Trustee Fees

The recovery process has not been without controversy. Some of Picard's largest recoveries have come from clawback lawsuits, where the trustee sought to recover funds from investors who withdrew more money from their BLMIS accounts than they initially invested. Picard defines losses based on the "net equity method" as "money paid in minus money paid out," meaning investors can only recover the initial money they gave Madoff, excluding any interest received (see Fig. 3). These lawsuits targeted institutional investors and individuals, including some who claimed they were innocent victims.

In 2015, the U.S. Supreme Court limited the scope of these clawback suits, ruling that the trustee could only recover transfers made within two years of the bankruptcy filing rather than the six years allowed under New York State law. This reduction in scope greatly limited the trustee's ability to reclaim assets from early withdrawals, leaving some potentially recoverable funds beyond reach and significantly reducing the amount of money the trustee could potentially recover for victims.

Another point of contention is the fees paid to the trustee and his legal team. As of March 31, 2024, the SIPA trustee and his law firm, BakerHostetler, had been paid $1.6 billion in fees, while other special counsel, consultants, and administrative costs totaled over $771 million. Critics have argued that these fees are excessive and divert funds away from Madoff's victims. However, proponents of the recovery effort point out that none of these fees are paid out of the Customer Fund, which is solely for the benefit of allowed claimants. Instead, the SIPC pays these costs through advances that are separate from the recoveries obtained for victims.

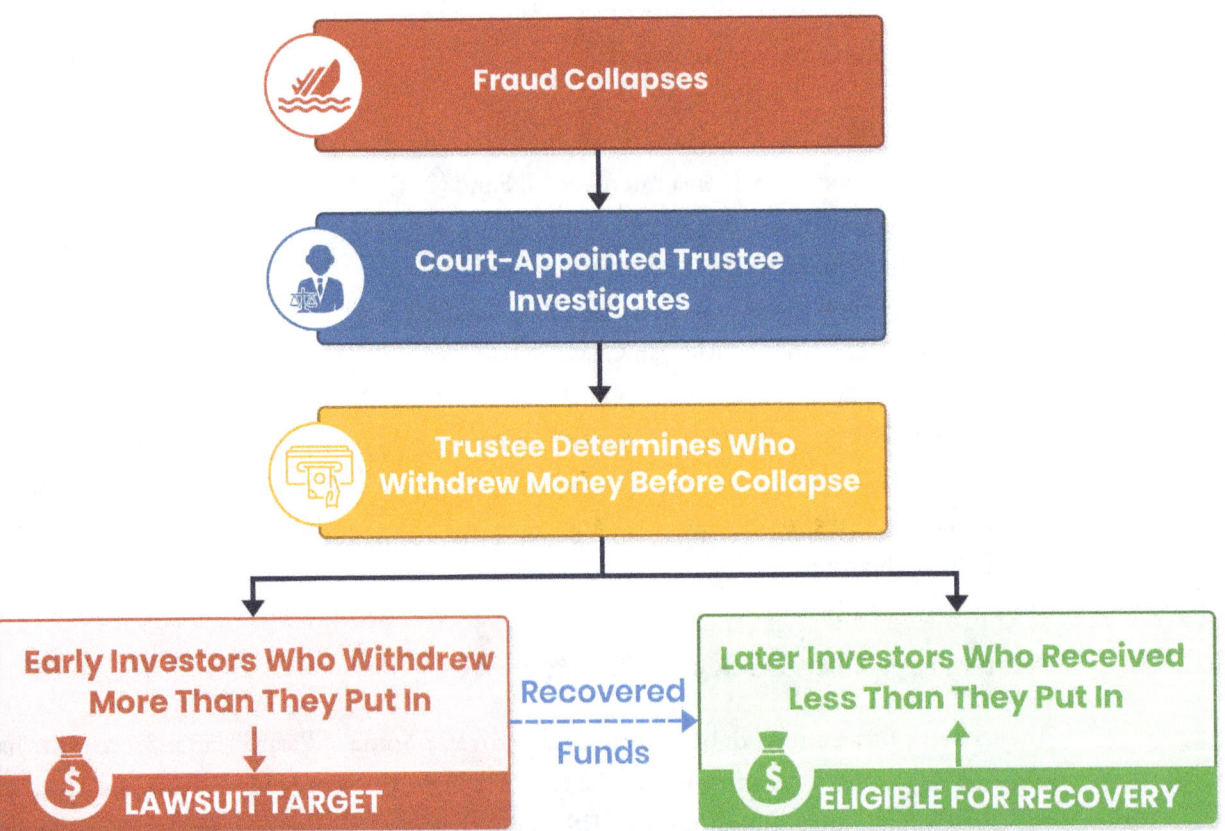

Figure 3: Clawback Lawsuits: Who Gets Sued?

INVESTING IN FRAUDULENT BANKRUPTCIES

Despite the challenges and controversies, the Madoff recovery effort stands out for its scale and success compared to other Ponzi scheme cases. The sheer magnitude of the fraud, the complexity of the recovery process, and the dogged pursuit of assets by Trustee Picard and his team have resulted in unprecedented returns for victims. Yet even with these remarkable recoveries, many of Madoff's victims will never be made whole. The fraud's impact extended far beyond financial losses, shattering trust, upending lives, and damaging numerous charitable organizations that had invested with Madoff.

While some sophisticated investors were able to profit from the Madoff case by buying claims or financing recoveries, the vast majority of those involved were victims who suffered significant financial and personal losses. The case serves as a stark reminder of the risks of financial fraud and the importance of a robust regulatory framework to protect investors.

The Madoff Ponzi scheme also underscores the importance of diversification, due diligence, and a healthy skepticism of "too good to be true" returns for fund investors. For regulators and lawmakers, it highlights the need for constant adaptation and strengthening of the rules and mechanisms designed to protect investors from fraud. As the recovery process winds down and the final payouts are made, the legacy of the Madoff scandal will continue to be felt by those who were directly impacted and those who study financial fraud.

For distressed investors, the Madoff case has been an absolute dream come true. First, returns have been spectacular. Second, because of the ample amount of product (Madoff investors), trading claims have been fairly liquid. There are the claims of direct investors ($17.9 billion) and those of investors in feeder funds. Some analysts have estimated that claims on these funds exceed $50 billion.

Looking back, it's remarkable how drastically the situation had changed. I still remember receiving a call in early 2009 from the attorney for a Madoff investor who wanted a bid for his client's claim. The conversation went something like this:

Attorney: Joe, you're never gonna believe this, but I have a client who holds a $2 million Madoff claim. How much do you think it's worth?
Me: The current market is 29 cents.
Attorney: 29 cents; oh boy, that seems low.
Me: Well, Picard only has a little over a billion dollars on $18 billion of claims; that's less than 10 cents.

This is how the dialogue goes in the beginning of all big cases: claims buyers do a quick back-of-the-envelope assessment of the amount of claims and the cash on hand and make projections.

In addition to buying and selling Madoff direct and feeder fund claims, some investors took another tack: financing trustees and law firms as they pursued recovery against parties involved in the Madoff case. These "litigation finance" opportunities proved to be a windfall for firms like Fortress and others.

When I ran the trade claims group at CRT Capital, our firm sourced hundreds of millions of dollars of Madoff claims at prices anywhere from 50 to 90 cents. We spoke and met with numerous investors and third parties involved in the case and made it our business to become as smart as possible about the marketplace. We also used the notoriety of the Madoff cases by giving quotes to the press and serving as valuation experts for institutional funds. This resulted in numerous "inbound" calls from investors and other professionals. Perhaps most significantly, Madoff led me to the Stanford International Bank case, one of my most profitable trading ventures ever. Let's go over it.

The Stanford International Bank Scandal

While the Madoff scandal remains the largest Ponzi scheme in history, it is far from the only case of large-scale financial fraud. Just as Madoff's web of deception unraveled under the weight of a financial crisis, other schemes were also exposed during the turbulent economic times of the late 2000s. One of the most egregious was the collapse of Stanford International Bank (SIB), a sprawling fraud led by Allen Stanford, whose deceitful practices and extravagant lifestyle rivaled Madoff's in audacity.

In the financial fraud world, SIB stands out as a particularly egregious example of greed, deception, and the betrayal of investor trust. At the heart of this scandal was R. Allen Stanford, a flamboyant Texas financier who built a sprawling financial empire that stretched from the Caribbean to Latin America and beyond.

Stanford's rise to prominence began in the 1980s when he founded Guardian International Bank on the tiny island of Montserrat in the British West Indies. He later moved the bank to Antigua, renaming it Stanford International Bank, and began aggressively marketing its primary product: certificates of deposit (CDs) that offered unusually high returns, often exceeding those of traditional banks by several percentage points.

For years, Stanford and his associates used the allure of these high-yield CDs to attract investors worldwide, particularly in Latin America and the Caribbean. Many of these investors were middle-class retirees or small business owners who entrusted their life savings to SIB, drawn in by the promise of steady, above-market returns and the bank's seemingly solid reputation. However, behind the veneer of success and stability, Stanford was orchestrating a massive Ponzi scheme that would eventually collapse, leaving thousands of investors with staggering losses. Instead of investing the funds from CD sales as promised, Stanford used the money to finance his lavish lifestyle, fund risky business ventures, and pay off earlier investors, all while providing fabricated account statements to maintain the illusion of profitability.

The scheme began to unravel in 2009, as the global financial crisis triggered a surge in CD redemption requests that Stanford couldn't meet. U.S. authorities, who had been investigating Stanford for years, finally moved to shut down his operations and seize his assets. Stanford was arrested and charged with multiple counts of fraud, money laundering, and obstruction of justice.

INVESTING IN FRAUDULENT BANKRUPTCIES

In the wake of Stanford's arrest, the true scale of the fraud came to light. Investigators discovered that SIB had sold approximately $7 billion worth of CDs to more than 21,000 investors in over 100 countries. However, the bank's actual assets were a mere fraction of this amount, with Stanford and his associates siphoning billions of dollars over the years. The fallout from the scandal was devastating for the thousands of individuals who had invested their savings with SIB. The impact was particularly severe in Antigua and other Caribbean nations, where SIB had been a major employer and a pillar of the local economy.

In the aftermath of Stanford's arrest, two main insolvency proceedings were initiated to try to recover funds for the victims. In the United States, a federal court in Texas appointed a receiver to take control of Stanford's U.S.-based assets and pursue claims on behalf of investors. Meanwhile, in Antigua, the Eastern Caribbean Supreme Court appointed joint liquidators to oversee the wind down of SIB and other Stanford-affiliated entities.

Over the years, the U.S. receiver and the Antiguan joint liquidators have worked to identify and recover assets related to the Stanford fraud. This process has involved a complex web of legal actions, negotiations, and asset sales spanning multiple jurisdictions.

To date, the U.S. receiver has collected nearly $2.7 billion for investors. The largest recoveries came from a settlement of a $5 billion asserted claim against TD Bank and a $155 million claim against HSBC in the United Kingdom. The basis for the receiver's claim against TD Bank was that they knew or should have known of Stanford's fraudulent conduct. This is a fairly common assertion in fraud cases against financial institutions by trustees. The fascinating thing is that the joint liquidator in Stanford made the same assertion and lost its case against TD Bank in Canada. The point to be taken from these disparate results is that litigation is fraught with uncertainty, and investors cannot safely assume that causes of action will ever be 100% successful.

There is another interesting dynamic in Stanford: the longevity of the case. Stanford started in 2009, and it took 15 years for investors to get the bulk of their recovery. Why? Because the majority of the recovery was dependent on a successful outcome of litigation against TD Bank. And guess what? Banks have plenty of resources to litigate.

An important difference between the Stanford and Madoff cases was the involvement of the DOJ. In the Madoff case, the DOJ pursued criminal investigations against financial institutions like JPMorgan, leading to major settlements. In contrast, the Stanford case did not involve similar criminal prosecution threats against banks. As a result, TD Bank's liability risk was purely civil, allowing it to prolong the litigation without the pressure of potential criminal charges. This fundamental difference made the Stanford case far more protracted than Madoff's.

Stanford was a great case for the patient investor for the following reasons. First, there was ample product. There were approximately 20,000 investors with about $5 billion in claims. Second, the initial picture of cash available for distributions was ugly, ugly, ugly—pennies. Accordingly, in 2011, when Stanford claims started trading, they sold for less than 10 cents on the dollar. As an investor paying 10 cents, the most one could lose was 10 cents. Furthermore, Stanford began to make what's known as "interim" distributions in 2014. The first distribution was one penny (that's right, 1%). That provided further leverage to claims buyers, because it confirmed just how dire the situation was.

Ultimately, Stanford creditors will receive approximately 40% of their net investment back.

Speaking of net investment: the concept of net invested capital is important for distressed investors to understand. In fraud cases where less than 100% of the investor's capital is being returned, fiduciaries look at the net amount of capital invested in determining a claim. That means if you invested $100 and were promised a 10% annual return and got back $50 during the life of your investment, your net invested capital and your allowed claim in the insolvency proceeding is only $50. The fact that you had lost opportunity costs is totally irrelevant.

The Enron Scandal: Complexities in Bankruptcy Claims Trading

The Stanford International Bank scandal was hardly the first time corporate giants have fallen via deceptive practices and mismanagement, and, alas, it certainly won't be the last. But while Stanford's fraud revolved around CDs and offshore accounts, the collapse of Enron showed how even sophisticated financial engineering and market manipulation within the corporate world can unravel spectacularly. The Enron scandal is also notable for how it transformed claims trading into a strategy for hedge funds and institutional investors.

The 2001 Enron collapse remains one of the most infamous corporate frauds in history and serves as a pivotal example of bankruptcy claims trading following a large-scale corporate scandal. Enron, once a titan in the energy sector, used off-balance-sheet special purpose entities and dubious accounting practices to hide massive amounts of debt and inflate profit figures. It was made possible because its outside audit team, Arthur Andersen, was complicit. The revelation of these practices led to a dramatic loss of investor confidence, a plummeting stock price, and eventually, Enron's filing for Chapter 11 bankruptcy.

Enron's bankruptcy resulted in a complex and protracted process. Thousands of creditors and investors were left vying for the remnants of the company's assets. In this chaos, the trading of bankruptcy claims spiked. Hedge funds and other investment vehicles saw an opportunity to purchase claims from smaller creditors who desired immediate cash rather than enduring lengthy bankruptcy proceedings.

The claims against Enron were initially valued based on pessimistic assessments of what the bankruptcy estate could recover. Accordingly, many creditors sold their claims at a fraction of the face value, expecting minimal recovery. However, the bankruptcy estate was able to liquidate assets more effectively than initially anticipated, leading to higher recovery rates. For instance, early in the proceedings, some claims might have traded for as little as 10% to 20% of their face value. But as the estate resolved its affairs and asset values became clearer, these claims sometimes appreciated significantly, realizing recovery rates much higher than the market had initially priced in. The Enron claims followed a generally predictable pattern (see Fig. 4).

TURNING DISTRESS INTO OPPORTUNITY: BANKRUPTCY CLAIMS TRADING

Savvy investors make money from the aftermath of financial collapse, not the collapse itself.

Figure 4: Turning Distress into Opportunity: Bankruptcy Claims Trading

Enron's bankruptcy involved numerous legal settlements that impacted the value of claims. For instance, Enron reached a $1.7 billion settlement with Citigroup and a $1.6 billion settlement with JPMorgan Chase, among the largest settlements in the case. These settlements increased the funds available to the bankruptcy estate, directly affecting the recovery for creditors. Investors who purchased claims before these settlements were announced often saw the value of their claims increase as the settlements raised expectations for the total recovery.

The sale of major assets also played a critical role in claim valuation. For example, the sale of Enron's pipeline assets and its interests in various energy plants brought in significant sums higher than initial estimates. These sales provided liquidity to the estate that was distributed to claim holders, enhancing the returns for those who had purchased claims at discounted rates. Furthermore, Enron's estate pursued strategic lawsuits that recovered additional funds, against various former executives and firms that had played roles in the company's financial collapse. The successful litigations added substantial amounts, positively impacting the recoveries of claim holders.

With its extensive legal and financial aftermath, the Enron scandal served as a precursor to other significant corporate collapses that involved complex financial mismanagement and regulatory oversights. One such case is the collapse of MF Global, a company that similarly fell through risky bets and regulatory failures. Both companies faced massive public and legal scrutiny, leading to a market for bankruptcy claims where investors sought to capitalize on the recovery processes. The transition from Enron, an energy giant wrapped in accounting fraud, to MF Global, a broker that disastrously overextended itself in European sovereign debt, underscores the breadth of industries and scenarios where bankruptcy claims can become viable investment opportunities.

The Collapse of MF Global: A Tale of Reckless Bets and Missing Funds

When it comes to the world of high finance, few stories have captured the public's attention quite like the spectacular collapse of MF Global.

Its fall reminds us how reckless bets and mismanagement can devastate even well-established financial firms. While the previous cases we discussed involved frauds built on deceit from the start, MF Global's downfall stands out as an example of a legitimate firm that faltered under poor leadership and excessive risk-taking. Under Jon Corzine's ambitious vision, the firm abandoned its conservative roots, chasing profits through complex financial maneuvers, only to fail spectacularly in 2011. The subsequent bankruptcy case offers a window into the unique challenges and opportunities involved in claims trading for distressed assets.

Once a respected global financial derivatives broker, MF Global faced a demise marked by a series of reckless bets, regulatory failures, and the mysterious disappearance of $1.6 billion in customer funds. At the center of the storm was Jon Corzine, the former Goldman Sachs CEO and ex-governor of New Jersey who took the helm of MF Global in March 2010. Corzine had grand ambitions to transform the sleepy commodities broker into a full-scale investment bank, and he wasted no time pursuing this vision.

Under Corzine's leadership, MF Global began taking on significant risk, particularly in the form of heavy bets on European sovereign debt through a complex financial instrument known as repurchase-to-maturity transactions. These transactions allowed MF Global to book profits upfront while keeping the transactions themselves off the balance sheet. However, as the European debt crisis intensified in 2011, MF Global's positions began to unravel. Margin calls mounted as the value of the sovereign debt securities fell, putting immense pressure on the firm's liquidity. Corzine's strategy had effectively backfired, leaving MF Global on the brink of collapse.

As MF Global's financial situation deteriorated, regulators began to take notice. In August 2011, FINRA raised concerns about the firm's capital treatment of its European sovereign debt positions, requiring MF Global to hold more capital against these assets. This regulatory action further squeezed MF Global's already-strained finances. The final nail in MF Global's coffin came in October 2011, when the firm reported a $191.6 million quarterly loss, largely due to write-downs on its deferred tax assets. This news, coupled with revelations about the firm's significant exposure to European debt, triggered a crisis of confidence among investors and counterparties.

The firm faced a massive liquidity crunch as MF Global's stock price plummeted and its credit ratings were slashed. Desperate to meet margin calls and fund its daily operations, MF Global began dipping into customer-segregated funds—a clear violation of industry rules. On October 31, 2011, after a frantic weekend of failed rescue attempts, MF Global filed for

Chapter 11 bankruptcy protection. It was the eighth-largest bankruptcy in U.S. history at the time. But the real shock came when it was revealed that $1.6 billion in customer funds—money that should have been kept strictly segregated—was missing.

The fallout from MF Global's collapse was immense. Thousands of customers, including individual investors, farmers, and small businesses, were left in limbo, unsure if they would ever recover their funds. Regulators, including the Commodity Futures Trading Commission and the SEC, launched investigations into the firm's actions. In the bankruptcy proceedings that followed, an important figure emerged: James Giddens, the trustee appointed to oversee the liquidation of MF Global's broker-dealer unit and recover funds for customers. Giddens and his team worked tirelessly to untangle the complex web of transactions and trace the missing customer money.

As the investigation unfolded, it became clear that MF Global had engaged in a dangerous game of "robbing Peter to pay Paul" using customer funds to cover its own mounting losses and margin calls. This practice, while blatantly illegal, had somehow escaped the notice of regulators until it was too late. Many observers have noted similarities between MF Global and FTX, with one glaring difference. The CEO of MF Global, Jon Corzine, escaped public ridicule and prosecution, while Sam Bankman-Fried was given an extended prison sentence and was the topic of newspaper article after late-night roast after another. Why one got off and the other did not remains an open topic for debate.

The MF Global case sparked intense debate about the adequacy of current financial regulations and the oversight of complex financial institutions. It also highlighted the risks posed by firms that engage in proprietary trading while also handling customer funds.

For distressed investors in MF Global, once the news of an investigation broke, the analytical work began. My firm built a recovery model based on public filings and numerous conversations with commodity traders. We began to reach out to these traders and share our model in order to test our recovery assumptions and build trust. This in turn prompted numerous traders to reach out to us to sell their claims, even at a massive discount. As one trader said to me with respect to his $9 million claim, "I can make more trading commodities in a day than I can by waiting out recovery in a bankruptcy case."

With that line, he had distilled the essence of a distressed trader's life. You want a counterparty who thinks just like that, who wants your cash to do what they do best and still leave you significant upside to recover in the bankruptcy process.

We developed a robust market in MF Global's bankruptcy claims. Many claims are traded numerous times, because some investors are willing to take more risk. Those are the investors who jump in when there's more uncertainty. Other investors, typically large multinational hedge funds, would rather enter the fray when there is more certainty on recovery.

Another aspect of the MF Global case that made it fascinating was that the claims-trading process took place in numerous countries where MF Global had operations, including the United Kingdom, Australia, and Asia. Trading claims in foreign jurisdictions presents numerous issues and requires counsel with expertise in those countries. It also creates risk for the buyer, specifically when it comes to the creditworthiness of the counterparty, in the event there is an issue with the claim. All this is factored into—you guessed it—the price one pays for the claim.

MF Global customers ultimately recovered about $8 billion, which was almost all their missing funds, thanks in large part to the efforts of the trustees and the claims-trading process.

Lessons from Fraud, Collapse, and Recovery

The collapse of MF Global underscores how delicate the line between legitimate business practices and reckless risk-taking can sometimes be. Although MF Global began as a respectable firm, misguided leadership, risky financial strategies, and regulatory pressures drove it into bankruptcy. In contrast, cases like Madoff and Stanford International Bank were fraudulent from the beginning, deceiving investors under the guise of stability and trust.

Each case illustrates different paths to collapse, but they all highlight a core truth: financial markets reward those willing to navigate uncertainty and risk (see Fig. 5). Whether through the trading of claims in bankruptcy or the recovery efforts that follow, sophisticated investors capitalize on moments of crisis. Yet, as these stories demonstrate, such opportunities come with ethical dilemmas, legal complexities, and prolonged uncertainty.

FINANCIAL COLLAPSES: WHAT WE LEARNED

Case Name	Fraud Type	Investor Losses	Recovery Rate
Madoff	Ponzi Scheme	$50B–70B	~70%
Stanford	Fraudulent CDs	$7B	~40%
Enron	Accounting Fraud	$60B	~50%
MF Global	Risky Trading	$1.6B Missing	~100%

Key Takeaways
- Recovery rates vary significanty based on fraud type and asset structure.
- Even in the worst cases, disciplined investors found opportunities for recovery.

Figure 5: Financial Collapses: What We Learned

INVESTING IN FRAUDULENT BANKRUPTCIES

For investors, the lesson is clear: even the most established and reputable firms are vulnerable to failure. Additionally, while due diligence, diversification, and skepticism are always required, they are no guarantee against losses. Fraudulent schemes, reckless financial bets, and outright deception have repeatedly reshaped markets, often at the expense of those who trusted too easily.

The aftermath of these failures, however, presents opportunities for those who understand the mechanics of distressed investing. Claims trading, litigation finance, and asset recoveries can yield substantial returns, but only for those who can assess risk, act decisively, and endure long periods of uncertainty. The line between losses and profits isn't just about timing; it's about understanding how markets react to crises, how legal frameworks shape recoveries, and how financial missteps create openings for those willing to navigate the chaos.

As long as markets exist, so too will fraud, failure, and collapse. And for those who can recognize the patterns, so will the opportunities.

In the next chapter, we will turn to crypto as a new frontier of distressed investing, where some of the largest collapses in recent memory have created chaos and opportunity. From Mt. Gox to FTX, the crypto landscape has been shaped by massive fraud, operational failures, and regulatory gaps, as well as by surprisingly sophisticated recovery efforts.

KEY INSIGHTS

1. The collapse of Bernie Madoff's Ponzi scheme revealed failures in financial oversight and reinforced the need for investors to recognize red flags, even in trusted institutions.
2. Clawback lawsuits in the Madoff case targeted both complicit and innocent investors, highlighting the legal risks of profiting from fraudulent schemes.
3. A 2015 Supreme Court ruling limited clawback actions to two years before bankruptcy, shaping future fraud recoveries and investor protections.
4. High trustee fees in Madoff's case sparked criticism, but SIPC advances ensured they did not reduce the victim fund, underscoring the complexity of recovery costs.
5. Madoff victims had to navigate both bankruptcy claims and the MVF, illustrating the logistical challenges of recovering losses.
6. Distressed investors bought Madoff claims at steep discounts, betting on legal proceedings to yield higher recoveries. This shows the speculative nature of claims trading.
7. The SIB scandal used fraudulent CDs to lure investors, exposing how financial schemes can mimic legitimate banking structures.
8. The SIB scandal collapse devastated the Caribbean economy, showing how distressed investments can ripple through entire communities.
9. Stanford's cross-border insolvency proceedings in the United States and Antigua revealed the legal challenges of international asset recovery.
10. Lawsuits against banks like TD Bank and HSBC underscored the risks financial institutions face when entangled in fraudulent operations.

11. Enron's collapse exposed how accounting manipulation and off-balance-sheet transactions can conceal insolvency, reshaping corporate governance standards.
12. Trading of Enron bankruptcy claims showed how investors profit from undervalued distressed assets, given patience and proper valuation.
13. Settlements with major banks added significant funds to Enron's bankruptcy estate, highlighting the role of litigation in recovery efforts.
14. Selling Enron's energy infrastructure provided liquidity for creditors, emphasizing the importance of strategic asset liquidation.
15. MF Global's failure, driven by risky bets on European sovereign debt, underscored the dangers of speculative trading and poor risk management.
16. CEO Jon Corzine's misuse of customer funds highlighted the consequences of weak internal controls and regulatory failures.
17. Cross-border claims trading in MF Global's bankruptcy demonstrated the complexities of handling international insolvencies.
18. Despite the turmoil, MF Global investors recovered nearly all their funds, showing how patient claims trading can lead to strong returns.
19. Unlike outright frauds like Madoff or Stanford, MF Global failed due to reckless risk-taking rather than deception, reinforcing the need for proactive risk assessment.
20. Successful distressed investing requires financial expertise, legal knowledge, and patience to navigate uncertainty.
21. The failures of Madoff, Stanford, and Enron stress the importance of vigilance, diversification, and skepticism, as even reputable institutions can collapse.

CHAPTER 12

Crypto: A Unique Opportunity in Distressed Investing

Every generation of distressed investors faces its own set of crises, but the mechanics of opportunity and risk remain surprisingly consistent. Whether it was railroads in the 19th century, real estate in the 1980s, dot-com startups in the early 2000s, or mortgage-backed securities in 2008, fortunes have been made and lost when entire industries faltered. Today, few sectors have produced more sudden, high-profile collapses than cryptocurrency.

Crypto presented something entirely new: an unregulated market with billions of dollars in assets, traded globally and held by everyone from Wall Street hedge funds to retail speculators. When crypto companies failed, they did so in dramatic fashion, often leaving billions in customer assets frozen, missing, or gone altogether. For distressed investors, these failures opened a unique window of opportunity, filled with extreme complexity but also the potential for enormous returns.

Unlike traditional bankruptcies, where assets are tangible (like factories, equipment, or real estate), crypto failures involve digital assets whose value can swing wildly and whose ownership is often hard to determine. The legal treatment of these assets is still being shaped in courts, and bankruptcy judges and trustees must decide how to handle property that exists entirely online. Investors must ask questions that have no clear answers. Can crypto deposits be treated as cash? Do customers truly own the coins in their accounts? How should assets that trade constantly and fluctuate in value be measured and distributed?

These are not small details. They are fundamental questions that will decide who recovers and who takes a loss. Investors who understand these issues have a chance to profit, while those who misjudge them may lose everything.

To understand how crypto distress has evolved and how investors can approach it, we will start with the collapse of Mt. Gox, the first major crypto bankruptcy and still one of the most complex and watched cases in the history of digital assets. Long before Celsius, Voyager, or FTX became household names, Mt. Gox showed the world what happens when a crypto exchange falls apart. Its story is not only a cautionary tale but also a roadmap for investors trying to navigate the next wave of crypto bankruptcies.

The Genesis of Crypto Distress: Mt. Gox

Mt. Gox, based in Shibuya, Tokyo, Japan, once handled over 70% of all Bitcoin transactions. Originally launched as a site to facilitate trading in a fantasy card game (hence the name "Mt. Gox," short for "Magic: The Gathering Online Exchange"), it pivoted to cryptocurrencies as Bitcoin began attracting more attention. By 2011, it was the largest platform for Bitcoin transactions worldwide.

Despite its early dominance, Mt. Gox unraveled in 2014 after a devastating hack. Hundreds of thousands of Bitcoins vanished, leaving the company short of assets to cover its account holders' funds. In February of that year, Mt. Gox filed for civil rehabilitation in Tokyo. At filing, its liabilities hovered around $65 million, with only $30 million in reported assets and approximately 127,000 creditors. Most of the "assets" were actually Bitcoins held on behalf of users, rendering the platform cash-poor in an instant. Founder Mark Karpelès was soon sidelined and later arrested, compounding the chaos and reinforcing the perception of widespread fraud.

In these early days of confusion, rumors ran wild. By May 2016, some creditors circulated unsubstantiated figures in the trillions of dollars, though official estimates later placed recovered assets at only a fraction of that amount. The Japanese trustee in charge of the proceedings located only $91 million in traceable assets at first, contradicting Mt. Gox's earlier claims of having more than $500 million. Then, unexpectedly, 200,000 Bitcoins resurfaced, creating renewed hope for creditors.

Between 2014 and 2018, professionals led by the liquidation trustee tracked down assets, sorted through creditor claims, and put some structure around what looked like a hopeless collapse. By March 2018, the trustee had sold enough Bitcoins to cover the nominal value of creditors' claims, though these sales took place sporadically, and often depressed Bitcoin prices when large blocks were offloaded. In the spring of 2023, however, the timeline for Bitcoin distributions suddenly shifted. Creditors expected payouts by the fall of 2023, only to learn the trustee had pushed that date to sometime in 2024 without a detailed explanation. This delay created new openings for distressed investors, including me, to acquire claims at around a 30% discount to the theoretical price of Bitcoin.

A central dispute in the Mt. Gox bankruptcy revolved around whether creditors should be paid in fiat currency or the cryptocurrency itself. Many investors who believed strongly in Bitcoin wanted their payout in digital coins rather than yen or U.S. dollars. By January 2021, the trustee, Nobuaki Kobayashi, revealed a plan to distribute much of the remaining Bitcoin as digital assets, thereby satisfying those who saw the future upside of holding onto cryptocurrency.

Eventually, this rehabilitation plan received near-unanimous support from creditors and was approved by the courts in late 2021. As of mid-2022, the trustee held around 142,000 Bitcoins, and the market value of these assets had soared far beyond earlier projections. For creditors, the shift from expecting little to possibly receiving a windfall reflected the broader volatility that defines the crypto market. By July 2024, the trustee began partial Bitcoin distributions; however, the final payout deadline has now been extended to October 31, 2025, due to ongoing legal and administrative delays. Prices had risen substantially, boosting the potential recovery for creditors, but the delay has added uncertainty and frustration for many who have been waiting, some up to a decade.

How Mt. Gox Established Themes and Implications for Future Crypto Cases

The Mt. Gox collapse revealed patterns that appear repeatedly in fraud-driven and crypto-related bankruptcies. At the outset, fear and rumors fueled investor panic, with some media outlets amplifying speculation that the losses would be insurmountable. Meanwhile, the professionals handling the reorganization—lawyers, accountants, and other advisors—sought payment in traditional currencies rather than in Bitcoin, often leading to forced sales of cryptocurrency assets at inopportune times. Over the years, however, Bitcoin's price rose dramatically, allowing creditors who ultimately received distributions in cryptocurrency to recover more than anyone had anticipated in 2014 (see Fig. 1).

By mid-2022, Kobayashi, the Mt. Gox trustee, formally announced that distributions would likely extend into 2024 due to the legal complexities of rehabilitation and the large number of claimants. While some creditors had hoped for an earlier payout, the revised timeline was already anticipated in part because of the ongoing legal negotiations and administrative hurdles. Japan's legal framework did require the trustee to issue periodic updates on the progress of asset recovery and distribution, in contrast to earlier perceptions that creditors had been completely left in the dark.

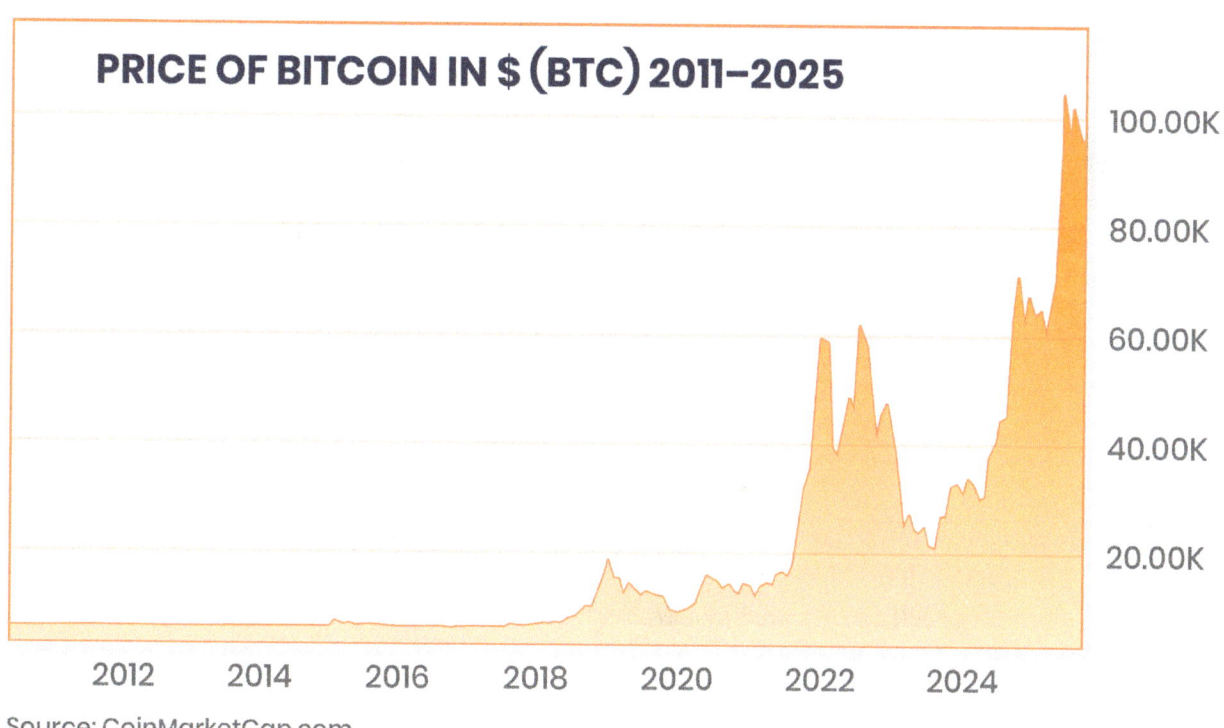

Figure 1: Price of Bitcoin in $ (BTC) 2011–2025

When distributions began in mid-2024, concerns about a sudden sell-off caused short-term volatility in Bitcoin's price, reflecting market jitters over how many creditors might immediately liquidate their recovered crypto. Despite these price fluctuations, those who held onto their Bitcoin distributions often benefited from its long-term appreciation. In addition, while distressed investors occasionally purchase bankruptcy claims at a discount in various insolvency cases, publicly available information does not confirm extensive or specific claim purchases related to Mt. Gox.

The Mt. Gox experience underscores a few enduring realities of distressed investing in crypto. First, legal systems differ across jurisdictions, and although Japan's disclosure standards may not mirror U.S. bankruptcy's high level of public filings, periodic trustee reports and creditor communications offered a degree of transparency. Second, the need for large cash reserves to pay professional fees can result in forced asset sales at lower prices, potentially leaving significant value on the table if crypto prices rebound. Third, the inherent volatility of cryptocurrencies means that what looks like a catastrophic loss can, in time, transform into a meaningful recovery for creditors. Finally, as seen in other cases of crypto failure (such as Cred, which we'll come to next), underlying issues of management, regulatory oversight, or alleged fraud can exacerbate instability, even if the exact nature of these failures differs from one platform to another.

The Mt. Gox failure and recovery remains a watershed event in crypto history. It showed how the absence of strong security measures and transparent operations could leave an exchange vulnerable to devastating hacks. At the same time, the eventual recovery process, though beset by delays, demonstrated that patient creditors might still recoup substantial value when cryptocurrency prices surge. As similar crises continue to unfold in the crypto sector, the lessons from Mt. Gox remain instructive for investors, regulators, and other market participants alike.

Cred: A Tale of Alleged Fraud and Misrepresentation

Founded in 2018 by Daniel Schatt and Lu Hua, Cred offered loans in U.S. dollars using customers' cryptocurrency as collateral and accepted digital deposits in exchange for a yield promise. However, beneath its promising exterior, Cred was mired in deceptive practices and poor oversight, leading to its abrupt collapse and the indictments of its top executives.

Cred's internal problems came to light in February 2020, when it emerged that James Alexander, the chief capital officer, had been scammed by a fake customer, causing an $8 million loss. Rather than disclose this openly, Cred's executives tried to hide it. By March 2020, cracks in the company's foundation were increasingly visible as a flash crash in the crypto market heightened pressure on its balance sheet. Despite this, Cred's CEO, Daniel Schatt, and CFO, Joseph Podulka, continued to reassure customers about the company's financial health, masking the reality that their hedging strategies had failed to safeguard against market swings.

The situation reached a tipping point in October 2020, when one of Cred's business partners, a cryptocurrency exchange that also used Cred's services, recognized the depth of Cred's financial distress during a routine call. This revelation triggered a crisis of confidence, prompting many customers to withdraw their assets. Within a month, Cred filed for Chapter 11 bankruptcy, exposing the gap between its public claims of "collateralized or guaranteed lending" and its actual practices, which were neither fully collateralized nor hedged.

By the time Cred entered bankruptcy in November 2020, it seemed that customers had lost everything. However, because the platform still held some cryptocurrency assets, there is now a chance that customers will recover at least 50% of their investments. Like many other crypto bankruptcies, Cred's case provides a reminder that initial perceptions of total loss may change once assets are marshaled and properly valued, even if the process is marked by allegations of deception.

Widespread Crypto Crises: A Chain Reaction

Mt. Gox and Cred were hardly the last of it. In 2022, a new wave of crypto bankruptcies emerged that underscored how contagion can spread when the market collectively loses confidence. One pattern that repeats itself over and over in distressed investing, especially in emerging industries, is that the bankruptcy of one company often results in the bankruptcy of other competitors.

With respect to FTX, the chain reaction can be traced to the broader crypto sell-off that began in May 2022 following the collapse of the Terra Luna coin and the related "stablecoin" TerraUSD. Within days, Terra Luna and TerraUSD both lost substantial value, prompting many crypto investors to withdraw their digital assets from various exchanges and brokerages.

This wave of redemptions contributed to the failure of crypto hedge fund Three Arrows Capital (3AC), which had significant exposure to Terra Luna. The ripple effects were enormous. Voyager Digital, a cryptocurrency brokerage, had loaned $665 million to 3AC, forcing it to freeze trading and then file for bankruptcy when 3AC defaulted on the loan. Around the same time, investors pulled over $1 billion from Celsius Network, a cryptocurrency lender, amid what the CEO referred to as a generalized "distrust of cryptocurrency." Celsius froze its platform for trading on June 12, 2022, then filed for Chapter 11 on July 13. Over the course of 2022, Bitcoin's value tumbled approximately 65%, amplifying liquidity pressures across the industry even more.

FTX Trading Ltd. froze trading on November 8, 2022, and filed for Chapter 11 on November 11. The freezing of the FTX platform significantly impacted the cryptocurrency lender BlockFi, which had $355 million of assets tied up in FTX. BlockFi had also made loans to Alameda Research, an FTX affiliate and hedge fund, which defaulted on approximately $680 million in collateralized loan obligations. BlockFi limited customer withdrawals on November 10, before filing for Chapter 11 on November 28. Meanwhile, Genesis Global Capital, yet another cryptocurrency lender, froze customer redemptions on November 16 and filed for Chapter 11 on January 20, 2023, after loaning significant sums to both 3AC and Alameda Research.

Most of these Chapter 11 filings unfolded with little preplanning, which is unusual for large corporate bankruptcies. In more traditional cases, a company might spend weeks or months negotiating with creditors to develop a workable path forward. Instead, each of these crypto businesses entered bankruptcy court in a "freefall" scenario, scrambling to respond to a sudden collapse in value and a surge in withdrawal requests. This lack of advanced restructuring prolonged the bankruptcy processes and added uncertainty for investors, but created more opportunities for distressed buyers.

Together with the earlier collapses at Mt. Gox and Cred, these failures highlight how quickly distress can spread when an entire market or asset class loses momentum. From Terra Luna's sudden downfall to the interconnected exposures of 3AC, FTX, BlockFi, and others, this chain reaction emphasizes the importance of monitoring broader market signals, particularly in an industry where regulatory and financial structures remain fluid.

Celsius Network: Rapid Rise, Sudden Fall

Celsius Network grew rapidly by promising reliable returns, offering high-yield interest-bearing accounts and loans backed by cryptocurrency deposits. At its height, the company managed more than $20 billion in assets and attracted a diverse global customer base, attracted to the idea of substantial passive income. But as its Chapter 11 bankruptcy filing made clear, the same ambitious growth that once elevated it also contributed to its downfall.

The trouble began in June 2022, when Celsius froze customer accounts and halted all withdrawals under the guise of "extreme market conditions." What was intended as a defensive measure instead caused panic among account holders, who saw their funds trapped on the platform. Court documents later revealed that the company, which claimed to have $4.3 billion in assets, actually faced liabilities of about $5.5 billion and counted more than 400,000 creditors on its books. CEO Alex Mashinsky acknowledged in a sworn declaration that Celsius had attempted to secure new financing but found no workable alternative to bankruptcy. Alameda Research, co-founded by Sam Bankman-Fried, emerged as one of Celsius's largest creditors, underscoring the intricate web of debt that tied many crypto firms together in 2022.

Celsius's failure exposed deeper issues that went beyond the plunge in crypto prices. The company had taken on significant risk through its investment decisions, betting heavily on speculative assets without sufficient hedging. Once volatility surged and investors grew uneasy about leaving their holdings on any one platform, Celsius discovered that its promises of above-market returns were built on shaky ground. Yet, for distressed investors, Celsius's bankruptcy presented chances to purchase discounted claims. With Bitcoin prices still fluctuating wildly, some claimholders were eager for an immediate payout, which created openings for buyers willing to take on the uncertainty of a drawn-out court process.

The court-approved restructuring plan in November 2023 outlined returning cryptocurrency to many customers and establishing a new entity focused on mining. By minting new Bitcoin and earning fees for validating blockchain transactions, Celsius's reorganized venture offered a sliver of hope to participants who had seen their crypto locked away for months on end. At the same time, the trading of bankruptcy claims became a mini-market. Sellers received at least 30% of the face value, which could be substantial cash for individuals who needed funds quickly, while the projected recovery of around 58% in crypto and stock left a potential margin for investors who were willing to wait.

One episode that vividly demonstrated the need for vigilance occurred after the plan of reorganization was approved and went into effect. Celsius sought to distribute cryptocurrency to certain large corporate creditors while issuing fiat currency to smaller creditors, an approach that was never sanctioned by the court. The company apparently aimed to minimize the cost and administrative burden of distributing crypto to every account, since each wallet verification required a third-party service that came with a considerable price tag. By paying smaller creditors in dollars instead of crypto, Celsius hoped to avoid these charges and, as critics argued, reduce its exposure to the future upside of Bitcoin.

When a group of smaller creditors realized they were being treated differently, they engaged legal counsel (the Sarachek Law Firm, no less!) and filed a motion in the bankruptcy court. Their argument was straightforward: distributing crypto to one subset of the same creditor class while forcing another subset to accept fiat constituted disparate treatment. The bankruptcy judge agreed that this move violated the principles set out in the reorganized plan. Celsius was forced to correct the disparity, leading to an additional distribution of around $75 million in value to the impacted creditors.

The takeaway for investors and observers alike is this: even after a plan of reorganization has been confirmed, there can still be surprising twists. The Celsius case shows that riding out a bankruptcy in the crypto world isn't just about tracking market conditions; it's about following every motion, filing, and distribution plan in real time. When a debtor tries to deviate from court-approved agreements, whether to save money, reduce complexity, or secure other advantages, those actions can have a real impact on how much creditors ultimately recover. Such developments underscore the importance of paying close attention throughout the process, whether by scrutinizing court dockets, sharing information in online forums, or staying in contact with legal counsel.

Voyager Digital: Overextension and Poor Risk Management

Voyager Digital's fall mirrored the mounting turbulence in the crypto landscape during the summer of 2022. Even as it promoted itself as a platform dedicated to "democratizing" cryptocurrency access through its interest-bearing accounts and a user-friendly app for trading, Voyager struggled behind the scenes with a precarious business model. Overconfidence in its rapid expansion left the company unprepared for the significant market downturn that struck much of the sector that year. By June 2022, the warning signs could no longer be hidden. Voyager abruptly suspended all trading, deposits, withdrawals, and loyalty rewards, citing (as Celsius had) "extreme market conditions," a move that swiftly eroded the trust of its sizable user base and foreshadowed the deeper crisis to come.

On July 6, 2022, Voyager filed for voluntary Chapter 11 bankruptcy in the U.S. Bankruptcy Court for the Southern District of New York. The filing revealed that one of Voyager's key vulnerabilities was its exposure to 3AC, the now-notorious crypto hedge fund that defaulted on approximately $675 million owed to Voyager. Compounding the pressure, the broader market freefall wiped out roughly $2 trillion in total cryptocurrency value in a matter of weeks. Voyager simply could not withstand that kind of shock, and the interconnected nature of crypto lending meant that one major default reverberated through many lenders and trading platforms simultaneously.

Further scrutiny of Voyager's business practices revealed other pitfalls. Rather than maintaining individual wallets for each customer, the company commingled all cryptocurrency assets into a single consolidated wallet and then swept them into a third-party custodian account. This approach raised concerns about whether users' funds were truly segregated and protected, an important question for anyone depositing assets onto an exchange or lending platform. For many observers, this lack of clear asset segregation heightened the perception that Voyager had grown too fast without implementing the structural safeguards necessary for a large-scale financial service.

Despite these shortcomings, Voyager's bankruptcy did not mark an immediate end to all value in its platform. Court documents indicated that the company still held about $1.3 billion in cryptocurrency and $350 million in a "For Benefit of Customers" account. These assets turned Voyager's demise into both a challenge and an opportunity for distressed investors. Those with deep expertise in bankruptcy proceedings and a nuanced grasp of crypto markets had the potential to acquire Voyager's remaining digital assets or claims at a discounted rate, depending on how the court ultimately ruled on asset ownership, liquidation procedures, and the feasibility of restructuring.

The aftermath of Voyager's collapse saw a scramble among various players eager to salvage whatever value remained. Sam Bankman-Fried's Alameda Research emerged as the company's largest single creditor, holding a $75 million unsecured loan that underlined, yet again, just how entangled major crypto firms had become. As Voyager's case proceeded, it became another telling example of the risks hidden beneath fast-paced growth and apparent stability. Like Celsius, this story showed that even platforms promoting themselves as user-friendly gateways to digital assets could harbor deep-seated liabilities, and that the same interconnected loans fueling the industry's rise could just as quickly hasten its decline (see Fig. 2).

From Voyager to FTX: A Fall That Shook the Crypto World

The collapse of Voyager Digital was only one of many cautionary tales unfolding in 2022. None, however, had a fall as far-reaching and reputationally damaging as FTX, once hailed as the gold standard for cryptocurrency exchanges. Its descent into bankruptcy exposed deep fault lines not only in the platform's operations but also in the broader oversight of digital assets.

Sam Bankman-Fried and the Rise of FTX

Behind FTX's meteoric rise stood Sam Bankman-Fried, widely known by his initials, SBF, who entered the crypto realm through Alameda Research, a trading firm he co-founded in

CRYPTO: A UNIQUE OPPORTUNITY IN DISTRESSED INVESTING

HOW CRYPTO BANKRUPTCIES TRIGGERED A CHAIN REACTION

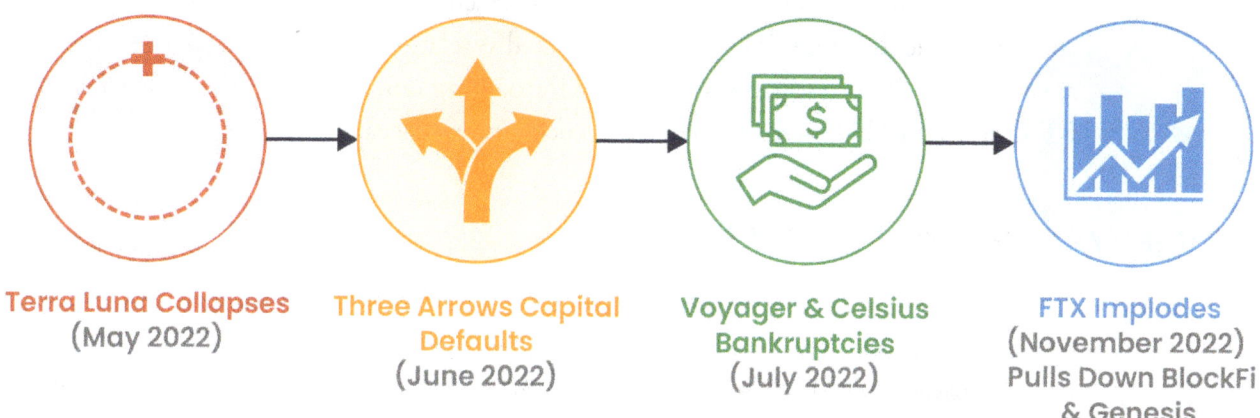

Figure 2: How Crypto Bankruptcies Triggered a Chain Reaction

California in 2017. Energized by early successes in exploiting price spreads across various markets, SBF launched FTX in 2019, positioning the exchange as a leader in crypto innovation. Leveraged tokens, advanced futures contracts, and a tech-savvy user experience quickly drew both institutional and retail clientele. By early 2022, FTX was valued at $32 billion, and SBF was frequently featured in major media outlets, depicted as crypto's accessible prodigy who grasped both Wall Street's culture and the crypto world's disruptive spirit.

In interviews and public appearances, SBF projected confidence and a commitment to the "effective altruism" movement, further boosting his reputation. He donated to political causes and contributed to various charities, painting himself as a benevolent figure who wanted to harness crypto for the greater good. Within the industry, his growing stature seemed to bridge old-guard finance and the new wave of blockchain-based innovations.

Revelations and the Beginning of the End

The first cracks in the SBF façade appeared on November 2, 2022, when Ian Allison of CoinDesk published an investigative report revealing that Alameda Research's balance sheet relied heavily on FTT, a token issued by FTX itself. Essentially conjured "out of thin air," FTT served as the backbone of Alameda's stated net worth. This revelation cast immediate doubt on both entities, suggesting that FTX's financial stability might be more illusory than real.

The situation accelerated on November 6, when Changpeng Zhao (commonly known as CZ), the CEO of rival exchange Binance, announced plans to liquidate Binance's FTT holdings due to concerns raised by the CoinDesk article. Rattled by CZ's move, investors began withdrawing funds from FTX at an unprecedented rate. Over the next 72 hours, an estimated $6 billion was pulled off the platform, swiftly depleting FTX's liquidity.

As FTX scrambled to raise emergency capital, SBF sought a bailout from Binance. Although Binance initially agreed in principle to rescue FTX, the deal fell apart once Binance conducted due diligence. Publicly, Binance cited revelations of deep financial issues at FTX and ongoing U.S. investigations as reasons for backing out. With no other rescuer in sight, FTX faced an $8 billion shortfall that it could neither conceal nor fix.

Bankruptcy and Unraveling of the Scheme

On November 11, both FTX and Alameda Research filed for bankruptcy. The filings laid bare a web of financial manipulations that included commingling customer funds, using those funds to cover Alameda's risky trades, and failing to abide by even the most basic compliance obligations. FTX's terms of service had assured users that their assets would remain separate and under their control, an assurance now shown to be false.

SBF's arrest in the Bahamas in December 2022 ignited one of the highest-profile financial fraud cases in recent memory. Extradited to the United States, he faced seven counts of fraud and money laundering. Though he maintained that he had not knowingly engaged in wrongdoing, often claiming ignorance of the specifics of Alameda's dealings, prosecutors presented evidence pointing to willful misrepresentation of the company's balance sheets and deliberate misuse of client assets. In media interviews, including a widely publicized BBC segment, SBF portrayed himself as an overextended manager, yet these attempts to shift blame did little to sway public opinion or the courts.

On March 28, 2024, a U.S. judge sentenced SBF to 25 years in prison, citing both the enormous losses by FTX investors and the founder's significant breach of trust. Observers noted that, unlike many white-collar fraud cases where convictions can be murky, the evidence here was stark: customer deposits that should have been held in reserve were instead used to patch holes in Alameda's balance sheet.

A Watershed Moment for Crypto

FTX's downfall sent shockwaves through the cryptocurrency ecosystem, prompting many to question the solvency and transparency of other exchanges and lending platforms. Investors' faith in "unregulated entities" took a major hit; finance professor Cesare Fracassi of the University of Texas remarked that skepticism around crypto wasn't new, but the FTX scandal underscored how lax oversight and opaque practices could converge to disastrous effect.

In the weeks following FTX's collapse, regulators worldwide began reassessing their stances on digital asset oversight, pushing forward proposals aimed at compelling greater transparency and accountability. The implosion also affected global sentiment; while some saw it as a short-term setback in an otherwise transformative technology, others viewed it as a defining cautionary tale that would reshape the industry for years to come.

Ultimately, the story of FTX and SBF illustrated the razor-thin line between ambitious innovation and outright fraud. By the time of its collapse, FTX was not just another crypto exchange but a symbol of how quickly fortunes could rise, and just as swiftly disintegrate, when billions of dollars in user funds were controlled by a select few operating in a largely unregulated environment. The lessons from FTX continue to reverberate, influencing not only how future exchanges will structure their operations but also how lawmakers, investors, and the public at large will approach the promises and perils of cryptocurrency.

The Surprising FTX Asset Recovery

The collapse of FTX, fueled by fraud allegations and mismanagement, appeared at first to be another harrowing entry in crypto's growing list of failures. Yet, in an unexpected twist, the exchange's post-bankruptcy turnaround became a story of near-miraculous asset recovery, something seldom seen in large-scale financial collapses. The effort was led by John J. Ray III, a seasoned corporate turnaround expert whose résumé included steering Enron through its infamous downfall. From the moment he took the helm at FTX as the newly appointed CEO and CRO, Ray pushed back against Sam Bankman-Fried's insistence that the company remained solvent, opting instead to file for bankruptcy in November 2022. SBF believed that enough time and favorable market conditions would eventually solve the liquidity crunch. Ironically, that belief turned out to be partially correct, but only after Ray and his team imposed rigorous controls to locate and consolidate every possible asset.

An Unprecedented Recovery Effort

Once bankruptcy proceedings began, Ray's group embarked on a meticulous hunt for FTX's holdings. They discovered billions in crypto assets, aided by a substantial rise in Bitcoin's token price, which shot up from approximately $16,000 in late 2022 to over $60,000 by March 2024. The team also uncovered investments in various startups, most notably a significant stake in Anthropic, an AI firm whose valuation soared after heavy backing from tech giants Google and Amazon. Valued at nearly a billion dollars, FTX's Anthropic stake formed a key pillar of the recovered asset pool.

Beyond digital assets, Ray targeted luxurious real estate in the Bahamas and even two private jets that had been purchased with customer funds. Although he tried to claw back political and charitable donations made by FTX, that facet of the campaign was met with mixed results as some recipients complied while others resisted or delayed repayment. Still, by the middle of 2024, Ray announced that FTX had gathered enough value to repay its customers in full, an almost unheard-of outcome for a meltdown of this scale (see Fig. 3).

THE DISTRESSED INVESTING PLAYBOOK

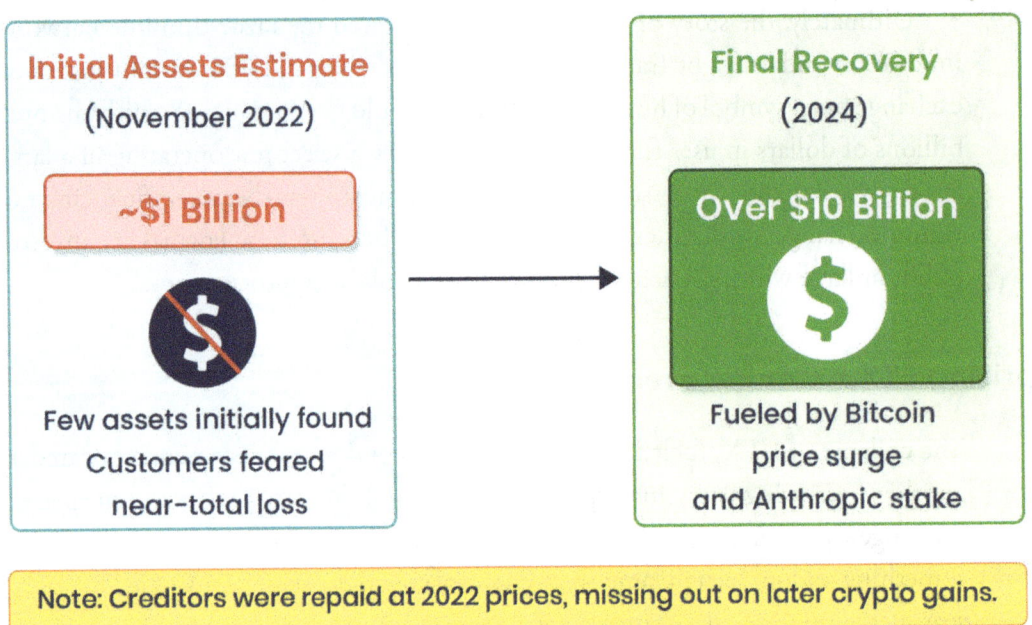

Figure 3: FTX: From Collapse to Recovery

A Caveat for Creditors

For the thousands of FTX users hoping to recoup their losses, Ray's announcement was momentous. Yet the relief came with important qualifiers. First, all creditors are being repaid the value of their cryptocurrency holdings as of the bankruptcy filing date in November 2022, when Bitcoin traded at around $20,000. With Bitcoin (and other digital assets like Solana) having climbed significantly since then, many depositors missed out on substantial gains they might have realized had their coins not been frozen.

Second, under a "convenience class" arrangement for claims under $50,000, certain FTX creditors may receive up to 118% of their original claims. This partial remedy helps bridge some financial gaps from the bankruptcy period, though it applies only to that specific class and does not cover all creditors. Even so, it does not fully account for the market's bull run following FTX's collapse. Even those receiving principal plus interest can feel shortchanged when they consider what might have accrued had they retained full control of their assets in a soaring crypto market.

As a result, while depositors can celebrate that much of their principal is being restored, or, in some cases, modestly exceeded, these outcomes have not erased the frustration of losing direct access to crypto holdings during a key growth period for digital assets. The FTX recovery stands out as a remarkable feat of asset tracing and liquidation, yet it also highlights the emotional and financial toll that comes with being unable to capitalize on a bullish upswing.

CRYPTO: A UNIQUE OPPORTUNITY IN DISTRESSED INVESTING

A Legacy for the Industry

Despite this fine print, FTX's turnaround left a profound mark on the cryptocurrency landscape. The rapid restoration of billions in assets underscored how crucial proper accounting, corporate governance, and transparent leadership can be in a market known for its opacity. It also offered a cautionary note about the perils of centralized exchanges that do not separate customer funds. While FTX once boasted about its innovation, it ultimately fell victim to the absence of strong operational safeguards.

Ray's success stands in stark contrast to recoveries in other epic financial frauds, such as Bernie Madoff's Ponzi scheme, where victims waited years, and, in some cases, are still waiting, to recover their funds. By finalizing the process within two years, Ray demonstrated that rapid and sweeping restructuring efforts can yield better outcomes when combined with favorable market conditions and a dogged commitment to tracking down hidden assets.

Although the FTX rescue story offered hope, it did not erase the broader questions lurking beneath the crypto industry's surface. As Fracassi suggested, the FTX scandal made investors warier of entrusting their money to unregulated or lightly regulated platforms. Since then, government agencies around the world have accelerated their pursuit of more comprehensive rules, drawing lessons from how easily FTX unraveled under the weight of insider abuses.

Ultimately, the FTX saga serves as a turning point, illustrating both the promise and perils of digital finance in equal measure. At one extreme lies the risk of collapse through opaque dealings; at the other, the possibility that strong leadership and transparent management can salvage value in ways few would have expected. The experience of FTX reminds us that while cryptocurrency may be groundbreaking, the fundamentals of ethical governance and regulatory oversight remain vital to the future of finance in whatever form it takes.

One of the more prescient investors in the distressed FTX claims market was NYU professor and commentator Scott Galloway, who saw an opportunity where many assumed total loss. "I actually bought claims against it," Galloway revealed in a conversation with Michael Lewis. He purchased them at 23 cents on the dollar, reasoning that FTX's investment in Anthropic alone was likely worth far more than most realized. "I valued Anthropic at approximately $40 billion...so just the stake in Anthropic, I valued at 44 cents on the dollar. Claims were selling for 22 cents. To me, this was the easiest trade I ever made."

His analysis proved correct, as crypto's resurgence and FTX's unexpected asset recovery pushed expected payouts to between 120 and 150 cents on the dollar. Galloway's experience underscores a central theme of distressed investing: when panic drives prices below intrinsic value, those who take a disciplined, analytical approach stand to gain the most.

Lessons from Crypto Distressed Investing

The high-profile collapses of Celsius Network, Voyager Digital, FTX, and Cred reveal how the rapid rise of a new market, powered by novel technologies and sometimes limited oversight, can generate both opportunities and pitfalls for distressed investors. Each case unfolded under distinct circumstances, yet the overarching lessons are instructive for anyone navigating industries prone to sudden legal, regulatory, or financial shocks (see Fig. 4).

First, speed and interconnectedness have a magnified effect in the crypto world. The downfall of one platform often leads to cascading failures, as seen with Terra Luna's collapse and its ripple effects on 3AC, Voyager Digital, and others. Even established players can be undone virtually overnight by runs on deposits, margin calls, or eroding public confidence. For investors, an ability to track these chain reactions in real time can be the difference between capitalizing on distressed assets and being blindsided by a market-wide squeeze.

Second, transparent governance and asset segregation matter enormously. Cases like Voyager Digital and FTX illustrated the dangers of pooling customer assets in commingled wallets, while Celsius showed that insufficient hedging and risk controls can trigger a liquidity crisis. Distressed investors who understand these technical specifics are better positioned to judge the real value of an enterprise, especially when official balance sheets may be murky or obscured by creative accounting.

Third, robust legal frameworks and regulatory clarity (or the lack thereof) play a defining role in recoveries. FTX's turnaround under John J. Ray III was driven not just by the rebound of crypto markets but by a disciplined process of tracing hidden assets and compelling disclosures. The Celsius bankruptcy, meanwhile, highlighted how even after court approval of a

LESSONS FROM CRYPTO BANKRUPTCIES

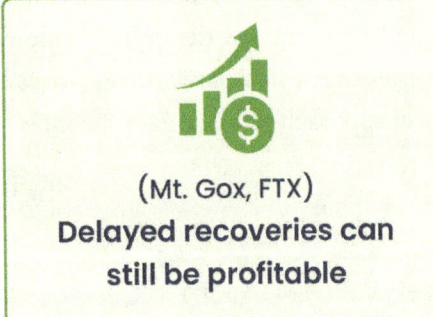
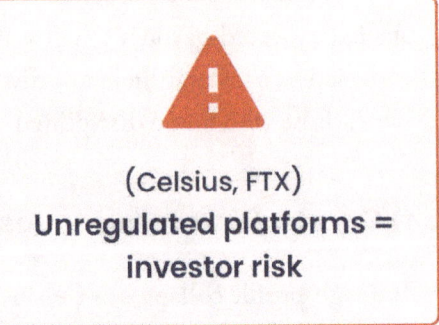

Figure 4: Lessons from Crypto Bankruptcies

plan, debtors may attempt revisions that could disadvantage certain creditor groups. In every instance, staying alert to ongoing proceedings, legal filings, and trustee announcements is paramount.

Finally, human nature and corporate culture, which transcend any single sector, loom large. Unchecked ambition, poor oversight, or a rush to market can expose investors to sudden and severe losses. Yet these same moments also create entry points for specialists who have the foresight and the fortitude to evaluate distressed assets objectively. When prices fall, and liquidity dries up, attentive investors can secure valuable claims that might later rebound, as evidenced by the unexpected recoveries in some crypto bankruptcies.

Although crypto presents challenges, many lessons from these bankruptcies apply across the broader world of distressed investing. Whether dealing with distressed retail, failed real estate ventures, or overleveraged companies in traditional industries, investors are always navigating uncertainty, conflicting claims, and shifting market conditions.

At its core, the collapse of platforms like Celsius, Voyager, FTX, and Cred reminds us that no level of innovation or market excitement can eliminate the need for careful oversight and rigorous diligence. Fast-moving markets and ambitious leadership are not substitutes for transparency and sound risk management. For investors willing to dig deep, monitor court filings, and carefully evaluate assets and liabilities, these bankruptcies offer opportunities to acquire claims and positions that may ultimately yield significant returns. But these cases also warn: when complexity, opacity, and hype outpace substance, collapse is often inevitable.

The next chapters will focus on how investors can take these lessons and apply them more broadly, emphasizing strategies for identifying distressed investment opportunities, conducting thorough due diligence, navigating legal complexities, and structuring deals to maximize recovery and minimize risk. From active and passive approaches to out-of-court restructurings and litigation funding, we will explore how sophisticated investors engage with distressed opportunities across industries.

KEY INSIGHTS

1. Opportunities for distressed investing follow recurring patterns across industries, from the offshoring of manufacturing in the 1980s to the tech bubble of the early 2000s and, most recently, the cryptocurrency collapse.
2. The fall of Mt. Gox was the first major crypto insolvency, demonstrating how poor security, lack of transparency, and inadequate asset controls can destroy an exchange and leave creditors uncertain about recoveries for years.
3. Crypto bankruptcies often follow cycles of misinformation, initial panic, and delayed but sometimes substantial recoveries, as seen in Mt. Gox, where early fears of catastrophic losses were later softened by rising Bitcoin prices.
4. Japan's legal system, while different from the United States in terms of disclosure, still mandated periodic updates in the Mt. Gox case, contradicting early perceptions that creditors were left entirely in the dark.

5. The rise and collapse of Cred illustrated the dangers of crypto lending platforms that promised high returns but concealed financial mismanagement, exposing how fragile unregulated lending models can be.
6. Crypto failures in 2022, including the collapses of Terra Luna and 3AC,, set off a domino effect, showing how interconnected financial obligations can rapidly destabilize an entire industry.
7. Celsius Network's downfall highlighted the risks of rapid, unhedged expansion, but its bankruptcy also demonstrated how distressed claim trading can present opportunities even in volatile markets.
8. Voyager Digital's commingled asset structure and reliance on high-risk loans exposed customers to hidden liabilities, reinforcing the importance of clear asset segregation and responsible lending practices.
9. FTX's dramatic collapse was fueled by the commingling of customer funds, mismanagement at Alameda Research, and false public assurances from SBF,, leading to one of the largest fraud cases in financial history.
10. John J. Ray III's leadership in FTX's bankruptcy led to an extraordinary recovery effort, securing billions in assets, including a valuable stake in Anthropic, though creditors were repaid based on the 2022 bankruptcy filing date, missing out on later market gains.
11. FTX's repayment plan offered some creditors in the "convenience class" up to 118% of their claims, but this benefit was not universal, highlighting the complexities of bankruptcy distributions.
12. The Celsius bankruptcy case revealed how debtors may attempt to restructure distributions in ways that disadvantage some creditors, emphasizing the importance of vigilance even after a court approves a reorganization plan.
13. Crypto bankruptcies frequently suffer from minimal preplanning, forcing companies into "freefall" restructurings that create uncertainty, prolong proceedings, and open opportunities for distressed investors.
14. Legal frameworks and regulatory oversight play a crucial role in shaping recovery outcomes, as evidenced by FTX's asset tracing success under a structured bankruptcy process.
15. Although the crypto sector has unique complexities, similar distressed investment opportunities exist in other industries, including opioid litigation, environmental liabilities, and struggling retail businesses.
16. The rapid rise and collapse of major crypto firms illustrate that no amount of technological innovation can eliminate the fundamental need for financial transparency, regulatory clarity, and prudent risk management.
17. Well-prepared investors who can identify and evaluate distressed assets objectively when others are panicking are often in the best position to capitalize on downturns and long-term recoveries.

CHAPTER 13

Turning Chaos into Opportunity

When I sit with successful distressed investors and ask how they identify prospects, one theme consistently emerges: the best opportunities are found in complexity and chaos that others find intimidating. What distinguishes great investors is their ability to keep the investment premise simple and focus on recovery value despite messy circumstances.

Distressed investing requires a sober and clear-eyed assessment of both risk and opportunity. For example, when American Express was rocked by the Salad Oil Scandal in 1963, most investors fled in panic as the stock plummeted 50%. Warren Buffett, however, took a different approach. Through boots-on-the-ground research, such as visiting local restaurants and banks to observe that customers were still using their American Express cards despite the headlines, he identified a disconnect between market perception and business reality. As we will explore, Buffett made a bold, concentrated bet at precisely the moment others were running scared—and made out handsomely.

This chapter explores the spectrum of approaches to distressed investing, from Buffett's high-conviction, hands-on style to more passive, diversified strategies. We'll examine the important decision between investing in debt versus equity through analyzing cases like Bed Bath & Beyond, where retail investors learned the hard way that equity claims vanish while debt holders often recover substantial value. We'll also consider the advantages and challenges of out-of-court restructurings, the complexities of the "holdout problem," and the growing importance of litigation funding in today's distressed landscape.

Whether you're drawn to active engagement with management or prefer a more hands-off approach, these strategies offer pathways to unlock value where others see only disaster. After all, in distress, price and value often diverge dramatically, creating asymmetric opportunities that can generate exceptional returns.

Active vs. Passive Investing Approaches

In distressed investing, one of the most fundamental choices investors face is how actively to engage with their investments. As I often tell my students, there's no universal "right" approach; what matters is finding the strategy that aligns with your resources, expertise, and temperament. Some investors thrive on deep involvement and concentrated bets, while others succeed through diversification and patience.

The distinction between active and passive approaches isn't merely academic; it shapes every aspect of the investing process, from sourcing to exit. To understand these contrasting styles, let's examine two iconic examples: Warren Buffett's hands-on approach with American Express during the Salad Oil Scandal, and, later in the section, Walter Schloss's more diversified methodology.

The Salad Oil Scandal: Young Warren Buffett Proves His Chops

In the early 1960s, American Express, a company renowned for its traveler's checks and charge cards, boldly moved into the field warehousing business. Through a new subsidiary known as American Express Field Warehousing, or Amexco, it issued warehouse inventory receipts that clients could use as collateral to secure loans from banks and financial institutions. Rather than directly providing credit, Amexco facilitated access to financing by certifying the existence of stored inventory. This venture eventually brought American Express into the orbit of Anthony "Tino" De Angelis, a notorious con artist whose elaborate fraud nearly toppled the company.

De Angelis had a storied career of schemes and swindles in the food industry, working his way up from a fish market laborer to executive roles at various meat-processing companies. His frauds included selling substandard lard to Yugoslavia and defaulting on a significant USDA pork contract. In 1955, De Angelis made his boldest move yet. He established the Allied Crude Vegetable Oil Refining Corporation in Bayonne, New Jersey, converting a dilapidated petroleum tank farm into a soybean and cottonseed oil storage facility. Allied's impressive inventory, however, was a fiction: De Angelis had filled many of the tanks with seawater, topped with a thin layer of oil.

Enter Amexco, a struggling subsidiary desperate for a lifeline. At the time, Amexco was operating at a loss and needed high-volume clients to stay afloat. De Angelis wooed Amexco representative Donald Miller, giving him VIP treatment and grand tours of the Allied facility and presenting himself as just the kind of client Amexco needed. Dazzled, Miller and his inspectors failed to detect the elaborate deceptions: phantom tank numbers, ladders to nowhere, fake pipelines, and even a requirement for twenty-four hours of advance notice before any inspections.

Based on Amexco's flawed certifications, Allied obtained warehousing receipts for nearly a billion pounds of vegetable oil—of which only a fraction existed. De Angelis used these receipts to secure loans from over 50 financial institutions, including Bank of America and Chase Manhattan. At its peak, Allied handled 75% of all U.S. soybean oil exports, an astonishing market share for a company built on lies. The house of cards began collapsing in November 1963 when the U.S. Commodity Exchange Authority investigated Allied's suspicious trading activity. Inspectors sent to verify Allied's inventory were shocked to find that tanks previously certified to be filled with valuable vegetable oil contained mostly seawater. Allied immediately declared bankruptcy and defaulted on its loans, kicking off a chain reaction that shook Wall Street.

When the fraud was uncovered, it turned out that the warehouse receipts issued by Amexco were based on nonexistent inventory. Since Amexco had vouched for the collateral, American Express was held financially responsible when the banks sought compensation for the worthless collateral. Essentially, Amexco's credibility and reputation were on the line, and as a subsidiary of American Express, the parent company bore the financial and reputational fallout. The Allied scandal hit American Express especially hard, causing its stock to plummet by 50%. The market situation worsened when, the very next day, President John F. Kennedy was assassinated in Dallas, sending the nation into mourning and the markets into a tailspin. The New York Stock Exchange shut down for four days, an unprecedented closure. When markets reopened, the losses were staggering. American Express faced $150 million in potential liabilities (equivalent to $1.3 billion today), a barrage of lawsuits, and a looming crisis of confidence. Sixteen companies were bankrupted, including Amexco itself. American Express's survival was in serious doubt.

One man, however, saw opportunity amid the chaos: Warren Buffett, then a little-known investor from Omaha, Nebraska. The thirty-three-year-old had been closely following American Express, and he came to a contrarian conclusion. Despite the scandal's severity, he believed the company's core businesses, traveler's checks and charge cards, remained fundamentally sound. So he decided to put his theory to the test. He visited local restaurants and banks, observing that customers continued to use their American Express cards and checks despite the negative headlines. This real-world data convinced Buffett to make a bold move: he started buying American Express stock.

The Allied scandal became a defining moment for Buffett, a trial by fire that showcased the effectiveness of his research-intensive, hands-on value investing. As Buffett's star rose to legendary heights in the decades to come, his American Express coup would be remembered as one of the early victories that helped forge the Oracle of Omaha's unparalleled investment legacy.

Importantly, Buffett's involvement did not stop at buying shares. He also actively engaged with American Express's management, including CEO Howard Clark, advocating for the company to settle the claims related to the scandal. Buffett understood that preserving the company's reputation was crucial for its long-term success. His influence helped push through a settlement of $60 million ($620 million in 2025 dollars), a strategic move that helped restore confidence and stability. This active role exemplified Buffett's approach to distressed investing. He took a significant, concentrated position, adding shares until he owned 5% of the company, and worked constructively with management to navigate the crisis. American Express's stock rebounded as the company recovered, and Buffett's investment grew substantially.

In a letter to his shareholders on January 24, 1968, Buffett reflected on the success of the American Express investment, noting that it had significantly outperformed the market and grown to 40% of his partnership's portfolio. He had purchased the shares at an average of $0.94 each and took some gains in the $5 range, marking an extraordinary return on investment. As of 2024, Berkshire Hathaway remained the largest shareholder in American Express, with a 21% stake.

The Salad Oil Scandal is a classic example of active, contrarian distressed investing. Buffett's ability to see through the near-term panic and trust his analysis of American Express's intrinsic value was pivotal. His high-conviction bet and hands-on involvement with the company's recovery underscore the potential rewards of this investment strategy.

As for De Angelis, he was convicted of fraud and conspiracy in 1965 and sentenced to 10 years in federal prison. Upon release, he dove back into the world of agricultural fraud, orchestrating a series of meat-packing scams that ultimately landed him back behind bars. He died in 2009 at age 93.

Passive Investing: Walter Schloss and the Rise of Index Funds

While Warren Buffett's hands-on and highly involved approach to distressed investing has garnered much attention, another strategy has quietly delivered remarkable success with a more passive method: the disciplined, diversified value investing of Walter Schloss.

A legend in the investment world, Schloss worked alongside Warren Buffett at Graham-Newman Corporation in the 1950s, where both learned the art of value investing from the father of the discipline himself, Benjamin Graham. However, while Buffett eventually evolved his approach towards more concentrated, high-conviction bets on quality businesses, Schloss remained true to Graham's original teachings throughout his career, which advocated seeking out undervalued stocks without becoming deeply involved in company operations (see Fig. 1).

Schloss's strategy was similarly simple: buy stocks trading significantly below their intrinsic value, specifically focusing on companies selling for less than their net current asset value. This approach, known as "net-net investing," required rigorous analysis to identify deeply undervalued stocks but did not require actively managing or influencing these companies. Schloss believed that by buying a diversified basket of these bargain-priced securities, the portfolio would deliver strong returns as the market eventually recognized their true worth.

The results speak for themselves. Over its 47-year investment career, Schloss's firm, Walter J. Schloss Associates, earned a remarkable 16% compound annual return after fees, significantly outpacing the broader market. Even more impressive, his actual portfolio returns before fees were even higher, with Buffett noting in his famous essay, "The Superinvestors of Graham-and-Doddsville," that Schloss had achieved a 21.3% annual return over 28 years.

What makes Schloss's approach particularly relevant to distressed investing was his comfort with unloved, out-of-favor companies that others avoided. While not exclusively focusing on distressed situations, his strategy of buying companies trading at deep discounts often led him to businesses experiencing temporary setbacks or market disfavor—precisely the types of situations where price and value diverge most dramatically.

Schloss's success was rooted in discipline, patience, and a focus on quantitative measures of value. He avoided the temptations of market timing and ignored the siren song of rapid growth. For Schloss, the key was to pay the right price for assets and to diversify widely, allowing the law

ACTIVE vs. PASSIVE DISTRESSED INVESTING

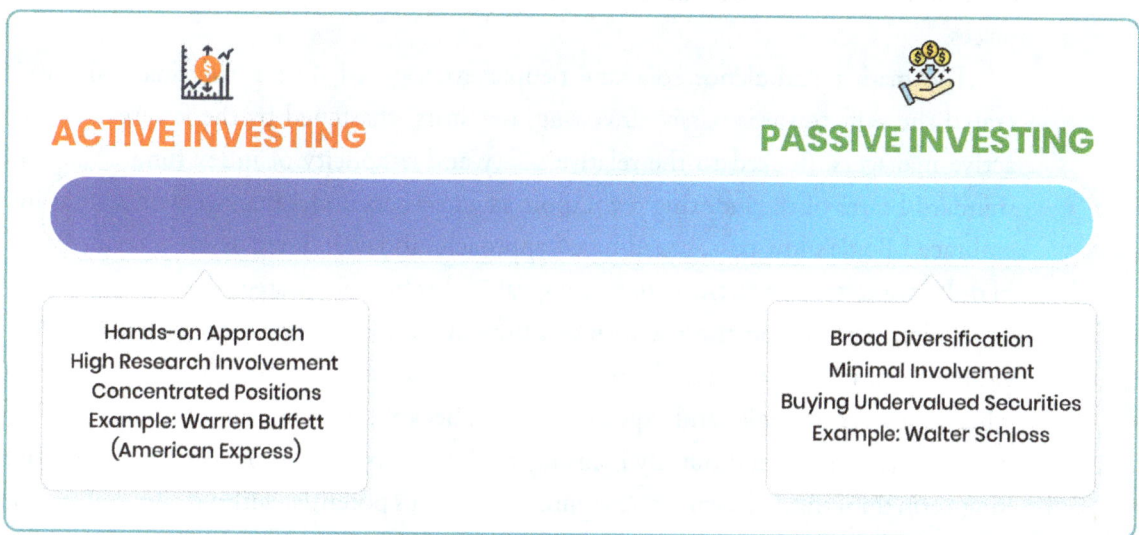

Figure 1: Active vs. Passive Distressed Investing

of averages to work in his favor. He recognized that not every investment would be a winner, but the odds were stacked in his favor by consistently buying stocks at a significant discount to their underlying value.

This passive, quantitative approach to value investing found its ultimate expression in the rise of index funds. Pioneered by Jack Bogle and his company, Vanguard, index funds took the basic premise of buying undervalued stocks to its logical conclusion: if trying to beat the market was a loser's game, why not simply buy the entire market? Bogle's first index fund, launched in 1976, aimed to track the performance of the S&P 500. His rationale was simple but powerful: most active managers consistently fail to outperform due to high fees and trading costs. By creating a low-cost fund that simply mirrored the index, investors could enjoy the market's long-term growth without the drag of excessive expenses.

Like Schloss's approach, index investing is based on recognizing the limits of individual stock-picking skills. Both strategies rely on the notion that, over time, the market tends to get valuations right and that a disciplined, low-cost, long-term approach can harness this tendency without the need for constant intervention.

The true test of this passive approach came during the crucible of the 2008 Global Financial Crisis. As markets plummeted and panic gripped investors, those who kept their faith in the market's long-term potential and invested in index funds reaped the rewards of the subsequent recovery. From the depths of the crisis in March 2009, the S&P 500 staged a historic rally, rising over 400% in the following decade. Those with the discipline to hold on to their indexed investments through the storm emerged unscathed and triumphant.

For distressed investors, this period demonstrated a critical lesson: broad market distress creates opportunities for those with patience and available capital. While Schloss might have approached this environment by selectively purchasing individual securities trading below their asset values, index investors achieved similar results by buying the entire market at depressed prices.

The market turbulence so many people experienced during the financial crisis accelerated the shift towards passive investing. Investors, chastened by the failures of high-flying active managers, flocked to the relative safety and simplicity of index funds. Vanguard, the standard-bearer of the indexing revolution, saw its assets under management soar as investors embraced Bogle's low-cost, broad-based approach. Today, indexed assets account for trillions of dollars, a testament to the enduring appeal of this humble strategy.

Walter Schloss and the rise of index investing offer powerful lessons for investors navigating the turbulent world of distressed securities. In a market often driven by fear and greed, where complex strategies and expensive experts beckon, the simplicity and discipline of these passive approaches stand out. By focusing on the core principles of value, diversification, and long-term thinking, investors can tap into the market's potential without succumbing to short-term volatility.

Debt vs. Equity: A Distressed Investor's Dilemma

The debt versus equity decision is where fortunes are made and lost in distressed investing. It's the high-stakes poker hand that separates the professionals from the amateurs, and it's often where retail investors get burned while seasoned players walk away with significant returns.

When a company begins its downward spiral, a quiet but ruthless game of musical chairs begins. Sophisticated investors start positioning themselves in the capital structure where they can maximize returns while minimizing risk. As one distressed fund manager told me, "In bankruptcy, it's not about what you think a company is worth. It's about where you sit at the table when the music stops."

Consider the company's capital structure as a building during an earthquake. The ground floor, secured debt, may suffer cracks but usually remains standing. The penthouse, equity, often collapses entirely. The creditors on the lower floors (senior secured debt) get the first claim on the assets, while equity holders must wait for everyone else to be satisfied before they see a penny. This is why experienced distressed investors obsessively study intercreditor agreements, loan covenants, and collateral packages before making their move.

The case of Bed Bath & Beyond illustrates this principle painfully well. As the retailer's situation deteriorated in 2022, vendors began demanding prepayments, exacerbating the company's liquidity crisis. While retail investors piled into the stock as a "meme play," the hedge fund Hudson Bay Capital Management structured a sophisticated deal that gave them preferred access to the company's remaining value. When the dust settled, equity investors were wiped out completely, while many debt holders recovered substantial portions of their investments.

The asset and cash flow analysis in distressed situations isn't merely academic; it's a matter of survival. Debt investors dig deep into collateral values because they know recovery will likely come from liquidation rather than ongoing operations. Meanwhile, equity investors making turnaround bets must realistically assess whether the company can generate enough cash to service its debt before equity sees any benefit. In Bed Bath & Beyond's case, empty shelves, disrupted supply chains, and dwindling cash reserves told the real story, one that social media enthusiasm and meme stock hype couldn't overcome. Despite retail investors piling into the stock, the company's fundamental financial struggles were too severe to be reversed by speculative trading alone.

Ultimately, the debt-equity decision forces investors to be brutally honest about their capabilities, time horizon, and stomach for risk. As one veteran investor once told me during a conference panel discussion, "Buying equity in deeply distressed companies is like trying to catch falling knives. Occasionally, you grab the handle and look brilliant, but usually, you end up bleeding." For those without the expertise to navigate complex bankruptcy proceedings or the capital to influence outcomes, debt positions often provide the safer path to capturing the distressed discount without betting on the most uncertain of outcomes.

CASE STUDY: BED BATH & BEYOND

The saga of Bed Bath & Beyond offers a textbook example of the debt versus equity dilemma in distressed investing and illustrates why capital structure position matters more than company potential when a business is circling the drain (see Fig. 2).

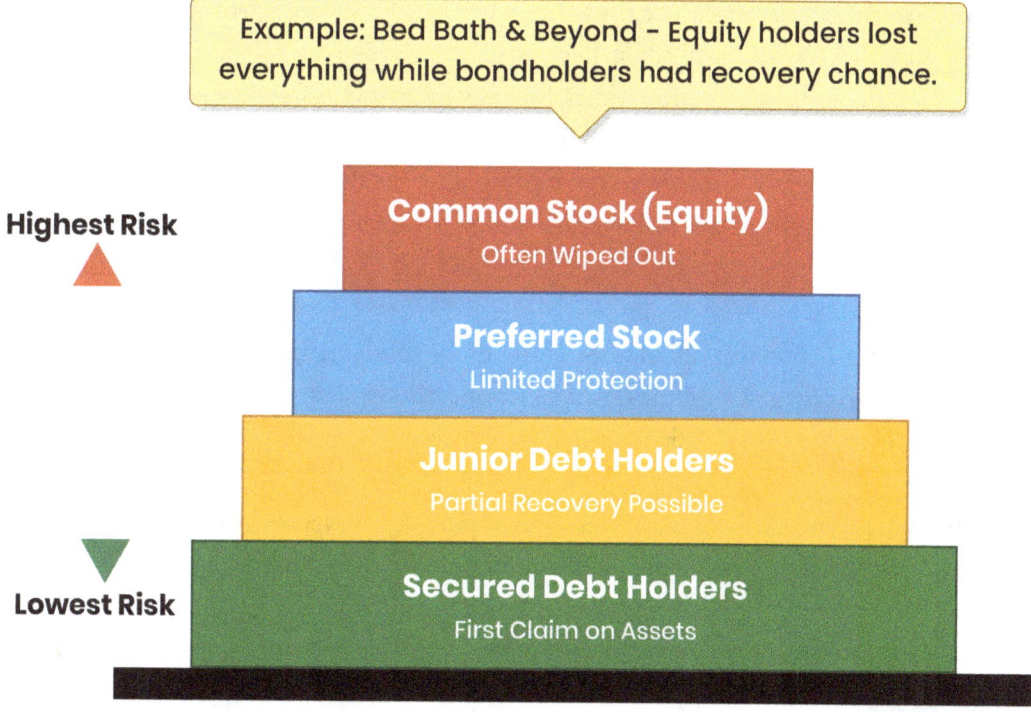

Figure 2: Debt vs. Equity in Distressed Investing

In early 2023, Bed Bath & Beyond was in dire financial straits. Once a dominant force in the home goods retail sector, the company had been grappling with declining sales, intense competition from e-commerce rivals, and the lingering impact of the COVID-19 pandemic. As the company's financial woes deepened, it made a series of last-ditch efforts to raise capital and stave off bankruptcy. These moves, all detrimental to equity holders, included multiple stock offerings and a structured deal with Hudson Bay.

What followed was a classic death spiral that sophisticated distressed investors recognized immediately but that trapped unwary retail traders looking for the next meme stock miracle.

In January 2023, Bed Bath & Beyond had approximately 117.3 million shares outstanding, trading at around $3.35 per share. Desperate for cash, the company launched a series of stock offerings that, by April 2023, had ballooned its share count to 739.1 million, while the stock price had plummeted to just $0.30. Hudson Bay seized the opportunity by paying Bed Bath & Beyond $225 million upfront in exchange for the right to receive discounted shares over time, with the option to re-up the trade eight more times at $100 million each. This deal raised about $360 million but issued 311 million new shares to Hudson Bay, representing 73% of the total outstanding shares.

This massive dilution was a red flag that professional investors recognized immediately. When a distressed company issues mountains of new equity at progressively lower prices, it's rarely trying to fund a turnaround; it's desperately trying to keep the lights on just a little longer.

As Bed Bath & Beyond's financial situation deteriorated, vendors began to demand prepayments, exacerbating the company's liquidity crisis. Bed Bath & Beyond was on the brink of collapse with empty shelves and dwindling cash reserves. Distressed investors looking at Bed Bath & Beyond during this tumultuous period had the choice between the company's debt and equity. Let's examine the situation in more detail to show why debt was the better choice.

Yes, Bed Bath & Beyond's structured deal with Hudson Bay gave the retailer much-needed cash. Still, it also resulted in a massive transfer of value from existing shareholders to Hudson Bay. The deal's structure, which allowed Hudson Bay to convert its preferred shares into common stock at a discount to the trading price, enabled the hedge fund to acquire a significant portion of Bed Bath & Beyond's equity at a steep discount. As the company's stock price declined, Hudson Bay was able to convert and sell its shares for a profit, while other investors suffered losses.

In late September 2023, Bed Bath & Beyond initiated a bankruptcy procedure that involved a managed winding down of its operations, with the remaining assets transferred to debenture holders. The shares were nullified and delisted, leaving shareholders with nothing. Despite warnings from the company's management, some retail shareholders remained hopeful for a last-minute rescue, speculating on potential buyers or restructuring plans.

The contrast between debt and equity outcomes couldn't have been starker. While equity investors were completely wiped out, bond investors stood to recover a meaningful portion of their investment, precisely illustrating the protection that positioning higher in the capital structure provides during distress.

TURNING CHAOS INTO OPPORTUNITY

For its part, Hudson Bay remains entangled in the aftermath. The hedge fund's transactions with "Section 16 blocker" provisions, designed to prevent Hudson Bay from being considered a 10% beneficial owner and thus subject to short-swing profit rules, have come under scrutiny. In a lawsuit filed in May 2024 by Bed Bath & Beyond's creditors, it is alleged that these blockers were "illusory" and that Hudson Bay repeatedly exceeded the 9.99% ownership cap. The creditors seek to recover more than $300 million in trading profits from Hudson Bay, arguing that the hedge fund's actions violated securities regulations.

Retail investors who participated in Bed Bath & Beyond's last-ditch stock offerings learned the risks of owning equity the hard way, as their investments were wiped out in the bankruptcy. It is the same hard lesson that amateur investors fail to learn time and again, whether it's with JCPenney, Hertz, Bed Bath & Beyond, or some other meme stock of the day touted by a day trader with a big social media following: shareholder value disappears because all creditors must be made whole before the equity owners get anything.

Bond investors in the Bed Bath & Beyond case will make out better insofar as they will likely recoup more than zero, but how much remains to be seen. In the meantime, a separate lawsuit is playing out for bondholders.

This isn't the end of the story, however. In an intriguing twist, the Pulte family, led by William J. Pulte Jr., entered the fray. After interacting with retail investors about the company through social media, Pulte, a philanthropist and the CEO of Pulte Capital Partners, expressed interest in purchasing Bed Bath & Beyond bonds. After extensive research, including hosting an event in Florida with retail shareholders, on January 18, 2024, Pulte purchased Bed Bath & Beyond bonds maturing in 2034 in the low single digits. His stated aim was to investigate potential irregularities behind the company's bankruptcy and hold those he believed had contributed to the company's downfall accountable.

Pulte's investigation and strategy are quite common in bankruptcy cases where the recovery to unsecured holders appears to be nothing. The motivation for pursuing something that at first glance seems to be pointless is because bankruptcies don't typically happen overnight. If there truly is malfeasance (i.e., behavior that may lead to the recovery of some amount of assets), the signs should have been evident long before a company files.

Who do claimholders look to blame? Directors and officers who guided the companies. And, because big companies typically have directors and officers liability insurance policies, even the seemingly worthless shell of a corporation can have unexpected assets worth pursuing. In the section on litigation funding at the end of this chapter and in Chapter 3, we discuss the opportunity to finance these types of lawsuits. But suffice it to say even in the bleakest-seeming bankruptcy cases able professionals may provide some hope of recovery.

The Bed Bath & Beyond case reminds distressed investors of a fundamental truth: in bankruptcy, your position in the capital structure typically matters more than your conviction about a company's future prospects. Debt investors may not capture the full theoretical upside of a miraculous recovery, but they also don't face the total loss that equity holders frequently experience when that recovery fails to materialize.

Taking Control Through Distressed Investments

Sharks don't apologize for their nature. When they detect blood in the water, they strike with cold precision. The most successful distressed investors operate with this same predatory instinct. They identify wounded companies, calculate their attack angle, and move decisively. This approach isn't for everyone. It requires nerve, capital, and the willingness to be vilified by those who don't understand that creative destruction is sometimes beneficial and necessary.

Eddie Lampert, the hedge fund manager who engineered the acquisition and systematic dismantling of Kmart and Sears, exemplifies this approach. While thousands lost their jobs and two iconic American retailers disappeared, Lampert and his investors made billions. His story demonstrates both the potential rewards and the moral complexities of taking control through distressed investments.

His success shows that while debt investments offer safer returns and equity plays offer potential upside, there's a third approach that can generate extraordinary returns: taking control. This strategy, acquiring enough influence to dictate a company's direction, sits at the aggressive end of the distressed investing spectrum. When executed successfully, it allows investors to extract value that others might miss. When executed ruthlessly, it can generate enormous profits while leaving destruction in its wake.

In some ways, the Kmart/Sears story is a playbook for success. In another way, it's a roadmap of what to be wary of. I think it's worth telling because it symbolizes what one man can do when he sees deep value in a group of assets. In Chapter 10, I described what happened to one of Sears's vendors, ShoeMe, who decided to sell their trade claim after being dragged through the company's agonizing bankruptcy process. In this chapter, I'll give you the rest of the gory details.

Let's start from the beginning.

In 2002, Kmart, a discount retail chain headquartered near Detroit, Michigan, filed for bankruptcy. Though it had approximately 1,200 stores at the time, it had been steadily losing ground to the likes of Target and Walmart in the mass retail marketplace. Shortly after emerging from bankruptcy with the assistance of Eddie Lampert, a hedge fund manager, it became clear that Kmart and its much larger competitor, Sears, could have a lot of synergies if they were combined. Around 2004, Lampert began amassing shares in Sears, which had approximately 3,500 stores. Seeking to cut costs and consolidate overhead, Lampert proposed merging Kmart and Sears into a super-retailer that could compete against Target and Walmart. At least, that was the public message. Lampert also saw that the stores of Kmart and Sears, not to mention venerable Sears-launched brands like Kenmore, Craftsman, DieHard, and Lands' End, had tremendous asset value.

This is where the distressed investor's mindset diverges from the typical business perspective. While industry analysts focused on whether the combined retailer could compete effectively with newer rivals, Lampert was playing a different game altogether: one focused on the underlying asset values rather than operational turnaround.

So in 2005, when the former competitors officially merged into a single company, Sears Holdings Corp., the new firm ranked as the third-largest retailer in the United States. Lampert, who controlled nearly 40% of the company, served as CEO and chairman, and soon after Sears Holdings' stock began trading, it became very attractive to the investment fund community because they realized what Lampert saw in the combined company. Although the holding company remained prosperous over the following years, sales at Kmart and Sears stores continued to decline, prompting Lampert to launch a major multimedia advertising campaign in 2008. He also oversaw the buyback of stock (which benefited him and his hedge fund greatly), which some shareholders claimed weakened Sears Holdings by leaving it low on cash.

The pattern that emerged over the next decade showcases the asset-stripping playbook in its classic form: gain control, selectively monetize valuable assets, and structure deals to ensure maximum benefit to yourself while maintaining the fiction of attempting a turnaround.

Under Lampert's oversight, the corporation subsequently began selling various assets, notably its Craftsman tool brand (2017), and in 2014, it spun off Land's End, one of Sears Holdings' profitable retailers, into an independent company. Furthermore, Lampert spun off real estate to a newly formed public entity, Seritage Growth Properties, which was focused on redeveloping old Sears and Kmart stores. In October 2018, Sears Holdings filed for Chapter 11 bankruptcy protection, and Lampert stepped down as CEO, though he continued as chairman. In February 2019, Lampert bought back the remaining 400 Sears stores; not long after, however, most of the stores closed (see Fig. 3).

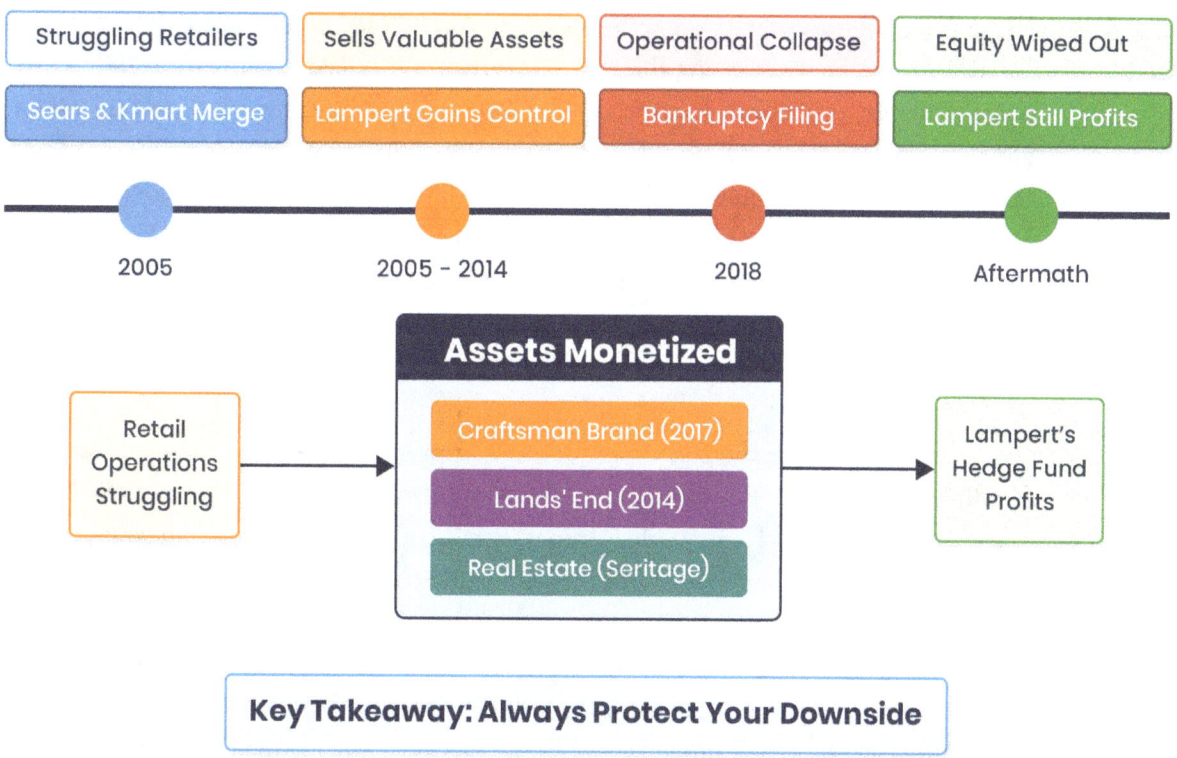

Figure 3: Distressed Investing Playbook: The Sears and Kmart Example

With all that as a preamble, here is your distilled distressed investing playbook takeaway: always protect your downside.

Lampert understood his downside protection from Day One, even as he started buying deeply discounted public shares. As he once reportedly told associates, "My worst-case scenario is better than most people's best-case scenario." Even if the retail operations failed completely, which they largely did, the underlying real estate, intellectual property, and brand value provided a floor that made the investment compelling. This approach, while controversial and devastating for employees and many other stakeholders, demonstrates how control-oriented distressed investing can generate returns even from businesses that ultimately fail as going concerns.

Asset Stripping Considerations

As I indicated, there are many lessons to be learned from Eddie Lampert's takeover of Kmart and Sears. First, he had an investment thesis: combining two struggling retailers seemed like a better idea than leaving each company to stand on its own. For a time, his strategy worked, but then the marketplace and the pressures of the internet on retailing became too great. Second, he understood complex financial mechanics and how to spin off and divest a company's assets, all while enriching his stakeholders. Third, he protected his downside by appreciating that because of the company's immense real estate portfolio, there was inherent value in the assets. This is the cornerstone principle of asset-driven distressed investing: always know your worst-case recovery scenario and make sure it exceeds your entry price. As the old Wall Street adage goes, "Figure out what something's worth when dead, and pay less."

Even while he was putting the pieces together and talked about revitalizing Kmart and Sears, Lampert probably felt quite certain that his investment would not lose money. He almost certainly calculated, even if on the back of an envelope, that if worse came to worst, the liquidation value of the combined real estate portfolio was worth considerably more than what he paid to acquire shares, a strategy known in distressed investing circles as "buy the assets, get the business for free." This approach was made famous by several prominent investors in the 1970s and 1980s who became known as "corporate raiders." These investors, viewed as villains by some and visionaries by others, recognized that America's corporate landscape was littered with inefficient conglomerates whose parts were worth far more than their whole.

The 1980s became the golden age of asset stripping as investors like Carl Icahn, Ronald Perelman, and Victor Posner deployed increasingly sophisticated tactics to unlock value. Icahn's dismantling of Trans World Airlines, Perelman's takeover of Revlon, and Posner's raid on Sharon Steel weren't merely financial transactions; they were seismic events that transformed American business culture. These investors forced corporate America to confront uncomfortable questions about efficiency, accountability, and shareholder value that still resonate today.

Besides his keen understanding of the value of Sears' and Kmart's real estate portfolios and the combined intellectual property and brand equity of the companies, Lampert recognized something fundamental that most retail investors missed: these storied brands were worth more as cadavers than as patients on life support. While mainstream investors fixated on quarterly sales figures and turnaround narratives, Lampert was coldly calculating liquidation values and divestiture options. Notably, one of Lampert's major suppliers of debt to his real estate company, Seritage, was none other than Warren Buffett's company, Berkshire Hathaway.

It's an open question whether he foresaw the end of one of America's most beloved retailers when he started acquiring shares. Some people claimed he never had any intention of running the companies as going concerns and restoring them to operational health. When his liquidation strategy became clear, however, he was quickly vilified by employees and the press. Numerous lawsuits followed, but after years of litigation, Lampert emerged as the financial winner. The price he paid, however, went far beyond dollars and equity stakes. Lampert became the face of hedge fund greed and the man who singlehandedly engineered the downfall of Sears.

Whether Sears would have toppled on its own is an open question. Considering that other major department stores like JCPenney failed and Macy's has teetered on the brink for decades lends credence to Lampert's contention that he had no choice. Distressed investors like Lampert will never win popularity contests, except perhaps with their own backers. And indeed, few people would have had the nerve, financial savvy, insight, and bravado to take over a company like Sears and liquidate it over multiple years, all while facing an onslaught of litigation and fierce criticism from vendors, employees, customers, and the press.

The Lampert saga illustrates the moral complexity inherent in control-oriented distressed investing. While his investors celebrated their returns, thousands lost their livelihoods, communities lost anchor stores, and an American institution vanished. Was Lampert merely accelerating an inevitable collapse, or did his asset-focused strategy prevent any chance of meaningful revival? The answer likely lies somewhere in between, and distressed investors must wrestle with these questions before pursuing similar strategies.

When done well, distressed investing can be a win-win, but when the object is maximum profit, the math can easily turn into a win-lose. I don't recommend that approach if for no other reason than that life is too short. Even today, the heirs to the Astor and Rockefeller fortunes may still feel a certain regret or even shame that their wealth came at the great expense of others. Andrew Carnegie may be one of the few "'robber barons" of his time whose conscience ultimately won out. The thousands of libraries and institutions named in his honor bear testimony to the fact that it's possible to both do well and do good. Maybe Lampert will donate his billions to a nonprofit organization that cures cancer, in which case history may judge him differently. At the time of this writing, however, few would choose to trade places with him despite his financial success.

Restructuring Approaches

When faced with financial distress, executives of companies like Sears and Kmart took bold and sometimes controversial steps, whether through asset stripping or creative debt restructuring. In both cases, they had to decide whether to resolve the issues privately or face the scrutiny of bankruptcy court. This isn't just a challenge for retail giants; it's a common dilemma for any business on the brink. The choice between informal restructuring and formal bankruptcy not only affects the company's future but also impacts potential investor returns. When a company finds itself in distress, a window of opportunity often still exists before formal bankruptcy becomes inevitable. During this period, stakeholders face a pivotal decision: attempt to resolve financial challenges outside the courtroom or prepare for Chapter 11. This choice, between informal restructuring and formal bankruptcy, shapes both the company's future and investors' potential returns.

For distressed investors, understanding the difference between these processes helps determine not only possible outcomes but also their influence throughout the resolution. Each path offers distinct strategic opportunities, risks, and timelines that savvy investors must navigate to maximize returns.

Out-of-Court Restructurings

When the threat of bankruptcy looms, companies may look for alternative solutions that minimize cost and reputational damage. Out-of-court restructurings and workouts are common choices that can provide companies with paths to adjust debt terms or capital structure without the formalities of bankruptcy. However, these approaches come with their own challenges, including the notorious holdout problem, which often complicates efforts to reach consensus among creditors.

Although the terms "restructuring" and "workout" are often used interchangeably, there is a subtle difference between the two. A restructuring typically involves a more comprehensive overhaul of a company's capital structure, which may include exchanging existing debt for new securities, such as equity or debt with different terms. On the other hand, a workout generally refers to a more targeted approach, focusing on modifying specific debt obligations without significantly altering the overall capital structure.

Out-of-court restructurings offer several advantages over traditional bankruptcy proceedings. By avoiding formal bankruptcy, companies can save substantially on professional fees, such as those for attorneys and financial advisors, costs that can quickly consume cash needed for operations. Participants in a workout are not bound by the strict rules and regulations of Chapter 11 bankruptcy, allowing them to create their own rules and terms if all parties agree. This flexibility can lead to more creative and tailored solutions.

Additionally, out-of-court restructurings are generally viewed more favorably by customers, suppliers, and employees, as they suggest that the company is taking proactive steps to address its financial challenges without the stigma of bankruptcy. In an out-of-court process, management also retains greater control over the company's operations and decision-making, unlike in a bankruptcy proceeding where a judge or court-appointed committees may have significant influence.

The automotive industry crisis of 2008–2009 provides a compelling study in contrasting approaches. In 2006, Ford Motor Company faced mounting financial challenges, including substantial losses and a weakening market position. To avoid bankruptcy, the company launched a comprehensive out-of-court restructuring plan it called "The Way Forward."

A major component of this plan involved securing a $23.5 billion loan, using most of Ford's assets, including its iconic blue oval logo, as collateral. This infusion of capital provided the liquidity Ford needed to fund its restructuring efforts. Also, Ford negotiated with creditors to reduce its debt obligations, working closely with lenders to modify terms, lower interest rates, and extend maturities wherever possible. Alongside these financial maneuvers, Ford implemented significant operational changes, such as closing unprofitable plants and reducing its workforce.

Together, these measures were designed to streamline operations and improve the company's overall financial performance. By executing its out-of-court restructuring plan, Ford avoided bankruptcy during the 2008–2009 financial crisis, unlike its domestic competitors, General Motors (GM) and Chrysler, which required government bailouts and ultimately filed for bankruptcy protection.

For distressed investors, Ford's successful out-of-court restructuring created different opportunities than those presented by GM and Chrysler. While the latter companies' bankruptcy proceedings offered clear entry points for claims trading and potential DIP financing, Ford's situation required more nuanced approaches, such as possibly purchasing debt at discounts or negotiating for equity-linked securities as part of creditor agreements.

The Holdout Problem

One of the challenges in out-of-court restructurings is the aforementioned holdout problem, which occurs when a group of creditors refuses to participate in the restructuring process, hoping to receive full payment on their claims while other creditors agree to accept reduced payments or modified terms. These holdouts can derail a company's efforts to achieve the minimum acceptance rate required for a successful restructuring (see Fig. 4).

The holdout problem creates a classic prisoner's dilemma, since each individual creditor has an incentive to hold out while hoping others will agree to concessions. If enough creditors follow this logic, however, the restructuring fails, and everyone potentially gets less in a subsequent bankruptcy proceeding. Smart distressed investors recognize both the risks and opportunities this dynamic creates.

To overcome the holdout problem and increase the likelihood of a successful voluntary exchange, companies can employ several strategies. First, they must thoroughly examine the firm's capital structure and identify the motivations driving various classes of claimholders. Understanding the priorities and incentives of different creditor groups helps tailor the restructuring proposal to address their specific concerns.

Companies should also investigate investors' views on the company's prospects by analyzing the pricing of its debt and equity securities. This approach provides insights into the market's perception of the company's creditworthiness and future performance, helping shape more effective restructuring proposals. Most importantly, successful restructurings make the new securities more attractive than the old debt while maintaining the seniority of the debt claims. This might involve higher interest rates, shorter maturities, or additional collateral to

THE HOLDOUT PROBLEM IN RESTRUCTURING

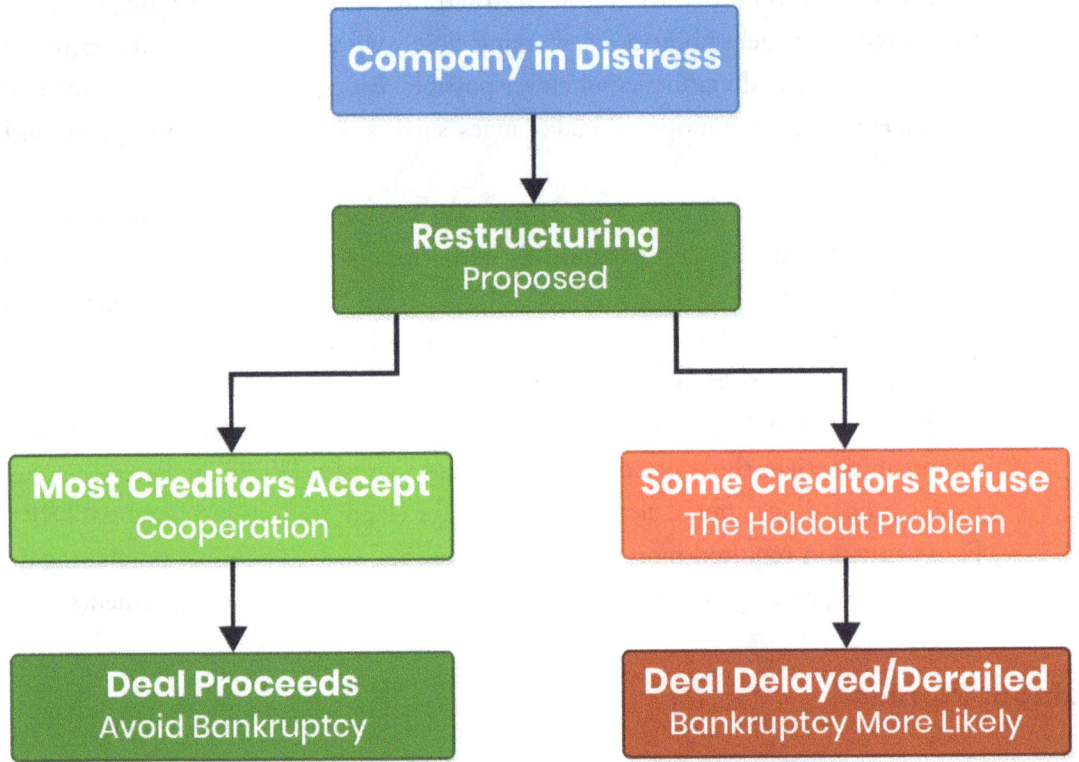

Figure 4: The Holdout Problem in Restructuring

encourage participation in the exchange, essentially creating a carrot to complement the stick of potential bankruptcy.

The holdout dynamic creates both challenges and opportunities. Being part of a blocking position in a key class of debt can provide significant negotiating leverage, potentially leading to better recoveries. However, this approach requires both capital and expertise to execute effectively. Smaller investors may find themselves at the mercy of larger creditors who control the direction of negotiations.

The success of an out-of-court restructuring depends on the company's ability to work through the complex web of stakeholder interests and overcome potential obstacles. By carefully examining its capital structure, engaging with investors, and crafting attractive exchange offers, a company can improve its chances of achieving a successful voluntary restructuring. As the case of Ford demonstrates, a well-executed out-of-court restructuring can be a powerful tool for companies seeking to avoid bankruptcy and position themselves for long-term success.

Legal Considerations in Distressed Investing

The legal landscape surrounding distressed investing resembles a chessboard where the rules occasionally change mid-game. To play the game intelligently, then, you need to not only understand current precedents but also anticipate how evolving case law might affect their positions.

Third-party releases in bankruptcy and litigation funding, for instance, are two areas of distressed investing that can be dramatically impacted by legal considerations. In both situations, a single court ruling or legislative change can transform a potentially profitable investment into a years-long struggle for minimal returns or, conversely, unlock unexpected value in previously undervalued claims. What may seem like little more than technical legal matters can significantly affect recovery amounts and timelines.

Third-Party Non-Debtor Releases

Third-party releases represent one of bankruptcy law's most controversial mechanisms. These provisions shield non-bankrupt parties, often company insiders, executives, or related entities, from liability related to the debtor's problems. Understanding when these releases are enforceable can mean the difference between recovering pennies on the dollar and pursuing potentially valuable claims against solvent parties.

Until recently, the bankruptcy world was divided on whether courts could approve releases that protected non-debtors without the consent of affected creditors. The Supreme Court's landmark 2024 decision in Harrington v. Purdue Pharma finally resolved this contentious issue, dramatically altering the landscape for mass tort bankruptcies and creditor recoveries. There are a few legal technicalities that might strike you as obtuse if you don't have the background, but let me walk you through the case. There are some important and useful facts to glean from Purdue that may help you come out ahead in other Chapter 11 situations.

CASE STUDY: SUPREME COURT DECISION IN PURDUE PHARMA

On June 27, 2024, the Supreme Court ruled in a 5–4 decision that bankruptcy courts lack the statutory authority to discharge creditors' claims against non-debtors without the creditors' consent. This decision in Harrington v. Purdue Pharma settled a long-standing dispute that will reshape how Chapter 11 reorganizations unfold, particularly in cases involving mass tort liability.

The Purdue Pharma saga began with the company's role in the opioid crisis through its marketing of the OxyContin painkiller. After pleading guilty to federal charges in 2007 for misbranding OxyContin as less addictive than other opioids, the company continued operations under the control of the Sackler family. Between 2008 and 2016, the Sacklers extracted approximately $11 billion from Purdue, diverting much of these funds to overseas trusts and family-owned businesses, actions that later became central to the bankruptcy controversy.

By 2019, facing thousands of lawsuits related to the opioid crisis, Purdue filed for Chapter 11 protection. The company and the Sacklers negotiated a global settlement where the family would return $4.325 billion (later increased to $6 billion) in exchange for comprehensive protection from civil liability. This protection came in two forms: consensual releases from creditors who agreed to the plan, and non-consensual releases that would bind even those creditors who objected.

The bankruptcy court initially confirmed this plan despite objections from thousands of creditors, including eight states and various municipalities. After a district court rejected the plan based on concerns about non-consensual releases, the Second Circuit reversed and reinstated the bankruptcy court's confirmation. The case eventually reached the Supreme Court, which had to resolve whether bankruptcy courts could approve such non-consensual releases.

The Court's majority concluded that the Bankruptcy Code does not authorize forcing non-consenting creditors to release their claims against non-debtors. The Court focused on Section 1123(b)(6), the catch-all provision allowing "any other appropriate provision not inconsistent with" the Code. The majority found that interpreting this provision to permit non-consensual third-party releases would grant powers far beyond what Congress intended.

The Court offered three additional reasons for its decision. First, such releases would effectively give non-debtors (the Sacklers) the benefits of bankruptcy discharge without actually filing for bankruptcy themselves. Second, the releases would shield the Sacklers from non-dischargeable claims (like those for willful misconduct) without requiring them to surrender all their assets. Finally, the Court noted that Congress had specifically authorized non-consensual releases only in asbestos cases, suggesting they weren't meant to be available in other contexts.

Despite this ruling, the Court carefully limited its decision's scope. It explicitly stated that consensual third-party releases remain valid, though it didn't define what qualifies as "consensual." The Court also declined to address whether its decision would affect plans that had already been substantially implemented.

The Purdue decision dramatically shifts the landscape for distressed investors. Creditors now have greater leverage in negotiations where third parties seek releases, as their explicit consent has become necessary. The Court's suggestion that non-consensual releases might still be possible in "full payment" plans also creates a new bargaining chip for creditors dealing with wealthy insiders or affiliates who desperately want liability protection.

The ruling has already prompted renewed negotiations in the Purdue case, with the Sacklers offering to increase their contribution to approximately $7.4 billion to secure broader consensual releases. It remains to be seen whether their better offer will be approved. Meanwhile, bankruptcy practitioners are exploring potential workarounds, including the use of Chapter 15 (cross-border bankruptcies) to recognize foreign proceedings where such releases might still be permitted.

For investors in distressed debt, particularly in cases involving mass torts or potential insider liability, the Purdue decision underscores the importance of carefully evaluating potential recovery channels. Claims against non-debtors that might previously have been eliminated through bankruptcy plans now represent a potentially valuable asset class in their own right.

Litigation Funding: Opportunities and Risks in Distressed Investing

Over the past decade, litigation funding has emerged as a compelling strategy in the distressed investing landscape, allowing investors to finance legal claims in exchange for a portion of potential recoveries. This approach has gained particular traction in high-stakes scenarios involving mass torts and corporate bankruptcies, including the Purdue case, where funders provided capital to law firms representing victims of the opioid crisis.

The basic mechanics of litigation funding in bankruptcy contexts take two main forms. In issue-specific funding, investors target particular legal claims with distinct recovery potential. For example, when officers and directors potentially committed fraud or improperly transferred assets, litigation funders might provide the $5 million needed to pursue these claims. In return, they might receive their capital back plus 20% of recoveries beyond a certain threshold, say $10 million. This creates a 2x return of capital plus an equity-like upside if the litigation succeeds.

Portfolio funding can also take a broader approach, financing multiple cases across a law firm's practice. A funder might back a mass tort firm handling cases against multiple defendants like Purdue Pharma, Boy Scouts of America, and others. This diversification spreads risk across various matters with different timelines and recovery prospects, potentially producing more stable returns.

A central feature of most litigation funding arrangements is their non-recourse nature. If the plaintiff loses, the funder absorbs the entire loss, with no obligation for the client or law firm to repay the funder. This structure effectively transforms legal claims into financial assets where the risk is clearly defined and limited to the capital deployed.

For distressed investors, litigation funding offers a unique angle on value creation in bankruptcy. While traditional approaches focus on trading claims based on expected distributions from the estate, litigation funding allows investors to participate in value creation through affirmative actions against third parties. This can be particularly attractive when the estate itself has limited assets but potentially valuable claims against solvent third parties.

However, litigation funding carries its own risks. Case outcomes remain inherently unpredictable, timelines can extend for years beyond initial projections, and regulatory scrutiny of funding arrangements continues to evolve. Successful investors in this space often have deep legal expertise and financial discipline. Considering the potential downside, they also quickly learn to balance portfolio construction to manage these uncertainties. In short, this is a game you shouldn't play unless you know all the rules and can anticipate and manage your downside risks.

Conclusion

The strategies and case studies presented in this chapter demonstrate the diversity and intricacy of distressed investing. From high-conviction, active approaches to passive, diversified strategies, each method has its place depending on the investor's goals, risk tolerance, and market outlook. The choice between debt and equity, for example, can dictate the level of control and potential returns, while out-of-court restructurings may offer cost-effective solutions if managed carefully and cooperatively.

The cases of American Express, Bed Bath & Beyond, and Purdue Pharma demonstrate how distressed investors must adapt their approaches to each unique scenario, harnessing industry knowledge, due diligence, and an understanding of market psychology to identify opportunities amid uncertainty. The emergence of litigation funding may have opened new doors to untapped value in complex legal environments, but the potential legal pitfalls involved in such situations underscore that deep pockets, nerves of steel, and high risk tolerance are required of any investors who wish to get involved.

As these cases and strategies show, distressed investing is never one-size-fits-all. It demands a flexible approach, an ability to assess risk from multiple angles, and a deep understanding of how different tools, from litigation funding to debt purchases, fit within the broader strategy. But theory and case studies can only take you so far.

In our final two chapters, we'll move from strategy to execution. We'll take the lessons learned so far and focus on how to build a practical framework for distressed investing, including how to source deals, analyze opportunities, manage risk, and position yourself for long-term success. Whether you're just getting started or refining an existing approach, these are the building blocks that can help you turn theory into actionable results.

KEY INSIGHTS

1. The best distressed investment opportunities are found in complexity and chaos that others find intimidating.
2. Successful distressed investing requires a sober assessment of both risk and opportunity.
3. In distressed situations, the line between business failure and misconduct often blurs.
4. Price and value often diverge dramatically in distress, creating asymmetric opportunities.
5. Distressed investing approaches range from high-conviction, hands-on styles to passive, diversified strategies.
6. Warren Buffett's American Express investment during the Salad Oil Scandal exemplifies active, contrarian investing with deep research and engagement.
7. Walter Schloss demonstrated that passive, diversified approaches focusing on undervalued assets can deliver remarkable returns in distressed scenarios.
8. In the capital structure hierarchy, secured debt typically suffers less damage than equity during financial distress.

9. Sophisticated investors position themselves in the capital structure to maximize returns while minimizing risk.
10. The debt-equity decision is crucial in distressed investing. Creditors on lower floors (secured debt) get the first claim on assets.
11. Bed Bath & Beyond illustrates why equity investors often get wiped out while debt holders recover substantial value.
12. Taking control of distressed companies can generate extraordinary returns but comes with moral complexity.
13. Eddie Lampert's Sears/Kmart strategy demonstrates how understanding asset values can protect the downside even when operations ultimately fail.
14. The cornerstone principle of asset-driven investing is to investing: know your worst-case recovery scenario and pay less.
15. Out-of-court restructurings offer advantages, including lower costs, greater flexibility, less stigma, and management retaining more control.
16. The holdout problem occurs when creditors refuse to participate in restructuring, hoping to receive full payment, while others accept concessions.
17. Successful restructurings make new securities more attractive than old debt while maintaining the seniority of claims.
18. Legal considerations dramatically impact distressed investing strategies and recovery amounts.
19. The Supreme Court's Purdue Pharma decision limited bankruptcy courts' ability to release claims against non-debtors without creditor consent.
20. Litigation funding transforms legal claims into financial assets with clearly defined risk, offering unique value creation in bankruptcy scenarios.

CHAPTER 14

The Distressed Investing Playbook in Action

There are watershed historical moments in our lives that become indelibly etched in our minds. I still remember exactly where I was at the moment Lehman Brothers collapsed. The date was September 15, 2008.

I was in my office in Rockefeller Center, New York, above where the *Today Show* is filmed, watching the news come in. Would the federal government come to Lehman's rescue? Would they let it fail? Would Goldman Sachs also go down?

I knew Lehman Brothers well because they made a lot of real estate loans, including on a housing development near my house. They also employed a lot of very smart people who I knew personally. With President George Bush at the end of his second term and little to lose, I thought there was a chance he and his administration would agree to let the federal government bail out Lehman. But somewhat unexpectedly, the powers that be decided there would be no bailout. Just like that, a 158-year-old Wall Street institution was gone, and within hours, the entire financial system started to unravel. Banks stopped lending. Markets crashed. Credit disappeared.

Many versions of the upheaval during that period have been recounted, but one observation I've heard repeatedly made is patently untrue: nobody knew what would happen next. Distressed investors knew that there was going to be plenty of opportunity.

That's what I find so fascinating about panic-selling at moments like this: nobody knows what anything is worth in real time. However, those with cash in their bank accounts have a multitude of options.

I watched guys who spent decades managing risk freeze up because what was happening around them wasn't in any of the textbooks. They were waiting for some instant certainty. That wasn't going to happen. The ones who made money, the ones who turned the crisis into an opportunity, didn't sit around and wait for someone to tell them what to do. They understood how to operate in uncertainty. They knew what to look for and had a playbook.

At the time, everyone was focused on Lehman itself. The bankruptcy. The court battles. The creditors fighting. But that wasn't where the real money was.

The real money was in everything Lehman had touched: Office buildings. Apartment complexes. Hotels. Businesses that were suddenly stranded, cut off from financing but still viable. Ancillary businesses that serviced these companies were also in trouble. That's where the opportunity was: in the ripples (see Fig. 1). The people who recognized it early, who knew how to structure deals and assess risk, made fortunes.

The Financial Crisis of 2008 was also the moment my thinking changed about distressed investing, because it wasn't just hedge funds and private equity firms making those deals. There were also individual investors: people who bought stocks when everything was collapsing, picked up rental properties for next to nothing, or stepped in when others were too afraid to move. It made me see that distressed opportunities weren't just reserved for institutions, that ordinary people who acted decisively could also reap substantial rewards. Still, there could have been more. A lot more.

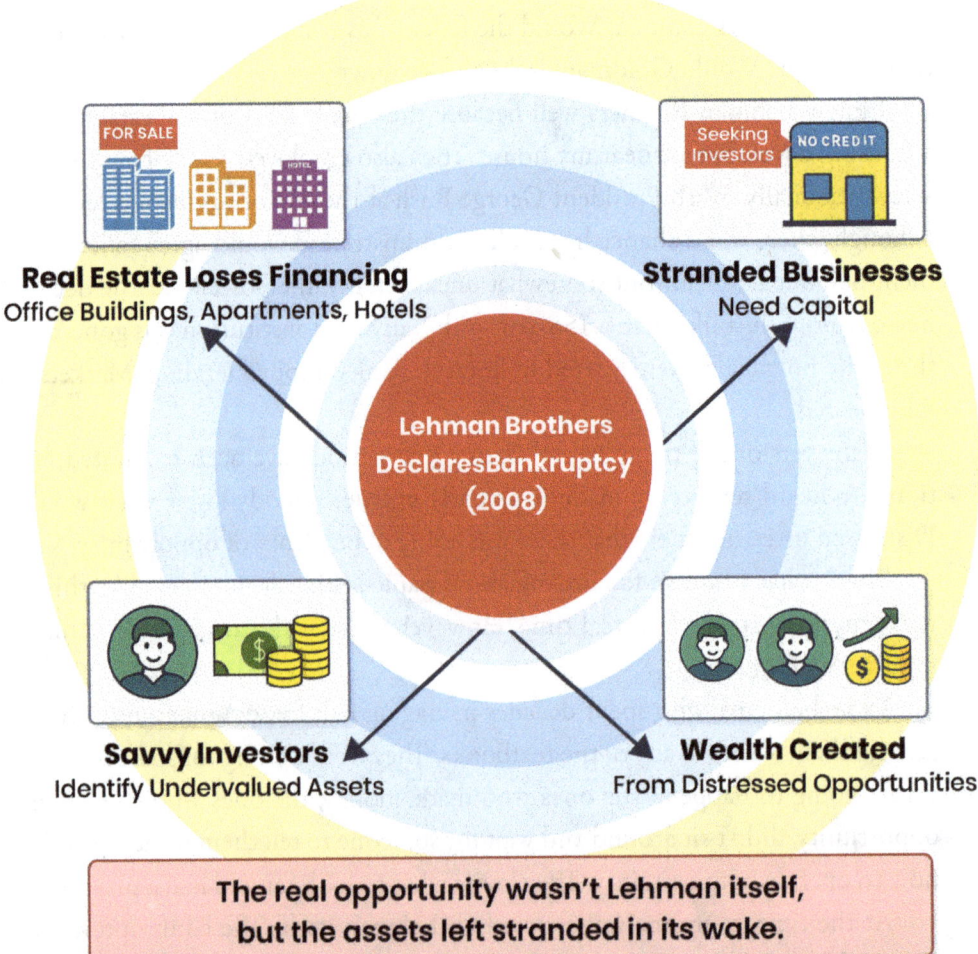

Figure 1: The Real Money Wasn't in Lehman—It Was in the Ripple Effect

THE DISTRESSED INVESTING PLAYBOOK IN ACTION

Most of the knowledge and principles I've presented in the pages of this book have surfaced through the result of relentless trial and error by many smart, dedicated people. The institutional investors I knew at the time of the crisis who were buying assets that most others wouldn't touch didn't win every time. Some of those buys didn't pan out, and others took years before they broke even.

In retrospect, investors who picked up assets at distressed prices made it look easy, but it was not. The individuals who had the courage, foresight, and knowledge to dive in while most were bailing out were prepared. They struggled for years, asked questions, made observations of human behavior, and made their share of mistakes. Like great poker players, they didn't win every time, but they heavily stacked the odds in their favor through relentless studying and effort. They met the moment by preparing well in advance.

In my own case, from my earliest days practicing law, I was fascinated by the arcane nature of distressed investments. Even with a legal education and experience in corporate restructuring at top firms, it took me more than a decade before I considered myself adept. A big reason why it took me that long was because the entire industry was opaque. At the time, if you wanted to buy shares of Xerox or IBM, all you had to do was set up an account at a brokerage firm and place a phone call. Your shares would arrive in your account the next day. Contrast that with someone who wanted to buy trade claims in a company that declared Chapter 11 bankruptcy. Where do you start? Who do you call? What are the steps? Yes, with enough persistence and effort it was possible to figure it out, but few people did. That disparity has always struck me as an inequity.

My students in the Executive MBA Program at the NYU Stern School of Business work selflessly during the day and go to school on weekends and nights. They are dedicated. As they take my class, which I call a "think tank" for distressed investing, they spend hours of their spare time reading, learning, talking with people in the field, and immersing themselves in details. They are smart, dedicated, and hardworking individuals. But most of them knew nothing about distressed investing before coming to Stern.

Ever since I learned the basics of corporate restructuring and bankruptcy, I firmly believed that everyday investors, the ones who buy stocks, mutual funds, or investment properties, can play in this space, too. No one needs a billion-dollar fund to think like a distressed investor. You just need to understand the playbook and to know how to execute when uncertainty creates opportunity.

Consider the recent FTX case, which I've cited multiple times in this book. According to the law firm Sullivan & Cromwell, the FTX bankruptcy filing involved *millions* of international creditor claims, and Xclaim estimated the number of creditors at more than *100,000*. Despite those massive numbers, a disproportionately small number of investors made a disproportionately large return on FTX claims.

I'm not saying that if you had read this book in 2022 you would have made a killing in FTX claims. What I am saying, however, is that if you had read this book in 2022 you would have at least known how to get started if you were interested in purchasing a risk asset like FTX claims.

THE DISTRESSED INVESTING PLAYBOOK

This is why I wrote this book. My hope is that the basic information I am providing will help level the playing field, make distressed investing more transparent, and in turn increase the market's efficiency. Coming up to speed takes time, energy, effort, and persistence.

Success is not guaranteed, and, moreover, no one should get involved without serious preparation. In each category of distressed investing, there are a few individuals who have dedicated years of their lives to understanding the nuances of certain assets. They bring as much intensity to what they do as any professional sports athlete. But instead of physical effort or manual dexterity, the distressed investor's game is intellectual capital—something each one of us can cultivate.

I can attest that at its highest levels, there is no more thrilling game on the planet.

Lessons from the Masters of Distressed Investing

Throughout my career, I've had the privilege of watching some of the most successful distressed investors in action. People like Carl Icahn, Howard Marks, Marc Lasry, Michael Leffell, Paul Singer, Steve Feinberg, David Tepper, David Bonderman, Leon Black, and Wilbur Ross. These people have built fortunes by understanding how to navigate distressed markets.

What makes these investors different isn't just their access to capital. It's their approach to uncertainty and their ability to see value where others only see chaos. Howard Marks of Oaktree Capital has a saying I've always appreciated: "The most dangerous words in investing are 'This time it's different.'" The best distressed investors understand that while each crisis has unique characteristics, the fundamentals of distressed investing remain constant: buy when others are fearful, understand the intrinsic value of assets, and focus on downside protection.

Each of these masters exemplifies specific principles we've covered throughout this book. Carl Icahn built his fortune by identifying companies where the market price significantly undervalued the underlying assets. His 1985 takeover of TWA started as a distressed play, as he recognized the airline's valuable routes and gates were worth far more than the company's depressed stock price reflected. Similarly, Wilbur Ross made billions in the early 2000s by purchasing bankrupt steel companies like LTV and Bethlehem Steel when everyone else had written off the industry. He understood what we discussed in Chapter 5: liquidation value creates a floor for your investment.

Marc Lasry and Avenue Capital demonstrated the power of trade claims investing during the Lehman Brothers collapse. He and his sister, Sonia Gardner, purchased claims from creditors desperate for immediate cash at 15 cents on the dollar, eventually recovering nearly 30 cents, a 100% return. I had the good fortune to work for Marc for a short time. His tactics show how uncertainty creates pricing inefficiencies in the trade claims market.

Perhaps the most instructive example comes from Howard Marks during the 2008 financial crisis. When mortgage-backed securities collapsed, Oaktree raised a $10.9 billion distressed fund, their largest ever. Marks didn't time the exact bottom like John Paulson; instead, he focused on what he called "the low enough point" and deployed capital steadily as assets reached their intrinsic value thresholds. By 2012, that fund had generated returns of approximately 19% per year.

These investors didn't become successful overnight. They developed a systematic approach to evaluating opportunities, managing risk, and executing deals. They built networks that gave them access to information and opportunities that others missed. And perhaps most importantly, they maintained emotional discipline when markets were in turmoil.

Consider David Tepper's audacious bet on bank stocks in early 2009. When Bank of America and Citigroup were trading at $3 and $1, respectively, most investors feared nationalization would wipe out shareholders completely. Tepper's Appaloosa Management conducted a detailed analysis of the specific scenarios under which these banks would survive versus collapse. That analysis gave him the confidence to invest heavily when others wouldn't, turning $2 billion into $7 billion in just one year.

What's particularly striking is how these masters apply the same principles regardless of market conditions or asset class. Leon Black's Apollo Global Management has excelled across distressed real estate, corporate debt, and struggling companies by adhering to a consistent framework: thorough diligence, appropriate leverage, and patience during restructuring. David Bonderman's TPG similarly demonstrates how disciplined application of fundamentals works across diverse scenarios, from acquiring Continental Airlines out of bankruptcy to restructuring troubled energy companies.

Learning from these examples, it's clear that success in distressed investing often comes down to a blend of rigorous analysis, strategic timing, and the ability to act when others hesitate. As we continue, we'll look at how to apply these principles in your own investment approach, building on the insights from these masters of the field.

CASE STUDIES: THE PLAYBOOK IN ACTION

The principles of distressed investing operate across all market levels. From individual investors working with limited capital to institutional giants deploying billions, the fundamental approach remains consistent. Let me share several real-world examples that demonstrate how the playbook works at different scales.

Start Small; Learn from Experience

The first time I purchased a bankruptcy trade claim was in 1997, right after I left my job as a young partner at the Chicago firm of McDermott, Will & Emery. At this point in my career, I was ten years out of law school, married, and with a small family. I could have stayed on the partner track, put in 70-to-80-hour weeks, and done well, but I realized that the demands of that schedule would eventually catch up with me. Instead, I had made up my mind to build a scalable investment portfolio, one that would work while I slept. I had knowledge and connections, as well as a little capital of my own, but I'd never before put my own money on the line in a distressed deal.

Eventually, the phone rang. The Chicago retailer Montgomery Ward, with several hundred stores and 37,000 employees, was feeling the pressure from rapidly growing competitors like Target and Walmart and had recently filed for Chapter 11. A Chicago lawyer who represented one of the retailer's landlords knew I had experience representing buyers of bankruptcy claims and called to see if any of my clients might be interested in purchasing the landlord's unsecured claim for damages. At the time, opening bids he was hearing were for 15 cents on the dollar. I listened carefully, but rather than calling one of my clients, I decided this was my opportunity to test my own theories by risking my own capital.

The landlord's attorney told me he already had an offer of 15 cents on the dollar for a $500,000 claim, which meant another potential buyer was offering $75,000. Time was limited, and there were several interested parties. I had to move quickly.

The burning question in my mind was: "What's the right bid?"

I had reason to believe this claim was worth more. Montgomery Ward was owned by GE Capital, a subsidiary of General Electric, one of the most respected financial firms in the world. That meant they had both the resources and motivation to resolve the bankruptcy efficiently. If the case dragged on for years, it would tarnish their reputation. I believed they would push for a swift resolution, which increased the likelihood that creditors would be repaid at a higher percentage.

After reviewing the landlord's lease documents, combing through the bankruptcy filings, and speaking to other professionals working on the case, I decided to offer 18 cents on the dollar—$90,000—knowing it was a significant sum of money for me to risk at the time. My logic was that the attorney had already shopped the deal at 15 cents to multiple bidders, and it seemed likely one of them would go slightly higher, maybe 16 or 17 cents. So, I upped the bid 20%. I reasoned that a bid of 18 cents gave me a good chance of being the highest bidder. Also, if my due diligence was correct, the upside was probably greater than the 20 cents most others were projecting. If my analysis was wrong, my worst-case scenario was that I would break even and get my money back, 18 cents, minus my time and legal expenses, in two to four years. Considering GE Capital's reputation in the financial world, I doubted they would let the case drag on or would be unable to liquidate enough assets to pay creditors.

By August 1999, Montgomery Ward confirmed a consensual reorganization plan that paid unsecured creditors 28 cents on the dollar. That meant my $500,000 claim was worth $140,000. In other words, I had turned my $90,000 investment into $140,000, a 55% return in 24 months. Annualized, that worked out to around 28%. It validated my strategy and boosted my confidence to keep going, but I never let myself believe I had some sort of magic touch. I had taken a calculated risk, structured the deal with a margin of safety, and had the patience to wait for the outcome.

Of course, not every deal would play out that well. Some investments took longer. Others were more complicated. And some, like the next one, didn't go quite as planned.

THE DISTRESSED INVESTING PLAYBOOK IN ACTION

The first time I loaned money directly to a bankrupt company, I thought my investment had a chance to double or even triple. The loan was to a small paper mill in Texas in the amount of $100,000, at a rate of 18% per annum, with interest to be paid at the time of repayment (I covered this briefly in Chapter 8). To improve my odds of success, I assembled a management team, including someone who sold paper for a living and knew how to make paper. I obviously knew about navigating bankruptcy cases, so that was the skill set I brought to the table. My group charged a relatively modest monthly fee that was designed to make sure that if all else failed, we'd come out of the deal with our expenses covered.

The value of the equipment in the plant and real estate was in excess of $2 million. The loan was approved by the bankruptcy court, and the paper mill started producing again. However, shortly thereafter, the price of natural gas, which powered the plant, unexpectedly skyrocketed. These costs could not be passed on to customers, and within six months, the plant was again out of money.

We gave it a good shot and proved that the mill's problems weren't due to mismanagement, but it became clear the business was not viable. Perhaps in a different location with lower overhead costs, it might have worked. We had no choice except to shut down the plant and sell the machinery and equipment, which we did first. We then sold the real estate. My $100,000 loan, now $118,000, was repaid. Creditors were repaid. Together, my business partners and I received $60,000 in management fees.

But was it worth the time, expenses, and aggravation? No! I don't regret the loan or consider it a disaster, but for nine months of sweat and toil, I don't consider the team's $78,000 total return on investment (time, travel, management, expertise) particularly good. The net return was approximately break-even.

Lessons Learned from Failure: When the Playbook Breaks Down

The paper mill experience taught me a hard truth that many investors eventually face: failure teaches more valuable lessons than success. Looking back, I can see several mistakes that contributed to the outcome, and over the years, I've seen these same patterns repeat themselves in both my own and others' failed investments.

First, insufficient due diligence is almost always at the root of bad deals. Whether it's overlooking operational weaknesses, failing to account for environmental liabilities, or ignoring pending litigation, missing these risks on the front end usually guarantees trouble later. I also learned the danger of overestimating management's ability to turn a business around. No matter how appealing a restructuring plan looks on paper, without the right leadership to execute it, the plan will fail.

Another mistake was underestimating the need for working capital. It's not enough to line up funds to buy the asset. The business also needs liquidity to operate and absorb shocks during the restructuring, like the spike in the price of natural gas we experienced. In this case, we failed to appreciate how much working capital would be needed beyond the acquisition price.

Timing is another common misstep. Bankruptcy cases rarely proceed on a predictable timeline, yet I assumed things would wrap up quickly. They didn't. I also failed to identify the vendor relationships that were essential to the company's survival. Once those vendors lost confidence and started tightening terms, the turnaround became much harder, if not impossible.

If I had taken the time to perform a proper sensitivity analysis on the paper mill's raw material costs, I would have seen how vulnerable the company was to swings in gas prices and other inputs. That alone might have convinced me to walk away. I thought I understood manufacturing, but I didn't fully understand this business, and that was a costly mistake. But that's how you learn. Every failure, if properly examined, becomes part of the next playbook.

Yes, every deal and every transaction, no matter how seemingly routine, will teach you something new. That's how life works. Lesson learned.

Mid-Market Example: The Turnaround Specialist

Sometimes, though, you get to see what it looks like when someone gets it right. Consider the case of a mid-market investor I'll call Michael, who specialized in distressed manufacturing businesses. Michael had previously worked as an operations executive in the automotive parts industry, giving him specialized knowledge that most financial investors lacked.

When a family-owned metal stamping business filed for Chapter 11 in 2018, Michael recognized an opportunity that perfectly matched his expertise. The company had modernized its equipment just three years earlier but was struggling with poor management and excessive debt from that capital investment. Their customer relationships remained strong, but cash flow couldn't support their debt service.

Michael's approach exemplified the core principles we've discussed throughout this book. First, he conducted thorough due diligence, spending weeks in the facility to understand operational bottlenecks and interview key employees. He developed relationships with the company's major customers to confirm they would maintain their business under new ownership.

Most importantly, he calculated the liquidation value of the specialized equipment, which established his downside protection. The machinery would be worth at least $3.2 million if sold piecemeal, creating a floor for his investment. With this knowledge, Michael formed a small investment group and submitted a bid of $4.5 million for the operating business.

After acquiring the company, Michael implemented targeted operational improvements while renegotiating supplier contracts. Within 18 months, he had doubled EBITDA to $1.2 million annually. Three years after his purchase, he sold the stabilized business to a strategic buyer for $9.6 million, generating over 100% return on the original investment. What makes this case instructive is how Michael leveraged his industry expertise to see value others missed, while still adhering to the principle of downside protection through hard asset valuation.

Navigating Risks

Throughout this book, we've focused on identifying opportunities in distressed markets. But the most successful investors I've encountered aren't just opportunity hunters; they're expert risk managers. They understand that the outsized returns in distressed investing come paired with substantial risks that must be properly identified, assessed, and mitigated.

As Howard Marks often says, "You can't predict, but you can prepare." This wisdom applies perfectly to distressed investing. While we can't know exactly which companies will fail or how market cycles will unfold, we can prepare for the inherent risks that accompany distressed situations.

I learned this lesson early in my career when I became involved with a seemingly straightforward distressed real estate opportunity. The property had solid fundamentals in a good location, and the previous owner's financial troubles appeared unrelated to the asset itself. What I failed to realize, though, was that it had environmental liabilities that weren't immediately apparent. What looked like a potential home run turned into a drawn-out battle with regulatory agencies that dramatically reduced returns and consumed countless hours.

That experience taught me that in distressed investing, what you don't see can hurt you far more than what you do. The most dangerous risks aren't the obvious ones that everyone's talking about. They're the hidden liabilities, the contingent claims, the regulatory issues that lurk beneath the surface.

Think of distressed investing as a game where the variables keep changing. Court decisions modify creditor priorities. Unexpected claimants emerge. Regulatory requirements shift. The investor who succeeds isn't necessarily the one with the most sophisticated financial models. It's the one who anticipates how these changes might unfold and positions accordingly.

In my decades of experience, I've observed that risk in distressed situations tends to cluster in several key categories. Understanding these risk categories, and developing specific strategies to address each, can mean the difference between spectacular success and devastating failure.

Below are major risk categories that every distressed investor must understand and mitigate. Each represents a potential pitfall that can derail even the most promising opportunity. But with proper preparation and vigilance, these risks can be managed, and sometimes even transformed into competitive advantages that less sophisticated investors fail to recognize.

Valuation and Collateral Risks

Within the broad category of valuation risks, the risks associated with collateral are often underappreciated in my experience. When a company files for bankruptcy, secured creditors face significant risks, including possibly being "jumped" in the priority line by tax liens, environmental liabilities, or other loans. These risks can drastically affect the recovery rate if a default or liquidation occurs. For example, a company with significant environmental liabilities might find that these obligations take precedence over other secured debts, diminishing the value of the collateral available to other creditors.

The quality and liquidity of collateral can vary dramatically, affecting both its value as downside protection and its role in potential reorganization. Equipment that's highly specialized may have substantial book value but minimal liquidation value if few buyers exist. Conversely, real estate in prime locations might retain significant value even when the business operating on it fails.

For distressed investors, relying on collateral is downside protection, but understanding whether the collateral is marketable is the next step. This means not just accepting appraised values at face value but conducting independent assessments of what assets would actually sell for in a forced liquidation scenario.

Disclosure Risk and the Fine Print

I'm a lawyer. I've spent an inordinate amount of my life reading contracts. I've seen what happens when people don't take the time to comb through them, and trust me, bad things happen.

So I know I've said this before, but permit me to state the obvious (again): *always read the fine print.*

One of my favorite guests in my classroom is Ira J. Perlmutter, an NYU MBA and CPA who has worked for the largest family offices in the country. Ira's motto is "Read Every Page." He calls his business "The Ira J. Perlmutter store," and he knows where every item in the store is and what it says.

As he will tell you, in distressed investing, reading every page of company-specific disclosures within financial statements, management's discussion and analysis, and auditors' reports is absolutely necessary for accurately assessing a company's financial health and potential risks. These documents become fully accessible to the public any time a company files for bankruptcy. Because court filings must be transparent and comprehensively reported, they provide deep insights into a company's ability to generate sufficient cash to fund operations, financial flexibility, and overall liquidity position.

Additionally, accountants and auditors are typically employed by the distressed company or contracted to conduct independent evaluations. Their role is to ensure that financial statements accurately reflect the company's condition. If they fail to identify or disclose obvious risks, they may face severe consequences, including lawsuits, loss of licenses, and damage to their professional reputations. To protect themselves, accountants and auditors often include cautionary language or highlight potential risks in their reports, even if those risks seem remote. This practice serves as a safeguard, even if they know most readers won't closely scrutinize every detail of their evaluations.

Disclosures are information gold mines, often containing detailed discussions about the company's plans to generate cash, such as cost reductions or restructuring strategies. They also highlight the impact of the bankruptcy plans on the company's capital and financial resources, offering a glimpse into the company's liquidity outlook. These elements, spelled out by accountants and lawyers, allow investors to understand the firm's potential for recovery and the risks involved in the investment.

Auditors' reports are equally significant, especially when they include a "going concern" paragraph. This section indicates whether the auditors doubt the company's ability to continue operating. If substantial doubt exists, the auditors will highlight the circumstances and refer to the company's footnote disclosures that discuss management's plans to address these issues. Conversely, a voluntary paragraph may be included when management's plans mitigate liquidity risks. While this does not indicate substantial doubt, it highlights uncertainties that could negatively impact the company's financial stability.

Interpreting these reports helps investors gauge the severity of a company's financial distress and the likelihood of successful restructuring. Paying attention to these disclosures and auditors' reports, whenever available, is often the only way to make informed decisions and mitigate risks associated with distressed assets.

Timing and Execution Risks

Even when your investment thesis is fundamentally sound, timing and execution can make or break your returns. Distressed assets rarely follow neat, predictable timelines. Bankruptcy proceedings get delayed, regulatory approvals take longer than expected, and market conditions shift during the holding period.

The investor who lacks sufficient patience or capital reserves may be forced to exit prematurely, leaving substantial value on the table. Conversely, those who become emotionally attached to their thesis may hold too long, refusing to recognize when fundamental conditions have changed.

Execution risk is equally challenging. Turnaround plans that look compelling on paper often falter in implementation. New management teams may struggle with organizational resistance, key talent may depart during restructuring, and competitors may seize the opportunity to poach customers during periods of uncertainty.

To mitigate these risks, successful distressed investors build substantial time buffers into their projections and maintain capital reserves to weather unexpected delays. They also develop clear milestones to track progress and establish predefined conditions under which they will reassess their position.

The Psychology of Successful Distressed Investing

Before we conclude, I want to address perhaps the most challenging aspect of distressed investing: the psychological component. Distressed markets can be emotional minefields. Fear, panic, and uncertainty create both incredible opportunities and incredible challenges. Managing your own psychology becomes as important as managing the financial aspects of your investments.

The most successful distressed investors I know share certain psychological traits that set them apart. They exhibit a remarkable comfort with uncertainty, recognizing that waiting for perfect information means missing opportunities. While others freeze in the face of ambiguity, they assess what they know, calculate reasonable ranges of outcomes, and act decisively within those parameters.

These investors also display genuine independence of thought. This isn't contrarianism for its own sake, but rather the willingness to develop and trust their own analysis even when it contradicts market consensus. I've watched investors make fortunes by maintaining conviction in their theses while markets moved temporarily against them.

This independence is paired with extraordinary patience. They understand that distressed situations often take much longer to resolve than anticipated, and they structure their investments accordingly.

Perhaps most importantly, successful distressed investors combine decisiveness with intellectual honesty. When the opportunity aligns with their criteria, they move quickly and with conviction, deploying capital while others hesitate. Yet this decisiveness exists alongside a rare ability to recognize when they're wrong and adjust accordingly. They don't fall victim to confirmation bias or sunk cost fallacies that plague many investors.

Developing these psychological traits takes time and self-awareness. I recommend keeping an investment journal that tracks not just your decisions but your emotions around those decisions. I also like ascribing a confidence factor to your investment decisions. Do you think that the probability of success is a 7 out of 10 or more? Review this journal periodically to notice patterns in your thinking and behavior that might undermine your success. Are you consistently exiting positions too early out of anxiety? Are you hesitating to act on opportunities that meet your criteria? These patterns, once identified, can be addressed deliberately.

Creating decision frameworks also helps maintain discipline when markets are chaotic. This might include pre-committing to certain actions, such as "I will invest X percent of available capital when assets reach Y valuation" or "I will reassess my position if these specific conditions change." Decision checklists ensure you consider all relevant factors rather than reacting emotionally to the latest headline or market movement.

In my experience, maintaining emotional equilibrium in distressed markets is perhaps your greatest competitive advantage. You think you'll be rational and calm when others lose their cool, but it often doesn't work that way. When panic sweeps through markets and drives irrational selling, it's like an infectious disease. The inoculated investor who can think clearly and act deliberately will find opportunities others miss. The best returns I've seen in my career came not from superior financial engineering or privileged information, but from the ability to remain psychologically balanced when markets were anything but.

KEY INSIGHTS

1. The collapse of Lehman Brothers in 2008 was a turning point in financial markets, demonstrating that the real money in distress often lies in the ripple effects rather than the immediate bankruptcy itself.
2. Successful distressed investors operate with a playbook, relying on experience, discipline, and structured approaches rather than reacting emotionally to crises.
3. Investors who thrived during the 2008 financial crisis understood that uncertainty creates opportunity and positioned themselves to buy undervalued assets when others hesitated.
4. The greatest distressed investors, such as Carl Icahn, Howard Marks, Marc Lasry, David Tepper, and Wilbur Ross, built their fortunes by recognizing intrinsic value in distressed situations, managing risk effectively, and acting decisively.

THE DISTRESSED INVESTING PLAYBOOK IN ACTION

5. Their success stories reveal recurring principles: buying when others are fearful, focusing on downside protection, and developing a systematic investment approach.
6. Distressed investing is not just for institutions; individual investors can apply the same principles on a smaller scale by leveraging their industry knowledge and networks.
7. Building a knowledge base, establishing a network, and understanding the distressed investment landscape are crucial first steps before committing capital.
8. Investors must choose a strategy that aligns with their expertise, whether it be trade claims, distressed real estate, or acquiring failing businesses.
9. Due diligence is the primary defense against catastrophic losses, requiring rigorous documentation, independent verification, and a structured valuation approach.
10. Deal flow is critical in distressed investing; successful investors build systems to consistently identify and assess opportunities before they become widely recognized.
11. Financing strategies in distressed investing vary, with investors leveraging personal capital, partnerships, private lenders, or structured deal arrangements to minimize upfront cash needs.
12. Maintaining emotional equilibrium is important in distressed investing, as fear and panic can cloud judgment. Successful investors develop psychological resilience, enabling them to act decisively when others hesitate.

CHAPTER 15

Bringing It All Together: Your Complete Playbook

In the previous chapters, we've dissected bankruptcy proceedings, analyzed liquidation values, explored capital structures, examined turnaround strategies, and so much more. But information without integration creates paralysis, not action. What separates the observers from the participants in distressed markets isn't just knowledge: it's the ability to synthesize disparate information into decisive action when others hesitate.

Every successful distressed investor I know has a mental playbook, a decision tree they've developed through years of experience that guides them when facing uncertain markets and complex situations. This final chapter will help you develop a playbook of your own, enabling you to transform theoretical understanding into practical execution when an opportunity appears.

The Distressed Investing Decision Framework

When I first entered this field decades ago, I approached each opportunity differently, relying more on intuition than process. That changed after watching seasoned investors consistently outperform through systematic evaluation. I learned that random approaches produce random results, while methodical analysis creates repeatable success. At its core, successful distressed investing isn't about heroic intuition or market timing; it follows a structured decision framework that transforms chaotic situations into manageable components (see Fig. 1).

This framework, acts as a compass through the fog of market panic and information asymmetry. Distressed situations may look chaotic, but there is a way to bring order to the mess. Once you build skills, knowledge, network, and dry-powder capital, you will be ready to execute a deliberate plan when opportunity beckons, like this:

- You start by spotting opportunity where others only see trouble. You scan bankruptcy filings, watch for cracks in specific industries, and pay attention to the signs that something is about to break. You move before the headlines hit.
- Once you see an opening, you focus on what matters most. You ask whether this is a business you understand. You think about where you would sit in the capital structure and who

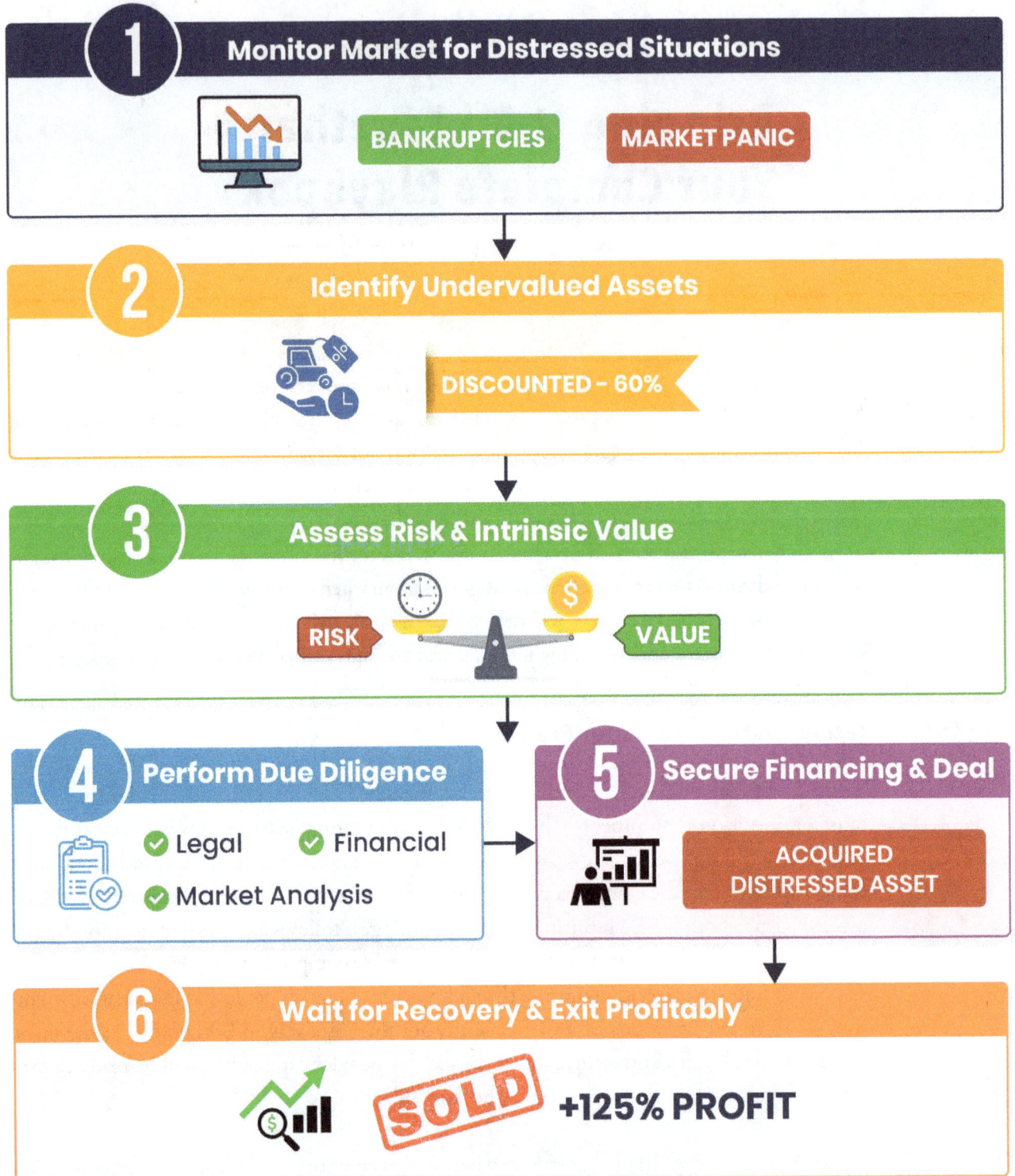

Figure 1: The Distressed Investor's Framework

BRINGING IT ALL TOGETHER: YOUR COMPLETE PLAYBOOK

else might be circling the same deal. You figure out quickly if it's worth going deeper. When it is, that's when the real work begins. You value the assets, assess the risks, and figure out who holds the power among creditors. You study management and ask whether the team running the business has the skills to turn it around. Most important, you think about how you will get out of the investment before you ever get in.

- Next, you structure the deal in a way that gives you protection and upside. Whether buying debt or equity, working alone or with partners, you make sure the legal side is buttoned up. You don't leave room for surprises.
- Even after the deal is done, you stay close to it. You follow court filings and business updates, track the market, and pay attention to shifts in creditor dynamics. You are ready to adjust if something changes. You never take your eye off the exit.

A framework isn't a magic formula—it's a way to think clearly when everyone else is paralyzed by uncertainty. And anyone can build one. You don't need a billion-dollar fund to start; you just need to commit to doing the work. Every deal, win or lose, makes you sharper. Over time, you will see patterns that others miss and develop the confidence to act when others hesitate.

The next wave of distressed opportunities is coming. There will always be another crisis. Another round of companies that borrowed too much or bet too big. The question is whether you will be ready when they start feeling distressed.

Your Distressed Investing Toolkit

Even the most brilliant strategist needs the proper tools to execute effectively. I've seen countless investors identify compelling opportunities only to stumble during implementation because they lacked the right analytical templates, information sources, or legal documentation.

To implement your framework, you'll need tools that are tailored to the unique demands of distressed investing. Some of these, like liquidation models, claim purchase agreements, due diligence checklists, and DIP term sheets, are included in the appendix; all are real-world templates used in deals I've worked on over the years. Others you'll develop as you gain experience and adapt to different types of deals. They can help you structure and formalize your investment approach, whether acquiring claims, negotiating financing, or evaluating collateral.

Your toolkit should also include financial analysis templates that help you model restructuring scenarios and estimate potential recovery rates. Tools that track legal developments, such as automated docket monitoring services and bankruptcy filing databases, are useful for staying updated on case progress, key motions, and emerging claims. Additionally, having templates for cash flow analysis and working capital projections will support your assessment of a distressed company's liquidity and operating viability.

Building a network of industry experts, including attorneys, accountants, or turnaround consultants, is just as important. These professionals can provide practical insights and help you identify red flags during due diligence. Maintaining these relationships can give you perspectives that numbers alone cannot offer.

Finally, develop your own decision frameworks and checklists to guide you through each stage of the investment process. These tools will help you consistently evaluate risks, consider different scenarios, and stay disciplined when markets are volatile. Integrating these resources with your strategic insights will position you to move from analysis to action while minimizing common pitfalls.

Your Next Steps

If you've made it this far, you understand that distressed investing is not just a concept. It's a discipline that requires action. But reading about strategies and case studies is only part of the work. The next step is deciding how to put this knowledge to use.

Start by taking inventory of what you've learned and the resources now available to you. The appendix contains practical forms, checklists, and templates. These are real tools that can help you move from theory to execution. Review them carefully so you are prepared when an opportunity arises.

Rather than trying to master every type of distressed opportunity, choose a focus that fits your interests, skills, and available capital. Whether it's trade claims, small bankruptcies, or debt of public companies, narrowing your attention will help you learn faster and make better decisions.

Relationships are another essential piece. Distressed investing is a relationship-driven business. Many of the best opportunities circulate quietly among professionals before they ever hit public filings. Take time to connect with attorneys, consultants, and experienced investors. If you approach them as a serious learner rather than a competitor, you'll be surprised how much people are willing to share.

You should also start building a system to monitor the markets you want to target. Set alerts for new bankruptcy filings, follow industry developments, and keep an eye on where credit is tightening. Patterns will begin to emerge as you sharpen your focus, and over time, you'll start to see opportunities others overlook.

Finally, get your house in order before you jump in. Line up your financial backing, legal support, and decision process now, not when a deal is already on the table. The investors who succeed in distressed markets are those who can move quickly and with conviction because they have already done the work to be ready.

The truth is that distressed investing isn't about predicting the next crisis. Crises always come. Success belongs to those who are prepared when they do. The people who made their mark in past downturns weren't fortune tellers—they were disciplined, patient, and ready to act when others hesitated.

If there's one lesson I hope you take from this book, it's that you don't need to run a billion-dollar fund to succeed in this space. You need curiosity, effort, and the courage to make your first deal when the time comes. There will always be another wave of distress, and there will always be opportunities for those who are prepared to see them. The only question is whether you will be one of them.

The Next 2008 Financial Crisis

I don't pretend to be able to predict the future, but I know with great certainty that there will be another massive financial crisis. No one knows when, why, or how it will unfold. When it happens, you'll think, *This is awful. It's a catastrophe. It will only get worse.*

And because everyone around you will be thinking the same thing, it may not occur to you, until much later, that hidden in that disaster is extraordinary opportunity.

In moments like those, when others are panicking, dumping assets, and forecasting endless doom, you should pause and ask yourself: "What would Warren Buffett or Charlie Munger do right now?"

In 2008 and 2009, when fear was everywhere, they were buying distressed assets by the truckload.

Now you have the same playbook they and other great investors have used. The principles laid out in this book have created billions in returns for those who knew how to use them. If you apply them with discipline, they can do the same for you, whether you're managing $5,000 or $500 million.

Remember, though, that distressed opportunities don't only appear in times of global crisis. Every day, companies file for Chapter 11. Assets are mispriced. Creditors are forced to sell. The cycle of distress never really stops. The only question is whether you'll be ready when opportunity appears.

Conclusion: Prepare for Opportunity

Throughout this book, I've shared with you the fundamental principles that guide successful distressed investing. What started as a set of lectures for my students at NYU has evolved into this playbook, a guide that I hope will serve you well whether you're just starting out or looking to refine your approach.

In Chapter 11, I discussed the Stanford Bank fraud case and how it illustrated a fundamental principle of successful distressed investing. It was also, as I briefly mentioned but will repeat here, a watershed moment in my career. After the massive Ponzi scheme collapsed, many creditors were desperate to recover even a small portion of their investments. Few expected significant returns. I saw an opportunity where others only saw devastation. Stanford was a disaster for a myriad of people, but it was a turning point in my life and career, giving me a jolt of confidence in my abilities to spot and capitalize on distressed assets.

After the first distribution, which was a mere 1% payout, investor psychology was at rock bottom. That minuscule return after years of waiting had degraded sellers' expectations so thoroughly that they were willing to sell their claims for pennies on the dollar. That's when I stepped in, purchasing claims at deeply discounted prices.

My approach wasn't based on blind optimism. It was calculated. When evaluating these distressed assets, I wasn't focused on how quickly I could flip them for profit. I was asking: "How quickly can I get my principal back?"

In the Stanford case, I projected that within three years of purchase, I'd recover my initial investment. And I did. Three years is a long time to wait, but from that point forward, every additional dollar was pure profit. At that point you are playing with house money. While the case dragged on for over 15 years total, this approach transformed what many viewed as a catastrophic investment into a significant success. Creditors eventually received around 40% of their net investment back, creating substantial returns for those who had purchased claims at steep discounts.

What makes this story powerful isn't just the favorable outcome. It's what it teaches us about psychology in distressed markets, patience, and focusing first on capital preservation before the upside. Sometimes the best opportunities emerge not from complex financial engineering, but from understanding human psychology when faced with apparent disaster.

I've witnessed countless cycles of boom and bust. I've seen once-mighty companies crumble under debt loads that seemed manageable just months earlier. I've watched sophisticated investors freeze when confronted with unprecedented market conditions. And I've seen ordinary individuals, armed with knowledge, discipline, and persistence, build remarkable wealth by stepping in when others stepped back.

The most successful distressed investors I know aren't necessarily the ones with the most capital or prestigious credentials. They're the ones who understand that this business is ultimately about people, about building trust with attorneys and other professionals who might bring you your next great opportunity, about understanding the motivations of creditors eager to sell their claims, about recognizing when management teams have what it takes to execute a turnaround. In distressed markets, relationships matter more than algorithms.

As I look to the future, I see a landscape rich with opportunity for those prepared to seize it. The combination of elevated interest rates, the aftermath of pandemic-era policies, and geopolitical tensions are creating conditions where distress is increasingly likely across multiple sectors. Whether it's overleveraged real estate, struggling retailers, or tech companies that grew too quickly on cheap capital, the next wave of distress is building.

When that wave crashes, whether through a sudden crisis or a slow, grinding decline, the principles in this playbook will serve as your guide. The specific circumstances will be different, but the fundamentals remain the same. Buy when others are fearful, focus on intrinsic value, and protect your downside.

I've shared these principles with hundreds of students over the years, and I've watched many of them build successful careers applying them. Some started small, purchasing individual trade claims and gradually building their expertise. Others joined established firms where they could learn from experienced practitioners. A few even launched their own funds, raising capital from investors who recognized their potential.

BRINGING IT ALL TOGETHER: YOUR COMPLETE PLAYBOOK

What unites these success stories isn't access to privileged information or extraordinary mathematical ability. The beauty of distressed investing is that opportunities exist at every level. While billion-dollar funds focus on large corporate restructurings, individual investors can find value in smaller situations that fly below the institutional radar. The principles are scalable, from trade claims of a few thousand dollars to complex transactions involving multiple asset classes and jurisdictions.

As we conclude this journey together, I want to emphasize that the most valuable asset in distressed investing isn't capital; it's knowledge. The investor who thoroughly understands the playbook will find opportunities others miss and avoid pitfalls others stumble into. This book is just the beginning. The real learning comes from application, from making your first trade, conducting your first due diligence, or negotiating your first claim purchase. Start small, learn continuously, and build on each experience.

I don't know what will trigger the next financial crisis or when it will arrive. But I know with absolute certainty that there will be another moment when markets panic, assets are mispriced, and the prepared investor finds extraordinary value amid the chaos.

When that moment comes, I hope the knowledge in these pages helps you recognize the opportunity, assess it accurately, and act with confidence.

The playbook is now in your hands. The opportunity will come. The question is: Will you be ready?

KEY INSIGHTS

1. Your first distressed investment should be treated as a learning experience. Starting small allows you to develop expertise without excessive risk.
2. Case studies illustrate that distressed investing works across different scales, from small individual transactions to large institutional plays, with the same core principles applied.
3. Failures in distressed investing often stem from inadequate due diligence, poor management assessment, insufficient working capital, and overestimating recovery timelines.
4. Valuation and collateral risks must be carefully analyzed, as distressed assets often come with hidden liabilities or overestimated book values.
5. Understanding financial disclosures, audit reports, and bankruptcy court filings provides investors with crucial insights into a company's true condition and risk profile.
6. Timing and execution risks are significant in distressed investing, as prolonged legal processes, restructuring delays, and shifting market conditions can affect outcomes.
7. The psychology of distressed investing is an important component of success. The best investors maintain emotional discipline, act independently of market sentiment, and remain patient in uncertainty.
8. Maintaining psychological resilience is fundamental for success in distressed investing. The best investors stay calm when markets are chaotic, act independently of market sentiment, and remain patient even when the process takes longer than expected.

9. Distressed investing is ultimately about preparation and execution, not prediction. Opportunities arise in every cycle, but only those ready to act can capitalize on them.
10. The playbook provided in this book is a framework for structuring investments, managing risks, and ensuring disciplined execution, regardless of the size or complexity of the opportunity.
11. The next financial crisis is inevitable, and those who apply these principles will be positioned to recognize mispriced assets, navigate uncertainty, and create value where others see only risk.

Appendix

To access the supporting materials referenced throughout this book, including downloadable documents, due diligence templates, and recovery models, please visit the online appendix.

These resources may be updated over time as the content evolves. You can scan the QR code or go to www.distressedinvestingplaybook.com/appendix for full access.

Glossary

363 Sale: Refers to the sale of a debtor's assets outside the ordinary course of business during bankruptcy, conducted under Section 363 of the Bankruptcy Code and often used to maximize value for creditors through a competitive bidding process.

Absolute Priority: The rule dictating that senior creditors must be paid in full before junior creditors or equity holders receive any recovery in a bankruptcy plan.

Accrued Interest: The amount of interest that has accumulated on debt but has not yet been paid as of a particular date, typically up to the bankruptcy filing.

Administrative Claim: A post-petition expense necessary for preserving the estate, such as legal fees or vendor payments, and has priority status under the Bankruptcy Code.

Allowed Claim: A creditor's claim that has been approved by the bankruptcy court, either because it was not objected to or because it survived an objection.

Article 9: A section of the Uniform Commercial Code (UCC) that governs secured transactions involving personal property, including how security interests are created, perfected, and enforced.

Asset Purchase Agreement: The formal contract through which a buyer acquires specific assets of a bankrupt company, typically negotiated as part of a 363 sale.

Assignment of Claim: The legal transfer of a creditor's claim in bankruptcy to another party, often used in claims trading.

Automatic Stay: A court-ordered freeze that halts all collection activities, lawsuits, and foreclosures against the debtor the moment a bankruptcy petition is filed.

Avoidance Action: A legal tool used by debtors or trustees to unwind certain transactions made before bankruptcy, such as fraudulent transfers or preferential payments.

Bankruptcy Code: The body of federal law (Title 11 of the U.S. Code) that governs bankruptcy proceedings, including rules for reorganization and liquidation.

Bankruptcy Court: A specialized federal court that handles all matters related to bankruptcy filings, including oversight of the debtor, creditor disputes, and plan confirmation.

GLOSSARY

Bankruptcy Trustee: An individual appointed to oversee the debtor's estate, often managing asset liquidation in Chapter 7 cases or ensuring compliance with a reorganization plan in other chapters.

Capital Stack: The hierarchy of claims on a company's assets, ranging from senior secured debt at the top to equity at the bottom, which determines the order of repayment in bankruptcy.

Carve-out: A negotiated exception in a bankruptcy case, usually allowing a portion of collateral to be set aside to pay for professional fees or administrative expenses.

Cash Collateral: Cash or equivalents (like receivables) that are subject to a secured creditor's lien; the debtor must obtain permission to use it during bankruptcy.

Chapter 7: A liquidation proceeding under the Bankruptcy Code in which a trustee sells the debtor's nonexempt assets and distributes the proceeds to creditors.

Chapter 11: A reorganization process that allows a company to continue operating while restructuring its debts, subject to court approval and creditor negotiation.

Chapter 13: A bankruptcy option for individuals (not businesses) that enables repayment of debts over time through a court-approved plan based on future income.

Chapter 22: A term used informally to describe a company that files for Chapter 11 bankruptcy twice, suggesting a failed or incomplete initial restructuring.

Claim Objection: A formal challenge raised in bankruptcy court disputing the validity, amount, or priority of a creditor's filed claim.

Claims Register: The official list of creditor claims filed in a bankruptcy case, maintained by the court or claims agent, and referenced for voting, distributions, and objections.

Claims Trading: The practice of buying and selling bankruptcy claims at a discount, allowing investors to profit from potential recoveries or influence the restructuring process.

Clawback: Refers to a contractual provision that allows an employer, investor, or regulator to reclaim money that has already been paid out, typically under certain conditions.

Comparable Companies (aka Comps): A valuation method that compares the distressed company to similar publicly traded companies, using financial metrics to estimate enterprise value and potential recovery.

Confirmation Hearing: A court proceeding in which the bankruptcy judge determines whether a proposed Chapter 11 plan meets the legal requirements for approval.

Cramdown: A legal process by which a bankruptcy court confirms a reorganization plan over the objections of certain creditor classes, as long as the plan meets statutory requirements.

Creditor Committee: A group of unsecured creditors appointed to represent the interests of all unsecured creditors in a bankruptcy case, often participating in negotiations and monitoring the debtor's actions.

GLOSSARY

Debtor in Possession (DIP): A debtor that remains in control of its operations and assets during Chapter 11 bankruptcy, subject to court oversight and fiduciary obligations.

DIP Financing Post-Petition: financing provided to a debtor during Chapter 11 proceedings, often with priority status or liens, to fund ongoing operations and restructuring.

Disclosure Statement: A detailed document that explains the debtor's financial condition, restructuring plan, and risks, designed to give creditors enough information to vote on the plan.

Distressed Debt Investing: An investment strategy focused on purchasing the debt of financially troubled companies, typically at a discount, with the goal of profiting from restructuring or liquidation outcomes.

Docket: The public record of all filings, motions, and court orders in a bankruptcy case, often reviewed by investors to track the case's progress.

Exclusivity Period: The initial period (typically 120 days) during which only the debtor has the right to propose a reorganization plan, often extended by court approval.

Executory Contract: A contract where both parties still have material obligations to perform; in bankruptcy, the debtor must either assume (continue) or reject (terminate) these contracts, subject to court approval.

Fiduciary Duty: The legal obligation of the debtor's management, trustees, and other parties to act in the best interests of the estate and its creditors during bankruptcy proceedings.

First-Day Motions Requests: Filed by the debtor immediately after a Chapter 11 case begins, seeking court approval for actions needed to stabilize operations, such as paying employee wages or using cash collateral.

Fraudulent Conveyance: A transfer of assets made with the intent to hinder, delay, or defraud creditors, or for less than reasonably equivalent value while the debtor was insolvent; these can be challenged and reversed in bankruptcy.

Impaired Claim: A claim that is not being paid in full or in the ordinary course under a bankruptcy plan, giving the claimant the right to vote on the plan.

Indenture Trustee: A financial institution that represents the interests of bondholders in a debt issuance governed by an indenture agreement; it plays a role in enforcing rights during bankruptcy.

Insider Creditor: A creditor with a close relationship to the debtor—such as an executive, board member, or affiliated entity—whose claims may be subject to additional scrutiny.

Intercreditor Agreement: A contract between multiple creditors that outlines how their respective rights and priorities will be treated, especially in a default or bankruptcy scenario.

Leverage: The use of borrowed funds to increase investment exposure; high leverage can increase returns but also amplifies the risk of financial distress or bankruptcy.

GLOSSARY

Lien: A legal claim or security interest in an asset, granted to a creditor to secure repayment; in bankruptcy, lienholders have priority over unsecured creditors.

Liquidation Preference: A provision in debt or equity agreements giving certain stakeholders priority in payment over others in the event of liquidation.

Liquidation Value: The estimated proceeds from selling a company's assets in a distressed or forced-sale scenario, often used as a floor for evaluating investment recovery.

Litigation Finance: A strategy in which investors provide capital to fund legal claims in exchange for a portion of any proceeds, often used in mass torts and bankruptcy-related lawsuits.

Litigation Funding: A financial arrangement where a third party covers the legal costs of a lawsuit in exchange for a share of any recovery. Commonly used by plaintiffs lacking resources to pursue claims, particularly in commercial, class-action, or insolvency-related cases. Also referred to as litigation finance; the two terms are often used interchangeably.

Loan-To-Own: An investment approach where a creditor acquires a company's debt with the intention of converting it into equity during restructuring, effectively taking control of the business.

Non-performing Loan: A loan in which the borrower is not making scheduled interest or principal payments, typically classified as non-performing after 90 days of delinquency. These loans are often sold at a discount in distressed markets.

Out-of-Court Restructuring: A negotiated agreement between a debtor and its creditors to modify debt terms without filing for bankruptcy, often used to avoid the costs and publicity of court proceedings.

Par: The face value or full claim amount of a debt instrument, usually expressed as 100 cents on the dollar. In distressed investing, buying a claim "at par" means paying its full value, while discounts (e.g., 40 cents on the dollar) represent purchases below par.

Petition Date: The official date on which a company files for bankruptcy protection. It marks the legal start of the bankruptcy case and sets the timeline for determining pre- and post-petition claims.

Plan Confirmation: The process by which a bankruptcy court approves a debtor's reorganization plan, after determining that it complies with the Bankruptcy Code and has received the necessary support from creditors.

Post-Confirmation Trust: An entity created after plan confirmation to handle remaining estate matters, such as pursuing litigation claims or distributing assets to creditors.

Post-Petition: Refers to actions or obligations that arise after the bankruptcy case is filed, typically given different treatment from pre-petition debts.

GLOSSARY

Pre-Arranged Plan: A bankruptcy plan negotiated with key creditors before filing, but not yet formally voted on, aiming to streamline the Chapter 11 process.

Preference Liability: A potential claim against a creditor who received payment shortly before the bankruptcy filing, which may be clawed back if it gave them an unfair advantage.

Preference Period: The look-back window—typically 90 days before the petition date (or one year for insiders)—during which certain payments may be deemed preferential and subject to clawback.

Pre-Packaged Bankruptcy: A Chapter 11 filing where the debtor has already solicited and obtained creditor votes on a plan before filing, enabling a faster court process.

Pre-Petition: Describes events or obligations that occurred before the bankruptcy case was filed; these claims are generally treated as unsecured debts.

Priority Claim: A type of unsecured claim that is paid before other unsecured claims, such as certain tax obligations, employee wages, or domestic support obligations.

Proof of Claim: A formal document submitted by a creditor stating the amount and basis of a debt owed by the debtor in bankruptcy.

Proof of Interest: A filing by an equity holder in a bankruptcy case asserting their ownership stake in the debtor. It is similar to a proof of claim but relates to stock or other equity interests.

Receivership: A legal process in which a court appoints a receiver to take control of a company's assets or operations, typically to protect creditors or enforce a judgment outside bankruptcy.

Recovery Rate: The percentage of a creditor's original claim that is ultimately paid out through the bankruptcy process, often used to evaluate investment outcomes in distressed scenarios.

Rejection Claim: A claim for damages filed by a counterparty when a debtor rejects an executory contract or unexpired lease. These claims are treated as general unsecured claims unless granted higher priority.

Remnant Asset: Assets of little value or overlooked in the bankruptcy process, such as small receivables or tax refunds, which are often sold in bulk at the end of a case.

Replacement Lien: A lien that is granted to a secured creditor during bankruptcy to compensate for the use or loss of existing collateral, ensuring the creditor remains adequately protected.

Restructuring Support Agreement (RSA): A contract between the debtor and key creditors that outlines the terms of a proposed restructuring plan and commits the parties to support it during the Chapter 11 process.

Roll-Up Financing: A DIP financing structure where pre-petition debt is "rolled up" into the post-petition facility, effectively elevating its priority and securing repayment ahead of other pre-petition creditors.

GLOSSARY

Rule 2004 Examination: A broad discovery tool in bankruptcy that allows any party in interest to investigate the debtor's financial affairs, transactions, and property.

Rule 3001(e): A provision of the Bankruptcy Rules that governs the procedure for transferring claims and the requirements for notifying the court and involved parties of a claim transfer.

Section 507 (Priority): A provision of the Bankruptcy Code that lists categories of unsecured claims granted priority for payment in bankruptcy, such as administrative expenses, employee wages, and certain taxes.

Secured Creditor: A lender or creditor with a legal claim (lien) on specific collateral securing the debt. If the borrower defaults, the creditor can enforce its rights against the collateral.

Special Situations: Investment opportunities arising from unique, complex, or event-driven circumstances—such as bankruptcies, spin-offs, or restructurings—that may lead to mispriced assets.

Stalking Horse: An initial bidder in a bankruptcy auction who sets the minimum purchase price for an asset sale. The stalking horse is often granted protections like breakup fees to encourage bidding.

Subchapter V: A streamlined form of Chapter 11 bankruptcy introduced under the Small Business Reorganization Act to help small businesses restructure more quickly and affordably.

Subordinated Debt: Debt that ranks below senior obligations in the capital structure. In a bankruptcy, subordinated lenders are repaid only after senior creditors have been paid in full.

Super-Priority Claim: A claim granted the highest level of repayment priority, typically for post-petition financing like DIP loans. These claims are paid before all other administrative and priority claims.

Term Sheet: A non-binding document outlining the key terms and conditions of a proposed investment or financing agreement, often serving as the basis for final documentation.

Trade Claim: An unpaid obligation owed by a debtor to a vendor or supplier for goods or services provided before a bankruptcy filing. These are typically unsecured and can be bought or sold.

Turnaround Specialist: A professional with experience in restructuring struggling businesses, often brought in to improve operations, reduce costs, and restore profitability.

Unexpired Lease: A lease that is still active at the time of a bankruptcy filing. Under Section 365, the debtor must decide whether to assume or reject these leases, subject to court approval.

Unsecured Creditor: A creditor whose claims are not backed by specific collateral. These creditors are lower in repayment priority and often recover less in bankruptcy proceedings.

Valuation: The process of determining the worth of a company or its assets, crucial in bankruptcy for negotiating claim recoveries, plan confirmation, and asset sales.

GLOSSARY

Vulture Investor: A term often used to describe investors who specialize in buying deeply distressed debt or assets at steep discounts with the aim of profiting from a turnaround or liquidation.

Waterfall: A repayment structure that outlines the order in which creditors and stakeholders are paid from available assets, typically based on priority and type of claim.

Workout Agreement: An out-of-court agreement between a debtor and its creditors to restructure debt terms, avoiding formal bankruptcy proceedings.

Yield-to-Maturity (YTM): The total return expected on a bond if held to maturity, reflecting both interest payments and any gain or loss relative to its purchase price.

Endnotes

1. Epiq Global, "Commercial Chapter 11 Filings Increase 20 Percent in Calendar Year 2024," accessed April 9, 2025, https://www.epiqglobal.com/en-us/resource-center/news/commercial-chapter-11-filings-increase-20-percent-in-calendar-year-2024.
2. Shane Shifflett, "Burger Chain Turns Pioneer for New Small-Business Bankruptcy Law," *The Wall Street Journal*, July 11, 2020, https://www.wsj.com/articles/burger-chain-turns-pioneer-for-new-small-business-bankruptcy-law-11594459800.
3. DailyDAC, "An Introduction to Bankruptcy Claims Trading," accessed April 9, 2025, https://www.dailydac.com/introduction-bankruptcy-claims-trading/.
4. James Altucher, "How to Succeed in Business and Politics | Wilbur Ross (39th Secretary of Commerce)," The James Altucher Show, September 17, 2024, podcast, 1:01:00, https://metacast.app/podcast/the-james-altucher-show/iYM257GO/how-to-succeed-in-business-and-politics-wilbur-ross-39th-secretary-of-commerce/B1LBOIu3.
5. National Pawnbrokers Association, "The History of Pawn," accessed April 9, 2025, https://www.nationalpawnbrokers.org/history-of-pawn/.
6. CBS News, "Traffic Stop Leads Police to Thief of Yogi Berra World Series Rings and Andy Warhol Artwork," April 7, 2024, https://www.cbsnews.com/news/thomas-trotta-crime-spree-from-beginning-to-capture-60-minutes/.
7. Corporate Finance Institute, "DCF Formula," accessed April 9, 2025, https://corporatefinanceinstitute.com/resources/valuation/dcf-formula-guide/.
8. Aswath Damodaran, "Dealing with Distress in Valuation," NYU Stern School of Business, accessed April 9, 2025, https://pages.stern.nyu.edu/~adamodar/New_Home_Page/valquestions/distresspaper.htm.
9. Katherine Doherty and Erin Hudson, "Jefferies' Ex-Navy SEAL Gains Edge in Distressed-Debt Deals," *Bloomberg*, March 27, 2024, https://www.bloomberg.com/news/articles/2024-03-27/jefferies-ex-navy-seal-gains-edge-in-distressed-debt-investing.
10. *Colonial Pac. Leasing Corp. v. N.N. Partners*, Casetext, accessed April 9, 2025, https://casetext.com/case/colonial-pac-leasing-corp-v-nn-partners.
11. U.S. Bankruptcy Court, endorsed order, accessed April 9, 2025, https://mcusercontent.com/cc1fad182b6d6f8b1e352e206/files/1ca0eb4f-0cbd-1950-fbaa-4369610d4570/17681244_140168062_endorsed.pdf.
12. Rebecca Trager, "J&J's Third Talc Bankruptcy Settlement Attempt Denied," *Chemistry World*, April 3, 2025, https://www.chemistryworld.com/news/jandjs-third-talc-bankruptcy-settlement-attempt-denied/4021242.article.
13. Adam Daniel, "The Blair Witch Project at 25: How One Film Changed the Horror Genre as We Know It," *The Conversation*, July 14, 2024,, https://theconversation.com/the-blair-witch-project-at-25-how-one-film-changed-the-horror-genre-as-we-know-it-233104.

NOTES

14. Sapna Maheshwari and Vanessa Friedman, "The Ghosts of Brooks Brothers," *The New York Times*, June 23, 2023, https://www.nytimes.com/2021/04/02/business/brooks-brothers-retail-bankruptcy.html.
15. Bruce Kelly, "Broker, Executive Hit with $1M Arbitration Loss over GWG Bonds," *InvestmentNews*, accessed April 9, 2025, https://www.investmentnews.com/alternatives/broker-executive-hit-with-1m-arbitration-loss-over-gwg-bonds/245130.
16. Alexi Horowitz-Ghazi, "Vulture Investors Who Bought Up Bankruptcy Claims from FTX Could See Huge Returns," NPR, May 3, 2024, https://www.npr.org/2024/05/03/1249036600/vulture-investors-who-bought-up-bankruptcy-claims-from-ftx-could-see-huge-return.

Works Cited

"Commercial Chapter 11 Filings Increase 20 Percent in Calendar Year 2024." Epiq Global. Accessed April 9, 2025. https://www.epiqglobal.com/en-us/resource-center/news/commercial-chapter-11-filings-increase-20-percent-in-calendar-year-2024.

Corporate Finance Institute. "DCF Formula | Guide to the DCF Formula with Examples." Accessed April 9, 2025. https://corporatefinanceinstitute.com/resources/valuation/dcf-formula-guide/.

DailyDAC. "An Introduction to Bankruptcy Claims Trading." Accessed April 9, 2025. https://www.dailydac.com/introduction-bankruptcy-claims-trading/.

Damodaran, Aswath. "Valuing Distressed Companies." NYU Stern School of Business. Accessed April 9, 2025. https://pages.stern.nyu.edu/~adamodar/New_Home_Page/valquestions/distresspaper.htm.

Deitch, Lindsay. "*The Blair Witch Project* at 25: How One Film Changed the Horror Genre as We Know It." *The Conversation*, April 8, 2024. https://theconversation.com/the-blair-witch-project-at-25-how-one-film-changed-the-horror-genre-as-we-know-it-233104.

Ferek, Katy Stech. "Burger Chain Turns Pioneer for New Small-Business Bankruptcy Law." *Wall Street Journal*, July 13, 2020. https://www.wsj.com/articles/burger-chain-turns-pioneer-for-new-small-business-bankruptcy-law-11594459800.

Gura, David. "Vulture Investors Who Bought Up Bankruptcy Claims from FTX Could See Huge Return." *NPR*, May 3, 2024. https://www.npr.org/2024/05/03/1249036600/vulture-investors-who-bought-up-bankruptcy-claims-from-ftx-could-see-huge-return.

Kelly, Bruce. "Broker-Executive Hit with $1M Arbitration Loss over GWG Bonds." *InvestmentNews*. Accessed April 9, 2025. https://www.investmentnews.com/alternatives/broker-executive-hit-with-1m-arbitration-loss-over-gwg-bonds/245130.

Lee, Lisa, and Jeremy Hill. "Jefferies' Ex-Navy SEAL Gains Edge in Distressed Debt Investing." *Bloomberg*, March 27, 2024. https://www.bloomberg.com/news/articles/2024-03-27/jefferies-ex-navy-seal-gains-edge-in-distressed-debt-investing.

Maheshwari, Sapna. "Brooks Brothers, a Faded Dandy, Fights to Keep Its Shirt On." *New York Times*, April 2, 2021. https://www.nytimes.com/2021/04/02/business/brooks-brothers-retail-bankruptcy.html.

WORKS CITED

National Pawnbrokers Association. "History of Pawn." Accessed April 9, 2025. https://www.nationalpawnbrokers.org/history-of-pawn/.

Notman, Nina. "J&J's Third Talc Bankruptcy Settlement Attempt Denied." *Chemistry World*, April 3, 2024. https://www.chemistryworld.com/news/jandjs-third-talc-bankruptcy-settlement-attempt-denied/4021242.article.

Trotta, Thomas. "Crime Spree from Beginning to Capture." CBS News, October 22, 2023. https://www.cbsnews.com/news/thomas-trotta-crime-spree-from-beginning-to-capture-60-minutes/.

U.S. Bankruptcy Court. Endorsed Order. Accessed April 9, 2025. https://mcusercontent.com/cc1fad182b6d6f8b1e352e206/files/1ca0eb4f-0cbd-1950-fbaa-4369610d4570/17681244_140168062_endorsed.pdf.

Index

A&G Real Estate Partners, 54
ABG-BB LLC, 122–123
ABI (American Bankruptcy Institute), 48, 50, 51, 53, 147
absolute priority, 17, 65–66, 138–139. *See also* priority of claims
academics, networking with, 49
accounts payable, trade claims on. *See* trade claims
acquisition mechanisms and strategy, 85–97. *See also* buyers
    asset vs. stock deals as, 86–89, 95
    case studies of, 85–87, 88–89, 90, 92–94
    choosing appropriate, 95
    DIP financing and, 123
    key insights on, 96–97
    overview of, 85–86, 95, 96
    prices and, 5, 196–198
    receiverships as, 86, 93–94, 95
    Section 363 sales as, 6–7, 85, 86, 91–93, 95
    trade claim investing, 33–34, 142, 152
    UCC Article 9 sales as, 86, 89–91, 95
active investing, 193–196, 197
adequate protection, 128
Adidas, 31
agreements. *See also* contracts
    Assignment of Claim, 152
    collective bargaining, 69, 140
    credit, 100–103
    joint operating, 112
    non-disclosure, 56
    restructuring support, 20–22
AI. *See* artificial intelligence
Alameda Research, 181, 182, 184–186
Alexander, James, 180
Alix, Jay/AlixPartners, 6
Allied Crude Vegetable Oil Refining Corporation, 194–195
Allied Pilots Association, 69
Allison, Ian, 185
Alto Ingredients, 89
Amazon, 187
American Airlines, 68–70, 140
American Bankruptcy Institute (ABI), 48, 50, 51, 53, 147
American Express, 193, 194–196, 212
American Express Field Warehousing (Amexco), 194–195
Anagram International, 92–93
Anthropic, 138, 187, 189
anti-money laundering checks, 152
antitrust issues, 70
Apollo Global Management, 102, 219
Appaloosa Management, 6, 219
Apple, 11–12, 32
Argo Partners, 142
Armstrong World Industries, 140
Arthur Andersen, 170
artificial intelligence (AI)
    distressed asset analysis and valuation by, 73, 75, 81
    opportunities found through, 51, 53
Asarco, 140
assets. *See* distressed assets
Assignment of Claim Agreements, 152
Association of Professional Flight Attendants, 69
attorneys. *See* legal counsel
Auction Advisors, 54
auditor's reports, 224–225
Authentic Brands Group LLC, 7, 31, 122–123
automatic stays, 17
Avenue Capital Group, 5, 218

BakerHostetler, 166
balance sheets, 63–64, 67
Balfour Investors, 6
Bankman-Fried, Sam ("SBF"), 45, 173, 182, 184–187
Bank of America, 145, 194, 219
bankruptcies
    advanced strategies for (*see under* Chapter 11 reorganizations)
    advantages offered via, 6–7
    business life cycle and, 11–12
    Chapter 7 (*see* Chapter 7 liquidation)
    Chapter 11 (*see* Chapter 11 reorganizations)
    current state of, 8–9
    distressed investing with (*see* distressed investing)

INDEX

bankruptcies (*continued*)
    filings as public information, 51–52, 146–147
    fraud leading to (*see* fraud cases)
    fundamentals of, 12–13
    key insights on, 26–27
    key legal concepts or levers for, 16–19
    management under (*see* bankruptcy management)
    number of filings, 8
    parties to, 13–16
    priority waterfall with, 65–66 (*see also* priority of claims)
    Subchapter V, 8–9, 110
    Trump, xviii–xx
Bankruptcy Abuse Prevention and Consumer Protection Act of 2005, 141
Bankruptcy Claim Exchange, 147
Bankruptcy Data, 50
bankruptcy management, 117–135
    Brooks Brothers, 118–120, 122–124, 130
    case studies of, 118–120, 122–130, 132–133
    cash collateral for, 127–129
    Chapter 7 liquidation despite, 126–127, 132–133
    DIP financing and, 121–127, 129, 130, 132–133
    executory contracts in, 126, 127, 130–131
    financial outcomes with, 117–118, 119, 126–127
    first-day motions setting stage for, 120–121
    GWG Holdings, 124–127, 132–133
    key insights on, 134–135
    overview of, 134
    QualTek Services Inc., 127–129
    reorganization plans and, 131–134
    ripple effects of bankruptcy and, 118–119, 124, 134
banks. *See* lenders
Barclays, 85–87
Barings LLC, 92
Barneys New York, 6
Bauer, Jon, 5
Bear Stearns, 161
Beckman, Jason, 8
Bed Bath & Beyond, 193, 198–201, 212
Beneficient Company Group, 132
Berkshire Hathaway, 196, 205
Bernard L. Madoff Investment Securities LLC (BLMIS), 161, 163, 164. *See also* Madoff Ponzi scheme
Berra, Yogi, 62
Bethlehem Steel, 218
Big Lots, 92
Binance, 185–186
Bitcoin, 178–180, 181, 182, 187–188. *See also* crypto distressed investing
Black, Leon, 218–219
BlackBerry, 32

Blair Witch Project, The, 118
BLMIS. *See* Bernard L. Madoff Investment Securities LLC
BlockFi, 181–182
Bloomberg Law, 50
BMC, 52
Boeing, 147
Bogle, Jack, 197–198
Bombardier, 147
Bonderman, David, 218–219
borrowers. *See* debtors
Boso, Jason, 9
BoxCo analysis, 63–64
Boy Scouts of America, 211
Brandt, William ("Bill"), 47–48
Breeden, Richard, 163
brokers
    cryptocurrency, 181
    networking with, 47, 54–55, 148
    pawn, 61–62, 77
    real estate note investments by, 38
    trade claim investments by, 142
Brookfield Asset Management, 31
Brooks Brothers, 7, 118–120, 122–124, 130
Buffett, Warren, xviii, 193, 194, 195–196, 205, 233
Bush, George W., 215
businesses
    bankruptcy of (*see* bankruptcies)
    distressed investing in (*see* distressed investing)
    life cycles of, 11–12
    operating (*see* operating businesses)
    restructuring of (*see* restructuring)
    small, 8–9, 110, 124
buyers. *See also* acquisition mechanisms and strategy
    bargaining power of, 81
    trade claim, 33–34, 142, 152

cancellation of debt (COD) income, 104
Cannondale, 57–58
CapitalIQ, 50, 75
Carnegie, Andrew, 205
case studies
    acquisition mechanisms and strategy, 85–87, 88–89, 90, 92–94
    active investing, 194–196
    asset-stripping, 203, 204–205
    bankruptcy management, 118–120, 122–130, 132–133
    cash collateral, 127–129
    Chapter 7 liquidation, 126–127, 132–133
    Chapter 11 reorganizations, 8–9, 22–26, 99–100, 102, 105–109
    control investments, 202–204

INDEX

crypto distressed investing, 177–191 (*see also* FTX)
debt vs. equity investments, 198–201
DIP financing, 23–25, 122–127, 132–133
distressed asset analysis and valuation, 61–62, 68–71, 79–83
distressed debt investments, 35
distressed investing playbook in action, 219–222
distressed opportunity sourcing, 45, 57–58, 221–222
distressed real estate investing, 32, 37–38, 204–205
fraud cases, 161–176
liability management exercises, 102
liquidation analysis, 68–71
litigation financing, 35
operating businesses, 41–43
out-of-court restructuring, 206–207, 208
passive investing, 196–198
receiverships, 93–94
Section 363 sales, 92–93
Texas Two-Step, 105–107
third-party non-debtor releases, 209–211
trade claims, 31–33, 137–138, 139, 154–158, 219–220
UCC Article 9 sales, 90
cash collateral, 69, 127–129
CBRE, 55
Celebration Bidco, LLC, 92–93
Celsius Network, 181, 182–183, 184, 189–191
Centers for Medicare & Medicaid Services, 112
CFTC (Commodity Futures Trading Commission), 173
Chapter 7 liquidation
    case studies of, 126–127, 132–133
    Chapter 11 reorganizations vs., 12–13
    overview of, 12
    trustees in, 110
Chapter 11 reorganizations
    absolute priority in, 17
    advanced strategies for, 99–115
    asset vs. stock deals in, 87, 88–89
    automatic stays in, 17
    bankruptcy management under, 117–135
    case studies of, 8–9, 22–26, 99–100, 102, 105–109
    Chapter 7 liquidation vs., 12–13
    claims in, 17, 18–19
    control in, 16
    CROs for, 20
    current state of, 8–9
    description of, 8, 12
    DIP financing with (*see* debtor-in-possession (DIP) financing)
    exclusive right to file, 15–16
    financial advisors in, 20
    First Day Declaration in, 52
    flexibility of, 15
    industry-specific issues for, 111–113
    investor's mindset and, 113–114
    key insights on, 26–27, 114–115
    key legal concepts for, 16–19
    legal counsel in, 19–20
    liquidation valuation in, 17, 19, 222
    LMEs in, 100–103
    mass tort litigation shields in, 105–107
    number of, 8
    operating businesses continuing under (*see* operating businesses)
    out-of-court restructuring prior to, 206–208
    overview of, 12
    parties to, 13–16
    priority of claims in, 17, 18, 100–102 (*see also* priority of claims)
    professionals in, 19–20
    reorganization plans for, 131–134
    RSAs in, 20–22
    Rule 3001(e) secondary market in, 17, 19
    Section 363 sales in (*see* Section 363 sales)
    Subchapter V, 8–9, 110
    tax issues and, 14, 103–105
    Texas Two-Step in, 105–107
    timelines of, 15, 109, 221
Chase Manhattan, 194
Cherokee Acquisition, 5, 137, 142
Chief Restructuring Officers (CROs), 20
Chrysler, 207
Cinecom, 117–118, 130, 131
Citigroup, 171, 219
claims
    Chapter 11, 17, 18–19
    definition of, 17, 18
    priority of (*see* priority of claims)
    trade (*see* trade claims)
    transfer of (*see* Assignment of Claim Agreements; secondary market)
Claims Market, 34, 147
claims trading platforms, 34, 147–149
Clark, Howard, 195
clawbacks
    for crypto asset recovery, 187
    distressed asset analysis and valuation considering, 67, 77
    fraud case, 163, 165–166
    liquidation analysis considering, 67
    trade claims and, 149, 154–156
Clinton, Bill, 48
COD (cancellation of debt) income, 104
CoinDesk, 185
cold outreach, 54

INDEX

collateral
    adequate protection of, 128
    cash, 69, 127–129
    crypto as, 181
    deficiency claims for lack of, 140
    distressed asset analysis and valuation of, 75–76, 198–199
    distressed real estate investing valuation of, 37
    operating business assets as, 39
    risks with, 223–224
    UCC Article 9 sales of, 86, 89–91, 95
collective bargaining agreements, 69, 140
Commodity Futures Trading Commission (CFTC), 173
communication
    cold outreach, 54
    networks of (*see* networks and networking)
    opportunities arising through, 46, 48–49, 53–54
comparable company analysis, 74–75
competition, 79–81
Continental Airlines, 219
contingent claims, 140
contract rejection damage claims, 140
contracts. *See also* agreements
    acquisition of, 89
    executory, 126, 127, 130–131, 140
    lease (*see* leases)
    trade claim, 34, 152
Contrarian Capital Management, 5, 142, 151
control
    in Chapter 11 reorganizations, 16
    DIP financing and, 121–122, 125–126, 127, 132
    distressed investing strategies for taking, 202–204
    by investment in operating businesses, 40, 202–204
    non-control investment vs., 40
Corporate Finance Institute, 73
corporate raiders, 204
Corzine, Jon, 172–173
Coty, 81
COVID-19 pandemic, 9, 22–23, 31, 79, 81, 118–119, 122, 151, 200
Craftsman, 202–203
cramdown provisions, 132
Cred, 180–181, 182, 189, 191
credit agreements, 100–103
Credit Investor's Handbook, The (Gatto), 66
creditors
    committees of, 14, 19, 70, 110, 131, 134, 150
    debt owed (*see* debt)
    holdout by, 207–208
    legal counsel for, 19
    as parties to bankruptcies, 14
    priority of (*see* priority of claims)

    Section 363 sales challenged by, 91
    third-party releases by, 209–211
    trade claims bought from, 33–34 (*see also* trade claims)
CROs (Chief Restructuring Officers), 20
crowdsourced platforms, 54
CRT Capital, 168
crypto distressed investing, 177–192
    asset recovery and, 187–188, 189
    in Celsius Network, 181, 182–183, 184, 189–191
    chain reaction of crises initiating, 181–182, 185, 186–187, 190
    in Cred, 180–181, 182, 189, 191
    due diligence on, 5, 149–150, 186
    fiat vs. digital currency payments in, 178, 179, 183
    fraud cases in, 173, 178–181, 186–187, 189
    in FTX (*see* FTX)
    key insights on, 191–192
    lessons from, 189–191
    monitoring status in, 183, 191
    in Mt. Gox, 177–180, 182
    overview of, 177
    patterns and generalities in, 179–180
    prices in, 5, 179–180, 182, 187–188
    regulatory environment for, 186–187, 189, 190–191
    sourcing of, 45
    trade claims in, 2, 137–139, 141, 143, 149–153, 188–189, 217
    transparency in, 180, 186, 190
    volatility in, 180, 182
    in Voyager Digital, 181, 183–184, 189–191
Cushman & Wakefield, 55
CVS, 79, 81

DailyDAC (Distressed Asset Central), 30
Damodaran, Aswath, 74
Davis, Peter S., 94
DCF (discounted cash flow) analysis, 72–74, 150
De Angelis, Anthony ("Tino"), 194, 196
debt. *See also* liens
    balance sheet of, 63–64, 67
    cancellation of, 104
    collateral for (*see* collateral)
    equity investments vs., 198–201
    equity swap for, 23
    investing in distressed (*see* distressed debt investments)
    LMEs restructuring, 100–103
    national, 3, 4
    priority over equity, 6, 65–66, 198, 199–201 (*see also* priority of claims)
    trade claims as (*see* trade claims)
Debt Exchange, The (DebtX), 55

INDEX

Debticate, 55
debtor-in-possession (DIP) financing
    acquisition advantage via, 123
    bankruptcy management via, 121–127, 129, 130, 132–133
    case studies of, 23–25, 122–127, 132–133
    Chapter 11 reorganizations and, 13–14, 17–18, 23–25, 112, 121–127, 129, 132–133
    control with, 121–122, 125–126, 127, 132
    court approval of, 122, 124
    definition and description of, 18, 121–122
    distressed asset analysis and valuation considering, 67, 76
    as emergency funding, 76
    executory contracts and, 126, 127, 130
    liquidation analysis considering, 67
    rescue financing as, 35
    small business, 124
    zero-interest, 122–124
debtors
    assessing financial condition and prospects of, 149–150
    DIP financing for (*see* debtor-in-possession (DIP) financing)
    legal counsel for, 19
    as parties to bankruptcies, 13–14
Debtwire, 50
decision framework, 226, 229–232
deficiency claims, 140
Delphi, 140
Delta, 70
Development Specialists Inc., 47
DieHard, 202
DIP financing. *See* debtor-in-possession (DIP) financing
disclosures, reading, 224–225
discounted cash flow (DCF) analysis, 72–74, 150
distressed asset analysis and valuation, 61–84
    advanced strategies for, 77–78
    balance sheets for, 63–64, 67
    bottom-up research for, 79–83
    case studies of, 61–62, 68–71, 79–83
    collateral and liens in, 75–76, 198–199
    comparable company analysis for, 74–75
    DCF analysis for, 72–74, 150
    distressed company structure and, 63–64
    financial model for, 66
    key insights on, 83–84
    liquidation analysis for, 66–72
    overview of, 62–63, 78
    priority waterfall for, 65–66
    PV-10 metric for, 111–112
    recovery risk evaluation in, 75–76
    trade claim due diligence with, 150

distressed assets
    acquisition of (*see* acquisition mechanisms and strategy)
    analysis and valuation of (*see* distressed asset analysis and valuation)
    asset-stripping strategy for, 203, 204–205
    clawbacks of (*see* clawbacks)
    crypto (*see* crypto distressed investing)
    investing in (*see* distressed investing)
    key insights on, 44
    liquidation of (*see* liquidation)
    operating businesses as, 3, 39–44 (*see also* operating businesses)
    overview of, 29
    real estate notes as, 2–3, 36–39 (*see also* distressed real estate investing)
    special situations creating, 3, 9, 34–36
    stock acquisitions vs., 86–89, 95
    trade claims as, 29–34 (*see also* trade claims)
    types of, 2–3, 29–44
distressed debt investments
    case studies of, 35
    equity investments vs., 198–201
    fraud cases and, 172
    in operating businesses, 40
    priority of claims in, 6
    as special situation investment, 35
    trade claims as, 142–143 (*see also* trade claims)
distressed investing
    acquisition in (*see* acquisition mechanisms and strategy)
    assets in (*see* distressed assets)
    bankruptcy and (*see* bankruptcies)
    beginning in, 3–4, 219–221
    case studies in (*see* case studies)
    characteristics for successful, xx, 4, 50, 113–114, 202, 218–219, 225–226, 234
    in cryptocurrency (*see* crypto distressed investing)
    in debt (*see* distressed debt investments)
    definition of, xvii, 1
    ethical issues with (*see* ethical issues)
    in fraud cases (*see* fraud cases)
    key concepts for, 2
    key insights on, 9–10
    legal issues in (*see* legal issues)
    market for, 2–3
    mindset for, 113–114, 146, 225–226
    overview of, xvii–xviii, 1–2
    playbook for (*see* distressed investing playbook)
    in real estate (*see* distressed real estate investing)
    risks of (*see* risks)
    rules for, 4–8
    sourcing opportunities for (*see* distressed opportunity sourcing)

INDEX

distressed investing (*continued*)
    strategies for (*see* distressed investing strategies)
    transparency in (*see* transparency)
distressed investing playbook, 215–227, 229–236
    case studies for, 219–222
    on decision framework, 226, 229–232
    on failure as learning opportunity, 221–222
    on financial crises as opportunity, 233, 235
    key insights from, 226–227, 235–236
    on lessons from successful investors, 218–222
    on next steps toward investing, 232–233
    overview of, xx–xxi, 215–218, 229
    on preparation for opportunity, 233–235
    on psychology of successful investing, 225–226
    reasons for creating, 215–218
    on risk navigation, 222–225
    on starting as distressed investor, 219–221
    on toolkit for investing, 231–232
distressed investing strategies, 193–213
    active investing as, 193–196, 197
    asset-stripping as, 203, 204–205
    control investments as, 202–204
    debt vs. equity purchases as, 198–201
    key insights on, 212–213
    legal considerations in, 209–211
    litigation financing as, 201, 211
    overview of, 193, 212
    passive investing as, 193–194, 196–198
    restructuring approaches as, 205–208
    for trade claims, 145–159
distressed opportunity sourcing, 45–59
    case studies of, 45, 57–58, 221–222
    characteristics for successful, 58
    cold outreach for, 54
    communication for, 46, 48–49, 53–54
    ethical issues and, 54, 56
    "Getting on First Base Approach" to, 46–59
    industry sector expertise for, 49, 113, 151, 222
    key insights on, 58–59
    networks leveraged for, 46, 47–49, 51, 53–55, 147–148, 231–232
    online searches for, 46, 51–53
    overview of, xviii, 45–46, 58
    profitability vs. personal interest influencing, 57–58
    public information for, 46, 50–53, 146–147
    seizing opportunity from, 56–57
    for trade claims, 146–148, 151
distressed real estate investing
    access to opportunities in, 38–39
    asset-stripping and, 204–205
    case studies of, 32, 37–38, 204–205

    Chapter 11 filings, 8, 113
    characteristics for successful, 39
    real estate notes as assets in, 2–3, 36–39
    risks in, 37–38, 223
    strategy for, 36
    timing of, 145–146, 218
Dodd, David, 66
Donlin Recano, 52
drop-down transactions, 101
dual restitution structure, 164
due diligence
    on collateral and liens, 76
    on credit agreements, 102–103
    on crypto cases, 5, 149–150, 186
    for distressed investing, 5
    on distressed real estate investing, 37
    failure with insufficient, 221
    fraud cases highlighting importance of, 167, 175
    for liquidation analysis, 68
    for LME navigation, 102–103
    on operating businesses, 43
    on Section 363 sales, 91
    on Subchapter V bankruptcies, 110
    on trade claims, 33–34, 148, 149–151, 220
    on UCC Article 9 sales, 90

earnings before interest, taxes, depreciation, and amortization (EBITDA), 67
eBay, 62
Elliott Management, 5, 35
EMC, 32
energy industry
    acquisitions in, 88–89
    Chapter 11 reorganizations in, 111–112
    distressed asset analysis and valuation in, 70–71, 82–83
    fraud case in, 170–172, 174
    trade claims in, 143, 151
Enron, 170–172, 174, 187
equity. *See also* stock
    balance sheet of, 63–64, 67
    debt investments vs., 198–201
    debt priority over, 6, 65–66, 198, 199–201 (*see also* priority of claims)
    debt swap for, 23
    distressed real estate investment in, 37–38
    Subchapter V treatment of, 110
Ericsson, 32
Estée Lauder, 79, 81
ethical issues
    asset-stripping raising, 205
    crypto distressed investing and, 189

INDEX

distressed opportunity sourcing and, 54, 56
    fraud case investing as, 164
exclusivity, of Chapter 11 right to file, 15–16
execution risks, 225
executives. *See* managers and executives
executory contracts, 126, 127, 130–131, 140

Falk-Wallace, Richard, 63, 66
Farallon Capital, 142
feeder funds, 162–163, 164, 167
Feinberg, Steve, 218
Femenia, Joe, 77–78
Fenty, 79, 80
film industry, bankruptcy management in, 117–118, 130, 131
financial advisors, 20, 147, 206
financial crisis (2007-2009)
    distressed investing opportunity growth in, 12, 215–216, 218–219, 233
    Ford restructuring during, 206–207
    fraud scheme exposures in, 161, 168
    future crises like, 233, 235
    government bailouts in, 207, 215
    Lehman Brothers in, 32–33, 85–87, 151, 153, 161, 215–216, 218
    liquidations from, 68–69, 90
    passive investing spurred by, 197–198
    prices in, 5, 187–188
    timing of investments with, 145, 218
    uncertainty during, 7
Financial Industry Regulatory Authority (FINRA), 127, 172
financial reports
    balance sheets as, 63–64, 67
    disclosures in, reading, 224–225
    opportunities found through, 52
    trade claim status monitored via, 153
Finbox, 75
Finchat, 73
FirstBank Puerto Rico, 107–108
First Day Declaration, 52
first-day motions, 120–121
First Financial Network, 55
Fitch Ratings, 50
503(b)(9) claims, 141, 154–157
Five Forces analysis, 79–81
Fontainebleau Las Vegas, 145–146
Ford Motor Company, 206–207, 208
foreclosures, 36–37, 90
Forever 21, 6
Fortress, 167
Fracassi, Cesare, 186, 189

fraud cases, 161–176
    American Express effects of, 194–196
    crypto-based, 173, 178–181, 186–187, 189
    dual restitution structure in, 164
    Enron as, 170–172, 174
    Fyre Festival as, 163
    impacts of, 162, 167, 168–169, 171–172, 173, 174–175
    key insights on, 175–176
    lessons from, 174–175
    liquidation analysis considering, 68
    liquidation in, 163–164, 169, 173
    litigation financing in, 163–164, 167, 211
    Madoff Ponzi scheme as, 9, 152, 153, 161–169, 174, 189
    MF Global as, 171–174
    payoff from investing in aftermath of, 163–165, 169–175, 233–234
    receiverships for, 93–94, 169
    risks from, 167, 172, 174–175
    Stanford International Bank as, 163, 168–170, 174, 233–234
    trade claims in, 152, 153, 167–174
Freund, Harry, 6
FRONTEO, 7–8
FTT, 185
FTX
    asset recovery from, 187–188, 189
    bankruptcy and unraveling of, 186
    chain reaction and demise of, 181–182, 186–187
    distressed assets of, 2, 150
    distressed opportunity with, 45, 217
    due diligence on, 5, 149–150, 186
    fraud by, 173, 186–187, 189
    investigations revealing problems with, 185–186
    launch and rise of, 184–185
    legacy of, 189
    lessons from, 189–191
    prices for, 5
    regulatory environment for, 186–187, 189, 190
    trade claims against, 2, 137–138, 139, 141, 143, 149–153, 217
Fyre Festival, 163

Galloway, Scott, 189
gap claims, 140
Gardner, Sonia, 218
Gates, Bill, 88
Gatto, Michael, 66
Gawker Media, 35
GE Capital, 220
General Electric, 220
General Motors, 207

INDEX

Genesis Global Capital, 181
Gerson Lehrman Group, 49
Giddens, James, 173
global financial crisis. *See* financial crisis (2007-2009)
Glossier, 79, 80
Goldman Sachs, 145, 172, 215
Goldsmith, Jay, 6
Google, 32, 51, 187
Gordon Brothers, 54
government
    bailouts by, 207, 215
    as party to bankruptcies, 14
    regulatory environment under, 82–83, 112, 124–125, 162, 167, 173, 186–187, 189, 190–191
Graham, Benjamin, 66, 196
Graham-Newman Corporation, 196
Great Financial Crisis. *See* financial crisis (2007-2009)
Guardian International Bank, 168
Guirguis, Karim, 48
GWG Holdings, 124–127, 132–133

Hanover, Louis, 6
Harrington v. Purdue Pharma (2024), 209–211
Hawaiian Electric, 83
healthcare industry, Chapter 11 reorganizations in, 112
Hecktman, Jeffrey ("Jeff"), 47–48
Herenstein, Andrew, 8
Heritage Village Assisted Living, 93–94
Hertz, 201
Hilco Trading Company (now Hilco Global), 48, 54
Hilton, Conrad, xvii, 1, 2
Hogan, Hulk, 35
holdout problem, 207–208
hospitality industry, Chapter 11 reorganizations in, 112–113
HSBC, 169
Hudson Bay Capital Management LP, 198, 200–201

Icahn, Carl, 7, 145–146, 158, 204, 218
index funds, 197–198
industries. *See also specific industries*
    bottom-up research on, 79–83
    Chapter 11 opportunities and challenges in specific, 111–113
    Five Forces analysis of, 79–81
    sector expertise for sourcing opportunities, 49, 113, 151, 222
    trade claim market and, 31–33, 143, 150, 151
    trade publications and news sources on, 51, 53
Inlow, Ronald J., 127
insider trading, 56

intellectual property
    acquisition of, 87, 89, 91
    asset valuation including, 150, 204
    Chapter 11 transfer of, 99–100, 101
    as collateral, 39, 75
    strategic investment attracted by, 11–12
    trade claims and, 31–32, 150
Internal Revenue Service, 11, 165. *See also* tax issues
inventory, 31, 39, 111, 119, 194

Jack Henry Loan Marketplace, 55
JCPenney, 31, 141, 201, 205
J. Crew, 22–26, 99–100, 101
Jefferies Financial Group, 77–78
Jelisavcic, Vladimir, 5, 137–138
JLL (Jones Lang LaSalle), 55
Joann Stores, 92
Jobs, Steve, 11–12
Johnson & Johnson (J&J), 105–107
joint operating agreements, 112
Jones Lang LaSalle (JLL), 55
journalists, networking with, 49, 148
JPMorgan Chase, 92, 165, 169, 171
J.S. Held, LLC, 94

Kannegundla, Bhagumshi, 137
Karpelès, Mark, 178
Keen-Summit Capital Partners, 54
Kenmore, 202
Kennedy, John F., 195
Kingate Euro Fund, 165
Kingate Global Fund, 165
Kmart, 202–205
know-your-customer (KYC) checks, 152
Kobayashi, Nobuaki, 178–179
Kroll, 52
Kylie Cosmetics, 79, 80

LaBonte, Chip and Rosanna, 119, 123
Lampert, Eddie, 155–156, 202–205
Lands' End, 202–203
Lasry, Marc, 5, 8, 218
leases
    Chapter 11 treatment of, 23, 111, 113, 119, 130
    deposits for, as priority claims, 140
    sourcing opportunities via, 56
Lee, 31
Leffell, Michael, 218
legal counsel
    Chapter 11 role of, 19–20
    for crypto cases, 183

INDEX

ethical advice from, 56
networking with, 47–48, 147–148, 231, 232
for operating business management, 39
out-of-court restructuring and, 206
for trade claims, 34, 147, 152
legal issues
agreements and contracts on (*see* agreements; contracts)
Chapter 11, key concepts, 16–19
counsel for (*see* legal counsel)
crypto distressed investing, 180
distressed investing strategies considering, 209–211
litigation on (*see* litigation)
operating businesses with, 39
protection from, 6
third-party releases as, 209–211
trade claim, 34
Lehman Brothers
Barclays acquisition of, 85–87
Madoff Ponzi scheme and, 161
ripple effect of, 215–216
trade claims against, 32–33, 151, 153, 218
lenders
debt owed (*see* debt)
networking with, 47–48, 54–55, 148
priority of (*see* priority of claims)
Section 363 sales financing by, 92
UCC Article 9 sales driven by, 90
Lewis, Michael, 189
LexisNexis, 50, 51
liabilities
asset vs. stock deals on acquisition of, 86–89, 95
balance sheet of, 63–64, 67
LMEs restructuring, 100–103
risks of hidden, 223
Section 363 sales shielded from, 91
Texas Two-Step transfer of, 105–107
third-party releases as shield from, 209–211
trade claims and, 140, 150, 154–156
UCC Article 9 sales and, 90–91
liability management exercises (LMEs), 100–103
liens, 75–76
life cycle
of businesses, 11–12
of trade claims, 138–139
liquidation
analysis of (*see* liquidation analysis)
Chapter 7, 12–13, 110, 126–127, 132–133
crypto case, 178, 180
fraud case, 163–164, 169, 173
valuation of (*see* liquidation valuation)

liquidation analysis, 66–72
balance sheet changes anticipated in, 67
case studies of, 68–71
determining liquidation value in, 66–67
due diligence for, 68
important features of, 72
price determination and, 5
liquidation valuation
asset-stripping and, 204–205
Chapter 11, 17, 19, 222
collateral risks and, 223–224
in liquidation analysis, 66–67
price determination and, 5
litigation
antitrust, 70
filings for, as public information, 52
financing of, 35, 163–164, 167, 201, 211
fraud case, 163–164, 165–166, 167, 169, 171, 211
mass tort, shielding from, 105–107, 209–211
litigation financing, 35, 163–164, 167, 201, 211
Littlejohn & Co., LLC, 92
LMEs (liability management exercises), 100–103
LoanStreet, 55
Lorber, Howard, 146
L'Oreal, 79, 81
LTL Management LLC, 105–107
LTV, 218
Lu Hua, 180

Macy's, 138, 205
Madoff, Andrew, 161
Madoff, Bernie, 9, 161–169. *See also* Madoff Ponzi scheme
Madoff, Mark, 161
Madoff Ponzi scheme
controversies in recovery from, 165–168
as fraud, 9, 152, 153, 161–169, 174, 189
methodology for Ponzi scheme, 162
overview of, 9, 161–163
payoff from investing in aftermath of, 163–165
recoveries from, 163–168, 174, 189
trade claims and, 152, 153, 167–168
Madoff Victim Fund (MVF), 163–164
Magic: The Gathering Online Exchange (Mt. Gox), 177–180, 182
Magna Servicing LLC, 125
managers and executives
bankruptcy management by (*see* bankruptcy management)
as debtor-in-possession (*see* debtor-in-possession (DIP) financing)
directors and officers liability insurance for, 201

INDEX

managers and executives (*continued*)
    failure with lack of appropriate, 221
    networking with former, 49, 148
    operating businesses run by (*see* operating businesses)
Marathon Asset Management, 6
Marks, Howard, 5, 8, 218–219, 223
Mashinsky, Alex, 182
Mayes, Kris, 94
McDermott, Will & Emery, 219
Merchant, Ismail, 117–118, 119, 130, 131
Merchant Ivory Productions, 117–118
MF Global, 151, 171–174
Microsoft, 11, 32, 88
Miller, Donald, 194
mindset of distressed investors, 113–114, 146, 225–226
Moelis, Kenneth/Moelis & Company, 6
Monarch Alternative Capital, 8
Montgomery Ward, 220
Moody's Analytics, 50
MountainSeed, 55
Moyer, Stephen G., 63–64
Mt. Gox (Magic: The Gathering Online Exchange), 177–180, 182
Mudrick, Jason/Mudrick Capital Management, 7
Munger, Charlie, 233
MVF (Madoff Victim Fund), 163–164

N&N Partners, LLC, 90
National Pawnbrokers Association, 61
NDAs (non-disclosure agreements), 56
negotiations
    bankruptcy process as structured, 15
    for DIP financing, 121
    for distressed real estate investing, 37
    holdout on restructuring as leverage in, 208
    labeling opponents in, xix
    for reorganization plans, 131
    for RSAs, 20–22
    third-party releases as leverage in, 210
    for trade claim purchases, 33, 152
net invested capital, 170
net-net investing, 196
net operating losses (NOLs), 103–105
networks and networking
    leveraging for opportunities, 46, 47–49, 51, 53–55, 147–148, 231–232
    trade claim status monitored via, 153
Neuberger Berman Investment Advisers LLC, 92
new entrants, as threat, 80
Newmark, 55
Nielsen, 79

Nike, 31
NOLs (net operating losses), 103–105
non-disclosure agreements (NDAs), 56
Nortel Networks, 31–32
Northgate, 54
note investing platforms, 38

Oaktree Capital Management, 5, 218–219
Obra Capital, 125–127, 132–133
online platforms
    claims trading, 34, 147–149
    comparable company analysis via, 75
    DCF calculators via, 73–74
    opportunities sourced via crowdsourced, 54
    real estate note investing, 38
online searches, opportunities through, 46, 51–53
open market purchase exceptions, 101, 102
operating businesses
    case studies of, 41–43
    Chapter 11 reorganization of (*see* Chapter 11 reorganizations)
    control investment in, 40, 202–204
    definition of, 3
    DIP financing for (*see* debtor-in-possession (DIP) financing)
    as distressed assets, 3, 39–44
    exit strategy from, 44
    liquidation analysis of, 67
    non-control investment in, 40
    risks of investing in, 39–40, 43–44
    turnaround process for stabilizing, 40, 43
opioid crisis, 209–211
opportunities
    sourcing (*see* distressed opportunity sourcing)
    strategies for creating (*see* distressed investing strategies)
out-of-court restructuring, 206–208
Owens Corning, 140

PACER (Public Access to Court Electronic Records), 50, 51, 52, 53, 146
Pacific Ethanol, 88–89
Pacific Gas and Electric (PG&E), 35, 82–83
Pacific Investment Management Company (PIMCO), 35, 63
Paperstac, 38
Party City, 92–93
passive investing, 193–194, 196–198
Paulson, John/Paulson & Co., 7, 218
pawn brokers, 61–62, 77
peer group analysis. *See* comparable company analysis
pension and OPEB claims, 140
Perelman, Ronald, 204
Perlmutter, Ira J., 224
PG&E (Pacific Gas and Electric), 35, 82–83

INDEX

Picard, Irving, 163–167
Picower, Jeffrey, 165
PIMCO (Pacific Investment Management Company), 35, 63
PitchBook, 50
Plaza Hotel, xviii–xx
PNC, 54
Podulka, Joseph, 180
Porter, Michael, 79
Porter's Five Forces, 79–81
portfolio funding, 211
Posner, Victor, 204
present value calculations, 111–112
price, buying at right, 5, 196–198
priority claims, 140
priority of claims
    absolute, 17, 65–66, 138–139
    Chapter 11, 17, 18, 100–102
    debt vs. equity, 6, 65–66, 198, 199–201
    DIP financing in, 121, 125
    distressed investing focus on, 6
    liquidation analysis considering, 67, 69
    reorganization plan addressing, 131
    trade claims, 138–139, 140–141, 154–155
    uptier transactions changing, 100–101, 102
    waterfall of, 65–66
professional associations, networking in, 48, 51, 53–54, 147
psychology of distressed investing, 113–114, 146, 225–226
Public Access to Court Electronic Records (PACER), 50, 51, 52, 53, 146
public information, opportunities through, 46, 50–53, 146–147
Pulte, William J., Jr./Pulte Capital Partners, 201
Purdue Pharma, 209–211, 212
PV-10 metric, 111–112

QualTek Services Inc., 127–129

Ray, John J., III, 187–189, 190
real estate. *See* distressed real estate investing
receiverships, 86, 93–94, 95, 107–108, 169
reclamation claims, 140–141
Refco, 151
Reorg, 50
repurchase-to-maturity (RTM) transactions, 172
reputation, 26, 39, 48, 56, 195
rescue financing, 35
restructuring
    Chapter 11 (*see* Chapter 11 reorganizations)
    formal vs. informal, 205–206
    holdout problem in, 207–208
    out-of-court, 206–208
    workout vs., 206

restructuring support agreements (RSAs), 20–22
retail industry
    asset-stripping in, 203, 204–205
    bankruptcy management in, 118–120, 122–124, 130
    Chapter 11 reorganizations in, 22–26, 111, 130
    control investments in, 202–204
    debt vs. equity investments in, 198–201
    distressed company signs in, 63
    distressed opportunity sourcing in, 56–57
    trade claims in, 31, 33, 143, 150, 151, 154–157
Revlon, 79–82, 204
Revson, Charles, 79
Richards, Bruce, 6
risks
    asset vs. stock acquisition, 87, 95
    collateral, 223–224
    debt vs. equity investments, 199
    disclosure, 224–225
    distressed real estate investing, 37–38, 223
    execution, 225
    fraud-related, 167, 172, 174–175
    litigation financing, 211
    navigating successfully, 222–225
    operating business, 39–40, 43–44
    protection from, 6
    receivership, 93
    recovery, analysis of, 75–76
    Section 363 sale, 91–92
    timing, 225
    tolerance for, xx
    trade claim, 30, 142, 143
    UCC Article 9 sale, 90–91, 95
    valuation, 223–224
Room with a View, A, 117, 130, 131
Ross, Wilbur, 6–7, 39, 218
RSAs (restructuring support agreements), 20–22
RTM (repurchase-to-maturity) transactions, 172
Rule 3001(e) secondary market, 17, 19

Sackler family, 209–210
Salad Oil Scandal, 193, 194–196
Salter, Jamie, 7
Sanders, Bernie, xix
S&P. *See* Standard & Poor's
Sarachek Law Firm, 183
Schatt, Daniel, 180
Schloss, Walter, 194, 196–198
Scrub Island, 107–109
Sears, 6, 141, 153, 154–158, 202–205
SEC. *See* Securities and Exchange Commission
secondary market, 17, 19, 62, 163

INDEX

Section 363 sales, 6–7, 85, 86, 91–93, 95
Section 503(b)(9) claims, 141, 154–157
Section 1129(b) cramdown provisions, 132
Securities and Exchange Commission (SEC)
    filings, as public information, 52, 53
    investigations by, 124–125, 132, 162, 173
    receivers approved by, 94
Securities Investor Protection Act (SIPA), 163–164
Securities Investor Protection Corporation (SIPC), 164, 166
Security Analysis (Graham and Dodd), 66
Seeking Alpha, 54
Seritage Growth Properties, 203, 205
Serta Mattress, 102
shareholders. *See* equity; priority of claims
Sharon Steel, 204
ShoeMe, 154–158, 202
SIB (Stanford International Bank), 163, 168–170, 174, 233–234
Silver Point Capital, 66, 142
Simon Property Group Inc., 31, 122–123
Singer, Paul, 5, 8, 218
SIPA (Securities Investor Protection Act), 163–164
SIPC (Securities Investor Protection Corporation), 164, 166
SLAQ, LLC, 142
small businesses, 8–9, 110, 124
Small Business Reorganization Act, 8. *See also* Subchapter V bankruptcies
social media, monitoring for opportunities, 53
Soffer, Jeffrey, 145
Solana, 188
Sony, 32
Southern California Edison, 83
special situation investments, 3, 9, 34–36
stalking horse bids, 91, 92
Standard & Poor's (S&P)
    500 index, 197
    CapitalIQ by, 50, 75
Stanford, R. Allen, 163, 168–170
Stanford International Bank (SIB), 163, 168–170, 174, 233–234
stock. *See also* equity
    acquisition of, 86–89, 95
    active investing in, 193–196, 197
    passive investing in, 193–194, 196–198
Stratosphere casino, 145
Stretto, 52
Stuart, Scott, 48
Subchapter V bankruptcies, 8–9, 110
subsidiaries
    asset transfers to, 99–100, 101
    liability transfers to, 105–107
substitute products, threat of, 81

Sullivan & Cromwell, 217
suppliers
    bargaining power of, 81
    as creditors, 14
    failure to maintain critical relationship with, 221
    payment terms for, 138–139
    Revlon's chain of, 79, 81
    trade claims of (*see* trade claims)

Taj Mahal casino, xviii, 7
Target, 202, 220
Tax Cuts and Jobs Act of 2017, 105
tax issues
    asset valuation including, 150
    cancellation of debt income as, 104
    Chapter 11 claims and, 14, 103–105
    investment implications of, 104–105
    net operating losses as, 103–105
    stock acquisition, 87
    tax identification numbers, 11
TD (Toronto-Dominion) Bank, 169
telecommunications industry
    cash collateral in, 127–129
    trade claims in, 31–32, 150
Tepper, David, 6, 218–219
Terra Luna, 181, 182, 190
TerraUSD, 181
Texas Business Organizations Code (2006), 106
Texas Two-Step, 105–107
Thema International Fund, 165
Thiel, Peter, 35
third-party non-debtor releases, 209–211
Thomson Reuters, 50
Three Arrows Capital (3AC), 181–182, 183–184, 190
time value of money, 73
timing of investments, 145–146, 151–152, 218, 225
Titan Solar, 70–71
TMA (Turnaround Management Association), 48, 50, 51, 53, 147
Toronto-Dominion (TD) Bank, 169
Toys "R" Us, 141
TPG, 219
trade claims, 137–159
    bankruptcy case and potential outcomes assessment for, 150–151, 153
    buying and buyers of, 33–34, 142, 152
    case studies of, 31–33, 137–138, 139, 154–158, 219–220
    contingent claims as, 140
    contract rejection damage claims as, 140
    contracts for, 34, 152
    crypto, 2, 137–139, 141, 143, 149–153, 188–189, 217

262

INDEX

debtor's financial condition and prospects affecting, 149–150
deficiency claims as, 140
definition and description of, 2, 29–30, 138, 140–141
due diligence on, 33–34, 148, 149–151, 220
executing and managing investments in, 152
exit strategies for, 143, 153–154
503(b)(9) claims as, 141, 154–157
in fraud cases, 152, 153, 167–174
gap claims as, 140
industry-specific factors affecting, 31–33, 143, 150, 151
investing in, 145–159, 218, 219–220
investment flow for, 30
key insights on, 143–144, 158–159
life cycle of, 138–139
market for, 30, 141–143
mindset for investing in, 146
monitoring status of, 150, 153
online platforms for, 34, 147–149
overview of, 138–139, 143, 158
pension and OPEB claims as, 140
priority claims as, 140
priority of, 138–139, 140–141, 154–155
proof of claim for, 149
rationale for investing in, 141–142
reclamation claims as, 140–141
risk with, 30, 142, 143
sellers of, 142, 152
sourcing of, 146–148, 151
strategies for investing in, 151
timing of investment in, 145, 151–152
transfer of ownership of, 152
transparency and, 138, 142, 146, 154
types of, 140–141
understanding, 138–139
trade publications, opportunities through, 51, 53
transparency
    in crypto distressed investing, 180, 186, 190
    in distressed investing, generally, 1
    ethical behavior and, 56
    networking with, 48
    of Section 363 sales, 91
    trade claims and, 138, 142, 146, 154
Transport Workers Union, 69
Trans World Airlines (TWA), 204, 218
TR Capital, 142
Tremont Group, 165
Tronox, 140
Trump, Donald, xviii–xx
trustees. *See also* U.S. Trustee
    Chapter 7, 110
    crypto liquidation, 178–180

fees paid to, 166
fraud case, 163–167, 173
Subchapter V, 110
Turnaround Management Association (TMA), 48, 50, 51, 53, 147
TWA (Trans World Airlines), 204, 218
Twisted Root Burger Co., 9

UBS, 6
UCC Article 9 sales, 86, 89–91, 95
uncertainty, 7–8, 143, 174, 215, 218, 225. *See also* risks
Uniform Commercial Code (UCC)
    Article 9 sales under, 86, 89–91, 95
    definition of, 90
    filings, on collateral and liens, 76
    reclamation claims under, 140–141
unions, 14, 69
United Airlines, 70, 140
Univision, 35
uptier transactions, 100–101, 102
US Airways, 70
U.S. Commodity Exchange Authority, 194
U.S. Trustee, 14, 19, 110

valuation of distressed assets. *See* distressed asset analysis and valuation; liquidation valuation
Vanderbilt, Cornelius, xvii, 2
Vanguard, 197–198
Van Heusen, 31
Verita, 52
Vida Insurance Credit Opportunity Fund III, 125
Voyager Digital, 181, 183–184, 189–191

Waldorf Astoria, 1
Wall Street Journal, 50
Walmart, 79, 81, 202, 220
Walter J. Schloss Associates, 196
Warren, Elizabeth, xix
waterfall concept, 65–66. *See also* priority of claims
WestLaw, 50
Witkoff, Steve, 146
WL Ross & Co., 39
workout, 206. *See also* restructuring
W. R. Grace, 140

Xclaim, 34, 147, 217

Yieldstreet, 38

Zell, Sam, 6
Zhao, Changpeng ("CZ"), 185–186

263

Acknowledgments

I have wanted to write a book ever since I was eighteen. I now realize much more is involved than my silly teenage self knew. For starters, books are generally not worth reading unless the author is an expert or at least has some way of imparting knowledge about a topic that isn't necessarily obvious or intuitive. It took me several decades, but I've finally mustered the confidence to assert that everyday investors can benefit from my knowledge and that I have the necessary perspective to provide significant value. Many different variables, people, timing, resources, and experience needed to line up for that to happen, and those elements began to align in 2019 when I was asked to teach graduate students at the Executive MBA Program at the Leonard N. Stern School of Business of New York University.

If you can't take my course in the EMBA Program, the objective of this book is to make this distressed investing skill set available to you, the reader of this book, whether you are an amateur investor interested in learning about distressed investing or the head of a corporation looking to profit from turmoil in the marketplace.

This book would not be possible were it not for the course I teach, "Turnarounds, Restructurings and Distressed Investments." I have the highest esteem for the students who earn their MBAs at NYU. They are full-time executives, managers, business owners, investment professionals, attorneys, doctors, engineers, veterans, and people committed to enhancing their academic credentials to advance their professional opportunities. At the same time, they are also mothers, fathers, husbands, wives, and partners balancing family life. Most of them come to my class with no bankruptcy expertise. They are "newbies" in the world of distressed investing. They come to the course with their diverse backgrounds, which, as I've explained in the book, are extremely useful in spotting investment opportunities others might overlook. They leave our class with the toolkit to enter the world of distressed investing. I am grateful to have interacted with each and every one of you in the NYU Stern EMBA Program. You have taught me as much as I have taught you.

Jens Thorsen, Will Frank, Robert Friedman, Lance Byers, Rory Rohan, Wilson Long, Karen Kuo, Nicole Sands, Joscelyn Read, Grace Ng, Marc Bucceli, Kristopher Kalibat, Guilhermo Gonzalez, Jacob Rheinstein, Michael Cimino, Lamont Conyers, and many others: thank you for your detailed comments.

Thanks also to guest lecturers Ira J. Perlmutter, Saul Burian, Steve Spitzer, David Marcus, Michael Gatto, Richard Falk-Wallace, Vladimir Jelisavcic, Dan Kamensky, Bill Brandt (obm),

ACKNOWLEDGMENTS

Phil Falcone, Jorian Rose, Richelle Kalnit, Jonathan Rosenfeld, and others who had an impact on teaching or who inspired parts of the book.

As with any book, it takes someone extraordinary to get the gears in motion. That person is J.P. Mark, my writing and publishing advisor. While writing this book, he has become my friend, confidant, and partner. J.P., your ability to transform my PowerPoint slides into a structured outline and your encouragement was instrumental in making this book a reality.

I'm also grateful to the team who worked on this project, including Adam Rosen, a gifted editor and author of a book about one of my favorite movies of all time. We were clearly destined to work together. I'd also like to thank Andrea Reider of Reider Books, whose art, technical skill, and attention to detail are displayed in this book's layout, as well as Wendy Dopkin and Christine Hoskin, the team's top-notch proofreader and indexer, respectively.

The winding path of my career would not have led me to where I am today without the guidance of many influential and wise individuals who counseled me along the way: Professor Karen Gross inspired me to pursue bankruptcy in law school. Sandy Mayerson suggested we write an article on trading in claims. Tom Mayer and Chaim Fortgang authored the seminal article on trading in claims. I'm also grateful to Jay Goldsmith and Harry Freund at Balfour Investors; my former employer, Marc Lasry and his sister, Sonia Gardner (the King and Queen of Claims Trading); Jim Carr, my former officemate at Kelley Drye & Warren; and Rob Heffes and Gail Rosenblum, my colleagues at CRT Capital, which was an incredible trading operation and taught me so much. (Can't we bring the band back together?)

Finally, I have to acknowledge other claims buyers: Vlad and Brad at Cherokee Markets, Matt and Andrew at XClaim, Jon Bauer at Contrarian Capital, Mike Singer at Argo, and Michael Linn at Farralon. The truth is competition keeps us honest, and we learn (or at least I do) from others. I have learned so much from all of you, sometimes by actually working with you and sometimes just watching you succeed and fail from afar. While it's always nice to succeed, and in the investment world, that means making a lot of money, there are many lessons to be learned from failure. The main lesson from failure is to figure out why you failed and not do it again, or you'll be out of business.

Obviously, the critical lesson to be learned from success is to replicate it. Over and over. Warren Buffett, Howard Marks, Marc Lasry, Paul Singer, and Carl Icahn, you guys are the grandmasters of distressed investing.

I also extend heartfelt thanks to my diligent and insightful colleagues at The Sarachek Law Firm and Strategic Liquidity Fund: Denise Fava, Zachary Mazur, Jarred Herzberg, Ryan Vollenhals, Freddie Smithson, and Paul Combe, and our summer associates Abhinav Vittal and Mendy Wolff. I would also like to acknowledge the efforts of Maury Bonime, our accountant, who has the Solomonic role of determining whether what we're doing passes muster. They say that if you love what you do, you'll never work a day in your life. Well, I don't know if that's true, because we work, a lot, but I do love what we're doing, and you guys are a large part of our success.

To Scott Stuart of Turnaround Management Association, you have been a long-time friend and fantastic representative for our business. It is particularly noteworthy that you

ACKNOWLEDGMENTS

created the annual Distressed Investing Conference in Las Vegas. And to Karim Guirguis, CEO, and Amy Quackenboss, Executive Director of American Bankruptcy Institute, I am highly confident you'll figure out a way to use technology to lead us in the next great age of the distressed industry. If readers of this book don't join these two organizations, they are crazy.

Two other inspirations for writing this book were my grandfather and namesake, Rabbi Joseph Sarachek, who wrote numerous books about medieval Jewish literature that analyze the pillars of Judaism. My sister, Maggie Sarachek, is also a motivating force for writing this book. Maggie is an incredibly caring social worker who co-wrote *The Anxiety Sisters' Survival Guide: How You Can Become More Hopeful, Connected, and Happy*, which is a roadmap for us all. If you don't have anxiety investing in distressed assets, just wait; you will.

I also want to thank my rabbis for their constant guidance. Rabbi Jonathan Morgenstern of the Young Israel of Scarsdale, whose beautiful voice resonates the words of G-d and inspires each of us to be better members of society. Rabbi Sholom Duchman of Colel Chabad, whose mission is to feed and clothe the less fortunate, and who recently told me that I have to make a lot of money because his charity needs it. Next, Rabbi Simcha Willig of Yeshiva University, whose generosity of self and spirit knows no bounds. Rabbi Nossen Fellig of Duke Chabad and his wife who are the spiritual leaders of the children of the Duke Blue Devils. Last but not least, Rabbi Zalman Deitsch and his wife, Sarah, who are building a different type of national championship dynasty at Ohio State to inspire generations of Buckeye students. There is simply no way I can stop working with all these rabbis in my life.

Finally, I want to thank my kids, Jake, Sydney, Josh, Jason & Spencer, for inspiring me to write this book; not that you ever mentioned it, but here's my legacy to you. Except for the two youngest (and your time is coming soon!), you guys each worked with me on distressed investments and are very capable sourcers (a word you all will learn soon). And, of course, my parents, Shirley and Julian Sarachek (obm), and my in-laws, Nancy and Harry Rosenstein (obm), you guys always love listening to a good distressed story, and I appreciate you more than you can ever know.

Of course, every married author should thank their partner; otherwise, they shouldn't be married. My wife, Heather, and I are blessed with a beautiful family, including in-laws who treat me like a son, but marriage is not without its challenges, and perhaps the greatest turnaround I have pulled off in my life is restoring a beautiful and thriving partnership with Heather.

Heather, you're a wonder, and you amaze me. I don't know how you do it. You remind me that there are only twenty-four hours in a day and to use my time wisely, but I am convinced you've found a way to squeeze in twenty-five. With everything you do for our family, for me, for your parents, for charity, and for your job, you somehow manage to give your best to all of it. Just as one person can change the outcome of an investment, one person, the right person, can change the course of a life. In my life, that person is you. You are the foundation that makes everything else possible. I am forever grateful.

ACKNOWLEDGMENTS

Because I'm a lawyer, I have to yet again provide a disclaimer that the lessons in this book are not intended as investment advice on any particular investment. Rather, they are a playbook to guide you in your journey in the world of distressed investments. Needless to say, any mistakes, factual or otherwise, are entirely my own.

Good luck.
Best, JES